The Eucharist as the Center of Theology

The Eucharist as
the Center of Theology

american
university
studies

Series VII: Theology and Religion
Vol. 237

PETER LANG
New York • Washington, D.C./Baltimore • Bern
Frankfurt am Main • Berlin • Brussels • Vienna • Oxford

Richard A. Nicholas

The Eucharist as the Center of Theology

A Comparative Study

PETER LANG
New York • Washington, D.C./Baltimore • Bern
Frankfurt am Main • Berlin • Brussels • Vienna • Oxford

Library of Congress Cataloging-in-Publication Data

Nicholas, Richard A.
The Eucharist as the center of theology: a comparative study /
Richard A. Nicholas.
p. cm. — (American university studies. Series VII, Theology and religion; v. 237)
Includes bibliographical references and index.
1. Mass. 2. Catholic Church—Doctrines. I. Title. II. Series.
BX2215.3.N53   234'.163—dc22   2005013276
ISBN 0-8204-7497-5
ISSN 0740-0446

Bibliographic information published by **Die Deutsche Bibliothek**.
Die Deutsche Bibliothek lists this publication in the "Deutsche
Nationalbibliografie"; detailed bibliographic data is available
on the Internet at http://dnb.ddb.de/.

The paper in this book meets the guidelines for permanence and durability
of the Committee on Production Guidelines for Book Longevity
of the Council of Library Resources.

Printed in Germany

To my parents, Anthony and Eileen Nicholas, who
were my first example of covenental love.

TABLE OF CONTENTS

PART II
THEOLOGY AND THE EUCHARIST IN THE THOUGHT
OF SAINT THOMAS AQUINAS

FOREWORD

Few things can be more gratifying to an author than to have his work taken thus seriously by a student as to have led him to devote most of a decade to a scrupulous examination of its merits and demerits. Inasmuch as Dr. Nicholas' criticism bears upon my view of theological method, his request that I write a foreword to his learned study and criticism of my proposed revision of the theological metaphysics of St. Thomas affords an opportunity to discuss and, it may be hoped, to clarify the role of theological method.

With Paul Tillich, I understand theological method as the formal cause of theological system, in that it provides the criterion or principle by which the congeries of statements comprising the material of the system are rationally unified, and thereby become coherent, discussable, and available to critical examination. Theological statements not submitted to methodological control lack the coherence, the intrinsic, intelligible unity, indispensable to their critical discussion. In brief, theology cannot but be systematic, methodologically controlled, if it is to be theology at all.

The first question of the *Summa Theologiae* is open to this interpretation by reason of St. Thomas' subordination of an otherwise autonomous rationality to the higher truth of the articles of faith; it is in this sense that I understand St. Thomas to be a systematic theologian. Not all agree that he is; e.g., Chenu and von Balthasar do not consider his thought to be thus methodologically unified.[1] This view of St. Thomas requires the discussion of his theological works to be other than theological. For example, St. Thomas' collected works may be regarded as a historical reality, thus as the object of historical

---

1 M.-D. Chenu, *Is Theology a Science?* Tr. A. H. N. Green-Armytage (New York: Hawthorn Books, 1959), at 113; H. U. von Balthasar, in *The Glory of the Lord*, I: *Seeing the Form*, at 75. Von Balthasar agrees with the limits placed by Chenu on the scientific aspect of St. Thomas' theology: see *The Glory of the Lord, I: Seeing the Form;* tr. John Riches (San Francisco: Ignatius Press; New York, Crossroad, 1982) at 75; in *The Theology of Karl Barth,* von Balthasar repeatedly describes St. Thomas as a transitional figure in the history of theology, *in via* from a cosmological to a historical mindset: see pp. 213 ff., 217.

study; they may be regarded as aesthetic or symphonic, in the sense
von Balthazar has given those terms, thus as the object of an artistic
appreciation. However, insofar as theology is viewed as St. Anselm
viewed it, which is to say, classically, with St. Thomas, as a *fides
quaerens intellectum*, it is a science, a quest for understanding on its
own terms, not as subordinate to a higher methodological control
such as history or aesthetics may be thought to provide. Thus viewed,
St. Thomas' theology is systematic, controlled by a distinctively theological method which makes it to be theology and not something else.

Nicholas' study has concluded that my distinguishing St. Thomas'
theology from all other theological or other academic enterprise, by
identifying it as the rigorous application of the act-potency metaphysics to the historical Catholic tradition, is in fact an impoverishment of
the reality: he believes the theology of St. Thomas to be richer than
this definition permits.

John Paul II has observed that St. Thomas' scholarship encapsu-
lated the Catholic culture of the thirteenth century Mediterranean
world.[2] Who could disagree? His published works, amounting to
twenty-five folio volumes in the Parma edition of the *Opera Omnia*,
preserve a Christian wisdom, a learned witness to the Catholic tradition, far more extensive than his metaphysical articulation of the
quest that is theology, the intellectual dimension of the worship in
Truth of the Truth. The *fides quaerens intellectum* is more than the system in which it finds an expression always inadequate, always seeking to transcend itself in order to remain faithful. St. Thomas' faith
drove him to a systematic expression of the *quaerens intellectum* integral to and inseparable from the faith. The Thomist *quaerens*, the
Thomist theology, transcends its systematization. However comprehensive the system achieved, it is always transcended by the *quaerens*
from which it proceeds, quite as the *quaerens* itself, the mind's worship
of the *mysterium fidei*, is transcended by the free gift of the free Truth it
seeks in freedom.

On the other hand, for more than seven centuries St. Thomas'
conversion of Aristotelian metaphysics to the task of theology has
been presented, for the most part uncritically, as at once inseparable
from his theological project and as the *norma normans et non normata* of

2 John Paul II, Address of John Paul II to the members of the Association for the
   Computerization of Lexicological Hermenutical Analyses, Friday, February 1,
   2002.

Catholic theology. This double methodological intransigence forced the *fautores* of its permanent Augustinian alternative to give a distinct methodological formulation to their distinct theological self-consciousness; at the same time, it forced St. Thomas' own supporters to seek within St. Thomas' thought and works the tools for their vigorous defense of his systematic understanding of the Catholic tradition. Their basic resource was the act-potency analysis, given theological application by St. Thomas' programmatic reformulation of Aristotelian metaphysics by way of his analysis of the contingency of creation in terms of essential potency actualized by existence. Aristotelian substance became existentially contingent by its submission to the doctrine of creation, and its consequent theological intelligibility is caused by the distinction St. Thomas made between essence and existence as between potency and act. This restatement of the act and potency analysis by its application to the doctrine of creation, unknown to Aristotle, made St. Thomas the first truly systematic theologian. However often he failed to apply his system to the doctrinal tradition, and however often he failed to grasp the full implication of his conversion of Aristotle, nonetheless the achievement is his. The failure of Thomist theologians to build upon it is comparable to a failure of physicists to advance beyond Newton's mechanics.

The various schools of Thomism may squabble, but not over the authority of the act-potency analysis, summarily, "the real distinction." Other methodological postulates may await their question, but not this. Those who reject its authority, as did Scotus and Suarez, reject Thomism: thus the Thomists. Those who accept the authority of that metaphysical analysis have been defending it for those seven centuries. I count myself among them: my *Covenantal Theology* is a reassertion of the permanent validity, the permanent necessity, of the Thomist method and the Thomist systematics. My revision of it is no more than the continuation of St. Thomas' conversion of Aristotle to the historicity of the Catholic tradition, a conversion initiated by his novel, concrete distinction between essence and existence as between potency and act.

However, insofar as Thomist scholarship has been concerned with his metaphysics, the concern has been for the most part philosophical: St. Thomas' act-potency analysis was understood to be intrinsic to "natural" rationality in the sense of being the work of reason uninformed by the doctrinal tradition. St. Thomas' understanding of a "natural" creation by the one God has been taken for granted; contemporary studies of the analogy of being, for example, never put this crucial matter in issue, quite as its dehistoricizing thrust has gone unchallenged by Thomist theologians. However, its impact upon Catholic theology is no longer acceptable; a series of recent papal initiatives has simply rejected St. Thomas' postulate of a "natural" creation.

In sum, Thomist scholarship has ignored the metaphysical surds which I have addressed and which, in my view, require not a rejection of Thomism, but a loyal enlistment in the project whose necessity he was the first to appreciate: that of submitting the *quaerens intellectum* that is theology to the twin demands of intrinsic coherence and intrinsic submission, which is to say, conversion, to the free, historical truth of the Catholic tradition. These postulates are proper to theological method as such, whether Thomist or Augustinian.

St. Thomas saw that the Aristotelian act-potency analysis, at once of being and of the human understanding of being, was the most capable device at hand for the goal he had in view, the coherent statement of the unity of the faith. Thus he undertook its adaptation, at once to construct a self-consistent theology, and to order and so to defend the tradition as it had been handed down to him, notably by the *Sentences* of Peter Lombard, reinforced by his own study of the Fathers, particularly St. Augustine. The unity of faith and reason was not in issue for St. Thomas; for him as for St. Augustine, these were distinct, and inseparable.

It is essential to Thomist theology that it continue to be self-aware, which is to say, that it continue to be as it has been from the outset, a *quaerens intellectum*, a questioning theology, not in the sense of an agnosticism seeking surcease, but of a Catholicism seeking an always further entry into a mystery of the faith, whose incomprehensibility is its invitation to the mind that can be satisfied only as *quaerens*, as freely seeking further to appropriate the Truth, Augustine's *pulchritudo tam antiqua et tam nova*, who has made us free to seek him, in his Church.

It may then appear that to identify Thomism as the Catholic *fides quaerens intellectum* insofar as freely submitted to the discipline of the act-potency analysis converted by its subordination to the faith, places only those limits upon the mind of St. Thomas which distinguish his theology from that of the followers of St. Augustine. One need only recall St. Thomas controversial stance toward Henry

Peckham to realize that thus to label his theology is not to circumscribe it, but to free it from a confusion with another *quaerens*, equally legitimate, but irreducibly distinct, as the Platonic hylemorphism underlying the Augustinian conversion of phenomenology to free historicity is irreducible to the Aristotelian act-potency analysis underlying St. Thomas' analogous conversion of metaphysics.

The Thomist project was controversial from the outset, simply because of its reliance upon discursive rationality, thus encouraging logical analysis. Theological subscription to "dialectic," i.e., to the use of discursive analysis as though formal logic as such were normative for the truth of an affirmation, had become a problem with the Carolingians; in the eleventh century it had been seen to underwrite the Berengarian heresy. With the death of St. Thomas, those theologians loyal to the older Augustinian phenomenology continued that opposition, contesting the legitimacy of St. Thomas' analytic use of "dialectic." The defensive reaction to this criticism tended not only to canonize the authority of St. Thomas, but also to set his text in concrete, as though itself canonical. Loyalty to St. Thomas became the alternative to the proto-Augustinian rejection of Aristotelian dialectic, to the Scotist refusal of the act-potency analysis, to the Nominalist confusion which followed close upon Duns Scotus and, later, the alternative to Suarez.

That loyalty produced commentators on St. Thomas' theology such as Cajetan, John of St. Thomas, Billuart and Billot; commentary on the text of St. Thomas became a qualification for theological scholarship, replacing finally the commentaries upon Peter Lombard's *Sentences* that had been *de rigueur* in the schools. The Thomist commentaries could not but differ in emphasis, and distinct schools of Thomist thought arose, controversy between which is illustrated if not typified by the notorious dispute *de auxiliis* between Dominicans and Jesuits over the reconciliation of human freedom with divine Providence. Such disputes had the effect of closing the ranks and also the minds of the disputants. Thomism became a loyalty, no longer an inquiry, but a weapon with which to arm oneself for controversy.

These loyalties are now passé, in part because they made systematic theology, i.e., theological metaphysics, monumentally boring. By the middle of the twentieth century the brighter minds had began to look elsewhere for theological occupation; and found in the philological disciplines a freedom denied to systematic theologians who, inso-

far as they raised novel questions, found themselves suspect of dis-
loyalty to St. Thomas, if not to the faith itself. On that unhappy time
we need not dwell. John Paul II, in *Veritatis splendor,* formally dissociated the faith of the Church from any theological system.[3]

The use of theological method did not vanish with the rise of positive theology. The new positive theological learning also required
methodological discipline, but the discipline in view was no longer
theological. "Historical-critical method" had been purified of all doctrinal reliance by the Enlightenment's Deist skepticism, to become another uncritical loyalty, another *armamentorium,* from the weight of
whose 'hermeneutic of suspicion' biblical exegesis and Church history
are only now freeing themselves. Liberated in principle from that doc-
trinaire historicism, those exegetes and Church historians now in
search of a significant past are still unfamiliar with the theology of
history, this having long since been discarded by the Enlightenment.
The systematic theological issues, e.g., in Christology, which had long
ago received a dogmatic resolution, are being newly raised by scholars evidently as unfamiliar with the dogmatic as with the theological
tradition: they are thus unable to do theology in the sense of a discipline possessed of its own methodology, its own identity. Thus ill- or
unprepared, they cannot be relied upon for the systematic exploration
of those dogmatic issues which St. Thomas left unresolved, these are
many, and pressing.

Perhaps the quandary before contemporary theology is best illustrated by Pope John Paul II's recent recognition of the nuptial order of
our creation to the image of God.[4] This doctrinal development was
unanticipated by St. Thomas; it is even foreclosed by his understand-

---

3 John Paul II, *Veritatis splendor, AAS 85* (1993), 1133–1228; at p. 1157 we read:

   Certainly the Church's magisterium does not intend to impose upon the faithful any particular
   theological system, still less a philosophical one.

   José Pereira has described the decline and the end of the papal attribution of
   doctrinal standing to Thomism in "Thomism and the Magisterium. From
   Aeterni Patris to *Veritatis Splendor," Logos* 5:3 (Summer, 2002), 147–183.

4 Its latest expression is in the "Letter to the Bishops of the Catholic Church on
   the Collaboration of Men and Women in the Church and in the World," published by the Congregation for the Doctrine of the Faith on July 31, 2004, where
   we read, with reference to the creation narrative in Gn 1:

   From the very beginning therefore, humanity is described as articulated in the male-female relationship. This is the humanity, sexually differentiated, which is explicitly declared "the image of God."

   Part II, § 5.

ing of the human person as natural, and as substantially complete. But this is only a single instance. The major defect of the Thomist metaphysical theology is its incomplete conversion from its nonhistorical, cosmological antecedents: viz., its continuing presupposition of the intrinsic necessity of being and of truth, a failure built into the Aristotelian metaphysics, whose conversion to the historicity of revelation and of grace St. Thomas left quite incomplete, and which his followers did not advance: e.g., they have not perceived that the conversion of act and potency in the case of the existence - essence polarity (the "real distinction) is equally a conversion of form and matter, of accident and substance, for the conversion frees the intelligibility of substance from immanent necessity under those analyses as well. This failure of methodological consistency has paralyzed the Thomist theological enterprise; one could hardly find more probative evidence of the identity of the Thomist theology with its theological method.

With this, then, I rest my case. It leaves untouched what is urged by Dr. Nicholas: viz., the enormous wealth of the religious tradition enshrined in St. Thomas' theological works, but at the same time insists that if this Golconda is to be mined theologically, it must be mined systematically.

Donald J. Keefe, S.J.
Fordham University,
August 18, 2004

ACKNOWLEDGEMENTS

Writing a book in itself, let alone one that focuses on covenantal union, has heightened my appreciation for the fact that human beings are most like God when they are in a personal relationship with one another. With this appreciation in mind, I should like to recognize several people who have assisted me in this writing endeavor. First, I wish to acknowledge my parents, Anthony and Eileen Nicholas, for the support and encouragement that only they could give. I am also indebted to Rev. Earl Muller, S.J. and Rev. Donald J. Keefe, S.J. for their love of knowledge, guidance, generosity, and loyalty to the Church. In addition, I am thankful for those who assisted with translations: Mr. Patrick Duffy, Mr. David Gritt, Rev. John Hinnebusch, O.P., Rev. Hugh Kennedy, S.J., Rev. Bede Kotlinski, O.S.B., and my brother, Robert Nicholas. My appreciation extends to Mrs. Barbara Baumgartner, who proofread the manuscript, Mr. David Baird, the copy editor, and Mrs. Maria Coletta, who located a copyright holder. Finally, I am grateful for all those unlisted here but whose names I carry in my heart.

Finally, I would like to recognize the following publishers and authors who granted permission to reprint material from their works. They are:

—Brill Academic Publishers (Donald J. Keefe, S.J., *Thomism and the Ontological Theology of Paul Tillich: A Comparison of Systems.* Leiden, Netherlands: E. J. Brill, 1971. Reprinted by permission of the publisher. All rights reserved.)

—Cambridge University Press (*Thomas Aquinas, Summa Theologiae.* Blackfriars edition. London: Eyre & Spottiswoode and New York: McGraw-Hill Book Company, 1964–1976. Reprinted with permission of Cambridge University Press.)

—Donald J. Keefe, S.J. (Donald J. Keefe, S.J., *Covenantal Theology: The Eucharistic Order of History. Revised edition with an appendix.* Novato, CA: Presidio Press, 1996. Reprinted with permission. All rights reserved.)

—James W. Kinn (James W. Kinn, *The Pre-eminence of the Eucharist,* Mundelein, IL. Copyright © 1961 by James W. Kinn.)

—Regnery Publishing, Inc. (From the book *Commentary on the Metaphysics of Aristotle* translated by John P. Rowan. Copyright © 1961. Published by Regnery Publishing, Inc. All rights reserved. Reprinted by special permission of Regnery Publishing, Inc., Washington, D. C.)

—*The Thomist* (John T. Dittoe, O.P., "Sacramental Incorporation into the Mystical Body." *The Thomist* 9 [October 1946]: 469–514; Frederick Jelly, O.P., "Review of *Thomism and the Ontological Theology of Paul Tillich: A Comparison of Systems,* by Donald J. Keefe." *The Thomist* 36 [January 1972]: 166–73; Donald J. Keefe, S.J., "Mary as Created Wisdom: The Splendor of the New Creation." *The Thomist* 47 [July 1983]: 395–420; James A. Weisheipl, O.P., "The Meaning of Sacra Doctrina in Summa Theologiae I, q. 1." *The Thomist* 38 [January 1974]: 49–80. Reprinted with permission of the publisher. All rights reserved.)

—*The Thomist Press* (William A. Wallace, O.P., *The Role of Demonstration in Moral Theology: A Study of Methodology in St. Thomas Aquinas.* Texts and Studies, vol. 2. Washington, D.C.: The Thomist Press, 1962. Reprinted with permission of the publisher. All rights reserved.)

—*Theological Studies* (Earl C. Muller, S.J., "Real Relations and the Divine: Issues in Thomas's Understanding of God's Relation to the World." *Theological Studies* 56 [December 1995]: 673–95. Reprinted with permission of the publisher. All rights reserved.)

—University of Notre Dame Press (*Thomas Aquinas and Karl Barth: Sacred Doctrine and Natural Knowledge of God* by Eugene F. Rodgers, Jr. Copyright 1995 by Eugene F. Rodgers, Jr. Published by University of Notre Dame Press, Notre Dame, IN 46556. Used by permission of the publisher.)

INTRODUCTION

1 Statement of the Problem

Conscious of the distinctive and perpetual problem Christian theology has faced in understanding and explaining the mystery of God as experienced by human beings, Donald J. Keefe, S.J. has proposed a new foundational ordering and governing principle of theology, that of the Eucharist, the sacramental manifestation of the New Covenant. He contends that the *prius*[1] of theology must be the free historical event of the immanence of God in history, the Word Incarnate, the New Covenant, the Eucharist. It is through the eucharistic *prius* that theology, according to Keefe, is a free inquiry into the free affirmation of the free Truth Who is the Christ, historically and sacramentally present within the Church.[2] This Christ-Church union is the accomplishment of the divine plan, namely, the Father sending the Son to give the Spirit. Hence, the Eucharist, as the *prius* of theology, is affirmed to be freely appropriated in history as Event and as Trinitarian—imaging the Christ-Church-New Covenant reality.

In contradistinction, St. Thomas Aquinas apparently locates his unity of theology or *prius* not in the Eucharist but in theology's object, God. In question one of the *Summa theologiae*, Aquinas states, "all things whatsoever that can be divinely revealed share in the same formal objective meaning....they are included under holy teaching as a single science."[3] Thus, there appears to be a divergence between

---

1 While a more detailed explanation of the term *prius* will follow in part I chapter one, an initial definition here is beneficial. The term can be defined according to two orders. In the order of logic, it means a presupposition, a postulate, or a condition of possibility. In the order of metaphysics, it is equivalent to a foundational cause that has no prior possibility.

2 This phrase will be explained in sections one and two of part I, chapter one.

3 St. Thomas Aquinas, *Summa theologiae*, Blackfriars Edition (New York: McGraw-Hill, 1964–1976), I 1.3. (Hereafter, referred to as *ST.)* The Benziger edition's

both men's positions as to the location of the theological *prius*. Keefe even objects that Aquinas' location of the *prius* in the *Deus Unus* distinguishes it from the *Deus Trinus* which emphasizes the relationality of God. This *prius* is developed, Keefe believes, in a necessitarian fashion that is apart from revelation and in the end a "cosmological monism again triumphs over the historical and covenantal revelation of the Trinity."[4] By dehistoricizing the One God, Keefe believes that Aquinas is ultimately confronted with the problem of how to relate such a God to history, to creation. Creation is in a real relation to God but not God to creation.

Hence, this present work is an analysis of Keefe's theology insofar as it is structured around a eucharistic *prius*. It will investigate the nature of a theological *prius*, why Keefe selects the Eucharist as the *prius*, and the implications of his doing so. In order to augment this analysis, Keefe's theology will be compared to that of Aquinas on this issue. Keefe's theology will provide the questions that are asked of Aquinas' theology. Consequently, a "testing dialogue" will ensue so as to establish the possibility of a limited convergence between the two theologians regarding this issue.[5] It will be shown that Keefe is generally correct in his assessment of Aquinas' *prius* when Aquinas' *corpus* is read in an "idealized" manner, that is, when Aquinas is strictly held to the consequences of his use of Aristotle's act-potency methodological system. It will be shown, however, that when Aquinas' *corpus* is read in a more "textual" manner, that is, when it is read more on its own terms and less in terms of the principles and dictates of the methodological system, there is more of a convergence in the thought of the two theologians than Keefe initially recognizes. There is "a movement toward" and not "an arrival at."[6] In the end, by reading

---

translation is also instructive: "whatever has been divinely revealed possesses the one precise formality of the object of science; and therefore is included under sacred doctrine as under one science."

4 Donald J. Keefe, *Covenantal Theology: The Eucharistic Order of History*, revised edition with an appendix (Novato, California: Presidio Press, 1996), 20.

5 The author is indebted to D. Thomas Hughson, S.J. for suggesting this language.

6 The author first learned of this understanding of convergence from Eugene F. Rogers, Jr., *Thomas Aquinas and Karl Barth: Sacred Doctrine and the Natural Knowledge of God* (Notre Dame, Indiana: University of Notre Dame Press, 1995) and James J. Buckley, review of *Thomas Aquinas and Karl Barth: Sacred Doctrine and the Natural Knowledge of God*, by Eugene F. Rogers, Jr., *The Thomist* 61 (April 1997): 320–25.

Aquinas in his own right, Aquinas provides more of what Keefe desires of a theological *prius* than Keefe initially realizes. This work will develop these Thomistic resources that theologians, Keefe included, are generally not aware of as being present.

There are two reasons why Aquinas has been chosen as a dialogue partner for Keefe's eucharistic or covenantal theology. First, one mode Keefe uses to express his theology is a converted Aristotelian metaphysics. Aristotle's metaphysics is fundamentally sound, according to Keefe, but it must be converted in order to articulate freely a free revelation. Aquinas holds to the same belief. The second reason is closely related to the first. Both theologians hold that metaphysics is to be subservient to revelation, the faith. Revelation has primacy over method. However, the relationship between revelation and metaphysics is one of correlation. Revelation is not a matter of methodological necessity, but philosophy does supply the method by which the revelation is articulated. Since the revelation is free and not necessary, the philosophy must be converted so that the correlation supports and maintains this freedom. Keefe believes that Aquinas made a noble attempt to convert the Aristotelian metaphysics in order that it freely articulate the faith but, in the end, the conversion was not complete. Keefe attempts in his work to take up again the challenge and strives to make the conversion more complete with the hope of moving Catholic systematic theology beyond the confines of Thomism.

2 Present Status of the Problem

In order to situate the present status of research into the problem mentioned above, the statement, "the Eucharist is the *prius* of theology," will be examined in three areas.

First, the statement itself is a methodological statement. Thus, what is the current status of theological method? Within this century, both Roman Catholic and Protestant theologians have given much attention to the function and use of method in theology. One methodological issue that is of concern here is the relationship between revelation and method. Among Protestant theologians, Karl Barth ad-

vocates a method that maintains the primacy of revelation.[7] Paul Tillich agrees but also holds that revelation can be correlated with a philosophical method (in Tillich's case, Platonic metaphysics) which
provides a means for articulating the revelation.[8] The revelation,
however, is not dominated by the method but is served by it. Catholic
theologians, like Bernard Lonergan and Karl Rahner, have used Aristotelian metaphysics to articulate the revelation. Keefe agrees with
this correlation principle and is comfortable in using either a Platonic
or an Aristotelian metaphysics. He, however, insists that it is important to recognize and delineate the *a priori*, the presuppositions that
undergird each metaphysics. This attention to meta-methodology
helps to avoid the imprecision, inconsistency, and incoherence that
has at times tainted different theologies when a system is not structured to allow for the freedom of revelation. Keefe holds that Aquinas
has not always been consistent in his application of the Aristotelian *a
priori* (e.g., the inclusion of the act-potency relationship of *esse*-
essence); therefore, he advocates the restructuring of his theology in
order to liberate it from the confines of necessity. To date, current
scholarship has not sufficiently reviewed Keefe's use of method in this
manner in order to join him in the challenge of jarring Catholic systematic theology from the confining methodological structures of the
Thomistic tradition and to set it on a new course.

The second area involves the status of the Eucharist in Keefe and
Aquinas' work. Keefe's treatment of the Eucharist is primarily laid out
in his major work, *Covenantal Theology: The Eucharistic Order of History*.
Again, scholarly reaction and review of Keefe's work has been sparse.
While the reviewers have a general understanding of Keefe's meth-
odological novelty, this general knowledge has not led to a specific
change in course. *Covenantal Theology* has been reviewed by Eugene
TeSelle, W. Charles Heiser, and B. R. Brinkman.[9] Of them, Brinkman

7 Karl Barth, *Church Dogmatics*, vol. I/1 The Doctrine of the Word of God, translated by G.T. Thomson (Edinburgh: T. & T. Clark, 1963), 11–13, 134–135, 339–
   344. Cf. Karl Barth, *Dogmatics in Outline* (New York: Harper & Brothers, 1959),
   16–17, 22, 83–84.
8 Paul Tillich, *Systematic Theology*, vol. 1 (Chicago: University of Chicago Press,
   1951), 59–64.
9 Eugene TeSelle, review of *Covenantal Theology*, by Donald J. Keefe, *America* 168
   (8 May 1993): 19; W. Charles Heiser, review of *Covenantal Theology*, by Donald J.
   Keefe, *Theology Digest* 38 (Winter 1991): 364; B. R. Brinkman, "Allargando Poco a

has a greater grasp and appreciation of the methodological shift that Keefe is proposing. He recognizes the importance of Keefe's assertion that the reality of revelation is above all not an abstraction. The divine Word comes to us concretely. Thus, "free substance" makes sense in a manner that "free being" does not. "Free substance" is given a significance by the divine action which confers on it autonomy and freedom (the New Covenant). This constitutes, in Brinkman's judgment, "a fresh theological principle." As such, "greater clarity in the work's construction might have given us a fresh classic, or at least a monument. As it is, Keefe, if not to be swallowed whole, is to be taken seriously."[10]

There has also been mention of Keefe in some recent books. Keefe's insistence that the New Covenant consists of a marital relationship between Christ and His Church, between the Head and the Body, between the masculine and feminine that is signed sacramentally is of interest to some who are engaged in feminist theology. Ralph Martin, in *The Feminist Question*, uses Keefe to further his explanation why women can not share in the active (masculine and, therefore, priestly) role of Christ as over and against the Church.[11] While she does not agree with this "spousal" position, Susan Ross, in *Extravagant Affections*, recognizes Keefe's contribution to its articulation and defense.[12] Herbert Vorgrimler cites *Covenantal Theology* in the bibliography of his book *Sacramental Theology*.[13] However, in all three cases, the references are brief and not substantial. The core methodological principles of Keefe's theology are not discussed.

To return to a broader context, scholarly work in Aquinas' eucharistic doctrine in the nineteenth and twentieth centuries may be understood in two stages. The first extends approximately from the time of Pope Leo XIII's *Aeterni Patris* to Pius XII's *Humani Generis*. In this stage, Aquinas' theology was accepted on the whole uncritically, for it was often used to defend the Church against challenges to such doc-

---

Poco: An Essay Review," review of *Covenantal Theology*, by Donald J. Keefe, *Heythrop Journal* 36 (January 1995): 65–72.

10 Ibid., 70.

11 Ralph Martin, *The Feminist Question: Feminist Theology in the Light of Christian Tradition* (Grand Rapids, Michigan: W. B. Eerdmans, 1994), 389–90.

12 Susan Ross, *Extravagent Affections: A Feminist Sacramental Theology* (New York: Continuum, 1998), 109.

13 Herbert Vorgrimler, *Sacramental Theology*, translated by Linda M. Maloney (Collegeville, Minnesota: Liturgical Press, 1992), 321.

trines, as the Real Presence (transubstantiation) and the sacrifice of
the Mass. Thus, scholarly work was largely apologetic and did not
systematically probe Aquinas' theology as theology. That is to say, it
did not ask systematic questions to test its consistency and cohesiveness. The manuals and commentaries by theologians such as Ludovico Billot, Emmaneul Doronzo, Giuseppe Filograssi, J. M. Hervé,
Reginald Garrigou-Lagrange, and Antonius Piolanti are good examples of the work during this period.[14]

The second stage, which in a sense runs parallel to the first,
started early in the nineteenth century when the theological faculty of
Tübingen began emphasizing the Church as communitarian and initiated a return to source studies of the Church's tradition. Also at this
time, the French Benedictine, Prosper L. P. Guéranger, called for a renewal of corporate rather than individual eucharistic worship.[15] A
century later, Édouard Le Roy, a Modernist, began pointing out problems with scholastic philosophy and stated that the Council of Trent
never intended to canonize one philosophy over another.[16] Aristotelian categories were seen to be mechanistic and unable to convey per-
sonalist considerations (*ex opere operato* vs. *ex opere operantis*). Trying to
avoid the rationalism and individualism of scholasticism, another
Benedictine, Odo Casel, relied on Ansgar Vonier and the phenome-
nologist Edmund Husserl to explain the eucharistic ritual as mystery.[17] By performing the ritual, the congregation entered into the
saving deeds of Jesus Christ. Maurice de la Taille gave some momentum to the emerging Liturgical Movement by discussing the meal as-

14 Ludovico Billot, *De Ecclesiae Sacramentis: Commentarius in Tertiam Partem S. Thomae*, 2 vols. (Rome: Gregorian University Press, 1931); Emmaneul Doronzo, *De Eucharistia*, 2 vols. (Milwaukee: Bruce, 1947); Giuseppe Filograssi, *De Sanctissima Eucharistia: Questiones Dogmaticae Selectae*, 6th ed. (Rome: Gregorian University Press, 1957); J. M. Hervé, *Manuale Theologiae Dogmatiae*, 4 vols. (Westminister, Maryland: Newman Bookshop, 1946); Antonius Piolanti, *De Sacramentis*, 3rd ed. (Rome: Marietti, 1951).
15 Prosper L.P. Guéranger, *Institutions Liturgiques*, 4 vols. (Paris: Société Générale de Librairie Catholique, 1880), esp. 3: 475, 481, 589–90; 4: 308.
16 Édouard Le Roy, *Dogme et Critique* (Paris: Bloud, 1907).
17 Odo Casel, *Le Mystère du Culte dans le Christianisme*, Lex Orandi, vol. 6 (Paris: Les Éditions du Cerf, 1946); Odo Casel, *The Mystery of Christian Worship and other Writings*, ed. Burkhard Neunheuser (London: Darton, Longman and Todd, 1962); Anscar Vonier, *A Key to the Doctrine of the Eucharist* (London: Burns Oates & Washbourne, 1925); and Anscar Vonier, *The New and Eternal Covenant* (New York: Benziger Brothers, 1930).

pect of the Eucharist even though his primary focus was on the relationship between the immolation on the Cross, the Last Supper, and the Mass.[18]

In the 1960s, Edward Schillebeeckx reiterated concerns over the accident-substance categories of scholasticism, especially in light of advances in modern physics.[19] Instead, he emphasized the insights phenomenology provided into sign-value and applied these insights to sacramental theology. Understanding how reality can be experienced *in* a sign rather than pointing *to* a sign, enabled him to reinterpret transubstantiation in terms of transsignification.[20] This development allowed Edward Kilmartin to speak of the Eucharist not in terms of an event (a change in substance) but as a sign of mystery.[21] With these new insights and the momentum of the ecumenical movement, other Protestant theologians (e.g., F. J. Leenhardt and Max Thurian) began to reshape their own understanding of the Eucharist and sacramental presence.[22]

While much more can be said with regard to the contributions of individual theologians, Protestant and Catholic, it is evident that Aquinas' eucharistic doctrine and his insistence on *ex opere operato* and the event character of the sacrament, in this stage of scholarly research, has been placed to the side. This is primarily due to a dissatisfaction with its use of the Aristotelian impersonal categories of accidents and substance.

---

18   Maurice de la Taille, *Mysterium Fidei* (Paris: Gabriel Beauchesne, 1921).

19   Edward Schillebeeckx, *The Eucharist*, translated by N.D. Smith (New York: Sheed and Ward, 1968).

20   Edward Schillebeeckx, "Transubstantiation, Transfinalization, Transignfication," in *Living Bread, Saving Cup*, edited by R. Kevin Seasoltz, translated by David J. Rock (Collegeville, Minnesota: Liturgical Press, 1982).

21   Edward J. Kilmartin, *Christian Liturgy: Theology and Practice* (Kansas City: Sheed & Ward, 1988), especially part III.

22   F. J. Leenhardt, "This is My Body," in *Essays on the Lord's Supper*, general editors J. G. Davies and A. Raymond George, Ecumenical Studies in Worship, vol. 1 (Richmond, Virginia: John Knox Press, 1958); Max Thurian, *The One Bread*, translated by Theodore DuBois (New York: Sheed and Ward, 1969); Max Thurian, *The Mystery of the Eucharist: An Ecumenical Approach*, translated by Emily Chisholm (Grand Rapids, Michigan: William B. Eerdmans, 1983); Max Thurian, "The Real Presence," in *Christianity Divided: Protestant and Roman Catholic Theological Issues*, Daniel J. Callahon et al. (New York: Sheed and Ward, 1961); and Max Thurian, "Toward a Renewal of the Doctrine of Transubstantiation," in *Christianity Divided: Protestant and Roman Catholic Theological Issues*, Daniel J. Callahon et al. (New York: Sheed and Ward, 1961).

The third area deals with the status of the *prius* of theology in Keefe and Aquinas. Scholarly reaction and evaluation of Keefe's work on this issue has been limited to five scholars' reviews of his book, *Thomism and the Ontological Theology of Paul Tillich: A Comparison of Systems*. The five reviewers are: A. D. Galloway, Frederick Jelly, Noel D. O'Donoghue, Vincent G. Potter, and John E. Zuck.[23]

Jelly, a Dominican theologian, presents a thorough and accurate summary of the book's purpose which he notes from the preface is to discern "the formal structural principles which make theology what it is." Jelly is appreciative of this endeavor:

> Such a work is of special significance in our age because the emphasis upon interdisciplinary studies in general, and upon the correlation of the secular disciplines and theology in particular, makes it imperative to distinguish them with sufficient clarity. Otherwise Christian faith becomes subject to the critical judgment of some humanistic norm, instead of the revealed categories of the Bible which, in the context of a living Tradition of the Church's teaching authority, must be the foundation for discovering their contemporary counterparts.[24]

Jelly notes that Keefe's study of the two diverse ontological methods of theology (Platonic Augustinianism and Aristotelian Thomism) should enable each tradition "to be in a better position of mutual enrichment by sharing insights in their common Christian problem of developing a viable theology in our secularized society."[25] In so doing, the book helps to clarify theology's "special role as a scientific reflection within the believing community as well as open up ecumenically

---

23 A. D. Galloway, "St. Thomas and Tillich," review of *Thomism and the Ontological Theology of Paul Tillich: A Comparison of Systems*, by Donald J. Keefe, *The Expository Times* 83 (July 1972): 313; Frederick Jelly, review of *Thomism and the Ontological Theology of Paul Tillich: A Comparison of Systems*, by Donald J. Keefe, *The American Ecclesiastical Review* 167 (June 1973): 423–24; Frederick Jelly, review of *Thomism and the Ontological Theology of Paul Tillich: A Comparison of Systems*, by Donald J. Keefe, *The Thomist* 36 (January 1972): 166–73; Noel D. O'Donoghue, review of *Thomism and the Ontological Theology of Paul Tillich: A Comparison of Systems*, by Donald J. Keefe, *Scottish Journal of Theology* 25 (August 1972): 354–56; Vincent G. Potter, review of *Thomism and the Ontological Theology of Paul Tillich: A Comparison of Systems*, by Donald J. Keefe, *Theological Studies* 34 (December 1973): 732; and John F. Zuck, review of *Thomism and the Ontological Theology of Paul Tillick: A Comparison of Systems*, by Donald J. Keefe, *Journal of the American Academy of Religion* 41 (June 1973): 271–72.
24 Frederick Jelly, review of *Thomism and the Ontological Theology of Paul Tillich: A Comparison of Systems*, by Donald J. Keefe, *The Thomist* 36 (January 1972), 166.
25 Ibid., 171.

different approaches to the inexhaustible riches of the Christian revelation."[26]

Such appreciation of Keefe's work does not, however, inhibit Jelly
from raising a few crucial issues which challenge some of Keefe's con-
tentions. There are three. First, Jelly takes exception with Keefe's insistence that pure nature is not a real possibility but only a conceptual
possibility and that it functions as a counter-concept by which the
gratuity of grace can be understood. For Jelly, "if we cannot conceive
of pure nature as a real possibility, then the reality of grace itself
seems to be somewhat compromised in that its distinctness would not
be discernible to us."[27] Rather, he holds that grace is able to elevate
and permeate that which would otherwise be pure nature in humanity, for potency does not cease to remain in a being even after its fulfillment.[28]

Second, by calling Christ the Prime Analogate of being because
He is the formal cause of the substantial actuality of the human race,
Keefe tends "to confuse certain formalities in the dynamic relationship between faith and reason that is the act of doing systematic theology."[29]

Third, Jelly questions whether Keefe's conclusion that Tillich's system differs from Thomism only *qua* system (i.e., in its logic, ontology,
and use of analogy), is entirely true. Keefe's "clarifications have certainly removed much misunderstanding and so are invaluable to the
ecumenical dialogue between various Christian theologians. However, it surely is not a service to authentic ecumenism if what is al-
leged to be common to the different faith-traditions is not so in
reality."[30]

In his review, O'Donoghue comments that Keefe "is engaged in
an ambitious project of systematic restatement" in his comparison of
the two systems which he views not as two different systems but as
two alternatives.[31] O'Donoghue, along with Jelly, recognizes that the
purpose of Keefe's book is not exegesis but the presentation of two
systems. Keefe does add "his own valuable insights to this general

---

26 Ibid.
27 Ibid.
28 Ibid.
29 Ibid.
30 Ibid., 173.
31 O'Donaghue, 354–55.

movement of thought"; however, O'Donoghue would prefer more references to the primary texts involved.[32] Consequently, he adds, "One is left wondering whether the term 'Thomism' should be applied to this system; perhaps it should be called 'post-Thomism.'"[33]

Potter, a philosopher, finds the purpose of the book (namely, to discern the formal structural and methodological principles which make theology what it is) to be "a live issue if there ever was one" and deserving of attention since "the question explored is hardly settled."[34] Potter not only has a good grasp of Keefe's contention that Christian theological method must be a method of correlation but also is perceptive in realizing that Keefe is ultimately dealing with "the problem of general hermeneutics, i.e., with the problem of metaphysics, which seeks to understand the structures of being which are isomorphic with the structure of knowing."[35] As a philosopher, he leaves then "the interested reader to explore, to judge, and to criticize....The conclusion he [Keefe] draws may be unexpected, controversial, perhaps even erroneous, but it is certainly worthy of consideration."[36]

While these reviewers present summaries and some critical comments on Keefe's first book, one is left wondering if they really grasp the impact of the transformation Keefe is proposing to make the revelation truly intelligible. Galloway, even though his review is the shortest, comes closest to this recognition by stating, "Both systems are open to correction and revision in light of the union of essence and existence, of concrete and universal, in Jesus Christ."[37] He believes that this correction and revision "could be of profound importance for the further elaboration of a Catholic-Protestant ecumenical theology."[38] One is left again, however, asking the question of whether this reviewer has made the fundamental metaphysical shift that Keefe is requiring. For Keefe, philosophy no longer dictates to the revelation. The revelation defines philosophy. The revelation is free, therefore, its articulation must be free and not necessary. Either of the

---

32 Ibid., 355.
33 Ibid.
34 Potter, 732.
35 Ibid., 733.
36 Ibid. Zuck's comments do not contribute anything further to the issues at hand and therefore will not be discussed here.
37 Galloway, 313.
38 Ibid.

two philosophical systems will impose necessity if they are not radically transformed by a free *prius* or prime analogate.

Joyce Little, in her book, *Toward a Thomistic Methodology*, has grasped the radicalness of Keefe's proposal.[39] There she deals with the limitations of Aquinas' transformation of the Aristotelian method with the introduction of the *esse*-essence distinction, which is fundamentally rooted in Keefe's understanding of a theological *prius*.[40] This is the only work to date which not only comprehends Keefe's thought in depth but actually goes about implementing and applying the proposed transformation. Thus, she does what Keefe has been calling for all along: to jar theology loose from the confines of past methodologies so that it may articulate the faith in a newer manner that respects the freedom of the revelation.

While much work has been done on the nature and even the terminology associated with theology and sacred doctrine (e.g., Marie-Dominique Chenu, Reginald Garrigou-Lagrange, Yves Congar, and Gerald Van Ackeren), the issue of the location of Aquinas' *prius* has only been approached tangentially. John H. Wright speculates that the *prius* may be identified with God as the final end.[41] Thomas R. Potvin raises the possibility of locating it with Christ as the source and exemplar of creation, while James W. Kinn proposes Christ present in the sacrament of all sacraments, the Eucharist.[42] More recently, Eugene F. Rogers, Jr. (in his book, *Thomas Aquinas and Karl Barth*, which relies on the work of Michel Corbin and, to a lesser extent, Victor Preller), closely approaches some of Keefe's major points by arguing that in the first question of the *Summa theologiae*, for Aquinas, a science is more Aristotelian the more it proceeds from first principles.[43] These first principles are Scripture and the Person of Jesus

---

39 Joyce A. Little, *Toward a Thomist Methodology*, Toronto Studies in Theology, vol. 34 (Lewiston/Queenston: The Edwin Mellon Press, 1988).

40 Little, 5–39.

41 John H. Wright, *The Order of the Universe in the Theology of St. Thomas Aquinas* (Rome: Gregorian University Press, 1957).

42 Thomas R. Potvin, *The Theology of the Primacy of Christ according to St. Thomas and its Scriptural Foundations*, Studia Friburgensia, nouvelle séri, 50 (Fribourg, Switzerland: University Press, 1973); James W. Kinn, *The Pre-eminence of the Eucharist among the Sacraments according to Alexander of Hales, St. Albert the Great, St. Bonaventure, and St. Thomas Aquinas*, Dissertationes ad Lauream, 31 (Mundelein, Illinois: Saint Mary of the Lake Seminary, 1960).

43 Rogers, 21–31; Michel Corbin, *Le Chemin de la Théologiae chez Thomas d'Aquin*, Bibliothèque des archives de philosophie, nouvélle seri, 16 (Paris: Beauchesne,

Christ. Sacred doctrine then has a "christoformity" about it (i.e., is Christocentric, the prime analogate being Christ). This dissertation will move this study of a theological *prius* even further.

3 Statement of Procedure

Keefe has constructed and presented a unique theology. This work will move the scholarly discussion to the next logical level. It will investigate and test the nature of such a theology by utilizing an analytical, comparative, and evaluative approach. First, this work will analyze the constitutive principles of Keefe's eucharistic theology. It will examine his methodological presuppositions, his conversion of Aristotelianism, the nature of a theological *prius qua prius*, and the reasons for identifying the Eucharist as the *prius*. A similar analysis will be undertaken with regards to Aquinas' Aristotelian transformation of theology, his method, and identification of a theological *prius*.

Once these constitutive principles have been delineated, they will be the focus of a comparison between the two theological systems. Based on the results of this comparison, this work will then evaluate whether Keefe's eucharistic theology is an advance over Aquinas' theology or rather a clarification of it.

Parts I and II are structured with this general description of procedure in mind. Since Keefe's theology provides the initial questions for the "testing dialogue" with Aquinas, Keefe's theology is analyzed first (part I) followed by an analysis of Aquinas' theology (part II). Part I is structured on the premise mentioned above that the relationship between revelation and metaphysics (philosophy) is one of correlation. Thus, the first chapter of part I deals with the revelation while the second chapter deals with the articulation of that revelation via philosophical methodology and metaphysics. The sections of the first chapter deal with the revelation as it is structured metaphysically by a *prius* and analogically by a prime analogate. These terms are defined first and then attention shifts to Keefe's identification of the *prius* as the New Covenant and how it plays out in the economy of salvation. The New Covenant is proleptically actual at the moment of the Incar-

---

1974); Victor Preller, *Divine Science and the Science of God: A Reformulation of Thomas Aquinas* (Princeton: Princeton University Press, 1967).

nation. It is offered and rejected in the Fall. The Fall does not thwart God's intention to establish a covenantal union with His creation; rather, it renders the Covenant redemptive. This union established on the Cross of Calvary is made accessible sacramentally through the Mass and eucharistic transubstantiation. In the end, this New Covenant is an image of the Trinity.

The second chapter of this part opens with an analysis of the methodological and metaphysical implications of Keefe's eucharistic *prius* or prime analogate. As the *prius*, transubstantiation is normative for metaphysics and thus, provides the intelligibility for all of the act-potency correlations that follow (i.e., *esse*-essence, accident-substance, and form-matter). Once this system is explicated, the analysis turns then to Keefe's critique and transformation of Aquinas' theological system in general and his theology of the Eucharist in particular. This analysis is done from the perspective of Keefe's own system.

Since Aquinas does not use the term *prius*, chapter three of part II begins with a study of his use of the comparable term "subject" as distinct from "object." An inquiry into the identification and function of the other philosophical disciplines' subjects provides a richer context for understanding Aquinas' subject of sacred doctrine. The first question of the *Summa theologiae* provides a detailed description of this subject, namely, God. Here Aquinas initially explains how sacred doctrine pertains to the revelation of God. Later, especially in the third part of the *Summa*, Aquinas identifies Jesus Christ as the revelation of God. The progression of his thought in this part constitutes, then, the remaining three chapters of part II. God is made knowable through the relationship His incarnate Son assumes with the rest of creation (chapter four). The Son reveals something of the Godhead through the various roles He performs (chapter five). In such roles, He shows Himself to be the most excellent exemplar by virtue of the fullness of grace He possesses as a result of the hypostatic union. He shares this grace as Head with those who are united with Him in His Mystical Body (chapter six). He, as second Adam, established this mystical union by undoing that which the first Adam did in sin. Grace and Redemption are channeled and applied to sinful humanity through the sacraments. Of the sacraments, the Eucharist is primary, for it is through this sacrament that Christ comes to communicate and unite Himself to the members of His Body by nourishing them with His body, blood, soul, and divinity. This salvific act is made present through transubstantiation. In the end, the Eucharist is the means by which God reveals Himself to His creation and by which He enters into relationship with it. It is the means by which one experiences God and all that is related to God, the subject of *sacra doctrina* (i.e., Christ is the primary referent of the first question of the *Summa theologiae*).

The concluding chapter is a synthesis chapter. Here the issues raised by Keefe's methodological pursuit of a theological *prius*, and asked in "conversation" or "testing dialogue" with Aquinas (throughout parts I and II), will be filled out and synthesized more formally. Included among these issues are: a) the function of two basic metaphysical systems (Platonism and Aristotelianism) in articulating the *prius* (prime analogate) of theology; b) the theological understanding of each theologian's *prius* (free versus necessary; covenantal versus monadic); c) a marital versus an organic understanding of union; d) real relation versus relation of reason; e) transubstantiation as a dynamic event versus static transformation of substances; f) the act-potency relations of being.[44] With this process, it will be possible to see if there are grounds for a convergence on these issues. "Convergence" here does not mean a consensus or an agreement but a shift in the status of previously perceived oppositions or tensions.[45] In so doing, there will be an exposition of resources in Aquinas of which many contemporary scholars are unaware.

---

44 It is important to note that the chronology of these issues is based on Keefe's understanding of theology (i.e., faith seeking understanding [Anselm]). Philosophy is subordinate to the faith and, as such, it provides an articulation of that faith for the sake of human understanding. The faith is organized by a theological *prius* which, for Keefe, is eucharistic. This identification fo the *prius* will have implications for the economy of salvation. Thus, issues of theology will proceed issues of philosophy and then the implications of a eucharistic *prius* will follow.

45 Cf. footnote 6 above.

PART I

THE EUCHARIST AS THE *PRIUS* OF THEOLOGY IN THE THEOLOGICAL AND PHILOSOPHICAL THOUGHT OF DONALD KEEFE

CHAPTER ONE

A THEOLOGICAL UNDERSTANDING
OF THE EUCHARIST

1 General Definition of *Prius*

1.1 Catholic theology: a metaphysics

For Donald Keefe, Catholic theology deals with metaempirical reality and truth and, thus, theology is at bottom a metaphysics.[1] This is due to the fact that once reality is considered contingent (i.e., non-necessary), one leaves the world of natural science where reality necessarily entails its own existence for the world of metaphysics where reality comes into existence and is not necessary.[2] As a metaphysics, Catholic theology's single interest and subject matter is not existence *per se* but existence in Christ.[3] For Keefe, Catholic theology does not

---

1 Keefe, *Covenantal Theology*, 19.
2 Little, 165–66.
3 For Keefe a metaphysics is or is not theological by virtue of its subject matter: to remain theological it must accept the control of that subject matter, which is to say, its theological method is a turn away from the necessarily immanent truth of Aristotelianism to the free and historically transcendent truth of the Christian revelation, the New Covenant which is sacramentallly realized in the Eucharist.

begin with some cosmological *a priori* or *prius* but with the Christ, the historical *a priori* Who is in covenantal union with all of created existence. To use a more classical motif, theology is faith seeking understanding. Therefore, Catholic theology is a free inquiry into the free affirmation of the free Truth Who is the Christ in His Church.[4] It is free to seek out, to inquire into, the mystery of the Christ, in whose life, death, and Resurrection the New Covenant is given and the world created in Christ is redeemed.[5] Consequently, we shall proceed in our investigation into Keefe's theological understanding of the term *prius* and its related term, "prime analogate."

While Keefe does not offer an explicit definition of *"prius,"* its meaning can be discovered by observing how it is used within the context of his theological method. From this context, one discovers that the term *prius* may be used in an order of logic where it can mean a presupposition, postulate, or a condition of possibility. In the order of ontology or metaphysics, it is equivalent to a foundational cause that has no prior possibility (for it is *ex nihilo sui et subjecti*).[6] It is a metaphysically antecedent condition, a cause of another reality by whose priority the second reality is intelligible.[7] Cause implies agency whereas "presupposition," "postulate," or "condition of possibility" do not. These latter terms denote a mere catalyst, which facilitates an effect but whose formality is not present in the effect (e.g., the second Adam is the *prius* of the Fall of the first Adam in so far as the freedom by which the Fall is possible is given only in Jesus Christ. He, however, is not the cause but the condition of possibility for the Fall[8]).

From a different perspective, Keefe also says that Catholic theology is a metaphysics because it has to account for the realism of the Church's worship. The free affirmations of that worship (e.g., the words of consecration, absolution, etc.) are objectively and historically true as causing real salvific events whose reality is on a level transcending sense knowledge. The truth of the free affirmation is neither ideal (in the sense of subjective) nor empirical (in the sense of tangible, visible, audible, etc.).

4   Keefe, *Covenantal Theology*, 10.
5   Ibid.
6   Ibid., 342.
7   Ibid., 346.
8   Ibid., 220–24, 335–37.

1.2 The *prius* as a prime analogate

Analogy is a principle characteristic of metaphysics, for if being were to be understood in a univocal manner, then all reality would be deemed to be in the same manner, which would ultimately lead to monism. Everything would be seen as identically one, and, therefore, there would be no difference between God and creatures.[9] For the realist and Christian, this is clearly not the case. Thus, when *prius* is related to an analogical structure where there is resemblance without identity, *prius* is often referred to as the "prime analogate." The "prime analogate" is that subject to which the perfection expressed by the predicate belongs primarily, *per prius*. It is the prime analogate which possesses the perfection completely and which also has the metaphysical priority which provides the basis for the analogical structure. "Secondary analogates" are those other subjects to which the perfection belongs because of a relation to the prime analogate.[10] They possess this perfection less completely, however.[11]

1.3 The prime analogate's relationship with the analogy of being

These terms are used by Keefe when he considers, in broad philosophical terms, the "analogy of being." The analogy of being deals with the problem of the One and the Many, how beings are individually different yet similar.[12] If the similarity between beings is over-stressed, a monism of some sort will result. If the difference between beings is over-stressed, an extreme pluralism will result. Thus, being is predicated of all beings neither univocally nor equivocally, but analogously. This philosophical consideration has immediate theological implications because it provides the metaphysics for an understanding of how God the Creator relates to creation, how relative participates in being relate to the Absolute Unparticipated Act of Be-

---

9 Tomas Alvira, Luis Clavell, and Tomas Melendo, *Metaphysics*, translated by Luis Supan and M. Guzman, Philosophy Book Series (Manila, Philippines: Sinag-Tala Publishers, 1991), 31.

10 Martin O. Vaske, *An Introduction to Metaphysics* (New York: McGraw-Hill, 1963), 241.

11 Keefe, *Covenantal Theology*, 394, 450.

12 This is the issue of the unity of being.

ing.[13] All other analogies presuppose this ultimate fundamental analogy for their very being and unity. There can be no relation between created beings, no relation between these created beings and the Creator, unless created beings exist. And for them to exist implies that their whole reality is dependently related to the Creator, the Primary Being, Who as their principle of being and unity is not related to a higher Being. The universe of being is united in Being.

When it is understood that the ultimate source of unity is existence itself, it is likewise understood, as well, that the only language adequate to speak of God is the language of the transcendental properties of being, i.e., those qualities which belong to any being insofar as it exists, namely, unity, truth, goodness, and beauty. God, as the source of all being, is one, true, good, and beautiful and the source of all these perfections in creatures who possess them in limited degrees through participation.[14]

1.4 The prime analogate, epistemology, and substance

If the prime analogate is the fullness of being, then it is related to substance and epistemology. Keefe explains:

> The prime analogate is the fullness of being, imparticipate and unlimited, at once the cause of finite being, as that in which the finite participates, and the cause of understanding of the finite, for in the prime analogate the empirical understanding participates. This prime analogate, from the epistemological point of view, is the agent intellect; from the ontological, it is substance in its widest, or unlimited, extension.
>
> The secondary analogate of being is of course substance in some lesser extension; this is the object of empirical knowledge. It has been seen that the potential intellect is actualized in this knowledge, and that any finite or empirical substance is potentially present in such an intellect. This presence is equivalently the actuality of the object known, i.e., its activity or operation.[15]

---

13 Keefe, 61–62. Keefe and Aquinas agree in postulating the analogous character of being, for the metaphysical reality of sacramental realism depends upon it; i.e., the created matter of a sacrament must be in metaphysical relation with the divine for it mediates the divine to the recipient.

14 John J. O'Donnell, *The Mystery of the Triune God* (Mahwah, New Jersey: Paulist Press, 1989), 118.

15 Donald J. Keefe, *Thomism and the Ontological Theology of Paul Tillich* (Leiden, Netherlands: E. J. Brill, 1971), 22.

Knowledge is a logical consequence of the analogy of being since analogy is the basis of knowledge and language. In an act of knowledge, the object is first perceived to be as existing. The human intelligence knows it as something which is. Second, given the initial knowledge *that something is*, human intelligence acquires a better understanding of that particular object by way of analogy, by way of comparison. The intellect measures the object against different entities so as to understand the object's specific essence. The object not only exists, but it exists as a particular kind of being. This essential knowledge is gained through discovering how the object relates and compares to other entities, multiplicities, and concepts. In other words, it is through experience that human beings learn to apply existence (*esse*) and essence (a specific mode of existence) analogously to reality in order to acquire knowledge.

As stated above, the prime analogate from the metaphysical point of view is substance in the widest extension; the secondary analogates are substance in a lesser extension.[16] Since the prime analogate is substance as such, it is the *a priori* unity of being, with being appropriated to the secondary analogates analogously. Consequently, the understanding and the reality of substance is identified with the understanding and the reality of being itself. Keefe holds that the particular notion of substance may be derived from either the logical method of Aristotelianism which asserts the materiality of substance or from the intuitive, dialectical method of Platonism which requires its immateriality. Yet, in either case, theology is concerned with an understanding of being and applies itself to the notion of substance.[17] The identification of this prime analogate, substance, or *prius*, is the concern of this work.

Theology is concerned with an understanding of being and so applies itself to the notion of substance, but, according to Keefe, it must identify its notion of substance with revelation, with the relation of being to God which is the true understanding of being. There is no Christian theology whose starting point is not a notion of substance which is revelation, and there can be no revelation which is not at least an implicitly metaphysical theology.[18]

---

16 Ibid., 22.
17 Ibid., 29.
18 Ibid.

1.5 Analogical structure: historical or nonhistorical

The substance or subject matter of theology, then, is revelation and from within this revelation a prime analogate is selected to provide an organizational structure to the entire content of that revelation. Choice of this prime analogate is limited to what is most fundamental to the revelation and which can be identified with the revelation, usually either God in His transcendence or Jesus Christ in His immanence. The former is non-historical while the latter is historical. An historical prime analogate is not the dehumanized "immanent *Logos*," but rather it is a divine expression, a communication, an historical event in the Person of Jesus Christ. History is transcended by way of the Lord's free historicity in the world, the sacramental presence of the God-Man to His creatures.[19] Thus, the immanence of Christ is not imposed upon subservient beings but rather is freely and knowingly appropriated by them.[20] Such a prime analogate does not have a prior possibility in some necessary analogy between a "natural" ungraced creation and God.[21] It is free—not despotic—concrete and historical and not the result of any prior necessity. In contrast, a non-historical prime analogate is usually understood to transcend the order of created history by being absent from it. It is absolute and incommunicable, having no real relation to the order of created history, although that order must have a real relation to it because it causes it to be. One consequence of such a prime analogate is a whole host of non-historical created secondary analogates whose historicity is not significant for their unity, truth, and goodness. In contrast, the secondary analogates of an historical prime possess unity, truth, and goodness as free, as historical, and as events.

1.6 The articulation of the revelation

Catholic theology in general is a metaphysics; metaphysics provides specifically a methodological structure in which to articulate coherently the revelation which is structured analogically by the prime analogate.[22] Such a resultant theological method must itself be a

---

19   Keefe, *Covenantal Theology*, 17.
20   Ibid., 12.
21   Ibid., 21.
22   Ibid., 119.

method of correlation, for by its attention to the interrelation of divinity and humanity in Christ (creator and creation [as in the analogy of being]), theology is inevitably involved in a dualist, correlated methodology.[23] Consequently, Keefe holds that there are two basic and equally valid metaphysical systems which can articulate and interpret the revelation in general or the prime analogate in particular: the discursive-analytical interpretation developed in Thomism and the intuitive-dialectical interpretation developed in Augustinianism (Tillichianism).[24] Each method has reason to lay claim to a "method of correlation" since each exhibits a theological metaphysics which is caused and intrinsically organized by the correlation of polar principles of being.[25] Keefe expounds:

> Each of these systems is the logical alternative to the other; in the ontology of Tillich, the polar principles are contradictory in the order of formal logic; in the Thomist ontology, they are contrary, not contradictory. These alternatives exhaust the logically possible modes of altereity. Thus, while both systems are ontological, in that they assume an isomorphism between the structure of being and of reason, their theological-ontological systems are radically different; the unity or systematic truth of each is caused by a theological method which in turn depends upon an ontological "point of view" in radical contrast to that underlying the alternative system.
>
> But the fact that each system uses a method of correlation causes them to be strikingly similar, and this similarity invites their comparison quite as insistently as their opposition provokes their contrast.
>
> The intrinsic unity of each system is caused by the method of that system in its correlation with the Christian revelation. In both systems, the theological method is theological by reason of this correlation to the revelation; systematic theology exists within this correlation, and not apart from it.[26]

1.7 The correlation: free or unfree

The correlation between the theological method and the revelation may theoretically be free or unfree. If it is free, the method is freely subordinate to the revelation, the prime analogate, as its prior truth and reality. If this were not the case, the prime analogate would then have a methodological *a priori* standing over it which can not be the

---

23 Keefe, *Thomism and Tillich*, xi.
24 Keefe, *Covenantal Theology*, 119.
25 Keefe, *Thomism and Tillich*, 3.
26 Ibid.

case by definition and by the fact that the prime analogate for a Christian theology is *ex nihilo sui et subjecti*.[27] Consequently, the theological statement which arises out of the correlation of the theological method and revelation and provides a response to the *quaerens* (a quest for knowledge of the faith which is an implicit, indispensable dimension of the mind's true worship[28]) that is asked of the revelation is hypothetical, a possible answer which is never definitive.[29] This hypothesis retains its theological truth only as a possible interpretation of the revelation and has value only as a potential truth relative to the actual truth of the revelation.[30] The theological statement is never to be identified with the truth of the *quaerens*. It is never doctrinal, for the formal cause of its truth is only the truth of method which provides for its coherency and cohesiveness. If this were not the case, theology could not continue to learn from a reality (revelation) which can be questioned but not controlled, not comprehended within any rational construct.[31] The freedom of the *prius* and the freedom of the correlation between the revelation and the theological method must be maintained. When this is indeed the case, the correlation is truly theological, *fides quaerens intellectum*.[32] Catholic theology is a free inquiry into the free affirmation of the free Truth; this inquiry, this affirmation, and this revelation rest upon no prior necessary possibility.[33]

If the correlation is unfree, the theological method is imposed upon the revelation. The necessities implicit within the method are worked out and control the revelation, rendering its content subservient to the method. The *prius* then is transcended by a higher source of being and truth from which the inquirer may learn, namely, the method.[34] Consequently, revelation is forced to submit to an autonomous methodological judgment as to the truth of its religious affirmations; these will now be judged according to some standard inherent in a consistent humanism.[35] Theology can only then regress into a

---

27 Keefe, *Covenantal Theology*, 119–20.
28 Ibid., 9.
29 Ibid., 15, 126–27, 132–33.
30 Ibid., 127.
31 Ibid., 132.
32 Ibid., 119–20.
33 Ibid., 10.
34 Ibid., 132.
35 Keefe, *Thomism and Tillich*, x.

cosmological format, whether Aristotelian or Platonic, and is, thus, pagan, non-Christian, and no longer a true Christian theology.[36]

In a free correlation between a theological method and the prime analogate, the method is at the service of the prime. The method, however, can not stand *per se*, for it is a theoretical expression of a pagan insight into the nature of being (the Absolute Being, the One can not be immanent within history, among beings, as one of the many).[37] It is enclosed upon itself and as such can not articulate the free reality with which it is freely correlated.[38] Kurt Gödel has proven that logical structures can never be closed, self-sufficient systems. The mind also can not be absolutized; it is a free coherence and it will not permit itself to be controlled by any logical system.[39] It must, therefore, be converted by the free expressive truth of the revelation so as to mediate revelation's content methodologically since by definition it is self-enclosed and forbidden by its own logic to deal with a free unnecessary truth.[40] With such a conversion, the revelation informs reason, the methodology. The two are freely interrelated and there is a mutual interpenetration. The revelation provides the content and the method articulates it according to its methodological principles and procedures which, after the conversion, respect the freedom implicit in the revelation. Without such a conversion, revelation will be dictated to by some sort of "natural reason" derived from the method.

1.8 Characteristics of the *prius*

To conclude, a brief mention should be made regarding primordiality and preexistence, the characteristics of the *prius*, the prime analogate. For Keefe, the two will coincide in meaning as do all equivalents, but each has its own linguistic flavor which finds expression in distinct usages. Both terms refer to that which is prior or previous in a metaphysical and historical context rather than in a temporal and cosmological context.[41] Even though the primordiality of the prime analogate is not temporal, this does not mean that it is a-historical. As

---

36 Ibid., 121–22.
37 Ibid., xi.
38 Keefe, *Covenantal Theology*, 14.
39 Ibid., 348.
40 Ibid., 9, 14, 384.
41 Ibid., 221, 279.

we shall later see in Keefe's theology, human fallenness is in the here and now. The constitution and offer of the New Covenant, historically realized as an event which brought about space and time, was consequently rejected by a free moral agent in an act of sin. Thus, primordiality, preexistence is neither a temporal nor a cosmological but a relational and historical notion, and, therefore, it has a metaphysical, relational, and historical meaning.[42] While this is the case for both terms, the referent for "primordiality" is usually the first or second Adam and Eve while the referent for "preexistence" is the Christ.

1.9 Section summary

Keefe holds that Catholic theology is at bottom a metaphysics because it deals with a metaempirical reality and truth. This reality and truth is not existence *per se* but existence in Christ. It is the encounter with a person Who transcends the empirical world and yet is immanent within this empirical world. Since we are dealing with existence (i.e., existence in Christ) and existence is neither univocal nor equivocal (cf. the analogy of being), one is dealing then with a *prius* or prime analogate by which all other beings or secondary analogates are intelligible. A *prius*, in the order of metaphysics, is an antecedent condition by whose priority the second reality is intelligible. With regard to the analogy of being, this *prius* is better labeled the "prime analogate." The prime analogate then is that subject to which the perfection expressed by the predicate or secondary analogate belongs primarily. It is the fullness of being and, as such, it is substance in its widest extension. It is that in which all finite beings participate.

Keefe applies this understanding of *prius* or prime analogate to theology. Theology, for him, is faith seeking understanding. It is divine revelation seeking to be proclaimed. The prime analogate provides an organizational structure to the entire content of divine revelation and then either a discursive-analytical or an intuitive-dialectical system methodologically provides for its articulation. The correlation between the revelation and the method is one of freedom because the revelation is freely given. God is not compelled out of necessity to reveal Himself. Consequently, the method must respect this

---

42 Ibid., 221.

freedom and be subordinate to the revelation. Catholic theology is a free inquiry into the free affirmation of the free Truth.

2 Identification of Keefe's *Prius* as the Eucharist

2.1 The identification of the *prius*

Having specified the general nature of a theological *prius*, focus will now shift to the identification and analysis of Keefe's *prius*. Keefe identifies the theological *prius* of Catholic theology to be the Eucharist. Keefe is very detailed and explicit in this identification:

> The Eucharistic Event is the Event of the New Covenant, instituted by the One Sacrifice of the Cross and inseparable from that Sacrifice: by the Eucharistic worship, this Event of covenantal Sacrifice is actual in history as the prime historical reality, the prime analogate of historicity, the concrete criterion by which all else is historically ordered, incorporated into the historical unity of the New Covenant, which alone is able freely to integrate the past, the present and the eschatological perfection of the Good Creation. As the actuality of the Eucharist is sacramental, so also is its historicity: i.e., history as such is intelligible only as the Eucharistic ordering of past, present, eschaton. No other free intelligibility of history has even been proposed.[43]

> The prime analogate…is then historical: the Christ of the New Covenant, as sent by the Father to institute the New Covenant in his nuptial and sacrificial union with his bridal Church in the prime Event which is the created, historical and covenantal imaging and revelation of the Triune God, and at the same time is the Good Creation in which the Immanuel, the Creator, because covenantally and irrevocably immanent in history, is also the redeemer of the fallen creation.[44]

> …the prime analogate, as historical, is not only Trinitarian, but is covenantal also, for it is the prime Event: the Father's sending of the Son to give the Spirit, the *Logos sarx egeneto* of Jn 1:14 by which is accomplished the radically free relation of total ontological dependence of the Good Creation upon the Trinity, a relation which must not be understood as structure but as Covenant, as free Event. From the side of God this relation is the sending, the mission, of the Son by the Father to give the Spirit; from the side of creation, it is the New Covenant in which that mission terminates. From the side of both it is free in the sacramental-historical sense which we have examined,

---

43 Ibid., 42.
44 Ibid., 388.

in which our free sacramental and Eucharistic solidarity in Christ is inseparable from our unfree solidarity in the first Adam, and from our eschatological solidarity in the Spirit....This Event of our solidarity in Christ (in creation, revelation, redemption, and Resurrection) is concrete and historical only as Eucharist; here we must begin, and end, with the Alpha and the Omega.[45]

The prime analogate of such a covenantal metaphysics is ineluctably the Eucharistic representation of the New Covenant in the objective sacramental Event of that representation, which is the Event of the Real Presence, the Event of the Sacrifice of the Mass, the Event of the One Flesh, and thus the Event of the *Logos sarx egenato.*[46]

As evidenced by these four identifying statements, holding such a position has profound implications. These implications include the issues of creation in Christ, His immanence, the Trinitarian mission and its *termini* of New Covenant and Good Creation, the consequences of the Fall which render that immanence sacramental, and solidarity in the redemptive acts of the second Adam. These are the issues that will be considered in the following pages.

The prime analogate is the fullness of being and at once the cause of finite beings. From a metaphysical point of view, this is substance in its widest extension. Theology, as systematic and metaphysical, is likewise concerned with an understanding of being and so applies itself to the notion of substance. Theology identifies its notion of substance with the revelation, with the relation of being to God which is the true understanding of being.[47] Revelation is the free self-communication of God in the Person of Jesus Christ. He is at once the one who mediates the revelation to creation (the means) and the divine reality who is the subject of the mediation, the revelation (the content). Thus, as revelation, He is identified with substance and is the fullness of being. The Christ-Event, as prime analogate, controls the meaning of being, which is the meaning of substance.[48] To put it in philosophical terms, metaphysics has to do with reality and all reality is in Christ.[49]

45 Ibid., 413–14.
46 Ibid., 650.
47 Keefe, *Thomism and Tillich*, 29.
48 Keefe, *Covenantal Theology*, 427.
49 Ibid., 653.

2.2 The prime analogate as immanent in Christ

Thus, the prime analogate for Keefe is immanent within history and is so because the revelation, the Christ, is likewise immanent within history. He is immanent not only as the historical Son of Mary Who is in covenantal union with all of humanity but also as the eucharistic risen sacrificial victim Who transcends and thus orders all of history. The Eucharist is the representation of the Immanuel in the fullness of His historical immanence in His people through the fullness of the New Covenant.[50]

This eucharistic immanence, moreover, is the result of God the Father sending the Son to give the Spirit. Christ is immanent within the universe because He was sent by the Father. Through this mission Christ is sent to constitute creation which, in its constitution on a primordial level, freely accepts the offer to be in covenantal union with its Creator. Mary, through the grace of the Holy Spirit, freely enters into a covenant with her Lord. Thus, the Good Creation responds to the divine initiative (which simultaneously provides for the grace of reception), the New Covenant is constituted, and Christ is immanent within His creation which causes it to be good. Thus, the *terminus* of the Trinitarian mission is creation which is constituted in and by the Son's immanence and as such, God freely enters into a covenant with this creation.[51] The *terminus* of the sending of the Son is not simply the Son incarnate in a "human nature" but the Son freely, covenantly incarnate in historical humanity which is created in and by His mission from the Father. The Son's immanence is the actualization of creation which has no other relation to the triune God than that which is actual in Christ. The free and covenantal immanence of the Son in creation is understood as the formal cause of creation which subsists totally in and by the Son.[52]

While Good Creation and New Covenant are identical substantially, a distinction can be made with regard to their formality. In both cases, the reality is the same, namely, Jesus Christ in His substantial completeness. This is to say, the divine Son of God is united with His humanity which is not to be understood simply in terms of His individual humanity regarded in a static and impersonal, nonrelational

---

50 Ibid., 425.
51 Ibid., 456.
52 Ibid., 442.

sense. Rather, it is the humanity with which He is in covenantal union and which is dependent upon Him for its existence.[53] Keefe states, "It is rather the One Flesh of the New Covenant that terminates the Son's mission, and consequently, the New Covenant is also the object of the divine creative will, which as divine is trinitarian: the sending of the Son by the Father to give the Spirit."[54] With this in mind, the formality of the Good Creation is the coming into existence *ex nihilo*. The formality of the New Covenant is free union with the Christ. Now, although coming into existence and free unity are two different ideas, they are, however, inseparable from one another. When considering the idea of covenant, freedom and entrance into a covenant are two of the leading notions. When considering creation, freedom is not one of the initial concerns but existence is. Yet coming into existence from the hand of God is inseparable from freedom, for they are both identified with Jesus Christ in His completeness.

2.3 Creation in Christ

The *terminus*, then, of the mission of the Son to give the Spirit is not simply the incarnate Christ but also the New Covenant which is the primordial creation in Christ.[55] All of creation and, in particular, humanity is totally dependent upon Him in the order of being.[56] Creation in Christ is, therefore, *gratia Christi*. According to Keefe, it is by, and only by, the free personal immanence of the Son that creation is actual. The Son's immanence is the actualization of creation, for creation *passive spectata* (i.e., the object which is produced by God's free action, in contrast to *active spectata*, creation as a divine act) has no other relation to the Trinity than that which is actual in Christ. This relation is understood to be the mission of the Son and, consequently, the free and covenantal immanence of the Son in creation is understood as the formal cause of creation. "[C]reation in its totality subsists in and by the Son, and not otherwise."[57]

If this is indeed the case, then the mission of the Son by the Father is not something subsequent to a creation which would by supposi-

53 Ibid., 433.
54 Ibid., 433, 442.
55 Ibid., 217–18, 442.
56 Ibid., 166, 178.
57 Ibid., 442–43.

tion have been created on some other basis than the mission.[58] It is the
cause of creation. Other proposed bases such as a "natural creation"
or a divine "intention" or "decree" suppose that the Christ is not
really primordial in the order of creation but was sent *propter pecca-tum*, with the implication that apart from sin the Son would not have
been sent by the Father to give the Spirit. Such a position undercuts
the New Covenant as the prime analogate, since these other bases are
not relational, not covenantal in and of themselves. According to
Keefe, they are monadic and cosmological, for they do not hold that
the Creator is immanent freely and covenantally in His creation.
Rather, God is a monistic divinity Who, as the One, is transcendent
simply, is closed in on itself.[59] This divinity is not relational intrinsi-cally and, consequently, it is not free. Thus, it creates on some other
basis which is not free but static and necessitarian. Even though this
divinity creates, it can not be in a real relation with that creation be-cause intrinsically it is not relational (in a monad there is no other en-tity in which to commit freely and in so doing, determine oneself) and
can not then cause a relational effect. Thus, such a God is not imma-nent covenantally with creation. Rather, for Keefe, creation is accom-plished by a tri-relational God, the trinitarian God Who creates the
world through the sending of the Son to give the Spirit; in other
words, by being immanent within it.

If creation is not grounded on any other basis than the mission of
the divine Son, then it likewise is not a "possible" in the sense of hav-ing an autonomous or "potential" intelligibility as disjunct from its
actual existential subsistence. Keefe considers it absurd to envision
the Absolute God choosing between an infinite number of "possible
objects of creation" held in the divine mind as ideas. This situation
implies potency in God; there is something in God which *can be* actu-alized (to create *this* possibility rather than *that* possibility). Rather,
everything in God is actual. If something exists in the mind of God, it
exists. The creative act of God does not involve choosing between
possibilities for there is no potency in God, Who is Pure Act. Here the
creative action does not involve choice among alternatives but self-commitment, a covenantal subsistent freedom whereby one affirms
one's reality by expending it on another, by committing to another.
This divine action is one of a commitment to creation or it is nothing,

58 Ibid., 232.
59 Ibid., 231.

for this is a strict implication of the *ex nihilo* character of creation. "The freedom of creation *active spectata* requires a cognate freedom in creation *passive spectata.*"[60]

2.4 Section summary

God reveals Himself by sending the Son to give the Spirit. The object of this divine creative mission is the New Covenant by which the Son mediates the revelation to creation and enters into covenantal union with that creation. It is the New Covenant that gives organizational structure to the entire content of divine revelation as the *prius* or prime analogate of theology. It is through the New Covenant that God is immanent within His creation not only as the historical Son of Mary but also as the eucharistic Lord of History Who is continually immanent within creation sacramentally. In other words, through the Trinitarian mission, Christ is sent to constitute creation (Good Creation) which, in its Christological constitution, freely accepts the offer to be in covenantal union with its Creator (New Covenant). This Covenant is maintained then through the sacrament of the Eucharist.

3 The Incarnation

3.1 The Son's covenantal Incarnation

It has been stated above that the *terminus* or object of the divine creative act of the sending of the Son is not simply the Son incarnate in a "human nature" but the Son freely, covenantally incarnate in historical humanity which is created in and by His mission from the Father to give the Spirit.[61] The subject of the Johannine phrase, "the Word became flesh" (*Logos sarx egeneto*; the primordial *Logos*), is not the prehuman, preexistent Son of God but rather the primordial Son of Mary, Who is the Son of God.[62] *Logos* is a personal name for the Christ and Keefe insists that it refers to the "one and the same" historical person

---

60   Ibid., 443–44.
61   Ibid., 442.
62   Ibid., 595.

رьт﹘

(declared by Chalcedon), Jesus Who is the eternal Son of the Father and the historical Son of Mary.[63]

Christ then is immanent in creation covenantally. He is the Son of God in covenantal union with humanity. We have considered this reality of Christ, so far, under the formality of the New Covenant and Good Creation. Both of these formalities, nonetheless, are established as historical events in the Incarnation. The mission of the Father sending the Son to give the Spirit terminates in the moment of the Annunciation whereby the New Covenant and Good Creation are actualized with Mary's *fiat mihi*.[64] It is with this event that creation is constituted and receives the Word addressed to it freely, completely, in covenant. The New Covenant is proleptically actual in the moment of the Incarnation.[65] It is with this event that Christ's personal unity as Son, at once of the Father and of Mary who is the *Theotokos* (thus, a divine and human sonship), is actualized.[66]

3.2 Mary's created *fiat*

It is as sent by the Father that the Son is incarnate and it is as incarnate that the Son's obedience to the Father is actual in the outpouring of the Spirit. It is through the power of the Spirit that Mary's freedom is created and is the grounds for her response to the angel Gabriel, *fiat mihi secundum Verbum tuum*.[67] Mary's response is a created one and without the divine initiative, she is not capable of it. This grace of reception is already a gift from God since there is no prior possibility for it. The reception is created by God as part of His assumption of humanity and it takes a very concrete form in Mary's *fiat*. Thus, as created, Mary is not in a state of equality with her Son but she is indispensable to His Incarnation. Apart from her unflawed and integrally free *fiat*, Christ's Incarnation could only be by some kind of imposition, some act of divine despotism, which would invoke an antagonism between humanity and divinity, pagan in meaning rather than Christian.[68] Keefe explains:

---

63 Ibid., 409.
64 Ibid., 316.
65 Ibid., 346.
66 Ibid., 449.
67 Ibid., 16.
68 Ibid., 216.

[T]he gift which is the New Covenant includes her feminine humanity as the created yet indispensable free correlative response to the created Personal *terminus* of His mission by the Father; the personal obedience of the *Logos* (at once and inseparably divine and human, "one and the same") meets the personal and entirely human obedience of the *Theotokos* in the New Covenant, with which Mary's free "*Fiat mihi*" is integral: i.e., her "*Fiat*" is an integrating *created* element of the New Covenant, the first effect of the outpouring of the Spirit of Christ....[69]

Thus, the gift of the Spirit terminates in Mary's primordial act of integral freedom, the *fiat mihi*, by which she appropriates her own reality as the created second Eve and in so doing is in covenantal union with her Creator in the virginal conception of her Son Who is paradoxically the Son of God, "one and the same."[70]

3.3 Mary's Immaculate Conception

Mary's integral freedom, exhibited in her *fiat mihi*, is constitutive of the New Covenant itself.[71] If this were not the case, then Christ's immanence could only be by some kind of imposition, some act of divine despotism which invokes an antagonism between humanity and divinity that is pagan in meaning rather than Christian.[72] God could only be present to His people as a despot, overcoming their "freedom" forcibly, suppressing their alienation.[73] To be so present would establish not a covenant but an obtrusion. In order to establish a covenant, only a freedom unsullied by sin can respond to the freedom of Christ's obedience to the Father. Thus, Mary is blessed with the unique plenitude of grace by which she, as the Immaculate Conception, is *freely* able to affirm the presence of her Lord to humanity.[74] In creating, God says to His handiwork, "Be good," and the only human being so blessed to respond in the affirmative is Mary, who is integral because she is *gratia plena*. In her, the Good Creation speaks and freely responds to God's offer of covenant.

Keefe holds that Mary's Immaculate Conception is an essential aspect of the New Covenant for without it the freedom of the cove-

---

69 Ibid., 372.
70 Ibid., 234.
71 Ibid., 216.
72 Ibid., 216, 374.
73 Ibid., 315–17.
74 Ibid., 216.

nant would be impossible. He also maintains that it provides for her integral femininity which affirms Christ's integral masculinity in the marital bond that results in the Incarnation.[75] Thus, correlative to Mary's Immaculate Conception is recognition that Christ's conception is not merely a physiological-biological occurrence but the covenantal relation itself. However, this covenantal relation is not only a bond between two parties. It is a marital union, a *mia sarx*, of integral femininity and masculinity. Femininity and masculinity are not merely accidental to this union, but are essential to it. Only integral femininity can be at once daughter, virginal bride, and mother to Him who is at once her Head and her Son.[76] By her *fiat mihi*, all that is constitutive of feminity (virginity, maternity, and nuptiality) is offered to integral masculinity so that two are in One Flesh, a union so intimate that He is virginally and physically conceived in her womb. The integral union of Christ and Mary is the *mia sarx* in which her Son's obedience to the Father is concrete and historically actual in the sending of the Spirit upon her whose humanity is due to that sending.[77]

3.4 A covenantal understanding of integrity

Integrity, unfallen humanity, is a reality that is verified in Mary, whose existence is, from the very moment of her conception, unfallen. The term itself, in Keefe's usage, is deep in meaning. First, to be integral is to be human totally, without ontological defect; it is to participate without reservation in the creative actuality of the Christ.[78] By this, Keefe means that the formal existential cause of the integral human person is Christ and the formal effect of Christ in such a person is a finite participation in the free, creative subjectivity of Christ.[79] This full participation in Christ is a substantial union with Christ, Who stands to the individual human person as actualization to potentiality.[80] Secondly, to be integral involves a continual expression of the wholeness in life which involves the harmony of mind and will in worship of Christ in whom one continually comes to be. This whole-

---

75 Ibid., 366–67.
76 Ibid., 344.
77 Ibid., 343.
78 Keefe, *Thomism and Tillich*, 105.
79 Ibid., 114.
80 Ibid., 105–06.

ness in life entails the gift, innate in one's substance, of transcendental freedom which is the primal freedom from which all else flows, namely, integral action.[81] It is created freedom, the correlate to divine creating freedom. As a result, integral humanity enjoys a unified self-presence or consciousness in which human nature is completely receptive to the illumination of it by Christ. The existence, *esse*, which actualizes the consciousness of an existing human being is the *esse Christi* in whom the person participates (i.e., existence is that which mediates Christ to the existing individual person).[82] In the state of integrity, then, the individual knows himself or herself to be orientated toward God Who is the highest Good and the highest Truth which are held as united within the person's consciousness.

3.5 Section Summary

The New Covenant is not abstract but a concrete actual reality. It was established as an historical event when the primordial *Logos* became incarnate through the Spirit-filled created yet indispensable free response of Mary. And yet in order to be a true and perfect covenant, only a freedom unsullied by sin can respond to the freedom of Christ's obedience to the Father. Thus, Mary is blessed with the unique plenitude of grace by which she, as the Immaculate Conception, is freely able to affirm the present of her Lord to humanity. The Immaculate Conception is an essential part of the New Covenant for without it the freedom of the covenant would be impossible due to the stain of sin.

In addition, the Immaculate Conception provides not only for freedom but also for a marital understanding of the convenantal union. Due to the plenitude of grace, Mary's femininity is integral and, as such, completely affirms Christ's integral masculinity. The union that occurs on account of this affirmation is not merely a physiological-biological occurrence but a marital one. The two become One Flesh, a flesh untainted by sin. Thus, the *prius* of theology is understood to be concrete, historical, untainted, complete, integral, and marital.

---

81   Ibid., 105.
82   Ibid., 113.

4 The Fall

4.1 The New Covenant as offered and rejected

The integral New Covenant is actual. It is not an abstract possibility of something that may be but it is objectively real, something that indeed is. It is a concrete, created reality: the free marital, covenantal bond between Christ and Mary whereby each freely affirms the other by self-donation and reception.

As actual, the New Covenant is metaphysically prior, is primordial as a condition precedent for the Fall. If the New Covenant (the primordial nuptial union of the second Adam and the second Eve) did not actually exist metaphysically prior to and independently of its refusal, the first Adam and the first Eve could not have freely rejected it and fallen from it.[83] The only other alternative would involve a fall from nothingness which is then not a fall at all or to render the rejected Covenant as merely prospective or eschatological.[84] Keefe renounces this alternative position by indicating that creation and history are good in the present. Creation reaches its completion in Mary's *fiat*. Otherwise, historical concreteness is the positive cause of all evil and thus is to be devalued and fled.[85]

For Keefe, the moment of the Fall is the moment of creation, the initial instant of created freedom ("in the beginning"). This is the moment in which the Covenant is both constituted, offered by the covenantal freedom of the second Adam and the second Eve, and rejected by the first Adam and the first Eve.[86] The integral existence offered by the second Adam and the second Eve is the term of the mission by the Father of the Son to give the Spirit.[87] This offer is refused by the first Adam and the first Eve in the primordial instant that is at once the term of the mission of the Son, the constitution of the *mia sarx* of the second Adam and the second Eve, the creation of the universe in Christ, and the free and sinful Fall of that creation.[88]

---

83 Keefe, *Covenantal Theology*, 242, 346.
84 Ibid., 237, 242, 337.
85 Keefe, *Thomism and Tillich*, 241–42.
86 Keefe, *Covenantal Theology*, 218.
87 Ibid., 339–40.
88 Ibid., 340.

The moment of the offer can not be distinguished from the moment of creation and the moment of the Fall; they are simultaneous.[89]

However, with the refusal, the Fall is actual concretely, in the here and now, at the primordial moment of creation. Since creation is fallen from "the beginning," there is no moment in the historical universe that is not fallen. The entire historical condition of the universe (with the exception of the second Adam and second Eve) is subject to the conditions of fallenness (namely, disunity, fragmentation, servitude, suffering, and death). Like creation, it is not to be held as some purely eschatological nonhistoric possibility (e.g., a fall from the Platonic realm of the ideas) which must be imagined nonhistorically and thus cosmologically in order for one to understand what is means to be fallen. Apart from the historical actuality, here and now, of the achieved New Covenant, it makes no sense, except by employing a dualistic pessimism, to speak of a fall, for then fallenness has no criterion which is not finally arbitrary or an abstract ideal.[90] If the New Covenant is actual in history, in fallenness, as the criterion of human fallenness, then it is thereby the concrete metaphysical *prius* of the Fall for if the criterion which is the New Covenant is not actual, then neither is human fallenness.[91] The Fall becomes, then, a metaphor for the materiality of the created order.[92]

Since creation and the Fall are actual, the refusal of the offer is the action of a real morally responsible agent.[93] The agent, by being created in Christ, is constituted as truly free and at this primordial moment of creation and offer, freely refuses the offer of freedom and, thus, renders creation unfree.[94] This moral act of the Fall is free by definition and not extrapolated from the empirical structures of a necessitarian universe.[95] The Fall is not to be understood as a prior possibility intrinsic to creation as though it were simply inherent in finitude.[96] The Fall is not cosmic but moral and, therefore, free.

Since the Fall is the action of a free moral agent, how is this human agent, who refused the New Covenant for all of humanity except

---

89 Ibid., 218.
90 Ibid., 220.
91 Ibid., 220–21.
92 Ibid., 287.
93 Ibid., 245.
94 Ibid., 219–20, 234–35.
95 Ibid., 333.
96 Ibid., 317.

for the second Adam and the second Eve, to be understood? First of all, we ourselves, whether as individuals or in whatever combination, are not this primordial agent. Our fallenness is not caused by personal sin for we are not freely fallen. Therefore, as fallen, our sinfulness is an effect rather than the cause of the Fall.[97]

Second, the primordial agent can not be the primordially covenanted couple, the second Adam and the second Eve who constitute the New Covenant. They are sinless by definition. While they constitute, by and in their marital union, the condition precedent for the Fall in that it is through them that the gift of integral existence is at once actual and actually offered, the rejection of the offer is not theirs, nor is the possibility of that rejection in any way entailed in that offer.[98]

Thus, Keefe holds that the first Adam and the first Eve, as the freely sinful agents of the Fall, are themselves fallen but, unlike their progeny, combine in themselves original sin both as active and as passive: as responsible for the Fall and as immanent in the fallenness of history which their sin alone has caused. They are understood to be *ex hypothesi* the sole causes and responsible agents of that Fall in that, although they have themselves never known an instant of integral existence, they alone are freely fallen and freely responsible for the fallenness of all humanity throughout all of history.[99]

Fallenness in not annihilation, for creation can not be undone by a creature. Thus, the fallen Adam is historical, having fallen into fallenness. The effect of this sin on the progeny, the solidarity in sin (*propagatione non imitatione*), would then require not only his reality within fallen history but also his primordial responsibility and authority as "head."[100] How is the headship of the first Adam, then, to be understood? How is it to be explained metaphysically?

---

97 Ibid., 222.
98 Ibid.
99 Ibid.
100 Ibid., 223.

4.2 The authority of the moral agents

Keefe holds that the free event of the Fall is beyond any theological reconstitution. The Fall is known by the revelation of its effects, which are a diminution in created reality, a negation of being. He explains:

> Consequently, any attempt at its reconstitution by theological speculation will be nonhistorical, thus cosmological: we can not by speculative *ratio* transcend our beginning. Otherwise put, the fall *originatum* or *passive spectatum* has no historical theological *prius* by reference to which we might construct the unfallen "original situation"; the fall is radically *ex nihilo*, the mystery of iniquity. The reparation of the degradation of the Good Creation by original sin is for God alone, who alone creates *ex nihilo sui et subjecti*. For the theologian to attempt this re-establishment of a primordial *status quo ante* is to re-enter systematically upon the original insolence.[101]

Therefore, the question raised regarding the nonhistorical *prius* of the Fall is not to be pursued, for, as Keefe points out, it is cosmological. The attempt to reconstruct the rejected headship of the first Adam and the integral humanity, those to whom the Son was sent, is futile since it is with the refusal of this headship and the integrity it connotes in head and body that the Fall is actual in history. Likewise, it is theologically impossible to deduce from a state of fallenness the features of the first Adam's unfallen headship of an integrally free humanity, for that is precisely what has never been actual; its reality has been refused. The problem of the responsibility for the Fall in the first Adam and the features of the first Adam can be dealt with only historically, only in the context of a covenantal metaphysics.[102] Keefe explains further:

> Consequently, over against the historical second Adam, the Christ in whom we are created and who, as immanent in our fallen history transcends it as the metaphysical *prius* of creation and redemption, there can be no historical first Adam who would be the primordial historical *prius* of our redemption from the fall. We can understand what has been refused by the first Adam only in terms of what has been affirmed by the Christ, whose headship in this world is not manifest, for its actuality is sacramental and Eucharistic.[103]

In summary, Catholic theology, according to Keefe, is forbidden "to get behind" the Fall by speculation. Theology's concern is for the

---

101 Ibid.
102 Ibid., 224.
103 Ibid., 224–25.

head whose headship is manifest in the Christ of the New Covenant: there is no other head in history, nor has there been, even in the first Adam. The moral freedom of the first Adam, the actuality of the primordial Fall, is implicit in the Redemption wrought by Christ, but it is to Christ that attention is turned in order to understand that moral freedom, that actuality of the Fall, not to the negation that is human fallenness, for that has no intelligibility as such.[104]

With this methodological warning, Keefe subsequently examines the authority proper to both the first Adam and the first Eve. Access to what this authority may mean, however, is only historical, that is, by way of sacramental symbolism due to the Fall.[105] In other words, that the symbolism is sacramental is due to the Fall; the reality, as such, is not due to the Fall, but it is rather the *prius* for the Fall. This authority is one of head and body which according to Paul's theology, sees in the husband-wife relation, a sacramental sign grounded in the relation of Christ to the Church which establishes and constitutes the New Covenant.[106] Since the New Covenant is the created term of Christ's mission, the image of the Trinity is contained within the head-body structure. More will be said with regard to this Trinitarian imaging later.

Based on this understanding, the first Adam, as head, is to be the source of the first Eve, who is His glory. His authority is to be her source, thus to be image, as her authority is to be His glory. She is created to be His equal: her authority is to be over Him, as His is to be over her, and, thus, the authority of each is to invoke the correlative but irreducibly distinct free responsibility or authority of the other.[107] Keefe explains:

> Thus, it belongs to Adam, as the head, to be the source of Eve and through Eve, as the mother of the living, to be the head and source of all humanity: the same paradigmatic role is proper to the second Adam, who through the Church, the second Eve, is the Head and source of all men. For the first Adam to accept the offer of the Covenant would be to exercise this integral and integrating authority, which is over Eve as hers is over him, but hers derives from his as from its source.
>
> Adam's sin in refusing the Covenant is therefore the violation of the integrally free order of the covenanted creation; it is a refusal at once to be the

---

104 Ibid., 226.
105 Ibid., 247.
106 Ibid.
107 Ibid., 252–53.

glory of the Christ and to be the head of Eve. Rejecting the gift of the life-giving *Spiritus Creator*, and with it the truth which would have made him free, Adam's refusal to be "head" also resumes the free, covenantal order of creation, and institutes instead the diminished realization that is *sarx*—which nonetheless remains, irrevocably, creation in Christ.

For the "sinful Adam" to exist as *sarx* is to exist in the grace of Christ, but defectively, as *simul justus et peccator*, as an image whose fallenness is revealed in the veiling of his glory. Eve's beauty now is veiled, obscure, a matter of shame, contradicted from within. Knowing himself as good and evil, he knows his wife not as his glory, flesh of his flesh, but as his unfree subordinate whose relation to her head no longer is free, and whose fecundity is now for her not joy unmixed but sorrow also. He knows the earth not as the source of life but of weariness and death. His relation to his own Head echoes that of his wife: Christ is to him the Image and Glory of the Father as law, not as love.[108]

The sin of Adam, consequently, deprives creation of its covenantal integrity. The integrity will be restored by the second Adam in the sacrifice instituting the New Covenant, whose manifestation is the raising of the Head from the dead which is a victory not only for the Head, but for the Body as well.[109]

The authority of the first Eve, like that of Adam, is available only insofar as it is sacramentally signed by the eucharistic sacrifice of praise and by feminine symbolism within the marriage covenant.[110] In this context, it is by the woman's authority that life, the summary gift of God, is mediated to His creation and it is for this reason that her primordial infidelity to her authority issues in a progeny of *sarx*, doomed to death.[111] Eve's sin, like the sin of her head, is typological; it is her rejection of the offered Covenant as Body.[112] Consequently, the punishment of the fallen Eve is the loss and the reversal of the authority that pertains to her integrity; she is now subject to rule by the man, and it is as his punishment that the woman who is his glory is now to be veiled.[113] When authority is simply reserved to men, it becomes unqualified and despotic, for it is then monadic and absolute. Its exercise is in the image of a false and despotic deity who can endure no freedom but his uncovenanted irresponsibility. An idolatry,

---

108   Ibid., 253.
109   Ibid.
110   Ibid.
111   Ibid., 254.
112   Ibid., 239–40, 254.
113   Ibid., 254.

thus, results and is the single alternative to the intended covenantal understanding of authority between two persons in marital union.[114]

In summary, the refusal of integrity is covenantal: it is that of both the head and the body. Offered "headship" and thus the ability to appropriate integrity for all humanity, the first Adam appropriated fallenness, i.e., existence as *sarx* rather than as *pneuma*. His use of freedom is decisive for the totality of humanity which, by the fact of his headship, is in solidarity with him; they are bonded with and by his sin.[115] The sin of the first Eve is the refusal of the responsibility to be integrally body. The body is fallen. The Fall is the negation of the freely appropriated covenantal integrity by which alone it is body. The offer of integrity is made to the head, the source of creation but the refusal also has effect in the body.[116] As has been stated above, head and body, by reason of the Fall, are real within fallen history only as in Christ, which is to say, only in the sacramental order by which the reconstitution of the Good Creation by the second Adam and second Eve is historically actual in the worship of the Church.[117]

4.3 Solidarity with the first Adam and Eve

Since the refusal of integrity is covenantal, all of humanity, with the exception of the integral Christ and Mary, are in solidarity with the original sin *originans* of the first Adam and Eve. That solidarity is original sin *originatum* in fallen humanity. In other words, the first Adam's sin, by the fact of his headship, affects all those who are in solidarity with him. Adam, as head, is to be the source of Eve and through Eve, as the mother of the living, to be the source of all humanity.[118] His sin as head affects the body. The Tridentine tag *"propagatione non imitatione"* affirms this solidarity, but this language is meaningful only upon the supposition that it exhausts the possible means of solidarity with original sin *originans*.[119] Keefe holds that due to the fact that the conciliar teaching insists upon the inadequacy of any notion of solidarity which would be merely extrinsic and thus

---

114 Ibid., 256.
115 Ibid., 235.
116 Ibid., 237, 239.
117 Ibid., 239–40.
118 Ibid., 235, 252–53.
119 Ibid., 332.

44   *A Theological Understanding of the Eucharist*

less than metaphysical, the weight of the teaching lies in the *non imita-tione*. This means that empirical physical observation (e.g., that as far back as history records, people have been killing each other) is not sufficient for explaining solidarity in sin. Empirical science can not account for the free moral character of an action. The world that is the subject matter of scientific inquiry is precisely a fallen world. The world as fallen can not explain itself for the cause of the Fall is moral and by definition a moral Fall is free and, therefore, is not capable of being abstracted from the empirical structures of the universe. If this were not the case, the Fall would not be a fall but a necessary implication of a dualistic cosmos and not a free and moral reality. *Propagatione* is a metaphysical rather than simply a physical notion, i.e., it refers to humanity's intrinsic *a priori* rather than to its unfortunate empirical situation. Solidarity is substantial and not accidental: it is noumenal and not phenomenal, moral and not an implication of human nature; its covenantal actuality is metaphysically prior to its unpleasant and ambiguous manifestations and so must be summoned to explain them, and not the reverse.[120]

Consequently, the theological account of humanity's fallen creation in Christ must find the fallen solidarity in the New Covenant, for no alternative is conceivable at the level of humanity's contingent substantial being. In an integral and unfallen world, that solidarity would be manifest; it is now given only in sacrament, which is to say, fallen humanity's solidarity with the second Adam, which is its unity as human, is historically actual but it is so only in the sign of His free eucharistic presence as the integral Head of the integral Body, the Church, in a fallen world. Therefore, to speak of a solidarity in sin with the first Adam is to risk forgetting that it is not in sin that we may find a substantial reality in which solidarity can be had. Sin is a negation and as such it has no substantial reality but is rather the diminishment of a substantial reality. Solidarity is in fallen humanity but fallen humanity is still substantial. Even with sin, humanity is still created in and through the Christ of the New Covenant, the prime analogate of being.[121]

Keefe holds that the Pauline understanding of *sarx* contains within it that unity which remains in human fallenness after the Fall and which links humanity *propagatione non imitatione* with the first

---

120 Ibid., 333–34.
121 Ibid., 334.

Adam and the first Eve. In pursuing this understanding, Keefe provides some prior negations indicating what this unity in *sarx* is not.

First of all, Keefe's concern is historical and, therefore, *sarx* is not to be considered in isolation from that which overcomes its isolation, namely, *mia sarx*. Of itself, *sarx* has no reality because it has no unity or freedom which are constitutive of a body by definition. These constitutive principles have been denied it when its head refused integrity. Its unity, rather, is *mia sarx*. Solidarity in *sarx* is solidarity in the absence of unity, in disunity, in the uncovenanted disintegration of all that is not one in Christ.[122] In other words, the issue at hand is a solidarity in disunity, which is an oxymoron. Solidarity can be arrived at if the individual sinners are held collectively by recognizing that one thing they all have in common is that they have committed sin. This solidarity not only has been arrived at through abstraction, but it is also a solidarity through imitation and not propagation. Such a solidarity is nonhistorical, for it is one step removed from the actual sin of the various sinners and, thus, postulates that the Fall is from a nonhistorical pure nature. This, then, is the ground for the imitation. Keefe holds that the only way to give this abstract commonality concrete historical reality is to refer it to the prime analogate of being, the New Covenant. Fallen individuals are propagated only in Christ, even as fallen.

Second, this solidarity is not a unity in sin, for the Word was made *sarx* and is *mia sarx* with His bridal Church. Solidarity in *sarx* is, thus, solidarity in fallen history, fallen flesh subject to death; it is as *sarx* that the Christ is historical, born of woman. It is as *sarx* that the Word is like us in all things but sin and it is as *sarx* that His Church is a Church of sinners, but she herself is sinless.[123]

Third, this solidarity is not in concupiscence since the doctrinal tradition of the Church has refused to attribute concupiscence to Christ or to Mary, both of whom are *sarx* in the covenantal union of the *mia sarx* of the second Adam and the second Eve.[124]

Fourth, solidarity in *sarx* is not to be understood as a community or society, for the solidarity spoken of here is one in disunity. "Rather it is solidarity in the refusal by the first Adam of the only human community that is real because it is integral, 'the holy society' of the

---

122 Ibid., 345.
123 Ibid.
124 Ibid.

New Covenant 'by which we belong to God.'"[125] Solidarity in *sarx* then is the dissociation of persons who by their solidarity are uncovenanted, unable in their unfreedom to enter into a dynamically free covenantal community or unity of distinct persons.[126] In other words, the refusal of the integrity of the New Covenant by the "head," the first Adam, renders that which is in solidarity with him, the "body," the first Eve, unfree, disunited and, therefore, incapable of being a community, properly understood.

For these reasons, the unity of *sarx* can not be autonomous but must rely upon an alternate source other than its own negation of unity, for of itself *sarx* tends only toward disintegration. Keefe holds, then, that what unity *sarx* possesses (and this is the unity of fallen humanity in fallen history) it has by its relation of dependence upon the pneumatic union of the second Adam and the second Eve, the risen Christ in His risen Church. This pneumatic union, the Kingdom, is immanent in *sarx* only by transcending its loss of integrity, its consequent disunity and unfreedom, and by being present as the integral and covenantal unity of the *mia sarx* of the Eucharist. The presence of Christ in history, the Event of the *Logos sarx egeneto*, has as its *prius* the primordial *mia sarx* of the New Covenant, historically actual by the response of Mary to the Annunciation by which she is the *Theotokos*, the bearer of the eternal Son of the eternal Father, and her Son as well.[127]

The "unity" of *sarx* then is the fallen creation. To exist as such is to be alienated from God, from the primordial goodness of creation, from one's own self, and from the rest of the race (man from woman, woman from man).[128] Fallen creation is also subject to destruction, sin, and death. *Sarx* has no unity of its own; of itself, it is only a negation of creation, of covenantal unity.[129] This negation is instituted by a fall, and it perdures in a consequent fallenness not as a static structure but as the ongoing dynamic event of the One Flesh of Christ and His Church.[130] This is a fallenness from reality: from the only unity that is real, the free unity of the Covenant, the prime analogate of being. It is

---

125 Ibid.
126 Ibid.
127 Ibid.
128 Ibid., 231, 237–38.
129 Ibid., 347.
130 Ibid., 346.

a fall from the integrally free covenantal unity offered by the *mia sarx* of the second Adam and the second Eve.[131] Thus, the original sin *originans*, the primordial refusal to be, does not, and can not annul the offer of the New Covenant, for the first Adam, as sinful creature, participates in the source of creation, the *esse Christi*.[132] Rather, it establishes the New Covenant in fallenness, in *sarx*: in the fallen history of humanity's Redemption by the blood of the New Covenant, offered in the second Adam's One Sacrifice on the Cross by which the New Covenant is instituted as the first fruits of Christ's Resurrection from the dead. Thus, the New Covenant is actual by the eucharistic *mia sarx* in which the One Flesh of the covenanted creation is actual in history by its veiled sacramental (eucharistic) representation. In summary, the reality of fallen creation has its solidarity with the second Adam, which is not undone by the Fall: only the freedom and the life of that solidarity is able to be refused.[133]

4.4 Section summary

The New Covenant is actual in fallenness meaning that the New Covenant is metaphysically prior, is primordial as a condition precedent for the Fall. If it did not actually exist metaphysically prior to and independently of its refusal, the first Adam and first Eve could not have freely rejected it and fallen from it. In other words, if the New Covenant is not actual, then neither is human fallenness. Keefe insists that both are actual and historical, not abstract and cosmological.

Since the *prius* is free, actual, and historical, the refusal to accept the offer of the New Covenant must be the action of a free moral agent. The agent is constituted as truly free and, at the primordial moment of creation and offering, the agent freely refuses the offer of freedom. Thus, creation is rendered unfree. This act is not extrapolated from the structures of a necessitarian cosmological universe but rather from a free universe. As such, the act is actual, historical, and moral.

---

131 Ibid., 347.
132 Keefe, *Thomism and Tillich*, 118.
133 Keefe, *Covenantal Theology*, 347.

The sin of the first Adam and first Eve is a fall from reality: the only unity that is real, the free covenantal unity offered by the *mia sarx* of the second Adam and second Eve. This original sin does not annul the New Covenant but rather causes it to be veiled, sacramental, eucharistic.

Solidarity in the sin of the first Adam and first Eve, who were asked to be head and body, is not due to their sin *per se*. Sin is a negation and, as such, it has no substantial reality but rather it is a diminishment of substantial reality. Strictly speaking, sin (*sarx*), for Keefe, has no unity. It can not. Thus, what grounds the solidarity of sinful individual persons is the primordial *mia sarx* of the New Covenant, the *prius*. The reality and propagation of fallen humanity has its reference to solidarity with the pneumatic union of the second Adam and the second Eve. Likewise, the roles of head and body offered to but refused by the first Adam and first Eve derive their being and meaning from the true Head and true Body, the second Adam and second Eve. Consequently, solidarity in *sarx* is solidarity in fallen history.

Being mindful of this understanding of the *prius's* role in the Fall, the discussion will now turn to its function in Redemption.

5 Redemption

5.1 Redemption through the New Covenant

Adam and Eve's refusal does not defeat the creative freedom of God; the will of God is not undone by sin, and original sin is not the undoing of the mission of the Son, nor of His covenantal fidelity which is irrevocable.[134] Rather the refusal makes the Creator's free covenantal union with humanity to be redemptive because it is first creative. Redemption (recreation) is implicit in creation, for the mission of the Son is single (namely, the free creative immanence of the Son in humanity), and it transcends the totality of what is not God, including sin and death.[135]

---

134 Ibid., 223, 247.
135 Ibid., 347.

As stated above, the immanence of God in humanity, by which humanity is constituted as covenanted, is the covenantal union of the second Adam and the second Eve.[136] Thus, the second Adam and the second Eve are freely immanent within fallenness (*sarx*); they accept a history that is fallen and in so doing, confront incongruously the un-freedom of "man-in-his-world" with their integral freedom. The in-congruity of the gift of the Good Creation confronting its refusal, of covenantal acceptance confronting obstinate aversion from God, of free obedience confronting concupiscent and servile disobedience is-sues in Redemption through the Cross.[137]

5.2 The triadic structure of Redemption

The Redemption won for fallen humanity by Christ is triadic in struc-ture: *sarx, mia sarx, pneuma*. It is upon this Cross that the entire history of fallen humanity is resumed, resolved, redeemed by a freedom which it can not master. This freedom is that of the last Adam, Who, by being "made sin for us," became obedient unto death on the Cross and offered His Blood for the establishment of the New Covenant.[138] It is upon this Cross that the *mia sarx*, the free union of the second Adam and the second Eve is fulfilled and becomes the redemptive dynamism of fallen history.[139] At the Annunciation the New Cove-nant is given proleptically (antetype): Christ's Spirit, given to Mary in its fullness, enables her conception of her Son, and His corresponding response to her freedom is precisely taking from her fallen historicity. Now on the Cross, that New Covenant, once given proleptically, is established.[140] It is here that Christ manifests that He is the Christ, the second Adam, in His One Sacrifice on the Cross for the Church. This sacrifice is at once the ultimate acceptance of His mission from the Father, and the unqualified gift of Himself and, thereby of His Spirit, to the Church, thus instituting the One Flesh of the New Covenant, the *mia sarx*.[141] On the Cross, He assumes the depths of fallenness (*sarx*), enters into the damnation that separates humanity from divin-

---

136 Ibid.
137 Ibid., 347.
138 Ibid.
139 Ibid., 341.
140 Ibid., 250.
141 Ibid., 249.

ity, and sacrifices Himself totally for the Church who by that sacrifice is free.[142] The New Covenant, established by this Sacrifice, is made manifest by the rising of the second Adam, the Head, from the dead. As the first fruits of the Spirit (*pneuma*), the victory over death of the Head is also the victory of His Body: the glory that had departed from the first Adam is restored by the risen second Adam Who, made a life-giving Spirit, as risen also raised the second Eve.[143] The Church, the new Eve, is now "the mother of all the living." As the Christ is the Head of the Church, so also He is the Head of each man and woman born of the Church and who now freely avail themselves to this newness of life in the Spirit.[144] The unfree solidarity in sin is now overcome by the free solidarity in Redemption.

To summarize, the immanence of the second Adam in nuptial union with the second Eve is the submission of the integral freedom of the *mia sarx* of the New Covenant to the "sarkic" burden of death which enslaves creation as fallen. This immanence of the Son is also the pouring out upon that fallenness the Spirit Whom it is the Son's mission to give. The gift is infallibly given and, by this gift, made irrevocable on the Cross. The new Adam, the One Who freely accepts the role of headship, is victorious over the fallenness which as Head He entered upon and as Head has overcome. His victory, salvation from sin and death, is offered freely to all who would appropriate it in the covenantal worship by which it is actual in their history and in the world's history. The second Adam and the second Eve are, therefore, present in history by the single obedience of the Son to the Father which constitutes creation as good and very good.[145]

5.3 The relationship between *sarx*, *mia sarx*, and *pneuma*

In the divine act of creation and recreation, we have seen how *sarx*, *mia sarx*, and *pneuma* have been operative. Keefe, however, draws some specific distinctions between these three elements of salvation history. First, unity in *sarx* is unfree, common to human beings and to beasts. Unity in *mia sarx* is by a free reentry into the New Covenant

---

142 Ibid., 250–51.
143 Ibid., 253.
144 Ibid., 251.
145 Ibid., 243.

and the New Creation. It is through this free unity in the One Sacrifice of the New Covenant that fallen humanity is redeemed, participates freely in the history of salvation. Unity in *mia sarx* is the freedom of the eucharistic worship of the Church: it permeates humanity as a leaven, but its source is the Son's gift of the *Creator Spiritus* Who in that worship creates and unifies the Church and, through the Church, the world.[146]

Second, the relationship between *sarx* and *mia sarx* is historical and, as such, it can only be free. The relationship is one of conversion to sacramental worship for one can not know the meaning of one's immersion in *sarx* except through the perspective given by the free appropriation of the *mia sarx* in the Eucharist. It is only in their free eucharistic mutuality that the reality of either one may be understood, for neither can be approached from some neutral and finally cosmological ground; the problem of stating their relationship is theological from the outset.[147]

Third, the conceptual isolation of one of the three from the others renders each of them false. As one can not understand Redemption except in the context of the sin, servitude, and death from which one is redeemed, so also one can not understand fallenness to be such except from the reality of the One Flesh given historically and actually in the Spirit. *Sarx* and *mia sarx* depend for their historical reality upon the fulfillment of that history as *pneuma*, in *pneuma* that is, in the risen consummated One Flesh of the second Adam and the second Eve. The consummation of the Son's mission is actual, objectively achieved, in the Resurrection, by which the Christ becomes a "living Spirit" historically present for the salvation of humankind through the Church's worship. Apart from this consummation, the historical relation of *sarx* to *mia sarx* collapses, and the history of salvation is not actual for salvation then is not mediated in history. History is not integrated as past, present, future or as *sarx, mia sarx, pneuma*.[148]

---

146 Ibid., 348.
147 Ibid.
148 Ibid., 348–49.

5.4 Section summary

The will of the Creator will not be thwarted by the sinfulness of creatures. The Son's mission will ultimately be accomplished, but the obstacle of sin must be dealt with first. Thus, the second Adam and the
second Eve freely embrace a fallen history (*sarx*) and confront the unfreedom of this sinful state with their integral freedom. Within the
context of fallen history, Christ became incarnate and assumed the
depths of fallenness (*sarx*) on the Cross. This sacrifice was at once the
ultimate acceptance of the Father's mission, the gift of Himself, and
the pouring forth of the Holy Spirit on the Church, thus, instituting
the One Flesh (*mia sarx*) of the New Covenant, the theological *prius*.
The New Covenant then is made manifest by the rising of the second
Adam. But this victory of the Head is also the victory of the Body. The
Church is now "the mother of all the living" for those who would
freely avail themselves of this new life. The unfree solidarity in sin is
now overcome by the free solidarity in Redemption. Thus, sin entered
the world through a refusal to enter into the New Covenant, the *prius*.
Now salvation is won and accessible through the same Covenant.

6 The Eucharist and Transubstantiation

6.1 Existence in Christ through *sarx*, *mia sarx*, and *pneuma*

It has been shown above that since the Fall is historical, its remedy is
likewise historical and finds its expression in the free unity of *sarx*,
mia sarx, *pneuma*. It is only in their free and redemptive covenantal
unity that they provide the free intelligibility of historical existence in
Christ.[149] This free association is given only in the eucharistic worship
of the Church in which *sarx* is "baptized" into the *mia sarx* of Christ
and the Church. By that baptismal entry into the Church's worship
fallen humanity receives the Spirit of eternal life (*pneuma*) so "that we
should not die."[150] Fallen humanity's free sacramental and eucharistic
solidarity in Christ is inseparable from its unfree solidarity in the first

---

149 Donald J. Keefe, "La 'Veritatis splendor' e il fondamento eucaristico della mo-
     rale," *Rivista di Teologia Morale* 110, no. 2 (Aprile-Giugno 1996): 218.
150 Ibid., 218–19.

Adam and from its eschatological solidarity in the Spirit (Old Covenant, New Covenant, Kingdom; *sarx, mia sarx, pneuma; sacramentum tantum, res et sacramentum, res tantum*).[151] This event of humanity's solidarity in Christ (in creation, Redemption, Resurrection) is concrete and historical only as Eucharist.[152] The New Covenant (the prime analogate, the One Flesh of Christ and His Church), by which humanity is redeemed, is a historical reality only as eucharistically represented, as redemptively transcending in sacrament the brokenness of the fallen spatio-temporality of the universe.[153]

6.2 The New Covenant's respect for history

If the New Covenant were not thus eucharistically represented, it would recede evermore into the past, to become evermore inaccessible, evermore merely a fading memory, obscured by the conditioning of a time unredeemed and, consequently, opaque to the risen Christ, finally forgotten. The Cross could not then be salvific except as merely eschatological: it would have no historical efficacy because it would lack all historical mediation. This supposition, however, would eliminate history as intrinsically intelligible: it would suppose time itself to be antagonistic to humanity, standing between it and its salvation. That pessimism with respect to historical existence implies the dualist and pagan world of personal irresponsibility: all evil there is accounted for as the fatal implication of temporality itself and all salvation must be by way of a flight from history rather than as mediated by history. Consequently, both *sarx* (flesh in need of Redemption) and *mia sarx* (the One Flesh by which humanity is redeemed) are then historical in the free relation by which Redemption is free. However, their unity is as yet incomplete for it looks to that eternal life which is the full gift of the Holy Spirit, poured out upon the Church by Christ's One Sacrifice.[154]

---

151 Keefe, *Covenantal Theology*, 413–14.
152 Ibid., 414.
153 Keefe, "La 'Veritatis splendor,'" 219.
154 Ibid.

6.3 A general definition of transubstantiation

The Fall renders the New Covenant as veiled, as a sacrament. It is through the Eucharist, then, that fallen humanity is able to avail itself (in solidarity and in sacrament) to the salvific New Covenant that is instituted on the Cross. To be more specific, it is through eucharistic transubstantiation that this availability is made possible. Transubstantiation is the *a priori* temporal event which provides the means for the metaphysical paradigm, the New Covenant, to be present sacramentally.

There are various aspects to transubstantiation. Transubstantiation is "that becoming" (*metabole*) which is the institution of the New Covenant, the New Creation.[155] Through it the event of the covenantal sacrifice on the Cross, which institutes the New Covenant (the New Creation), is actual in history. The transubstantiated bread and wine are the historical, sacrificed, and risen personal reality (body, blood, soul, and divinity) of the sacrificial victim and priest, Jesus Christ.[156] But the transubstantiated bread and wine are so concretely as the *mia sarx*, the free, sacrificial, nuptial union of Christ and His Church, within which the transubstantiated bread and wine, the One Sacrifice of the Christ, at once signify and cause to be correlatively present, the Church, for the eucharistically-signed sacrifice of the Christ is inseparable from the Church's sacrifice of praise.[157] In short, it is through the eucharistic transubstantiation that the second Adam, in One Flesh with the second Eve, is immanent within history.

6.4 The Mass as a representation of the Cross

The doctrine of transubstantiation upholds the event character or historicity of the eucharistic representation of the One Sacrifice of Christ. It is through the means of transubstantiation that the Eucharist is the Event of the New Covenant instituted by the One Sacrifice of the Cross on Calvary and represented actually in history through the Sacrifice of the Mass. As stated above, transubstantiation is the *a priori* temporal event which provides the means for the metaphysical para-

---

155   Keefe, *Covenantal Theology*, 434.
156   Ibid., 428.
157   Ibid., 428–29.

digm to be present sacramentally. Through transubstantiation, the redemptive sacrifice which was once offered on the Cross is made present in the sacrifice of the Mass. This is so because the Sacrifice of the Cross is a single unique event and is not repeated. Keefe explains in two separate but related statements:

> The One Sacrifice of the Cross and the One Sacrifice offered in the Church in the person and by the authority of Christ are a single unique Event, distinct only in the manner of their offering. They cannot be thought of as in isolation or as objectively different. Each includes the other, for without the Eucharistic representation of the One Sacrifice of the Cross, that One Sacrifice could not be redemptive: it transcends history, and so redeems it, only as Eucharistically represented. The Event of the Eucharist is the Event of the Cross: they are indissociable, concretely and numerical identical, a single Event.[158]

> The One Sacrifice offered Eucharistically is identical to that offered on the Cross; there is no question of repetition. As the Sacrifice is the institution of the New Covenant of the second Adam and the second Eve, Christ and the Church, its Eucharistic representation is the historical actualization of the New Covenant by the sacrificial and sacramental presence of the Christ in union with his bridal Church, the sacrament of the eschatological Kingdom, the risen Body of which Christ is the risen head.[159]

If the sacrifice of the Mass were a repetition of Christ's sacrifice on Calvary, then the only thing that could integrate these repetitions is a nonsacramental *prius*, an idea, a remembrance.[160] Ideas, however, operate by way of subjectivity, in terms of personal experience and consciousness. The presence of Christ and His sacrifice is, then, thought to be effected not *ex opere operato* but *ex opere operantis*. If this is the case, then Christ's sacrifice is immediately rendered non-sacramental and non-historical, for, as an idea, it is within a person's consciousness. It is private and not a public, historical event capable of being sacramentally signed and appropriated in worship. Christ's sacrifice has no reality as an event except as ideal, as some sort of remembrance or repetition and can only ground then a spiritual and not a "real presence," an historical immanence. Consequently, apprehension of that remembrance occurs in faith, *sola fide*. Keefe holds, rather, that the Mass is a representation, a rendering present of the One Sacrifice of Calvary. As quoted above, the sacrifice of Calvary is made

---

158 Ibid., 662–63.
159 Ibid., 43.
160 Ibid., 42.

historically present in the Mass and it is not repeated to every new age of people. It is an "event," for concrete events are required by free physical presences.

6.5 Presence *per modum substantiae*

The free physical presence involved here is a presence *per modum substantiae*. It is a "history-transcending historical presence" whereby the one present is not submitted to the before and after, the here rather than there of fallen space and time. The Sacrifice of Christ is accessible to fallen creation by being transcendent to all history—to location in space and time—while at the same time being in history. In the Eucharist, Christ is not present locally or empirically (*per modum accidens*), yet He is present concretely, historically, and actually (*per modum substantiae*). Transcending and unifying all of history is the function of the prime analogate for all historical metaphysics.

It must be remembered, however, that this prime analogate is covenantal and historical. The Eucharist, as prime analogate, informs all of history as its beginning, its center, its meaning, and its end not as some dehumanized transcendent *Logos* of an immanent Trinity but as a God-Man freely and covenantally immanent within humanity.[161] Christ transcends history not as an abstract *Logos* but as an historical human being Who is the eternal *Logos*. Christ's role as the ordering principle of history is actual only as *mia sarx*, in the One Flesh of the second Adam and second Eve, in the recapitulation of the Good Creation, in the Event of the institution of the New Covenant in history.

6.6 Sacramental realism

With such a free, covenantal, historical prime analogate in place, personal action and "works" (secondary analogates) have sacramental significance indicating profound personal dignity and responsibility. The salvation worked by the risen Christ can then be mediated by fallen human activity in history, which is to say, in the sacraments (thus, sacramental realism). If this were not the case and the nonhistorical Word integrates history, as the Protestant reformers claimed,

---

161   Ibid., 17, 42, 243, 661.

then the Eucharist is simply a recollection of Calvary, the single significant event in history. Consequently, the Eucharist has no event character and, in a corresponding manner, individual works have no present meaning. History then collapses into the eschaton. The single deed of the One Sacrifice, "by effecting our redemption, exhausts the meaning of history, leaving no remainder, no redemptively significant 'works,' to be achieved by the worshiper whose worship is reduced to the passivity of a nonhistorical *sola fide* lacking any reliable historical expression or significance."[162] Between Calvary and the eschaton, then, there are no events with salvific meaning. Rather, individuals living in this in-between time participate on an ideal level mediated to them by the Word. The ultimate issue regarding sacramental realism, then, is whether Christ's redemptive work can be mediated by the sacraments in history, or, on the contrary, whether the historical order is so totally corrupt as to prevent the sacramental and historical representation of Christ's salvific sacrifice within it. Keefe answers that the Roman Catholic Church lives on the concrete representation in fallen history of the One Sacrifice of Christ by which the world is redeemed; the Reformation hinges upon Luther's abandonment of this confidence and the subsequent development of the pessimistic implications that all concrete actions in history and their mediatory powers are ambiguous because of the historical order's fundamental corruption. Keefe holds that this disagreement is over what both Catholics and Protestants must understand to be an *articulum stantis et cadentis ecclesiae.*

6.7 The definition and role of sacrifice

According to the doctrine of sacramental realism, the sacrament of the Eucharist renders present in history the One Sacrifice of Christ. The purpose of this sacrifice is to institute the New Covenant by which the Church is caused to be. The Church then is the *sancta societas quae inhaereamus Deo* (the holy society by which we belong to God). This achievement is the result of sacrifice as understood by Augustine. Keefe adopts Augustine's definition of sacrifice since covenant is integral to it, "Thus the true sacrifice is offered in every act which is designed to unite us to God in a holy fellowship (*sancta societas*) that is,

---

162 Ibid., 42–43.

which is directed to that final Good which makes possible our felic-
ity....This is the sacrifice of Christians, who are many making up one
body in Christ."[163] Sacrifice is defined by its purpose, the achievement of the *sancta societas*, the "Whole Christ," *Christus totus, intergar,
plenitudo Christi*, the covenantal, marital union of Christ with His
Church. Christ's obedience to God the Father is His sacrifice, His irrevocable self-donation to and for the Good Creation, the Church
which is His Body, the Holy Society by which human beings belong to
God as the "Whole Christ," the marital One Flesh of Christ with His
Church.[164]

According to Keefe, this is the primary meaning of sacrifice since
Christ's sacrifice does not wait upon the Fall (i.e., occur *propter pecca-
tum*). Rather, the Fall changed the manner in which His sacrifice, His
self-donation to the second Eve and to the *sancta societas* would occur.
The Son's sacrifice would become redemptive (taking the form of a
slave, obedient unto death, even death on a cross) so that its goal
might be achieved. The work of Redemption, then, was a condition
precedent to the fully creative outpouring of the Spirit, which is the
purpose of the creative mission of the Word. Life can not be given to
those who are as yet constitutionally unable to live.[165] Sin is a rejection of life and an affirmation of death. By embracing and transcending death, Christ put an end to its cause, namely, sin, and thus
reconstituted humanity substantially. With this redemptive sacrifice,
the Spirit of Life was poured out within the Church so that human
beings could then choose to live in the *sancta societas*, the original *telos*
of Christ's sacrifice.[166] Consequently, for Keefe, sacrifice is primarily
defined by its purpose and only secondarily defined by its means of
achievement.

6.8 Christ's One Sacrifice as grounds for the Church's sacrifice of praise

Thus, the New Covenant, the prime analogate, is instituted by the
One Sacrifice of Christ; it is the *Totus Christus*, the union established

---

163 Augustine, *De civitate Dei*, vol. 47 of *Corpus Christianorum Latinorum*, Serie
      Latina (Turnholt 1, 1953 ff), 10:6.
164 Keefe, *Covenantal Theology*, 343.
165 Keefe, *Thomism and Tillich*, 126.
166 Keefe, *Covenantal Theology*, 66.

by the One Sacrifice between the primordial Adam and the primordial Eve. Even though it is a single reality, abstractions may be made to highlight its covenantal, marital character. Thus, Christ the Head offers Himself in sacrifice to establish the One Flesh. His sacrifice is offered totally for His Body, the Church. He acts both as priest and victim. This sacrifice evokes, causes, and creates the Church whose actuality is her worship, her own sacrifice of praise, the distinct self-offering of the Body in One Flesh with her Head. Apart from Christ's self-offering, there can be no Church and no reciprocal offering by the Church, for the Church does not initiate the sacrifice of the One Flesh; Christ does this by His One Sacrifice.[167] The Church responds to Christ's act by an action that utters—and in uttering receives—her whole reality. The offering of Christ's sacrifice, in instituting the New Covenant, can not be distinguished from the creation of the Church and of her response which results in the One Flesh Union. The Church's sacrifice is turned as totally upon her Lord as His sacrifice is offered totally for her.[168] The sacrifice of the Church is conjoined to—and inseparable from—the sacrifice of Christ and, thus, is acceptable to the Father only because it is One Flesh with His.[169]

Due to sin, Christ's self-donation, His sacrifice, would now take on the added dimension of immolation in the form of crucifixion. Christ's sacrifice now ineluctably establishes the *sancta societas* through the immolation on the Cross. However, since His sacrifice causes the Church whose actuality is her worship, her own sacrifice of praise, she, too, must undergo a type of immolation. Since the One Flesh, the *mia sarx*, is given in actuality, she is subject to the suffering, inseparable from *sarx*, that similarly afflicted Christ.[170] Her sacrifice is at one with His sacrifice due to the *mia sarx* union in which she is taken from His wounded side.

Similarly, the suffering of the *Mater dolorosa* is Mary's covenantal response to His redemptive suffering and death. This sacrifice of Mary is understood by Keefe to be triadic. As *sarx*, her "fiat" is the culmination of all the worship of the *Qahal*. Hers is also the suffering of the *Mater dolorosa* whose heart a sword shall pierce and the Daughter Zion whose virginal bearing of the Promised One fulfills all that

---

167 Ibid., 393–94.
168 Ibid., 18.
169 Ibid., 18, 166.
170 Ibid., 343.

was prophesied in the barren woman of the Old Testament. She belongs with her Son by the freedom in which He is conceived, One Flesh with her: integrally and, thus, irrevocably she is the *Theotokos*. Finally, having been joined to Him in the agony of His Cross, Mary is also One Flesh with Him in His Resurrection. By the gift of the Spirit (*pneuma*), Who is bestowed by Christ to establish the New Covenant, she also is risen, assumed into the Kingdom where her risen Son is Lord and where she also reigns with Him. She is present there not in the *sarx* of the time of the Old Testament, nor the *mia sarx* of the New Testament, but *pneuma* simply, for she shares there the triumph of her Son over death.[171] Apart from her Assumption, her eschatologically complete union with her risen Lord, the New Covenant is not fulfilled, and there can be no eucharistic representation of the One Flesh of the risen second Adam and second Eve; a Christomonism will then result.[172] The New Covenant is achieved and salvation is complete in sign. The Church is reigning in heaven through the risen Mary, who is One Flesh with the Redeemer.[173] Thus, Mary's sacrifice and, subsequently, the Church's sacrifice, is essential and indispensable to the New Covenant, but it is dependent upon the grace of Jesus' sacrifice, His institution of the One Flesh.

6.9 Section summary

The New Covenant, the means by which humanity is redeemed, is a historical reality only by being sacramentally represented. As a sacrament, it transcends the brokenness of the fallen spatio-temporal universe and its efficacy and meaning does not recede into the past. The New Covenant is historically efficacious because it embraces history and is mediated by it (i.e., sacramental realism).

To be more specific, it is through transubstantiation that the New Covenant is present sacramentally. Through it the event of Christ's sacrifice of the Cross, which institutes the New Covenant, is actual in history at the celebration of Mass. Both the sacrifice of the Cross and the sacrifice of the Mass are concretely, indissociably, and numerically

---

171 Ibid., 264.
172 Ibid., 265. For Keefe, a Christomonism reduces all to Christ through the submersion or annihilation of another's personhood.
173 Keefe, *Thomism and Tillich*, 102.

identical (i.e., a single unique event). As such, the Mass is not a repetition of Calvary. If the Mass were a repetition, the only thing that could integrate the two would be a nonsacramental principle, an idea, a remembrance. Ideas, however, operate in terms of personal subjective experience and consciousness. They are not historical for they are in the person's mind. They are not public and can not be signed and appropriated in worship because they are private. In short, the Event character of Christ's sacrifice would be undercut and, consequently, render the New Covenant nonhistorical.

Events require free physical presences. Through transubstantiation, the Body and Blood of Jesus Christ is really present in the Eucharist. This presence transcends all of history not by being removed *from* history but by being *within* history. Christ is not present locally or empirically (*per modum accidens*) but He is present concretely, historically, and actually (*per modum substantiae*). Thus, the Eucharist unifies all of history by transcending it. It informs all of history as to its beginning, center, meaning, and end. This is a function of an historical *prius*.

Christ's sacrifice forms a holy society (*sancta societas*), one that is replete with marital love. But this love is even more profound in that Christ's sacrifice makes it possible for the Church to responds in sacrifice as well. His sacrifice is one in which He offers His entire self for the sake of the Church. The Church's sacrifice of praise is then Her entire self-donation back to Her Lord. Due to sin, both sacrifices are freely offered in immolation. Thus, the union achieved in the New Covenant is not only marital, but sacrificial and marked with a suffering, freely accepted and embraced.

7 The Mass

7.1 The sacramental *ordo*

History, for the Christian, is free, since salvation, which is a free gift, can not be present in history if history is not the realm in which freedom is possible. The ordering principle, the prime analogate, of history is not only free but it is sacramental as well. This is the case since, according to Keefe, every other analysis of freedom reduces it to necessity or randomness. Thus, as has been discussed above, the Eucharist orders history in such wise that its existence is understood as *sacramentum tantum, res et sacramentum, res tantum*, the fundamental sacramental *ordo* that underlies all of history.

This fundamental sacramental *ordo* can take a number of forms: when Redemption is the focus, it may integrate history as *sarx, mia sarx, pneuma*; when salvation history is the focus it is integrated as Old Testament, New Testament, Kingdom of God. When the faithful seek to appropriate in the sacrifice of the Mass the salvation Christ accomplished for them by His One Sacrifice on Calvary, then the form is offertory, canon, communion.

Since the New Covenant, the prime analogate, is instituted by Christ's One Sacrifice on Calvary and the sacrifice is numerically identical (one and the same) with the sacrifice of the Mass, then it is important to analyze the sacramental order. In so doing, a better understanding of the prime analogate will result.

7.2 The offertory

At the offertory, ordinary bread and wine are presented by the members of the Church. Up until this point they are neutral food stuffs, but in this action they become the Church's *prosphora*, the Church's sacrifice of praise.[174] The Church has chosen *this* bread and *this* wine from among that which is generally available and assigned to them a new meaning extrinsically; they are now symbols (*sacramentum tantum*) of the Church's self-offering.

The meaning of the unconsecrated bread and wine, however, is not of nonhistorical, passive, and value-free cosmological "substance." They are the free historical sign, the *sacramentum tantum*, of that which they are to become, the New Covenant, the *res et sacramentum*. They, as the historical *prius* of the eucharistic representation of the One Sacrifice of Christ, are in an historical, active, and value-filled relationship with that sacrifice. Therefore, according to Keefe, the bread and wine represent all that the New Eve has to give her Lord (her self-donation), all that she has received from the Old Covenant as the Daughter of Zion; concretely, this is her historicity, her free offer of

---

174 Ibid., 427.

her free humanity as radicated in the people of God of the Old Covenant.[175] Keefe explains further:

> This offering, as in union with her Lord's, subsumes all the failed sacrifices of the Old Law, whose failure is that they are not yet offered *per Ipsum et cum Ipso et in Ipso, in Christo.* In the Offertory the Church prays as the Daughter Zion, and in her prayer gathers the long history of salvation into that focus which of itself, when abstracted from history, is nothing, but which, in the objective nuptial union with her Lord's One Sacrifice—effected by his creative initiative, his giving of the Spirit, not hers—is the New Covenant. In the Offertory, she also prays prolepticaly as the Church, celebrating her own reality, that of the sacrament of the Bride whose eschatological union with the Bridegroom, in the New Covenant, is complete, for the Church also is fulfilled as *pneuma* in the Resurrection of the Lord.[176]

The Church's offering, her sacrifice of praise, is, therefore, comprehensible only as *sacramentum tantum* in covenantal relationship with the other two elements of the sacramental *ordo*. This is to say that the *sacramentum tantum*, although entirely distinct from the *res et sacramentum* and the *res tantum*, nonetheless is unintelligible apart from them, as they are unintelligible apart from the *sacramentum tantum*. This offering is related to the consecration (the *res et sacramentum*) in the Canon of the Mass as the whole historical era of the Old Covenant relates to the institution of the New Covenant. In that historical relation, which is an Event and not a static cosmological structure, the bread and wine do not lose their significance as food and drink (as *sacramentum tantum*), but now, as will be discussed shortly, signify and make historically present, by the deed of Christ alone, the Event which is the One Flesh.[177] It is by His giving of the Spirit that this One Flesh is instituted and thus present to be appropriated in communion by the faithful.

7.3 The Canon and consecration

At the offertory, the Church's sacrifice of praise is offered, and its acceptance is its transubstantiation. The bread and wine are transubstantiated during the Canon of the Mass into the historical, sacrificed, risen personal reality of the Christ; they are the body, blood, soul, and

---

175   Ibid., 428.
176   Ibid.
177   Ibid.

divinity of Jesus Christ.[178] This presence is not, however, a static presence of His body, blood, soul, and divinity. He is present as priest and victim offering His One Sacrifice. His presence and His Sacrifice are immediately effective in that He institutes the Church in offering Himself for the Church. The transubstantiated bread and wine, thus, make present the One Sacrifice of Christ which is the institution of the Church with whom He is in covenantal union (Christ's One Sacrifice causes the Church and also is the mediation of the New Covenant). The transubstantiation of the bread and wine do not result in a static Real Presence but in a Real Presence that is the dynamic sacrifice of the Christ of the Covenant.[179] Keefe explains:

> Thus transubstantiated, the bread and wine are the historical, sacrificed and risen personal reality of the Christ; they are the physical Body and Blood, soul and divinity, of Jesus the Christ, *semper interpellans*, but they are so concretely as *Una Caro*, the free, sacrificial, nuptial union of Christ and his Church, within which the transubstantiated bread and wine, as *res et sacramentum*, the One Sacrifice of the Christ, at once signify and cause to be correlatively present the Church, the sacramental sign of the risen Bride, for the Eucharistically-signed Sacrifice of the Bridegroom is inseparable from her sacrifice of praise. This sacramental union is the sacrament of the One Flesh of the last Adam and the last Eve: the Church in her historical reality, her Eucharistic worship, in sacramental union with her Eucharistic Lord.[180]

Clear distinctions exist in Keefe's understanding of transubstantation. Transubstantiation causes the presence of Christ and not that which the presence of Christ causes, namely, the Church. The transubstantiated bread and wine do not include the Church. They cause it, but they do not include it. The same can be said of the New Covenant. The New Covenant is caused, signed by the transubstantiated bread and wine and is not immanent within them. What is immanent within them is the body, blood, soul, and divinity of Jesus Christ. They are, however, *res et sacramentum*, and as such are not just effects but causes here of the Church and, subsequently, the New Covenant. The Body and Blood of Christ present, signified by the bread and the wine, causes the Church. The Church is an immediate consequence of the eucharistic presence of the Christ. Where Christ is present, there is His bride in covenantal union.

---

178   Ibid.
179   Ibid., 415.
180   Ibid., 428–29.

According to Keefe, the sign of the Church is the Church's worship which is sacramental. The Church exists in this worship and has no reality other than its worship. Its worship is the offering of its prayers in union with the One Sacrifice of Christ. In that union, which is the One Flesh of the Church and Christ, the Church's prayers are acceptable to the Father because they are in union with Christ's sacrifice. It is the Church's entire worship that is the essential sign of the Church, since her sacrifice of praise, presented at the offertory, is transubstantiated into Christ's Body and Blood and ceases to exist.[181] The Church and the Church's worship are metaphysically dependent upon the One Sacrifice of Christ for their existence even though the offertory, the sacrifice of praise, is temporally prior.

The Church's sacrifice of praise, as *sacramentum tantum*, is her offering of all that she has, of all that she has received (her love, freedom, obedience, loyalty), turned totally to Christ as her source upon whom she is dependent ontologically. By the action of the risen Christ, the Church's gift of herself (the gift and not the giver)—*per Ipsum et cum Ipso et in Ipso ad Deum Patrem omnipotentum*—becomes His One Sacrifice, but does so only as in the union of One Flesh with her whose gift is thus transubstantiated by His obedience to the Father, in the eucharistic representation of that obedience unto death on the Cross. The Church herself is not transubstantiated into the Christ.[182] She does not stop being herself. It is by turning toward Him, Who is metaphysically prior, that she indeed becomes herself. Her gift, an expression of all that she has, is what is transubstantiated. Keefe says, "The subject of transubstantiation is the offering, not the one who offers."[183] If this were not the case, a Christomonism would result whereby the second Eve is "merged" with the second Adam into a single person, *una persona*. There is no assimilation of the second Eve's person or her sacrifice of praise to His Person or to His sacrifice, for that would undercut the New Covenant and ultimately the divine mission of the Father sending the Son to give the Spirit.[184]

Transubstantiation proceeds *ex nihilo*, for there is no prior possibility in the bread and wine to become the Body and Blood of Christ of-

---

181 Ibid., 436.
182 Ibid.
183 Ibid., 453.
184 Ibid., 438.

fered in sacrifice.[185] Similarly, the New Covenant is not an implication of the Old but rather the Old Covenant receives its meaning and unity in light of the New.[186] The New Covenant is objectively given. Transubstantiation, which brings about the eucharistic representation of the New Covenant, is thus novel and unique objectively. Its explanation can not be by assimilation to some prior metaphysical analysis. Such an analysis supposes a necessity intrinsic to a prior intelligibility that is not free and historical. Consequently, transubstantiation can only be understood *a posteriori*, from within the objective truth appropriated in the worship of the Church. This worship is the *ordo*: the Eucharist, the prime analogate by which reality, as free, as history, is articulated.[187]

Keefe holds that there is an analogy between transubstantiation and the event by which Mary, as the second Eve, conceived her Lord at the Annunciation. This analogy is exact for it is the analogy of covenantal worship.[188] Mary's *fiat mihi* corresponds to the Church's offering of bread and wine. Both acts of worship are created by Christ's gift of the *Spiritus Creator* and as a result of this gift, the offering of Mary's fecundity and the Church's bread and wine are received, and, simultaneously, Christ is immanent within humanity.[189] By being immanent, by taking on flesh, Christ subjects Himself, then, to suffering and death so as to fulfill the Father's mission.

Just as Christ's obedience in becoming flesh is at one with Mary's obedience in conceiving Him in her free expression, *fiat mihi*, so, too, His One Sacrifice is never disjunct from the Church's sacrifice of praise. In the Eucharist, the two sacrifices are One Flesh, never to be dissociated or identified. Thus, due to the consecration, Christ's Body and Blood are eucharistically present in the species and consequently, Mary is correlatively present not in the species but in the eucharistic worship which the Church offers Who, in so doing, is One Flesh with Her Lord, understood covenantally and not monistically. As Keefe states:

> In the Church's Eucharistic worship, the Christ is present as Event: as Sacrifice, as Risen, as King. By the sacramental representation of his Sacrifice, his

---

185 Ibid., 435.
186 Ibid., 435–38.
187 Ibid., 436.
188 Ibid.
189 Ibid., 17.

> Bride is present under the sign of the Church; it is thus that the second Eve, assumed in heaven, is made present in history where she has a sacramental event-presence correlative to her Lord's. This is the sacramental representation of the event of her worship, her sacrifice of praise.[190]

According to Keefe, the eucharistic presence of the Christ has its source in the Whole Christ, the historical as well as the risen Christ. Keefe states:

> It would be a most serious mistake to suppose that the creative causality exercised by the Eucharistic presence of the Christ has its source simply in the Christ as risen: its ground is historical, inseparable from the Son's historical Sacrifice on the Cross, his obedience unto death; similarly it would be...a most serious mistake to suppose that the presence of the Christ is only that of the historical Jesus who died on the Cross, for he is present in the Eucharist as the risen Lord of history.[191]

The eucharistic presence, then, has its source in the entire Christ: risen and historical. This Christ is what is present in the Eucharist and as sacrament is what provides for the free unity of history. Yet the Christ Who is present is historically immanent in His people and in the fullness of the New Covenant of which He is the Sacrifice (as inseparably *sarx, mia sarx, pneuma*). Otherwise, the eucharistic presence of Christ would not cause the Church (militant) to be actual as the sacramental presence of the risen Kingdom (Church triumphant) inseparable from the sacramental presence of the risen King. The Eucharist is the sacrament of the Whole Christ (*Christus totus*), of the Head and Body which fills the universe, not as an immanent *Logos* which is cosmological in structure, but as the free Event of the free immanence in fallen history of the Immanuel in the Event of the One Flesh.[192]

Since both Christ and the Church are present in the Eucharist as sacrament, the Church is sacramental in the same correlative manner as Christ is, namely, as historical and risen. The sacramental Church has the event-structure of sacramental worship, the historical articulation of *sarx, mia sarx, pneuma*: as *sarx* the Church is the Old Testament *Qahal*; as *mia sarx* she is the historical Church, whose sacrifice of praise is One Flesh with Christ's One Sacrifice; as *pneuma* she is the Queen of Heaven, risen and fulfilled.[193]

---

190 Ibid., 265.
191 Ibid., 424–25.
192 Ibid., 425.
193 Ibid., 265.

7.4 The priesthood

Since the Church's worship is instituted by Christ's Own Sacrifice, the Church offers the Mass in Christ's name and by His authority, for the Church knows but one high priest. Consequently, a priest of the Church, acting *in persona Christi*, offers the sacrifice in His name and not in his own. The words of consecration which the priest speaks over the gifts of bread and wine, which cause and sign the One Sacrifice, are Christ's uttered in His Person and with His authority and not his. Only as uttered by Christ are the words effective of His sacrifice and His presence to His Church. On no other authority can the words be spoken in truth. As Keefe states, to act in the person and with the authority of Christ is to do so in the Person of the Head whose One Sacrifice is His nuptial union with His Body, the bridal Church. The priest acts, then, as the Bridegroom in relationship to the Church which is represented by the congregation.[194] He acts as head with regard to the body. The priest does not cease, however, to be a member of the Church by reason of his ordination to offer the One Sacrifice. If that were the case, then he would be excluded from the salvation which is offered only to the body of those for whom Christ died.[195]

7.5 The communion

During the Canon of the Mass, the death of Christ on the Cross is sacramentally (therefore, in the real actuality of an historical Event) represented as the unsurpassable fulfillment of the prophecies of the Old Covenant, as the pure sacrifice of the Christ Who alone establishes the New Covenant, and as the eschatological consummation of the Old and the New Covenant. It is through this One Sacrifice that we have communion with the Second Adam, raised by the Spirit, Who now pours out the Spirit upon His bridal Church.[196] By entering into eucharistic communion with the risen Lord of the Kingdom and by receiving the fullness of the Good Creation in that sign and symbol of the One Sacrifice of the One Flesh by which we are redeemed, one enters into the only reality there is: the New Covenant, the prime

---

194 Ibid., 43.
195 Gerald Emmett Cardinal Carter, *"Do This in Remembrance of Me:" A Pastoral Letter on the Sacrament of Priesly Orders* (Toronto: Mission Press, 1983), 45.
196 Keefe, *Covenantal Theology*, 424.

analogate.[197] It is by entering into the One Flesh that we are freed from the slavery of sin and are thus free to appropriate the New Covenant freely. We are freed to be free freely. In Keefe's words:

> Free participation in this Eucharistic worship is the personal appropriation of the New Covenant in fallen history: this can only be the free integration of the individual communicant into the covenantal and marital order which is the free unity of substantial being, the covenantal imaging of the Triune God. By this historical integration, human beings become truly personal, subsisting in unique and irreducible relations to other analogously unique persons whose uniqueness and dignity is precisely their self-donation to each other....This free personal appropriation of the New Covenant is then Eucharistic, and its intrinsic intelligibility is that of the sacramental *ordo* which we have seen: the *sacramentum tantum*, the *res et sacramentum*, the *res tantum*. It culminates in the fulfilled freedom of the eschatological Kingdom of God, but as our personal historical freedom it is enabled and sustained only by solidarity with the sacramental immanence of the Immanuel....[198]

The *res tantum* of the Eucharist is the communion which is not a sign, not a visible reality, but a final effect (a *res*) merely (*tantum*). It is the free *ex opere operantis* effect of the efficacious signing (*ex opere operato*; i.e., by the work of the Spirit poured out by the risen Christ) of the *sacramentum tantum* of the sacrificial presence of the risen and sacrificed Christ and by the *res et sacramentum* of the achieved full bestowal of the Spirit by which all things are made new and the Kingdom of God is fully realized. In short, the *res tantum* is the free personal union with the risen Christ in His Kingdom. It is entry into the "holy society by which we belong to God."

Since this effect is covenantal freedom and all union with Christ is free, it must be freely appropriated by the individual recipient of the Eucharist.[199] While original sin in each fallen human being (*originatum*) is not voluntary, acceptance of the offer of Redemption must be voluntary and not imposed for it to remain free. By the redemptive action of Christ, fallen humanity is no longer unfreely unfree (a solidarity in sin) but freely free if he or she so chooses. The freedom of the New Covenant that Mary accepted and which now is offered to the rest of humanity can not be imposed, because it is marital freedom which recognizes mutual dignity. Thus, it must be a matter of personal acceptance. The unfreedom that the first Adam chose can be

---

197 Ibid., 414.
198 Ibid., 458.
199 Ibid., 235.

imposed, for it is unfreedom which recognizes no mutual dignity. Keefe explains:

> To be fallen is to be unfree, so that a free solidarity in fallenness would be a contradiction in terms. The inverse is also true: had there been no fall our solidarity in the integrity of the first Adam would have been effective in each of us as a spontaneous, personally free commitment, as finally our redemption must be.[200]

Thus, a person freely appropriates the New Covenant through reception of Holy Communion. We know from Paul that reception is free, since the Eucharist may be received to one's detriment if one so chooses. Proper reception, however, includes what the Alexandrine school has always understood, since the time of Clement and Origen, to be a divinization: the medicine of immortality, the triumph over sin and death. Thus, the *res tantum* is the gift of incorporation in the Body of Christ: the earthly Church, the heavenly Kingdom. It is the passage from the hopeless fallenness which is mere *sarx*, through the Redemption given in the *mia sarx*, the One Flesh of the New Covenant, to the *pneuma* that is eternal life in union with the risen Christ.[201] This is given in pledge in the eucharistic communion.[202]

7.6 Section summary

The theological *prius* structures history according to the fundamental sacramental *ordo* of *sacramentum tantum, res et sacramentum,* and *res tantum*. In reference to the Mass, this *ordo* takes the structure of offertory, canon, and communion.

At the offertory, the Church's sacrifice of praise is exemplified by bread and wine (the *sacramentum tantum*). They represent all that the New Eve has received from the Old Covenant as the Daughter of Zion and all that she gives to Her Lord in sacrifice. The bread and wine are not static cosmological structures but rather they signify and make historically present the eucharistic Event which is the One Flesh during the canon and communion of the Mass.

At the canon, the Church's offering of bread and wine are accepted by their being transubstantiated into the personal reality of

---

200   Ibid., 236.
201   Ibid., 437.
202   Ibid., 415.

Jesus Christ (*res et sacramentum*). This presence is indeed one of Christ's body, blood, soul, and divinity, yet Keefe emphasizes that it is not a static presence. He is present as priest and victim actively offering His One Sacrifice which institutes the Church with whom He is in covenantal union. In other words, the transubstantiation of the bread and wine does not result in a static Real Presence but in a Real Presence that is the dynamic Sacrifice of Christ. This sacrifice of the Body and Blood of Christ institutes the Church and the New Covenant. The Church is then free to worship and by offering prayers in union with Christ's sacrifice, upon which She is dependent, the Church's worship is acceptable to the Father. In the Eucharist, the two sacrifices of Christ and the Church are never dissociated or identified.

Communion is the *res tantum*; it is not a sign, not a visible reality, but a final effect. It is the effect brought about by the risen Christ Who pours out His Spirit upon His Church and makes all things new in the Kingdom of God. Slavery to sin has been broken and now human beings are freed to be freely free. The freedom of the New Covenant that Mary accepted is now offered to the rest of humanity. It must be freely accepted and not imposed because it is grounded in freedom, integrity, and mutual dignity.

Each one of the three elements of the sacramental *ordo* is interdependent upon the other two. All three are interconnected. The conceptual isolation of one from the others renders each of them mute. This relational aspect is also evident and essential within each one of the three elements themselves. The offertory, canon, and communion each have constitutive principles that are divine and human. The covenantal presence of Christ and the Church is evident in each one. This fact is a manifestation of the marital nature of the *prius*.

8 The New Covenant as an Image of the Trinity

8.1 An introduction

According to Keefe, creation is the object of a free decision by God the Father to send His Son to give the Holy Spirit. God creates, however, through the offer of the New Covenant. Creation is dependent upon—and is the formal effect of—the New Covenant as offered. The

New Covenant is the object of the divine creative will, which as divine, is Trinitarian: the sending of the Son by the Father to give the Spirit.[203] Thus, the New Covenant is the free image of God. That is, the Trinity is imaged only in the actuality of the Good Creation which is the historical activity of the New Covenant.[204]

Keefe holds that the New Covenant, as prime analogate, grounds and establishes the revealed analogy between the divine and the human. It permits one to speak of the divine substance and to use of God such terms as "tri-personal," "tri-relational," and "triune." Consequently, the Person of the Father is Father in terms of His total donation of all that He has, His divinity, to the Son. The Son is Who He is in receiving all that He has from the Father. As standing relations, they pour forth the Holy Spirit Who is the Spirit of the Father and the Son. He is distinct from both in His relations to them. Thus, neither the Godhead nor the Persons possessing that Godhead are monadic but are interrelational. The Father is not simply a divine Person in isolation from the other two Persons. He is the Father Who sends the Son to give the Spirit. Thus, for Keefe, Boethius' definition of person as an individual rational substance is rejected on grounds that it is not relational, not trinitarian. He likewise rejects the Thomistic definition ("a person is for himself and for his purposes and not a mere utility to be subordinated to the purposes of some other being,") on the same grounds. Rather, personhood is defined in terms of relationality, that which is incapable of formal replication due to a unique and unrepeatable relation of origin.[205] In other words, the ground for the personhood of the Son is that He is the unique Son of the Father. The ground for my personhood is that I am in a unique relationship to my parents and to God.

8.2 Freedom within the Trinity

The Father does not generate the Son by an act of will, by a free choice, for that would render the Son a creature. The Father also does not act out of necessity for God would then no longer be God. There would be an extrinsic agent standing over and against God control-

---

203 Ibid., 433.
204 Ibid., 6.
205 Ibid., 387, 450.

ling God which can not be. Rather, the Father generates the Son by nature. It is the nature of God to be infinitely eternally fruitful in the act of divine generation and spiration. While this action is by nature (an intrinsic "necessity"), it is freely willed by God for all eternity. There is no compulsion that constrains God's will. His will is His nature and this nature is free.

In speaking here of the freedom that is constitutive of the Trinity, Keefe obviously does not envision here what is called "categorical freedom." This is the freedom that is exercised in this or that way, between this or that choice. Neither is he referring to noncovenantal freedom which is an aspect of "substantial freedom" or that freedom by which one affirms or denies one's reality or substantial being. Rather, he is referring to covenantal substantial freedom which is constitutive of the Trinity. This freedom is the freedom by which one affirms one's reality by expending it on another, by committing to another. This freedom is a relational freedom *for* rather than a monadic freedom *from*. The only freedom a monad has is the flight to self-enclosure, to alienation, for it is free to the extent that it is not touched by other monads.[206] The monolithic, monadic person is not a person by relation but by identity with substance. The person has withdrawn to such an extent that he or she is absolute, the only such person, the only such substance. It is a removal from all that is not self. On the other hand, in covenantal freedom (freedom *for*, the freedom of the Trinity), the person determines himself or herself by transcending the self in committing to another. This freedom involves the affirmation of a particular unique and irreducible other with whom one is in a relationship. This relationship is free. Neither partner in the relationship is in servitude to the other. One's identity is actualized and reciprocally affirmed in acts of mutual self-donation.[207]

8.3 The Trinitarian response to the problem of the One and the Many

As stated above, the One Godhead is variegated on a personal level and this variegation is utterly free. Personhood is freely determined by a unique relation of origin and is freely affirmed by the other per-

---

206 Ibid., 28.
207 Ibid., 29, 388.

sons in that one divine nature. Consequently, the Triune God utterly transforms the ancient problem of the One and the Many. By the faith-affirmation of the revelation which is in the Christ of the New Covenant, the unity of being is seen to be trinitarian, and the many are discovered to be in a free, historical, positive, and covenant relation to the One.[208] This conversion of the One from Monad to Trinity eliminates the time-honored antagonism between the unity of the Creator and the multiplicity of the created order.[209] The New Covenant, then, is that means by which the One God relates to His creation. The New Covenant is in itself (as prime analogate) that by which there is a unity of being in creation, and that unity of being is an image of the triune God. In short, the New Covenant is that by which God relates to His creation and the New Covenant is that which unites all things in creation and in so doing is an image of the Trinity.

8.4 The New Covenant as a marital image

The New Covenant is the sole mediation of the Father's sending of the Son to give the Spirit and as such is the image of the Trinity.[210] It submits only to the norm of the Trinity.[211] God's definitive presence to His people is constituted by the One Flesh union of the New Adam and the New Eve. In other words, the *sine qua non* of the mission is the Incarnation of the Son through the motherhood of her by whose *fiat* the Uncreated and Created Wisdom are united in a bond which is at once the definitive presence of God in the world and the equally definitive imaging of God.[212] Mary's *fiat* is integral to the New Covenant; while it is created, it is the indispensable free correlative response to the created personal *terminus* of Christ's mission by the Father in the Incarnation.[213] Yet this free correlative response is essentially tied to her feminine humanity. Inasmuch as the Incarnation has united the Son personally with His masculine humanity, the Son's

---

208 Ibid., 350.
209 Ibid.
210 Donald J. Keefe, "Mary as Created Wisdom: The Splendor of the New Creation," *The Thomist* 47 (July 1983): 406, 409.
211 Ibid., 406.
212 Ibid., 409.
213 Keefe, *Covenantal Theology*, 236.

personal unity includes His masculinity and is, thus, essential to the New Covenant as well.[214]

Keefe argues that this view of the New Covenant as marital, which is taken up by the Pauline adaptation of the Yahwist "one flesh" of Gen. 2:24 in Eph. 5:31, is inseparable from the notion of covenant itself, whether in the Old Testament or the New.[215] He also holds that it is inseparable from the reality of created freedom:

> As the Old Testament is the record of the summons to freedom, of the liberation, of the People of God, that freedom is more and more clearly presented, from Hosea to the final chapters of Isaiah and in the later Wisdom literature, as the response to a love which is marital. God's love for his people is the continual offer, by the Lord of the living, of the gift of life: He evokes the bridal return, the mediation, of that love, and condemns its betrayal as a prostitution, i.e., as betraying not only God, but the splendor and beauty of the Good Creation, whose reality is forsworn when its one purpose and truth, the mediation and imaging of God, is refused. Any interpretation of the relation of God to Israel which does not take very seriously, and not as mere metaphor, the bridal symbolism by which that relation is increasingly stated in the later levels of the Old Testament can not avoid an impoverished and finally inadequate view of the New Covenant as well.[216]

This covenanted freedom finds its primary expression in the *fiat mihi* of Mary by which she as second Eve, as the *Theotokos*, reverses the refusal of the first Eve and in so doing occasions the inception of a radically new relation of the Lord of history to the world, the New Covenant. As unfallen, immaculate, integral, Mary fulfills totally the mediatory role of her people: a role at once virginal and maternal, Daughter of Zion, Mother of God, Bride of Yahweh.[217] Thus, the Trinitarian imaging proper to the marital society which is the New Covenant takes a variety of forms: New Adam-New Eve, Bridegroom-Bride, Incarnate *Logos*-Mother of God, Christ-Church, Head-Body, etc. Yet in all of these images, the eschatological perfection is uniquely symbolized by marriage rather that by one of the other polarities found in human sexuality (father-daughter, son-mother, brother-sister, etc.) for of these sexual polarities, only marriage is a sacramental sign and a Trinitarian symbol.[218]

---

214 Ibid., 78.
215 Keefe, "Mary as Created Wisdom," 406–7.
216 Ibid., 407.
217 Ibid., 408.
218 Ibid., 410.

Keefe holds that the Trinitarian structure of the marital symbol is rather evident: the total self-donation of two persons to each other is constitutive of each, as husband, as wife, and is productive of a third reality, the marriage bond itself. This bond is the substantive love of each for each which can not be undone and whose self-subsistent character is evidenced by its irrevocability. This love or covenant can not be identified with either of the covenanting persons for this, and its radical permanence as a relation, makes the marital covenant of husband and wife the Trinitarian image and sacrament *par excellence.* It is only within this context that the Trinity is in fact "imaged."[219]

Since Trinitarian imaging is the basis of the New Covenant, Keefe locates the meaning of the masculine-feminine polarity of the New Covenant there. According to Keefe, the language of subordination by which this sexual polarity is designated is rooted in the Trinitarian subordination of the Son to the Father and, therefore, does not carry with it an implication of ontological inferiority.[220] The masculine is that which is actual by a holistic reference and donation to the feminine; the feminine is that which is actual in a reciprocal self-donation to the masculine: neither possesses any autonomous significance.[221] The one's significance is rooted in and mutually affirmed by the other.

While it must be remembered that the New Covenant is a single Event (the marital One Flesh established by the One Sacrifice of Christ between the second Adam and the second Eve), abstractions can be made in order to highlight its covenantal imaging of the Trinity. Thus, Christ as Head and image of the Father, offers Himself in sacrifice to establish the One Flesh. His sacrifice is offered totally for His Body, His glory, the Church. His sacrifice evokes, causes, and creates the Church whose actuality is her worship, her own sacrifice of praise, the distinct self-offering of the Body in One Flesh union with her Head. Apart from Christ's self-offering, there can be no Church and no reciprocal offering by the Church, for the Church does not initiate the sacrifice of the One Flesh; Christ does. The Church responds to Christ's action by an action that utters—and in uttering receives—her whole reality. The offering of Christ's sacrifice in instituting the New Covenant, can not be distinguished from the creation of the Church

---

219 Ibid.
220 Donald J. Keefe, "The Sacrament of the Good Creation: Prolegomena to the Discussion of the Ordination of Women," *Faith & Reason* 9 (Summer 1983): 132–33.
221 Ibid., 133.

and her response which results in the One Flesh. The Church's sacrifice is turned as totally upon her Lord as His sacrifice is offered totally
for her.[222] The sacrifice of the Church is conjoined to and inseparable
from the sacrifice of Christ and, thus, is acceptable to the Father only
because it is One Flesh with His.[223] Thus, there are two inseparable
sacrifices: that of the Head and that of the Body.

All three elements of the New Covenant instituted by the One
Sacrifice of Christ, considered in abstraction—the Church's sacrifice of
praise, the sacrifice of Christ, and the One Flesh union—are integral
to the imaging of the Trinity. To understand the One Flesh as merely
one sacrifice (either Christ's sacrifice or the Church's sacrifice) is to
undermine the distinction between the spouses who freely constitute
the New Covenant and so to barter the reality for a false simplicity, an
image that is non-nuptial. Likewise, the nuptial imaging of the Trinity
is equally destroyed if the Church's sacrifice is understood to merge
with Christ's sacrifice in a Christomonism. There is rather no merger,
to the point of lost identity, of the Church with Christ into *una persona*
(mia physis); there is no assimilation of her person or her sacrifice to
His Person or His sacrifice; no single or monadic reality is formed.[224]
The union between Christ and His Church is not organic so as to constitute a single physical reality but, rather, marital, a relationship between two free nuptial persons.[225] In other words, the New Covenant
as prime analogate is to be conceived nuptially not monadically or
Christomonadically.[226]

Consequently, the image, the nuptially ordered New Covenant
must contain the three elements of the *ordo*, for it has no other basis
for its actualization than the Trinitarian mission of the Father sending
the Son to give the Spirit.[227] Through His sacrifice, Christ creates the
free response for the free acceptance and actualization of the One
Flesh union. While the Church's sacrifice is indeed dependent upon
Christ's sacrifice, the two are never to be identified. Head and Body
are distinguishable because they are nuptially distinct as masculine

---

222 Keefe, *Covenantal Theology*, 18.
223 Ibid., 18, 166.
224 Ibid., 52, 438, 447.
225 Keefe, "The Sacrament of the Good Creation," 135.
226 Keefe, *Covenantal Theology*, 179.
227 Ibid., 18.

and feminine but yet are inseparable due to the nuptial bond uniting the two.

The nuptial distinction of masculinity and femininity in sacrifice is analogous to the distinction in the sexual polarity of the New Covenant's imaging of the Trinity. Following upon Christ, the nuptial role of the masculine is seen to be sacrificial: to offer the sacrifice which institutes the covenant. The man does this as a head from whom the Bride proceeds as a "glory" so as to constitute with him one flesh, a holy society by which humanity belongs to God. The self-donation that is the offering of sacrifice by the head is at the same time an election: it is for the exclusive benefit of the bride, the body of the head. The exclusiveness of the covenant is mutual, for in neither the man nor the woman is there any reservation of self. The offerer of the sacrifice and the offering are the same: the sacrifice is an unconditional self-donation without reservation to a unique bride, and in that sense is a passage from a fragmentary condition of flesh (*sarx*) to the nuptial union of "one flesh" (*mia sarx*). There is no remainder in the head or the glory which is his body that is available for any other commitment. Thus, the meaning of masculinity is complete in Christ's sacrificial relation as Head to the Church, the Body, and the meaning of feminity is uttered in the Church, as Body, as Glory.[228]

8.5 Irrational creation's imaging of the Trinity

Keefe holds that created imitation of the Trinity extends to the irrational dimension of creation, but only as vestiges rather than images.[229] Due to the Incarnate Christ, the universe's sole intelligibility and actuality is human and covenantal.[230] The universe is actual in and by the actuality of the human being which is brought about itself through the prime human actuality, Jesus Christ.[231] In other words, the intelligibility of the universe is identified with the intelligibility of the human species. If the human species is created through Christ, then so, too, is the universe. The universe is actual by its participation in the actuality of humanity, for matter is implicit in the material crea-

---

228 Donald J. Keefe, "Sacramental Sexuality and the Ordination of Women," *Communio* 5 (Summer 1978): 250.

229 Keefe, *Covenantal Theology*, 389.

230 Ibid., 447.

231 Keefe, *Thomism and Tillich*, 90.

tion of humanity as given in the Incarnation.[232] The universe is provided for when God became a human being, took on material form.

Obviously, irrational creation has no free will by which to determine itself freely in a covenantal relationship, but it is ordered to humanity which then supports humanity's self-determination. Materiality, nonetheless, is novel, free in its own proper order, according to Keefe. Materiality is not necessitarian, "pre-programmed." It is not deterministic as the pagan Stoics held. If it were deterministic, then eventually science would reduce physical truth to mathematical rationality and that would entail the methodological nullification of the scientific inquiry into the physical universe. The scientist would eventually have no need for experimental science for the intelligibility of the universe would be reduced to mathematical equations. If, on the other hand, the universe is chaotic, it has no intelligibility to be discovered. The scientist has no need to inquire. He or she has undercut his or her own discipline. Rather, scientific investigation functions only as long as there is an expectation of finding something new. This expectation is based on the Christian doctrine that the physical universe is free, intelligible, and inexhaustibly interesting.[233]

Keefe considers the recognition of the revelation of the Trinity and the covenantal creation in the image of God "the single theological task of importance." Upon the postulate "finite reality is intelligible only as covenanted because only as free" rests the entirety of free historical rationality and the entirety of Catholic theology. "Apart from its covenantal quality, which is the free order of a free or historical event, finitude is not only *a priori* incapable of mediating the infinite God; it can not even be the object of inquiry."[234] Finite material reality then would not be recognized as gratuitous, as a free covenantally ordered gift from God with which it is in covenant. Rather, it would be rendered monadic and its intelligibility abstract, nonhistorical, and deterministic. Ultimately, the scientist's method undermines its rationale for inquiring into historical finitude, and when it is applied to theology, the finite is incapable of mediating the infinite.

---

232 Ibid., 92.
233 Ibid., 135.
234 Ibid., 6.

8.6 Section summary

According to Keefe, the New Covenant, as *prius* or prime analogate, grounds and establishes the revealed analogy between the divine and human. It permits the divine substance to be spoken of in terms such as "tri-personal," "tri-relational," and "triune." Thus, the Person of the Father is Father in terms of His total donation of all that He has, His divinity, to the Son. The Son receives all that He has from the Father. As standing relations, they pour forth the Holy Spirit Who is the Spirit of the Father and the Son. Consequently, neither the Godhead nor the Persons possessing that Godhead are monadic but are inter-relational. Personhood must now be defined in terms of relationality (i.e., that which is incapable of formal replication due to a unique and unrepeatable relation of origin).

The Father generates the Son not by an act of the will or by free choice because that would render the Son a creature. He also does not act out of necessity because there is no necessity or potentiality in God. Rather, God acts out of covenantal freedom by which the person determines himself or herself by transcending the self in committing to the other. This freedom, in contrast to categorical freedom, involves the affirmation of a particular unique and irreducible other with whom one is in a relationship.

Keefe argues that because the Trinity is inter-relational, the New Covenant, which is an image of the Trinity, is best symbolized by marriage. In marriage, the total self-donation of two persons to each other is constitutive of each, as husband, as wife, and is productive of a third reality, the marriage bond itself. The gift, affirmation, and reception of one spouse to the other is so real that it takes the form of a marital bond (and, at times, even a child).

Keefe locates the meaning of the masculine and feminine in the New Covenant as well. The nuptial role of the masculine is to offer sacrifice. The man does this as a head from whom the bride proceeds as a glory so as to constitute with him one flesh. The self-donation that is the offering of sacrifice by the head is at the same time an election of this particular woman from among all other women. By affirming and receiving this election, she is called to be the body of the head in her reciprocal act of total self-donation to her husband. She is subordinate but not inferior. One's dignity and significance is rooted in and mutually affirmed by the other.

Created imitation of the Trinity also extends to irrational creation not as images but as vestiges. The intelligibility of the universe is identified with the intelligibility of the human species. Since the human species is created through Christ, then so, too, is the universe. Obviously, irrational creation has no intellect or free will, but it does have a freedom in its own proper order. It is not deterministic; its truth can not be reduced to a mathematical rationality. It is not chaotic since there is an intelligibility to be discovered. Rather, the physical universe is free, intelligible, and interesting. Recognition of this fact is of the utmost theological importance because without it, materiality and historical events would not be able to mediate the divine. If the New Covenant is the *prius* of theology as Keefe proposes, this can not be the case.

9 Chapter Summary

A *prius*, in the order of metaphysics, is an antecedent condition by whose priority the second reality is intelligible. With regard to the analogy of being, the *prius* (or more precisely, the prime analogate) is that subject to which the perfection expressed by the predicate or secondary analogate belongs primarily. It is the fullness of being and, as such, it is substance in its widest extension. It is that in which all finite beings participate.

When this understanding of *prius* or prime analogate is applied to theology (i.e., faith seeking understanding), it provides an organizational structure to the entire content of divine revelation and then either a discursive-analytical or an intuitive-dialectical system methodologically provides for its articulation. Keefe identifies the New Covenant, the Eucharist, as the *prius* of theology. Such a *prius* is historical, free, actual, sacramental, and covenantal. It is the *terminus* of the Trinitarian mission: the Father sends the Son to give the Holy Spirit. The Father creates the universe through the Son and the Son becomes immanent within this creation through the Incarnation. The primordial Covenant is offered to the first Adam and the first Eve; however, it is rejected. The sinful actions of a creature, however, will not thwart the divine will. The obstacle of sin is dealt with by the incarnate Christ embracing the depths of fallenness and sin (*sarx*) on the

Cross. Through the complete and perfect sacrificial offering of Himself and the pouring forth of the Holy Spirit on the New Church, the One Flesh (*mia sarx*) of the New Covenant is instituted and made manifest. Human beings are now free as moral agents to appropriate and live within this Covenant. This is done within the sacramental *ordo* of the Mass by which the Church offers her sacrifice of praise to the Father in union with Christ's sacrifice. Here materiality and historical events are able to mediate freely divinity to humanity in a covenantal manner that reflects the inter-personal relationship within the Trinity. All of this is expressed in a eucharistic theological *prius*.

CHAPTER TWO

A PHILOSOPHICAL UNDERSTANDING OF THE EUCHARIST

1 A Covenantal Transformation of Act-Potency

1.1 A recapitulation

We have seen that Keefe regards all reality, all truth as free. No necessary being, no necessary truth is actual anywhere in the created or the uncreated order precisely because the creation, whether as a divine act or as the object of that act, is a free order. The unity, truth, goodness, and beauty of the created order (whose creation is in Christ) are known only as revealed in Christ, that is, only as given *ex nihilo* and, consequently, as free gift, not as intrinsically necessary. This creation has a Trinitarian order which is imaged covenantally: this free order (or free unity of the Trinity) is imaged in the One Sacrifice of Christ for His Bride, which is the institution of the New Covenant. This New Covenant is the prime creative act of the Trinity (the Father sending the Son to give the Spirit) and its actuality in history is only eucharistic. If it were not the eucharistic representation of the One Sacrifice, it would cease to be redemptive because it would be no more present in history or transcendent to it than any other event that has receded into the past. In short, the revealed intelligibility, unity, truth, goodness, beauty of created being demands a prime analogate which does not contradict its intrinsic freedom. This analogate must be an event, not a thing, not a structure, not an idea, for none of these can be understood as free or as the principle of such freedom. The only free order of being is nuptial: the institution of the One Flesh by the One Sacrifice of Christ.

1.2 Transubstantiation as normative of metaphysics

For Keefe, then, the immediate implication of the recognition of the New Covenant as the prime analogate of substantial being is that eucharistic transubstantiation must be seen to be normative for metaphysics, as only an *a priori* can be normative. Thereupon, transubstantiation is not an exception to metaphysical intelligibility arbitrarily inserted into reality as a requirement of faith, but it is the very criterion of metaphysical intelligibility. Thus, for Keefe, a properly theological task is one that understands reality under the eucharistic criterion of historical objectivity, namely, under the *a priori* of the prime historical objectivity, the eucharistic event of transubstantiation and of sacrifice. The task is not to attempt to understand transubstantiation within the *a priori* context of a cosmological notion of objectivity, for this notion will control *a priori* what transubstantiation might be. In other words, the task of theology is to develop an historical and theological metaphysical analysis of being as intelligible, immanent freedom in the covenantal terms which are manifest and effective in eucharistic transubstantation and not to develop an account of transubstantation in terms of a metaphysical analysis of the intelligible immanent necessity of being. Consequently, since this work is focusing on the Aristotelian-based methodology of Keefe's systematic theology, this section will analyze how he applies the act-potency analysis of being under the norm of the historical prime analogate (the eucharistic representation of the New Covenant) which, consequently, is the reverse of prior attempts of trying to fit transubstantiation into a prevailing necessitarian act-potency system.[1]

1.3 Act-potency

With such a new understanding of the prime analogate, the entire range of terms and meanings associated with it must reflect this understanding. In this case, since Keefe applies an act-potency analysis to the prime analogate, the meaning of act-potency must be controlled by this analogate. Consequently, since the prime analogate is not necessary but free, the theological act-potency correlations are free and do not refer to the "conditions of possibility" which are supposed by a cosmological act-potency analysis to be necessarily immanent in a cosmic metaphysical structure.[2] For Keefe, potency is a free potency which means that while it is a precondition, it is not a necessary precondition nor is it a sufficient precondition. It is simply a temporal *prius*, a temporal antecedent, an historical potentiality. Potency is understood as potency only insofar as it freely points to its actualization. An act is an actualization of a potency, the actuating cause of the potency.

The act-potency analysis is transcendental in that it bears upon the intrinsic intelligibility of being. There are three modalities of this analysis. As developed by Aristotle, the first, namely form-matter, replies affirmatively to the question of whether intelligible form can inhere in matter. The second, namely accident-substance, replies affirmatively to the question of whether the resultant material substance can undergo change and remain itself. To these Aristotelian analyses, Aquinas added a third, which responds positively to the question of whether a finite substance can exist contingently (i.e., whether it can be created). The affirmative response to these three questions amounts to setting out in terms of act and potency the intrinsic conditions of possibility of the immanence of form in matter (matter is potency as to form), of accidental change (substance is potency as to accident), and of contingent existence (essence is potency as to *esse*).[3]

---

1 Keefe, *Covenantal Theology*, 429.
2 Ibid., 426.
3 Ibid., 430.

In each of these three modalities of the act-potency analysis, the object of the analysis remains constant (i.e., the New Covenant) while the questions posed are different. Insofar as the questions are historical and metaphysical, they refer to the New Covenant in its historical presentation which is the Eucharist. Consequently, all the act-potency analyses of Keefe's Aristotelian-based system are analyses of the fundamental reality, the eucharistic Event which is the historical and sacramental representation of the One Sacrifice of Christ. While this is a novel systematic method in which to deal with the Eucharist, Keefe holds that it is the only way to honor the *ex nihilo* aspect and the primordial freedom it possesses.[4]

1.4 The *esse*-essence correlation

Keefe understands, as Aquinas himself did, that the *esse*-essence relation is an implication of an act-potency analysis of creation. It is an analysis which presupposes that the radical contingency of creation, occurring on the level of subsistence, possesses intrinsic intelligibility and that the cause of a novel and free subsistence must itself be free. This free cause can only be a free Event, for we have seen that Keefe holds that only events, not structures, ideas, and so forth, are free. This Event can only be the free immanence of the Creator in creation, the New Covenant: only in the concreteness of its exercise is a free cause actual. The free immanence of the substantial cause of creation demands not only the freedom of the Creator, which is accounted for in the contingency of the *esse*-essence relation, but also the freedom of creation. Keefe explains, "The creation itself must be historically free, constituted by the free and affirmative response of humanity to the free human immanence of the Creator, whose immanence would otherwise be despotic and finally a dualist overcoming of a demonic principle of passivity or resistance."[5] As a result, the freedom of creation pervades all three act-potency relations but it is the *esse*-essence relation that specifically addresses the intrinsic character of divine freedom which is the contingency of substantial being, of creation.[6] Keefe continues to say, "The esse-essence analysis looks then to the

---

4   Ibid., 432.
5   Ibid., 441.
6   Ibid.

freedom of the covenantal relation between God and creation in such wise as at once to uphold the divine transcendence over the historical order and to refuse every 'necessary reason' that would imply an essential metaphysical dualism in the creation."[7] This analysis focuses on the contingency, which is free because it is historical, of the relation between the Son and His human immanence in humanity.[8]

In Keefe's analysis of the covenantal prime analogate, *esse* designates the covenantal immanence of the eternal Son of the eternal Father (Keefe holds that *esse* likewise connotes Christ's humanity. This will be discussed later). This *Esse*, as eternal Son, is Being-Itself for only Being-Itself can be the source of being. As a result, all created reality participates in this actuality. Thus, Keefe does not understand Being-Itself as simply and only transcendent to creation because the concrete individual Jesus Christ transcends creation by being immanent within creation sacramentally (*per modum substantiae*). The essence correlative to the *esse* refers to the subject of His immanence: the integral personal humanity, "one and the same," which also can be the transcendental correlative of the personal freedom of His immanence and, therefore, can support this immanence as its correlative within the personal unity of the incarnate Son. The *esse*-essence correlation is primarily proper to and constitutive of the second Adam of the primordial Good Creation, but it is also constitutive of the One Flesh of His covenantal union with the second Eve and at the same time is constitutive of historical humanity at large in which He is freely immanent. Recall that for Keefe, the *terminus* of the divine creative act of the sending of the Son is not simply the Son incarnate in a "human nature," but as the Son covenantally incarnate in historical humanity which is created in and by His mission from the Father.[9] The *Logos* Who "became flesh" is not the pre-human, preexistent Son of God but rather the primordial Son of Mary Who is the Son of God.[10] He is Jesus Christ, the "one and the same" historical person of Chalcedon, Who is immanent in creation covenantally.[11]

---

7   Ibid., 442.
8   Ibid.
9   Ibid.
10 Ibid., 595.
11 Keefe rejects the patristic two-stage image of creation: the first being that of the cosmic preexistence of the Father eternally alone with His Word and Spirit, and the second being that of the historical economy of creation and Incarnation (Ibid., 58).

In identifying *esse* as such, Keefe reiterates that it is the New Covenant, not simply the immanence of Christ, that is created by the Trinitarian mission of the Son, and the present concentration upon the *esse*-essence relation intrinsic to His Person should not obscure that fact. Nevertheless, it is by the free personal immanence of the Son that creation is actual, for creation *passive spectata* has no other relation to the Triune God than that which is actual in the Christ, its formal cause. The appropriation of creation by every creature, then, is by participation in that *esse*, but it is a participation that is historically and humanly mediated by Christ as One and the Same. Creation has no relation to existence except in the Christ, in Whom humanity and divinity are so joined that of Him it must be said that one and the same is the eternal Son of the eternal Father, the human Son of the Virgin Mary. There is no immediate participation of creation in *esse* but only in Christ.[12]

The "essence" of the *esse*-essence correlation is the New Covenant. Keefe insists that essence is not to be dissociated from *esse* and given some autonomous meaning of its own. Rather, it is only by its correlation to *esse* that essence has actuality as covenantal and so has actual intelligibility. As such, essence has no antecedently intelligible possibility: it is not possible in the sense of a possible object of creation or having an autonomous or potential intelligibility as disjunct from its actual existential subsistence. This is an implication of the *ex nihilo* character of the Good Creation and the New Covenant. The freedom of creation *active spectata* requires a corresponding freedom in creation *passive spectata*. Thus, Keefe rejects the notion of creation as involving a divine choice to create one among an infinite number of divine ideas as limiting the free covenantal immanence of the Creator in His creation, as assigning potency in the Godhead (one idea is actualized while others are potentially possible), and as ultimately nominalistic.[13]

Essence, for Keefe, is an intrinsically free transcendental relation. The intrinsic (act-potency) analysis of essence looks to the free conditions of essential intelligibility and finds them in the form-matter correlation which applies them to the existentially contingent substance of creation *ex nihilo*.[14] The analysis bears upon substance and not

---

12 Ibid.
13 Ibid., 443.
14 Ibid., 443–44.

upon some supposed component of substance such as an essence divorced from existence. The intelligibility and, thus, the substantial reality of a created substance can not but be free: if form and matter correlate as act and potency to compose it, that correlation must be free. This is due to the fact that the prime analogate of such a composite substance is the free union that is the New Covenant. Keefe rejects the notion that these conditions of essential intelligibility are necessary, for that would render the essence a monad, existing in abstraction from the historical, existential, and covenantal contingency of creation.[15]

Consequently, Keefe insists that the free intelligibility of the historical prime analogate, the substantial New Covenant, must be upheld and not allowed to disintegrate into dissociated elements, whether of *esse* without reference to essence or of essence as intelligible *in se*, apart from the reference to *esse* whereby it is actual in the actuality of a created substance. Keefe explains to the contrary:

> There is then neither an Esse nor a created essence which might be studied in isolation from the correlation by which Esse-essence is actual in the world, in order that a nonhistorical core of "pure" intelligibility might be isolated in essence or in Esse alone. The only analysis which can serve as theological metaphysics is that which remembers that the formal cause of the freedom of the Covenant is he whom Irenaeus and the tradition after him insisted upon naming, in his humanity as in his divinity, One and the Same, the second Adam.[16]

The New Covenant, as we have seen, is an historical relation between two irreducibly distinct persons: their acts of existence are distinct within this substantial union.[17] Of these distinct acts of existence, only the Christ's is that which is designated in this context with a capital, *Esse* (in the quote above). Mary's *esse* is by the participation in His which is her creation, her total metaphysical dependence upon her Son. Thus, there is neither a divinization of the *Theotokos* by the assimilation of her concrete existence to the Son's existence, nor is there a Christomonism whereby the marital union of the two is understood as the physical unity of One Person. Rather, created exis-

---

15 Ibid., 445.
16 Ibid., 446.
17 Ibid., 446–47.

tence is characterized by the simultaneity of the created freedom of the creature with metaphysical dependence upon the Creator.[18]

The New Covenant, as a covenantal prime analogate, designates God as the Trinity, as historically revealed to be immanent in history by the Father's mission of the Son to give the Spirit. This analogate designates the preexistent God, but not as subsistent Being-Itself dissociated from history and, therefore, impossible to relate to history except by some method of necessity.[19] For Keefe, the prime analogate designates preexistence in the Johannine and Pauline sense of the primordial Son of Man, Who, as Word, is man (the second Adam) freely and covenantally immanent in the metaphysically primordial unfallen goodness of creation. The preexistence of the Word is not upon the cosmic timelessness of the Son as proper to an "immanent Trinity" in an *a priori* disjunction of the Trinity from immanence in humanity. Such an understanding of a dehumanized or dehistoricized Second Person of the Trinity is untenable for an historical, covenantal theology. Rather, the preexistent Christ is the term of the Trinitarian immanence in creation by which the creation "in the beginning" is at once constituted and is good by reason of its covenantal relation to the Creator.[20]

Keefe maintains that analytical metaphysics must distinguish systematically between radical and dependent contingencies. The radical contingency is the mission of the Son, and this is to be distinguished from the dependent contingency of the historical institution of the New Covenant in which the One Sacrifice is actual in fallen creation and represented sacramentally by the historical Event of the Sacrifice of the Mass, the transubstantiation. For Keefe, it is clear that, concretely, the Event of creation and the event of the Fall are the same due to freedom and not to necessity. If the distinction between the two levels of contingency is not systematically maintained in terms of the analysis of its intrinsic intelligibility, then their relation is considered to be extrinsic by default. In other words, if the two levels of contingency (mission of the Father and the Fall) are not distinguished, then they will be related in an extrinsic fashion. The Fall occurred, and Christ came extrinsically to redeem it and, thus, is not intrinsic to creation. Keefe, however, argues that Christ is intrinsic to the uni-

---

18 Ibid., 447.
19 Ibid.
20 Ibid., 448.

verse's intelligibility and this is not altered by the fact of the Fall. Given sin, the solution is itself intrinsic to the universe through the historical and sacramental immanence of the Christ. To put it succinctly, the mission of the Son is not to be thought of as adventitious, a mere *propter peccatum* remedy for a fall which is in itself devoid of any reference to the Christ.[21]

This systematic requirement is met by the distinction between the primordial actualization of the New Covenant which is the *esse*-essence correlation of the Christ in union with His Bride (the *Christus totus*) and the historical accident-substance analysis of the economy of salvation in the pattern of *sarx, mia sarx, pneuma*. The *esse*-essence correlation looks to the Good Creation, to the primordial institution of the New Covenant, not to fallen history, while the accident-substance correlation bears upon the historical order and the integrity of the order's sacramental representation in the Eucharist.[22] Thus, the pattern of *sarx, mia sarx, pneuma* is to be held by both contingencies. These three elements deal not only with fallenness but also with the Good Creation. *Sarx* is not fallen explicitly, even though it relates to death and suffering. Christ takes on *sarx*, humanity, and becomes one with it (*mia sarx*) so as to give the Spirit (*pneuma*). In short, the issue is whether the immanence of Christ is intrinsic to the intelligibility of the universe or is it only *propter peccatum* and, thus, not constitutive of that intelligibility. Keefe holds that Christ is intrinsic to the intelligibility even of fallen humanity rather than the reverse, i.e., fallenness as intrinsic to the intelligibility of Christ.

With this distinction in place, the *esse*-essence analysis supports the covenantal notion that the preexistent *Logos* of the Johannine and Pauline literature is immanent "in the beginning" of creation by reason of His personal unity as the Son, "one and the same." It is in His personal unity as Son (at once Son of the Father and Son of Mary) that His divinity and humanity relate as *esse*-essence. *Esse*, according to Keefe, connotes His humanity as well as His divinity. Aquinas, while respecting the Christ's personal unity, finds in either His divinity or His humanity the ground for his suffering or His preexistence. Keefe rejects the cosmological aspect of this position on the basis that it invokes a quest for some nonhistorical *status quo ante* which would be the radical ground of the real intelligibility of the mission. Rather,

---

21 Ibid., 449.
22 Ibid.

Aquinas' position must be augmented by the recognition that the freedom of the *Logos'* immanence in humanity by His personal obedience to the Father is also human, for his obedience is historical and covenantal. In other words, the *Logos* is not to be regarded as only divine and then this divine Son obeys the Father. Rather, the *esse* is human as well as divine; therefore, obedience is human and divine. The Second Person of the Trinity, this human person, is obedient to the Father. Furthermore, the Son is not imposed but freely received by Mary's act of obedience (her *fiat mihi*). In His humanity, He is freely conceived by Mary to become her human Son in the Event of the Incarnation which is the paradigm of transubstantiation and creation, for only the integral freedom of Mary's conception of her Son is consistent with a covenantal immanence of God in history.[23]

The created object of the divine creative mission, the human universe, exists, then, by the divine *Esse* of the Lord of the Covenant. Only the immanence of the Creator in creation satisfies both the demand within an Aristotelian-based system for the intrinsic intelligibility of contingent substance and the requirement, proper to a Good Creation *ex nihilo sui et subjecti*, that this immanence be historical in the sense of free. "This can only be a covenantal immanence, whose intrinsic intelligibility and unity is that of a free order, not a necessary structure."[24]

As was stated in the introductory material on the prime analogate, secondary analogates have their free and objectively true reference to the prime analogate and, as such, participate in it metaphysically. In this context, the secondary analogates participate not in *Esse* simply, i.e., in Being-Itself which has no real relation to the universe, but in the prime analogate, the essence which is the New Covenant. This participation is free; it is the free affirmation and appropriation of covenantal existence by all that depend upon the Trinitarian mission of the Son to give the Spirit.[25]

---

23 Ibid., 447.
24 Ibid., 451.
25 Ibid., 450.

1.5 The form-matter correlation

For Keefe, the form-matter analysis, like the other two act-potency analyses, is concerned with the intrinsic free intelligibility of historical substance, of the New Covenant.[26] It is concerned with the immanence of "form" in "matter," but unlike classical Aristotelian metaphysical systems, these terms will undergo a covenantal transformation similar to that which affects the other two analyses.

Form, as covenantal, is the free immanence of God in history. This understanding alters the Aristotelian postulate that matter is the potentiality for form and so reduces their relation to a necessity immanent in material substance. The Christian affirmation that Jesus is the Lord of History does not at all rest upon the supposition that history is in any determinist or rationalist sense the potentiality for the Christ but, instead, reads the Old Testament as the prophecy of a Messiah Whose coming it could not command, Who comes out of obedience to the Father and not out of some rational necessity. The Old Testament is in fact the temporal *prius* of the New Testament but it is dependent upon the New as its metaphysical *prius*. It is the temporal *prius* in the free order of the economy of salvation and to isolate it from the freedom derived from that historical unity with the New would be to falsify it, for its truth is historical, incapable of abstraction from the history of salvation which has its center in the Christ of the historical New Covenant.[27]

God is freely immanent in history when the new Eve's (the Old Testament's) *fiat mihi*, her sacrifice of praise, is seen to be in covenantal union with her Lord's One Sacrifice, and thereby is transubstantiated in the Event of the Word becoming flesh. The subject of transubstantation, we have seen, is the offering and not the one who offers. Thus, the marital, nuptial aspect of the covenant is maintained by the fact that the second Eve is not transubstantiated into the second Adam. It is through His covenantal union with the *Theotokos* that the Lord of History is consubstantial with historical humanity. Consequently, the form of the New Covenant is not the cosmic *Logos*, Who in some cosmic moment assumes humanity, but it is the immanence of the Christ Who offers the One Sacrifice so that a holy society may be formed by which human beings belong to God (Augustine's *sancta*

---

26 Ibid., 452.
27 Ibid., 453.

societas inhereamus Deo).[28] It is an immanence that is free and covenantal, not despotic. Keefe elaborates:

> "Form" is therefore to be summed up in the Pauline title, the second Adam, which includes primordiality, the Old Covenant preparation, the New Covenant One Flesh of Christ and the Church, and the eschatological fulfillment of history that is the Kingdom. All this is resumed, represented, in the eucharistic worship of the Church, concentrated in the Event of the offering in his Name of the One Sacrifice by which we are redeemed.[29]

Since the prime analogate governs the transformation of the meaning of form from a cosmological understanding to a covenantal understanding, it too will govern the transformation of the meaning of matter. If form is the Christ of the One Sacrifice, then matter is the free correlative of His covenantal immanence in history: the second Eve who is Mary and who is the Church. This transformation continues to assign to matter the connotation of femininity and to form the connotation of masculinity which it inherited from the Greek cosmological tradition. It is obvious, however, that Keefe has divested these connotations of all the pessimistic and antihistorical implications of Aristotelian dualism by basing their meaning on the New Covenant. These implications are displaced by the eucharistic worship of the Church whose own set of implications are profoundly optimistic and historical because they are rooted in the utter gratuity and freedom of the New Covenant.[30] Masculinity and femininity are no longer seen as a paradoxical, incompatible, and yet irreducible polarity but as a marital covenant, an image of the Trinity, wherein the husband and the wife each encounter in the other's concrete free historicity a solitary and irreplaceable personal dignity that is utterly unique, irreducibly different from their own. This personal dignity is encountered as good, i.e., as responsive, responsible, complementary, and indispensable to their own reality. In this covenant and only here, the free responsibility of a man evokes the free responsibility of a woman, and the free responsibility of a woman evokes the free nuptial responsibility of a man. In this mutual recognition, each affirms not oneself but a personally irreducible other in a moment of selflessness by which the irreducible unique masculine or feminine self is realized, received, made actual in the convenantal self-forgetful free-

---

28 Ibid.
29 Ibid.
30 Ibid., 454.

dom that is love. Mutual submission creates a common authority held by the husband, wife, and the marital bond as subsisting relations constituting an analogously trinitarian human substance whose reality is free, sacramental, objectively and historically concrete.

Keefe expresses this same reality using head-body language. In this community, the husband is irrevocably joined and committed to this woman, who is his glory by being uniquely chosen by him from among all others, excluding all others. It is he who leaves his family for her. In the resultant marital bond, the glory (who is "bone of his bones, flesh of his flesh") gives meaning to and, in fact constitutes, his own dignity as her head, her source precisely as his glory. The woman irrevocably chooses this man above all others and excluding all others, affirming and constituting his unique masculine dignity and authority over her, that of the head, affirming him to be the very source of her feminine dignity as his glory, his body. The free, irreducible and constitutive affirmations by both spouses of the other's nuptial dignity are constitutive at the same time of their own dignity, and of the irrevocable marital covenant in which alone those irreducible dignities are actualized, i.e., in the "one flesh" of their marital community, whose existence and perdurance waits upon no permission or approval but their own. Thus, masculinity and femininity are seen as mutually related and are not seen in terms of order-chaos as paganism would have it. Mutual relatedness is intrinsic to the meaning of humanity. Male and female do exclude each other, but they relate as form and matter, as covenantal principles of intrinsic intelligibility.[31]

1.6 The accident-substance correlation

In the classic Aristotelian metaphysics, the accident-substance analysis underwrites the changeability of material being by accounting for the intrinsic intelligibility of that change in terms of act and potency. In Keefe's transformation of this metaphysics, the contingency of existence concerns not only the *esse*-essence correlation, but the form-matter correlation (which has been discussed previously) and the accident-substance correlation, as well. The contingency of creation (*esse*-essence) must pervade all that is created (form-matter and accident-substance); otherwise, such contingency remains purely nomi-

---

31 Ibid., 248–354.

nal, without intrinsic intelligibility. The only way for contingency to pervade creation is for the Creator to be immanent within the creation. When this immanence is established and given a metaphysical standing in terms of immanent causality, then a creationist act-potency metaphysics can proceed with consistency and pervasiveness. This immanence was given metaphysical standing when it was identified as the prime analogate. The paradigmatic Event of the New Covenant and its sacramental representation in the Mass control the meaning and historicity of accident-substance.[32]

Keefe bemoans the fact that there is a standing ambiguity in the act-potency terminology which finds "substance" used concretely in two quite irreducible senses. He recognizes and then transforms the cosmological aspects of the first meaning which refers to the plenary unity of being, that subject of all predication which itself can never be predicated, that unity which is *indivisum in se et divisum ab omni alio* (indivisible in itself and divisible from all others). In covenantal metaphysics, it is used differently because it is understood historically; substance in this plenary sense now designates the free *plenum* which is the Father's sending of the Son to give the Spirit, a fullness of being which is at once Trinitarian and covenantal, for it terminates in the free and historical immanence of the Christ in the creation which is created in and by His immanence. Substance in the secondary sense designates the potentiality which stands over and against the actuality of accident in a bipolarity with this accidental perfection, constituting substance in the first sense of the word. "Thus, the act-potency analysis appropriate to the examination of the immanent activity of substantial being is that of accident-substance."[33] This analysis bears upon a free intelligibility, that of the New Covenant; consequently, "accidents" are not antecedently contained in the potentiality of "substance" on an *a priori* basis. The correlation of the two is free and not the logically necessary expression of an immanent prior possibility.[34]

With this understanding in place, what has been stated earlier about the sacramental *ordo* may be understood more deeply. Thus, the Old Covenant is the potentiality of the New Covenant, as substance is potentiality to accident. Their composition is also free: the integration of salvation history that is the Old Covenant, the New Covenant, and

---

32 Ibid., 455.
33 Ibid., 456.
34 Ibid.

the Kingdom which is the fullness of the New Covenant, its final achievement, but only in terms of the substance-accident correlation of the Old Covenant-New Covenant. Similarly, the *sacramentum tantum* of the eucharistic Sacrifice has the character of substance when understood as signifying (freely causing) the *res et sacramentum*, the Body and Blood of the eucharistic Sacrifice which has the character of accident, and the *res tantum* which is the communion with the risen Christ, the character of substance in the plenary sense of the term (the final effect of the substance-accident causality intrinsic to historical substance). The *sarx, mia sarx, pneuma* of, respectively, fallen humanity's solidarity with the first Adam, its eucharistic solidarity with the second Adam as in sacrificial union with His Church, and its risen solidarity with the risen Christ in His Kingdom, are integrated historically, as free events, in accordance with the same paradigm. This paradigm rests upon the same prime analogate, the New Covenant that is the liturgical integration of the Old Covenant, the New Covenant, and the fulfilled Kingdom of God. With this covenantal paradigm of accident-substance in place, it is evident that transubstantiation conforms to the accident-substance analysis.[35] It does so, however, not as an exception to the rule, but as the rule itself, by reference to which all history achieves its objective free significance and apart from which it has none.[36]

In its covenantal sense, "accident" must be understood historically as the free actualization of the potentiality of substance. The substance-accident analysis bears upon the intrinsic intelligibility of the New Covenant as historically active. The accidents, which are freely correlative as act to the potentiality of the substantial New Covenant, are immanent to its plenary substantiality, for "outside" this plenary substantiality (the prime analogate) is only nothingness. This is the case because substance, understood theologically as denoting the New Covenant in its plenitude, embraces the entirety of all reality, the entirety of the free relation between the Creator and creation. The accidents are immanent not from the non-historical vantage point *sub specie aeternitatis* (under the species of eternity) which attempts to see all things at once in one thought without any past or future as a species of eternity, but historically, by its own intrinsic dynamics. The paradigm of plenary covenantal substantiality is the his-

---

35 Ibid., 356.
36 Ibid., 457.

torical representation of the One Sacrifice and the representation of
the objective passage from potency to act in freedom from Old Testament to the New, from the Offertory to the Canon, from solidarity
with the first Adam to solidarity with the second, from cosmology to
history.[37]

This passage from potency to act is a free conversion to a free
truth; plenary substance is now understood to have the unity, truth,
goodness, and beauty of a free Trinitarian and covenantal *ordo*.[38] Consequently, its accidents are not simply latent in a supposedly static
and ideal structure of substance which as potency would be a necessary *prius* of the accidental change. The substance as potency, which is
the free *a priori* of the accidents, is itself no longer conceived of as the
static material species in which the substantial form is immanent in its
fullness. For Keefe, the whole species, all of humanity, is not immanent in its fullness within the substantial form. The species is free and
not simply the working out of intrinsic necessities immanent within
the form. Plenary substance is no longer the fullness of the human
species but the covenantal and historical union of historical being, the
New Covenant whose formal substantial cause is the freely immanent
Christ in union with the material cause of that free immanence, His
Church.[39]

"Accident" denotes the immanent activity proper to the historical
covenantal community, its sacramental worship. This is the historical
response to the immanence of Christ in the world. Worship is obviously not to be viewed as *sub specie aeternitatis* because it is a free historical conversion from the potentiality which is our necessary
solidarity in *sarx*, to the sacramental actuality of our free solidarity in
the *mia sarx*, to the fulfilled actuality with the risen Christ in the
Kingdom. Free participation in this eucharistic worship is the personal appropriation of the New Covenant in fallen history, and by this
integration, human beings become truly personal, subsisting in
unique and irreducible relations to other analogously unique persons
of faith whose uniqueness and dignity are precisely their self-
donation to each other. This is their unity in the Church, whose

---

37 Ibid.
38 Ibid.
39 Ibid., 458.

source is the Spirit of the risen Christ, poured out upon the Church precisely in her worship.[40]

This free personal appropriation of the New Covenant is then eucharistic and its intrinsic intelligibility is that of the sacramental *ordo*: the *sacramentum tantum, res et sacramentum,* and *res tantum*. It culminates in the fulfilled freedom of the eschatological Kingdom of God, but as an individual person's historical freedom, it is enabled and sustained only by solidarity with the sacramental immanence of the Church, by reception of Holy Communion.[41]

The accident-substance correlation as historical and covenantal is, then, the personal appropriation in worship of one's objective reality and one's freedom, since it is an appropriation of the free unity of being, the prime analogate. It is the hominization of the world in that it is the historical and responsible actualization in the world of the free actuality of the unity, truth, goodness, and beauty of the Christ in whom and by whom the world is created and subsists.[42] This correlation embraces the whole of responsible human activity in history. The achievements of history witness to Christ and have no meaning apart from Him. Any attempt to do so is a vain attempt to construct, out of personal vacuity and incoherence, a surrogate universe which has some other center than Christ.[43]

1.7 Section summary

A fundamental implication of identifying the New Covenant as the theological *prius* or the prime analogate of substantial being is that eucharistic transubstantiation is not an exception to metaphysical intelligibility but is normative of it, as only an *a priori* can be. Thus, theology's proper task is to understand reality in terms of this eucharistic *prius* and not vice versa. The methodology used by Keefe to understand this reality is that of discursive-analytical Aristotelianism.

The fundamental correlation of an Aristotelian analysis is act-potency. The correlation itself is not necessary but free. Potency is understood as a free potency which means that while it is a pre-

---

40 Ibid.
41 Ibid.
42 Ibid.
43 Ibid., 458–59.

condition, it is neither a necessary nor a sufficient one. It freely points to its actualization. Act, then, is an actualization of a potency or the actuating cause of a potency.

The object of the Aristotelian analysis remains constant (i.e., the New Covenant); however, there are three modalities of act-potency that can be applied to it. The first is *esse*-essence which both Keefe and Aquinas hold to be a proper implication of a created universe. The free cause of a contingent universe can only be a free Event for only events, not structures or ideas, are free. This Event can only be the free immanence of the Creator in creation, the New Covenant.

In Keefe's work, *esse* is the covenantal immanence of the eternal Son of the eternal Father. This *Esse* is Being-Itself since only Being-Itself can be the source of being. As a result, all created reality participates in this actuality. And yet, Being-Itself transcends creation by being immanent within creation sacramentally (*per modum substantiae*); it participates in created reality. The essence of this correlation is the subject of this immanence, namely, His integral personal humanity. The consequence of His free immanence in creation is not simply a disjointed Christ but a Christ Who is in covenantal union with creation. "The Esse-essence correlation is of course primarily proper to and constitutive of the second Adam of the primordial Good Creation which is the New Covenant, but it is also constitutive of the One Flesh of his covenantal union with the second Eve, and the same time is constitutive of historical humanity at large, in which he is freely immanent."[44] The *terminus* of the divine creative act of the sending of the Son is not simply to have the Son incarnate in a human nature but to have the Son incarnate in historical humanity which is created in and by His mission from the Father. Creation does not participate in the preexistent Son of God but in Jesus Christ Who is immanent in creation covenantally, the "one and the same" historical person of Chalcedon. In other words, the secondary analogates participate not in *Esse* simply (i.e., in Being-Itself which has no real relation to the universe) but in the prime analogate, the essence which is the New Covenant. This participation is the free affirmation and appropriation of covenantal existence by all that depend upon the Trinitarian mission of the Son to give the Spirit.

---

44   Ibid., 442.

The second modality of act-potency is the matter-form correlation which is concerned with the question of whether intelligible form can inhere in matter. This modality is interested in the free intrinsic intelligibility of historical substance, the New Covenant.

Form, as covenantal, is the free immanence of God in history. History here is not to be read in any determinist or rationalist sense of a potentiality for the coming of Christ. Rather, the Christian faith reads the past of the Old Testament as the prophecy of a Messiah Whose coming history could not command, Whose coming is out of obedience to the will of the Father and not out of some rational necessity. The form of the New Covenant is the immanence of the Christ Who freely offers the One Sacrifice so that a holy society may be constituted by which human beings belong to God. Form refers to an immanence that is free and covenantal and not despotic.

Matter is the free correlative of Christ's covenantal immanence in history: the second Eve who is Mary and who is the Church. Matter connotes femininity and form connotes masculinity but the ancient pessimistic and antihistorical implications associated with pagan dualism is replaced by the optimism, historicity, and freedom of the New Covenant. Masculinity and femininity are no longer seen as a paradoxical, incompatible, and irreducible polarity but as complementary constitutive principles of the marital covenant. Each person recognizes and affirms not oneself but a personally irreducible and unique masculine or feminine self and, in so doing, the marital covenant is formed.

The third modality of act-potency is the accident-substance correlation which is concerned with the question of whether a material substance can undergo change and still remain itself. In a cosmological sense, "substance" refers to that subject of all predication which itself can never be predicated, that unity which is indivisible in itself and divisible from all others. In a covenantal sense, it refers to the free fullness of being which is the Father's sending the Son to give the Spirit, a fullness which is at once Trinitarian and covenantal because it terminates in the free and historical immanence of the Christ in the creation which is created in and by His immanence. In a more specific sense, substance designates the potentiality which stands over and against the actuality of accident in a bipolarity (an entity) with this accidental perfection. Substance in reference to theological *prius*, then, is the fullness of the New Covenant which is the total integration of the Old Covenant, the New Covenant, and the fulfilled Kingdom of God (i.e., the intelligible unity of salvation history).

In a covenantal sense, "accident" is understood historically as the free actualization of the potentiality of substance. It indicates the free immanent activity that is proper to the historical covenantal community. To be more specific, the accident of this accident-substance correlation is the Church's sacramental worship. It is an historical worship whereby a person freely actualizes and appropriates the solidarity of the *mia sarx*. A person who enters into worship is acting as a free moral agent whose uniqueness and dignity is one's donation to the other. The accident is immanent to the substance not in a nonhistorical, determined, and static manner but in a historical, free, and dynamic manner.

2 Keefe's Critique and Transformation of Aquinas' System

2.1 A free prime analogate

It has been stated above that Keefe takes the doctrinal tradition seriously in regard to creation *ex nihilo*. Thus, all reality, all truth is free. There is no necessary truth or being actual anywhere in the created or uncreated order precisely because creation is a free order. As a free order it has a Trinitarian order that is imaged nuptially or covenantally. It is imaged in the One Sacrifice of Christ for His Bridal Church, which is the institution of the New Covenant, the One Flesh of the second Adam and the second Eve. This sacrifice, this One Flesh, this Covenant, is the prime creative act of the Trinity: the Father sending the Son to give the Spirit. As the *terminus* of the Trinitarian mission, the New Covenant is the means by which God is immanent in history, in creation, as the free cause of being as being, as the free ordering cause of the free order of the historical creation.[45] It is the free community of God and creation; it is the free and public event, at once sacrifice and transubstantiation; it is the prime analogate.[46]

45　Ibid., 390–91.
46　Ibid., 19–20.

According to Keefe, there is no other conceivable free prime analogate, for freedom requires community in unity. The only free community, the only free unity, which has ever been proposed, is that which is affirmed in the Church's eucharistic worship: the nuptial, covenantal unity of the second Adam and the second Eve, the New Covenant, instituted by Christ on the Cross, effectively presented by the event of transubstantiation, and represented objectively, sacramentally, and historically in the central act of the Church's worship.[47] This analogate must be an event, not a thing, not a structure, not an idea for none of these can be understood as radically free or as the principle of such freedom. An event is an objective occurrence that engages; it is not subjective or dependent upon the believer. Only the eucharistic prime analogate is at once concretely historical (i.e., in space and time) and transcendent to history (i.e., not limited to space and time) as the ordering and integrating cause by which the past, the present, and the future are a single history of salvation.

2.2 Keefe's general reasons for rejecting Aquinas' prime analogate

It is on the account of freedom that Keefe rejects what he identifies as Aquinas' prime analogate, the *Deus Unus* or, in classical Thomism, *Ipsum Esse Substistens*.[48] According to Keefe, the *Deus Unus*, as a non-Trinitarian (non-relational) monad, is locked into the immanence of the ideal notion of unity. The unity of divinity is absolutely unqualified, for God must be the Absolute, the Transcendent by definition. Consequently, God can not be related to anything that is not Himself, since this is what is meant by the term absolute; God is absolutely unrelated to whatever is multiple until that multiplicity is recognized as nonbeing, an illusion.[49] There can be no nexus, no connection between the Absolute and what is relative. God is incapable of any real relation to that which He has created; thus, He can not be in history.[50] While Thomists will hold this position, they seek to diminish its impact by saying that historical creation can be in a real relation to the Creator. Keefe, however, refuses this position on grounds that Aqui-

---

47   Ibid., 12.
48   God is understood to be the First Cause, the transcendent ground of being, and so Being at its ultimate is: *Ipsum Esse* and, as Person, *Ipsum Esse Subsistens*.
49   Ibid., 143.
50   Ibid., 143, 425.

nas' metaphysics of creation by the *Deus Unus* is unable to overcome the cosmological antagonism which its logic places between the Absolute and the relativity of creation.[51] According to Keefe, if it is supposed that the *Deus Unus* can not be related to creation but creation can be related to God, when this is applied to Christ, divinity then can not be related to humanity in the Person of Jesus Christ.[52] Such a position on Aquinas' part (even though he gives no indication that he explicitly was aware of it) bars the historicity of the "one and the same" upon which the Council of Chalcedon was so insistent.[53] The personal unity of Jesus Christ insists that there is a single self that is at once divine and human, inseparable but quite distinctly two natures. However, if one supposes that humanity is related to God but God is not related to humanity, then the self of Jesus Christ is either divine or human. It can not be both, according to this logic.

Likewise, this relation of the relative to the Absolute is not revealed, but is necessary, for the mere process of rational discourse brings to light the logical necessity of the Absolute. Without the Absolute, human knowledge of contingent and relative entities is impossible: humanity knows of them only in the context whose intelligible unity is provided by, and logically dependent upon, the Absolute in the "five ways"[54] (which Aquinas develops in his proofs for the existence of the Absolute which, as he says, "men call God"). This Absolute, however, whose existence Aquinas shows to be a necessity of thought, is thereby shown to be necessarily immanent to thought.

---

51 Ibid., 425.
52 Ibid., 195, 300.
53 Ibid., 195.
54 According to Keefe, these "five ways," which are illustrations of the analogous predication of being, take for granted that one can argue from the knowledge of the existence of material entities to the existence of God. If no foundation for the analogy here in use is provided—as it is not provided by Aquinas—these proofs for the existence of God are the equivalent to arguing from the existence of creatures to the existence of the Creator. This obviously is a question-begging argument, since it presupposes the existence of the Creator-God when it supposes that the material entities of the world are created. In other words, Aquinas does not grasp the circularity of his postulate of the analogy of being (between the Prime Analogate, God as *Ipsum esse subsistens* and the secondary analogates, the substances of the created order) and so of his proofs, because they all depend upon the analogy. And this analogy begs the whole question: obviously if there is an analogy of being, one is dealing with a creation and a Creator-God. But this is what is to be proven, not assumed at the outset as the postulate of the analogy assumes it (*Covenantal Theology*, 22, 140, 290).

This insight led Aristotle to postulate an agent intellect, a "thought thinking itself," incapable of learning because it is already the full actuality of understanding with no potency whatever for further learning; such an intellect is fully in act, an intellectual substance without accidents of any kind. The inference of the necessary existence of the agent intellect raised even more unresolvable ambiguities. Aristotle noticed them but did not resolve them and Aquinas' solution, which made the agent intellect to be multiple within the species, a distinct reality immanent in each individual mind, did not resolve them either, for if each human person possessed his own agent intellect, each person would be equivalent to an angelic species. Each human person would be an incommunicable intellectual universe, a self-enclosed mind, an intellectual monad knowing nothing but the self. The individual is complete in the order of *intellectus*, and thus in the order of substantial actuality. Consequently, such an identification of material and existential individuation is fatal to Thomist metaphysics, because it merges the form-matter correlation and the *esse*-essence correlation.[55] This same point will surface later in the context of the existential analogy of being, where such an understanding of the agent intellect can not support the analogous predication of being, for such a predication obtains only in the potential or discursive understanding proper to potential intellects (and yet Aquinas speaks of human knowledge as potential).

Yet, the alternative, as Aquinas saw in his debate with the Averrhoists, viz.—to make the agent intellect a specific perfection, necessarily immanent not in the individual but somehow in the many-membered human species—would be to deprive the individual human person of moral freedom: the person would be no more than a function of a specific process to which he or she is entirely assimilated as a member, without remainder. To the extent that this were the case, the person could never know it, for that would be to rise above the species, to transcend the Absolute, which would be simply impossible: as a matter of definition, the Absolute can not be transcended. Hence, Keefe perceives this dilemma as pervading Thomistic epistemology; it is one incapable of the rational resolution which the use of the analogy nonetheless presupposes. On these accounts, Keefe consequently dismisses the *Deus Unus* as the prime analogate in favor of

---

55 Keefe, *Thomism and Tillich*, 85.

a free historical one that transcends history from within history and does so eucharistically. There is no resolution of this dilemma which does not involve a prime analogate that is immanent in the human species. If theological epistemology is to be loyal to the Catholic doctrinal tradition, this species-immanent prime analogate must be historical, freely immanent in humanity and human history: again, only the Incarnation provides this free immanence, but it does so as the antetype of the New Covenant, for the freedom must be proper to the humanity in which the Christ is immanent and to the obedience by which the Son is thus Incarnate. The Event of the Son's immanence itself can not be subject to the determinism of the fallen temporality constituting human history, but must transcend it redemptively from within time: only a sacramental, eucharistic immanence meets the case.

Keefe holds that Aquinas' choice of the *Deus Unus* as the prime analogate is symptomatic of the Neoplatonism that was prevalent in theological thought during the thirteenth century. A consequence of the synthesis of Platonic cosmology and Aristotelian logic is the dictum, *bonum diffusivum sui*. God is the Good and as good, can not but be diffusive of Himself.[56] Thus, necessity is built into God. God must create and in so doing falls into a necessary material world, a world composed of material things that are less than God, less than good. While Aquinas tried to mitigate the necessity to make it compatible with Christianity by saying that creation is not necessary but appropriate, Keefe holds up Aquinas' prime analogate as an indication that it was not sufficient. Keefe rejects this prime, because it is rooted in Neoplatonism which relies ultimately on necessity. This necessity sets up a dualism between formal immaterial Being and material non-being and, consequently, devalues the physical order and its historicity.[57]

2.3 The analogy of being

According to Keefe, it is the free facticity of the New Covenant, as prime analogate, which warrants and controls the analogy of being. On no other basis may an analogy between the unity of Being itself

---

56 Keefe, *Covenantal Theology*, 7, 170.
57 Ibid., 170.

and the multiplicity of that which is not Being itself, be affirmed.[58] Such a prime analogate circumvents the problems that have traditionally plagued the analogy of being as essential and the analogy of being as existential.

2.3.1 The essential analogy of being

In an analogy of being, one seeks a principle of unity or commonality that can be used to relate multiple individuals. What accounts for the multiplicity? What is the principle of individuation? And then, what accounts for the unity, the commonality? Since there is no *esse*-essence correlation within an essential (Aristotelian) analogy of being, multiplicity is not located with *esse* but with essence only insofar as it is part of the intelligibility of this essence to be material. What accounts for the unity is likewise only found in the essence in terms of the intelligibility of the entire species. This type of analogy of being functions, then, as necessitarian, as non-gratuitous, since essence is a necessary intelligibility. It is necessary insofar as it is entirely actual, without correlation to any formal cause of actuality (It has no gratuitous contingencies because there is no *esse*-essence correlation). This essence must be entirely actual, for if it were not, then it could not actualize the potency of any of the individual members of the species, and some other reality would be its actuality, thus producing an infinite regress. The prime analogate of being, then, is essential; it is the *agens intellectus* ("Thought thinking itself"; the supreme Understanding, the fullness of Truth, the Absolute intelligence which possesses the totality of Truth); it is the substantial cause of participate essential being, the individual secondary analogates of being.[59]

In this understanding of substance as necessary being (pure nature), the prime analogate is the cause of the unity of substance, the cause of formal intelligibility. It is the *intellectus*, the ground of being, that is the formal cause of the potential *intellectus*, the potential subjectivity, of the individual human person. This completely actual *intellectus*, the transcendental ego, is thus the prime analogate of actual being. This prime analogate, in the pure nature situation, is the *a priori* of participate subjectivity and, as such, is located where that partici-

---

58 Ibid., 20.
59 Keefe, *Thomism and Tillich*, 82–83.

pate subjectivity is achieved, in the human community. By participating in communal subjectivity, the individual achieves his or her own ego in the act by which he or she affirms the communal *a priori* and appropriates it personally. By doing so, one is inserted into the continuing communication which is communal subjectivity. Outside this correlation of actual and potential *intellectus* lies only the unthinkable: absolute non-being.[60]

Consequently, this is the necessary, non-gratuitous function of the essential analogy of being. It is caused by the correlation of matter and form which constitutes human nature, for matter provides multiplicity when united to and correlated with substantial form. The analogy is not caused by the gratuitous correlation of *esse* and essence which constitutes existential human substance. At this point, the requirements of an intelligible pure nature have been met on the level of immanence: pure nature is a possible object of thought which can not be thought of except as eternally necessary, as uncreated.[61]

If one holds nature to be "pure," then it is the *a priori* precondition, the *prius*, of grace and, thus, it may be discussed in isolation from grace. Such a position can and has resulted in interpreting nature as substance and grace as accident.[62] According to Keefe, Aquinas and his followers proceeded, in effect, "to deduce grace from nature: the New Covenant was seen to have a prior possibility in a 'natural' nexus, a necessary because 'natural' analogy, between a 'natural' creation and God."[63] That which is "ungraced" is incoherently the cause of "grace." This is to mistake effect for cause. It is to interpret nature as substance and grace as accident, to make nature the *prius* of grace. Ultimately, this is to displace the historical freedom of the revealed truth of the New Covenant with the immanent necessities of a cosmology.[64]

The unprofitableness of this situation is patent, for it is based on a premise that is systematically inconsistent with the Thomist act-potency analysis.[65] A natural potency (the substantial creation) is incompatible with a graced or supernatural actuation when potency

---

60 Ibid., 83.
61 Ibid., 83–84.
62 Keefe, *Covenantal Theology*, 210.
63 Ibid., 21.
64 Ibid., 21, 210.
65 Ibid., 22.

and act are conceived in terms of substance and accident, wherein substance as potency governs what accident as act may be. This is to contradict the *ex nihilo sui et subjecti* gratuity by which grace is grace.

"Nature" rather has a free and historical sense: it is freely fallen and freely redeemed. It is created in Christ and its relation to grace is free rather than necessary, the relation of the human person to his or her prospective conversion and personal renewal. As *sarx* is unintelligible apart from the *Logos sarx egeneto* of the Incarnation and the *mia sarx* of the New Covenant, so the historical sense of nature is unintelligible apart from grace. The conceptual isolation of nature from grace amounts to the normalization of an unredeemed *sarx*, which is its de-historicization. Yet it is by this rational isolation and its abstraction from history that nature becomes "pure nature." It is purified, precisely, of grace. "Pure nature" is the unreal reflex of the real, of the supernatural because it is cosmological. "Nature" is the unreality from which one is converted, the determinism from which one is freed and, by comparison with which, *ex post facto*, the gratuity, the freedom, and the gift-character of historical actuality may be known to be such. The normative criterion of reality is, therefore, supernatural, not natural.[66]

2.3.2 The existential analogy of being

With the introduction of Aquinas' real distinction between *esse* and essence, the analogy of being may be understood existentially. *Esse* is distinct from essence. It is not something that is part of the necessary intrinsic intelligibility of essence. If it were, then this essence would necessarily exist, but existence is gratuitous. The intelligibility of this existence can not be found in the all-embracing intelligibility of essence. Thus, *esse*, along with essence, is an option as the principle of individuation. For Aquinas, there is a materially (essence) determined individuation and a personally (*esse*) determined individuation. *Esse* is the actuation of the essence. *Esse* also accounts for the unity of being, for all individuals are existing, are beings; they participate in being itself.[67]

---

66 Ibid., 176.
67 Keefe, Thomism and Tillich, 86.

A problem arises, however, when one applies the *esse*-essence correlation to the analogy of being. The analogy is seeking necessary connections between individuals, and yet the correlation is gratuitous. According to Keefe, if the analogy remains necessitarian, then the *esse*-essence correlation is undermined in one of two ways. The correlation may be understood as necessary rather than gratuitous. If this were the case, then the correlation would collapse into essence, for essence is the realm of necessity. *Esse* would be intrinsic to essence; it would in effect be identified with accident. To use the language of participation, participation is what grounds the analogy of being, because it is that which allows a particular being to be simultaneously united in and separated from. This applies to both participation in *esse* and essence. Within Aristotelianism, an individual human being participates in the species (essence) of humanity, and the individual's participation in the essence is what guarantees the unity of the species. Since Aristotle does not have an *esse*-essence distinction, participation in *esse* is simultaneously a participation in essence. *Esse* is understood as an accident of essence. Thus, an intrinsic contradiction results: the gratuity of *esse* but the necessity of essence. There is participation in both *esse* and essence, and when they are identified intrinsically, contradiction results. The material individual participates in being-itself (being- gratuity) but does so as material (essence- necessity). Thus, the analogy of being would be involved in the intelligibility of the created species (essence), as intrinsic to the created species, for essence is of necessity. An existing individual would be of a certain species (essence), because it is a participate substance. The analogy of being is simultaneously a participation in being and a participation in essence.[68] In other words, participation in being is understood as an accident of the essence. Thus, an intrinsic contradiction: the gratuity of *esse* but the necessity of essence.

On the other hand, the correlation may be understood as gratuitous. The analogy of being is located then in *esse*, the principle of gratuity. *Esse* is an external cause to the essence. Unity is in *esse* and, in order to explain multiplicity, the essence is divided in existence by *esse*. As a result, it is "uncorrelated" from and opposed to essence. Essence is fragmented by *esse*; the two no longer compose but oppose. Thus, the correlation is destroyed. To use the language of participa-

---

68   Ibid., 85–86.

tion, an individual human being's actuality is in terms of participation in being-itself. Participation in transcendent being is what grounds humanity. Thus, participation is understood as distinct from and transcendent to the human species, the human essence. Participation in being is separated from participation in the essence. Under the conditions of existence, essence is shattered into many existing entities. Individuation is imposed upon the essence according to an intelligibility that is not implicit to essence but implicit to *esse*. Particular existing individuals are manifestations of a transcendent idea that is contradicted, opposed, and ultimately fragmented in existence.[69]

An existential analogy of being may be understood to identify the actuality of substantial being with participation in *esse*, in *Ipsum Esse*. Inasmuch as individual members of the human species participate in existence, it follows that each member is substantially complete in the order of existence. The fundamental objection Keefe makes is that individual members of a species can not be substantially complete; they are not *indivisum in se et divisum ab omni alio*, for their actuality is achieved in common; considered as *divisum ab omni alio*, they are not actual, but potential. As members of a finite species, they participate in existence by participating in the existential actuality of the species, and not otherwise. Human individuals participate in *esse* secondarily, by means of the primary participation of the species; only the latter participation is properly substantial.[70]

All of this is implicit in Aquinas' decision to place the agent intellect in the individual, for then the individual is complete in the order of *intellectus* and substantial actuality. It is impossible, then, to avoid the implications of the identity of *intellectus* and substantial actuality; if materially individuated human persons can be and are substances, there is no reason to deny *intellectus* to any member of any species. Consequently, as Keefe points out, the conclusion is fatal to the Thomist metaphysics, because it identifies material and existential individuation; it merges the form-matter correlation and the *esse-*essence correlation.[71] The ones known to be logically distinct are treated as ontologically identical.[72]

---

69 Ibid., 86–87.
70 Ibid., 85.
71 Ibid.
72 Ibid., 87.

2.4 Keefe's alternative solution

With these metaphysical problems in mind, Keefe proposes a solution that does not identify the *esse* with essence but rather maintains a correlation between them. *Esse* and essence have their own proper analogy of being and they do not contradict each other as long as they are kept in a free, non-necessitarian correlation.[73] One analogy grounds participation in being itself (*esse*), and the other grounds participation in humanity (essence) rather than collapsing the two into one analogy of being. The existential human person participates in existential intelligibility by participating in the existential human substance, i.e., by participating in the *esse*-essence correlation of human substantiality.[74]

The formal cause, the existential intelligibility, of humanity is the revelation. According to the revelation, the *Logos* correlates to the human nature of Jesus Christ as *esse* correlates to essence to constitute the man Who is Jesus Christ, the existential substance. This correlation occurs in the creative act of the Incarnation and not apart from it. Through the Incarnation, the existential truth and actuality of humanity is caused.[75] Keefe elaborates:

> Christ, as human, is a created participation in human substance; as a divine Person, He is the uncreated actuality of that participation; i.e., He is the creator of His, and of all, humanity. The terminus of His creative act is substantial humanity, the human race....But His creative act is the Incarnation, by which His divinity, as *Esse*, is correlated to His participated human nature. This correlation is thus the creation of all men; it is the contingent existential actuality of the human substance, in which all human persons participate, and by participating in which they are human persons. The human substance is therefore actual by the actuality of Christ; He is the formal cause of substantial actuality of men. Graphically expressed, humanity is actual by its tangency with the Logos, at the tangential point which is Christ.[76]

Divine participation in His creation, in humanity, is through Christ. He participates in the spatio-temporal continuum of that creation; His human life submits to human history. As the Incarnate *Logos*, however, He remains causally prior to the humanity He shares, for His humanity is not the ontological *prius* of the Incarnation; rather, the Incarnation is the ontological *prius* of humanity, for it is identical

---

73 Ibid., 90–91.
74 Ibid., 89–90.
75 Ibid., 90.
76 Ibid., 91.

to the contingent actuality of humanity, to the creation of the human substance. The ontologically prior humanity of Christ and the Incarnation are not separated, but they are simultaneous.[77]

The existential human person is human by participating in the *esse*-essence correlation of the existential substance, Jesus Christ. Through participation in the divine *Esse* of Christ, the human person is simultaneously participating in the human substantial form; i.e., by being an existentially contingent person.[78] The divine *Esse* actualizes humanity and participation in it is not diverse from but correlated with participation in the human essence, for they are correlated as act and potency in Christ. This participation is not an activity for Keefe. Rather, it constitutes the individual as a member of the substantial species whose actuality is the formal effect of *esse* not of essence. The human person is human by one's participation in the *esse*-essence correlation of human substantiality.[79] In summary, the prime analogate is a human prime, the Incarnate *Logos*, in whose actuality men and women participate by being human as well as by having a participation in existence.[80] With such a prime analogate, either one avoids identifying *esse* with essence (Aristotelian essentialism) and allows for existential participation or one avoids being forced into Platonism where that in which one participates is immanent within the world.

2.5 The alternative, covenantal understanding of substance

This alternative covenantal understanding of the analogy of being avoids the metaphysical difficulties outlined above regarding the essential and existential (cosmological) analogies of being. Consequently, the Aristotelian cosmological meaning of substance as the *a priori* unity of metaphysics generally, and specifically of the metaphysics of the Eucharist, is abandoned and replaced with that historical notion which is drawn from the eucharistic liturgical tradition: the One Flesh of the representation of the Sacrifice of Christ.[81] Substance is now historical, and its contingency is that of a free Event.[82] More

---

77 Ibid.
78 Ibid., 89.
79 Ibid., 89–90.
80 Ibid., 88.
81 Keefe, *Covenantal Theology*, 423.
82 Ibid., 230.

specifically, substance, when applied to humanity as created, denotes the dynamic actuality of created human freedom and history, whose concrete actuality is marital. The created human substance, thus, is a substantially free society, a community constituted by three subsistent relations (husband, wife, marital bond), whose free historical unity (the covenantal One Flesh) images not a cosmic *Deus Unus* but the Trinity of Persons Who are Father, Son, and Spirit, each irreducibly unique by reason of the unique relation each bears upon each of the other Persons.[83] Substance can not be understood to denote either the solitary individual or the collective, concrete universe which is the Aristotelian species, for the perennial cosmological and rationalist dilemma of whether to assign entitative unity to "the One or the Many" is overcome in the covenantal revelation of the Trinity which is the Son's imaging of God.[84] Keefe explains further that a theologically informed metaphysics, created human substance "denotes the covenantal marital community of Head and Body, whose members are constituted as Body and as real in their free and covenantal interrelation to the Head, and this out of no necessity whatever, whether intrinsic or extrinsic to their creation, to their substantial Trinity— imaging constitution—for the imaging is free."[85]

2.6 Section summary

Keefe rejects what he identifies to be Aquinas' prime analogate; namely, the *Deus Unus*. According to Keefe, the *Deus Unus* is a non-relational monad that is locked into the immanence of the ideal notion of unity. This means that the unity of the divine is absolutely unqualified. God must be the Absolute, the Transcendent. Consequently, God can not be related to anything that is not Himself because He is absolute. God is incapable of any real relation to His creation. Thus, He can not be in history. According to some Thomists, creation, however, can be in a real relation to the Creator.

Keefe rejects this position on grounds that Aquinas' metaphysics of creation by the *Deus Unus* can not overcome the cosmological antagonism between the Absolute and the relativity of creation. When

---

83 Ibid., 320.
84 Ibid., 321.
85 Ibid.

this logic is applied to Christ, divinity then can not be related to humanity in the Person of Jesus Christ which is a violation of Chalcedon's doctrinal declaration of Christ being "one and the same." Christ is a single self that is at once divine and human. If one supposes that humanity is related to God but God is not related to humanity, then the self of Jesus Christ is either divine or human.

Another reason why Keefe rejects Aquinas' prime analogate is because Aquinas holds that the Absolute is a necessity of thought and necessarily immanent to thought. These insights lead Aquinas to adopt Aristotle's postulate of an agent intellect, but he makes it multiple within the species rather than singular. This deals with the problem of the relationship between the Absolute and the relative (the One and the Many); however, Keefe perceives yet another problem. If the agent intellect were multiple within the species, if each person possessed his own agent intellect, then each person would be an incommunicable intellectual universe, a self-enclosed mind incapable of knowing anything but itself. This is not the case. Aquinas recognized this point to some degree in his debate with the Averrhoists. The alternative was to make the agent intellect a specific perfection necessarily immanent not in the individual but somehow in the many-membered human species. This alternative is unacceptable for Keefe because it would deprive the individual human person of moral freedom. The person would be no more than a function of a particular species. The only resolution Keefe holds as possible is one in which the prime analogate is immanent in the human species and transcends history from within history.

According to Keefe, the free facticity of the New Covenant, as prime analogate, must control the analogy of being in order to avoid the traditional problems that have plagued the analogy of being as both essential and existential. If one adopts an essential (Aristotelian) analogy of being, as Keefe believes of Aquinas, whereby multiplicity and unity are located in the essence, then the analogy of being functions as necessitarian, as non-gratuitous. This essence must be entirely actual, for if it were not, then it could not actualize the potency of any of the individual members of the species, and some other reality would be its actuality. Consequently, a necessary, non-gratuitous analogy of being (pure nature) results.

Keefe sees that a logical implication of such an analogy of being in theology is that pure nature becomes the *a priori* condition of grace.

According to Keefe, Aquinas does in fact deduce grace from nature; that which is "ungraced" is the cause of grace. A major problem with this position is that it mistakes an effect for a cause. Nature is understood to be a substance and grace an accident. This violates the act-potency analysis. A *natural* potency is incompatible with a *supernatural* actuation when potency and act are conceived in terms of substance and accident, wherein substance as potency governs what accident as act may be.

Keefe responds by saying that nature, rather, is free and historical: it is freely fallen and freely redeemed. It is created in Christ and its relation to grace is free rather than necessary. It is unintelligible apart from grace just as *sarx* is unintelligible apart from *mia sarx*. Rather, nature is the unreality from which one is converted, the determinism from which one is freed and, by comparison with which the gratuity and the freedom of historical actuality is known to be as such. The normative criterion of reality is supernatural and not natural.

When Aquinas introduces the *esse*-essence correlation to the analogy of being, a problem arises. The analogy of being is seeking necessary connections between individuals, and yet the correlation is gratuitous. According to Keefe, if the analogy remains necessitarian, then the *esse*-essence correlation is undermined in one of two ways. First, if one insists that the correlation be understood as necessary rather than gratuitous, then *esse* would be intrinsic to essence. Second, if the correlation is understood as gratuitous within a necessitarian analogy, then *esse* would be external to essence. As a result, *esse* and essence end up being opposed to each other and uncorrelated. These problems are consequences of Aquinas' decision to place the agent intellect in the individual.

Keefe proposes a solution which does not identify *esse* with essence but rather maintains the correlation between the two. Each has its own proper analogy of being and they do not contradict each other as long as they are kept in a free, non-necessitarian correlation. One analogy grounds participation in being-itself (*esse*), and the other grounds participation in humanity (essence) rather than collapsing the two into one analogy of being. The existential human person participates in existential intelligibility by participating in the existential human substance, i.e., the *esse*-essence correlation of human substantiality.

How does this take shape in particular? To put it simply, the *Logos* correlates to the human nature of Jesus Christ as *esse* correlates to essence in order to constitute the man Who is Jesus Christ, the existential substance. "Christ, as human, is a created participation in human substance; as a divine Person, He is the uncreated actuality of that participation; i.e., He is the creator of His, and of all, humanity. The terminus of His creative act is substantial humanity, the human race of men."[86] The existential human person is human by participating in the *esse*-essence correlation of the existential substance, Jesus Christ. The prime analogate of being is a human prime, the Incarnate *Logos*, in whose actuality men and women participate by being human as well as by having a participation in existence.

With such a prime analogate in place, Keefe holds that all the metaphysical difficulties that arise regarding the essential and existential (cosmological) analogies of being are rendered moot. Substance is now historical, and its contingency is that of a free Event.

3 Keefe's Critique of Aquinas' Theology of the Eucharist

3.1 Reasons for rejecting Aquinas' understanding of transubstantiation

We have seen Keefe's critique of Aquinas' cosmological understanding of substance. Now attention will be turned to how this understanding affects Aquinas' theology of the Eucharist. Keefe holds that in the end his theology is flawed by the cosmological implications of its form-matter analysis which are the reduction of the formal content of the sacrament to the words of consecration and the historicity of the sacrament to the moment of transubstantiation.[87]

Keefe points out that the form-matter analysis of the eucharistic sign, as Aquinas uses it, places all sacramental efficacy in the words of consecration. As a result, the bread and the wine signify and cause what they signify only by the words of consecration (the form).[88] Keefe points out that Aquinas insists that bread and wine are indis-

---

86 Keefe, *Thomism and Tillich*, 91.
87 Keefe, *Covenantal Theology*, 422.
88 Cf. *ST* III 78.1.

pensable to this efficacy but he provides no act-potency explanation for their indispensability. The words of consecration are truly the formal content of the sacramental sign, while the matter is insignificant, and does no more than individuate the sign in space and time, for which purpose any matter would suffice.[89]

The words of consecration are indispensable and are effective of the *res et sacramentum*, but that taken in isolation exhausts the formal significance, yet bread and wine have a formal significance of their own and this can not be conceded. Keefe recognizes that Aquinas knows this, for he distinguishes between the *sacramentum tantum* and the *res et sacramentum* of the Eucharist in numerous places and assigns distinct causality to each. Aquinas' argument, however, that the words "take ye and eat" and "drink ye all of this" of the institution formula are not an element of the form risks isolating the canon from the offertory and the communion of the Mass. The offertory and communion are not consecratory, but they are not on that account any less integral to the efficacious sign-character of the sacrament itself, whose efficacy is more than consecration, as the Mass is more than canon. Keefe notes that Aquinas is well aware of this point, but his form-matter analysis does not account for it; only when he uses the classic Augustinian language does the dimension of the Eucharist that is its historicity find room in his theology.[90]

Consequently, Keefe holds that this theology of the Eucharist is defective in that it effectively bars the sign-function of the bread and wine by which they are the *sacramentum tantum*. The species of the bread and wine, understood as metaphysical accidents, are efficacious only as intrinsic causes, for this is their sole reality within the intrinsic analysis of historical reality that is the Thomist metaphysics: the causality of accidents is only effective by their being transcendental relations to the substance which is the term of their relation.[91] In other words, the species can have no sign value because signs are causes only to the extent that they are transcendentally related to some substance in which they inhere. If there is no substance in which they inhere, then they have no causal power. Accidents have sign-value only to the extent that they are related to substance transcendentally.

---

89 Keefe, *Covenantal Theology*, 422.
90 Ibid., 422–23.
91 Ibid., 424.

Keefe points out that the difficulty with this definition of accident is that it is not relational. While it is obvious that after consecration the remaining accidents can not be thought of as substantial, they likewise can not be thought of as accidents in such a manner that the notion that they are supported by divine power makes metaphysical sense. An accident is not a composite entity which might be created or otherwise held in being; its only *esse* is an *esse ad*, and to suppose otherwise is to deny its meaning.[92]

Absent a subject of inherence, accidents can exercise no causality within this metaphysical framework, while to depart from that framework is to depart from systematic theological explanation. For this reason, Keefe rejects Aquinas' theology of transubstantiation. Keefe explains that Aquinas has left intact the static character of the transcendental relations which he acquired from Aristotelianism and, even under his command, this cosmological analysis has failed when applied to the historical Event which is the Church's eucharistic worship.[93]

Similarly, Keefe rejects Aquinas' theology of transubstantiation on grounds that it does not involve a change effected by the consecration from bread, understood as a cosmological substance, to a historical substance which is the sacrificed and sacrificing Christ whose sacrifice is the institution of the New Covenant. Keefe explains that this is the case for two reasons. First, there is and has been no factual reality corresponding to the cosmological notion of substance, for the actuality of substance, its creation in Christ as measured by the covenantal *a priori* of a theological metaphysics, is contingent and created, as cosmological substance is not. Keefe illustrates this point by stating that the classic Thomist metaphysics of creation by the One God is unable to overcome the cosmological antagonism which its logic places between the absolute *Deus Unus* and the relativity of creation and continues to insist that God so conceived is incapable of any relation to that which He has created. This conclusion is inconvenient for a theology of Incarnation and can not but be equally so for the highly concrete historical realism of a covenantal metaphysics.[94]

Second, transubstantiation as a free Event can not be made congruent with any intrinsically necessary analytic structure by way of

---

92 Ibid., 420.
93 Ibid., 423.
94 Ibid., 425.

the transcendental relations which would set out the *a priori* intrinsically necessary conditions for its historical presentation as Event. This is due to the fact that a free Event is utterly novel in its creation *ex nihilo sui et subjecti*, and it can not be understood in the cosmological context of analytical metaphysical necessity. Such a reality would not be free, for it could not possess the intrinsic ground for the intelligibility of freedom which that analysis demands.[95] Transubstantiation is the basis for the transcendental relations and not vice versa.

Thus, in conclusion, two metaphysical frameworks, one cosmological and the other relational, can not coexist. In the end, real transubstantiation that is the eucharistic *metabole* is to be understood to possess an analytic and intrinsic intelligibility only insofar as the analysis submits to the uniquely valid historical criterion of theological intelligibility, the New Covenant.[96] Transubstantiation is simply unintelligible in the static context of a necessitarian cosmological metaphysics, and it is absurd to seek the conditions of its possibility within such a framework, according to Keefe.

Keefe commends Aquinas for recognizing as few had done before that the relation between the temporal before and after of transubstantiation could not be as between one monadic identity and another without abandoning the sign (*sacramentum tantum*) dimension of the eucharistic bread and wine. "Before" transubstantiation is the bread and wine and "after" transubstantiation is the Body and Blood of Christ. If they are understood as two independent monads, they can not be related to each other as signs ought, by definition. This acknowledgement placed Aquinas in inextricable difficulties, for the species (the signs) had as "accidents" no correlative substantial subject of inherence (i.e., they act as monads).[97] His reply is nominal. It is an attempt to reduce "accident" to an abstract definition, while the reality of an "accident" in his metaphysics is that of a transcendental relation whose reality is intelligible only as an *esse ad*.

Keefe holds that there is no escaping this dilemma based on Aquinas' cosmological framework. While Aquinas rejected the notion that the eucharistic species conceal rather than manifest the presence of Christ (for signs manifest rather than conceal), he was nevertheless unable to provide for their effective signing, because the dynamism of

---

95 Ibid.
96 Ibid., 425–26.
97 Ibid., 426.

that sacramental efficacy is historical, not cosmological, and his metaphysics remained a cosmology. He provided the intrinsic freedom of the substantial transcendental relations with no intrinsic cause, with no intelligible account, although his transcendental method requires precisely that intrinsic ground if the contingency of creation is to be in fact intelligible.[98] His transcendental method requires an intrinsic cause, but he provides the *esse*-essence relation with no intrinsic cause because the cause of being for a created thing is extrinsic and not intrinsic to it. For Aquinas, the Creator has to be extrinsic for there to be a creation since there is no real relation between the Creator and creation.

In conclusion, Keefe holds that Aquinas considered transubstantiation to be a unique exception to the ordinary cosmological pattern of substantial change.[99] The problem that presented itself, then, was how to accommodate the reigning act-potency analysis. How was transubstantiation to be understood within the *a priori* context of a cosmological notion of objectivity? Keefe holds that the problem is not that of fitting transubstantiation into a prevailing act-potency system, but of reinterpreting the act-potency analysis of being under the norm of the historical, liturgical *a priori*, the historical prime analogate that is the eucharistic representation of the New Covenant.[100] As he sees it, the task of a Thomist eucharistic theology is not to develop an account of the Event of transubstantiation in terms of a metaphysical analysis of the intelligible immanent necessity of being, but to develop a historical and theological metaphysical analysis of being as intelligible immanent freedom in the covenantal terms which are manifest in eucharistic transubstantiation.[101]

3.2 Section summary

Keefe makes several points in his critique of Aquinas' theology of the Eucharist. According to Keefe, Aquinas places all sacramental efficacy in the words of consecration. The words of consecration for him provide the formal content to the sacramental sign while the matter itself

---

98 Ibid.
99 Ibid., 428.
100 Ibid., 429.
101 Ibid., 430.

is insignificant and does no more than individuate the sign in space and time. Keefe insists that the bread and wine have a formal significance of their own. Keefe believes that Aquinas knows this fundamentally but that this form-matter analysis does not account for it. In the end, Keefe is of the opinion that Aquinas effectively bars the sign-function of the bread and wine. The accidents (species) have no sign value because signs are causes only to the extent that they are transcendentally related to some substance of inherence. If they have not substance of inherence, they have no causality. For Aquinas, the accidents (species) have no subject of inherence after transubstantiation. For Keefe, they need to be related to a substance for they are only effective by their being in a transcendental relation with substance.

Keefe also takes the position that Aquinas has a mistaken understanding of transubstantiation which holds that the consecration effects a change from the cosmological substance of bread to the historical substance which is the sacrificed and sacrificing Christ whose One Sacrifice institutes the New Covenant. First of all, there is no reality corresponding to the cosmological notion of substance. Substance is contingent, created, and free. Second, transubstantiation is a free Event which lacks any antecedent possibility. It can not be made congruent with any intrinsically necessary analytic structure (e.g., form-matter, accident-substance, *esse*-essence) which would set out the *a priori* intrinsically necessary conditions for transubstantiation's presentation as an Event.

In the end, if the *prius* of theology is free and historical, then it sets the norm by which all metaphysics is structure. Transubstantiation is not to be explained in terms of some *a priori* necessitarian structure but rather the structure is to be reinterpreted in terms of transubstantiation (and the free historical *prius*).

PART II

THEOLOGY AND THE EUCHARIST IN THE THOUGHT OF SAINT THOMAS AQUINAS

OVERVIEW

As indicated in the "Statement of Procedure" of the introductory chapter, this second part is an inquiry into the identification and function of Aquinas' "subject" of sacred doctrine, a comparable term to Keefe's *"prius"* or "prime analogate," and its relationship to the Eucharist. The part is divided into four chapters. Chapter three will discuss how sacred doctrine pertains to the revelation of God. Chapter four will establish that Aquinas identifies Jesus Christ as the revelation of God by first inquring into Aquinas' treatment of God's knowability (section 1). Once God is recognized to be knowable, then the implication that there is a relation between the knower and the known is made immediately by definition (section 2). This relation (i.e., a real relation) between creatures and God is mediated by the incarnate Jesus Christ. As a result, humanity has personal access to God through the God-Man. This God-Man reveals the Godhead through various roles (e.g., prophet, Word, teacher, mediator, and priest) of which He is the culmination or the most excellent (chapter five). Chapter six discusses that this excellence is due to the fullness of grace He possesses, both substantially as an individual man by virtue of the hypostatic union and accidentally by virtue of sanctifying grace as an effect of the hypostatic union. Consequently, by the grace of this union (*gratia unionis*), Christ received personally the fullness of grace (*gratia habitualis* or *gratia santificans*) which He freely bestows upon rational creatures as their Head (*gratia capitis*) (section 1). By such a bestowal, a union is formed between Christ the Head and the members of the Mystical Body (section 2), whereby all that fell as a result of the first Adam's sin is reestablished by the second Adam (section 3). Redemption and salvation are predicated, for Aquinas, upon the premise of the mystical union between Christ as Head and the Church as Body (section 4). This union is established and secured through the sacraments which serve as channels of grace. Of the sacraments, the Eucharist has primacy, according to Aquinas, because its ultimate effect (*res tantum*) is union with Christ (section 5).

Thus, while Aquinas holds that God does not have a real relation with His creation,[1] which initially seems to preclude a covenantal *subjectum* of *sacra doctrina* (chapter three), there is evidence that Aquinas moves in this covenantal direction by holding that Jesus Christ is the incarnate revelation of God (chapter four). In Christ, there is a real relation between the created nature and the Person of the Word. By extension, humanity now has personal access to God through the Incarnate Christ. This access is established and maintained by His role as mediator. He reveals God by assuming various roles through which people come to know and then commit themselves to God. In these roles, Aquinas holds that Christ is the culmination and the most excellent of all those who share in them (chapter five). As such, He has primacy (to use a Keefian expression, He is the "prime analogate"), and those participants in the roles (i.e., the secondary analogates) derive their significance from Him. This primacy is tied to His Headship and, as Head, He draws creatures into mystical union with Him by bestowing salvific grace upon the members of His Body via the sacraments (chapter six). The Eucharist has primacy among all the sacraments because, by containing Christ sacramentally (*res et sacramentum*), it effects the mystical union (*res tantum*) between Christ and His Church. In the end, there is a movement in Aquinas' thought from God and all that is related to God as the subject of *sacra doctrina* to the eucharistic Jesus Christ Who effects a mystical union with the members of His Body as the subject.

---

1 God has instead a relation of reason with creation.

CHAPTER THREE

SAINT THOMAS AQUINAS' SUBJECT OF SACRED DOCTRINE

1 The Terms *Subjectum* and *Objectum*

While Aquinas does not use the terms *prius* and prime analogate in the way Keefe does, he does have an analogous term, *subjectum*. This section will investigate the way in which Aquinas understands this term and how it relates to the term *objectum*. By such an investigation, grounds will be set for comparing and contrasting Keefe and Aquinas with regard to the subject of theology (i.e., the *prius*).

1.1 Aristotle's influence.

In article seven of the *Summa theologiae* (I 1), Aquinas raises the question whether God is the subject (*subjectum*) of this sacred science. Aquinas' understanding of the term was shaped by Aristotle who, for quite some time, had already been regarded in the Christian world as the logician *par excellence*.[1] From the eleventh century on, Aristotle's *Categories* and *Propositions* were read with some continuance. The term *subjectum* was initially understood in the context of Aristotelian logic. In both of these works, Aristotle speaks of the "subject" and "predicate" of a proposition, that of which something is predicated. In a sentence, the subject denotes the bearer of a property while the predicate denotes the property itself. Aristotle explains:

> It is evident from what has been said that, of things said of a subject, it is necessary for both the name and the definition [corresponding to that name] to be predicable of that subject. For example, man is said of an individual man, which is a subject; so the name 'man', too, is predicable [of the individual man], for one would predicate 'man' of an individual man. And the definition of man, too, would be predicable of the individual man; for an individual man is a man and also an animal. Thus both the name and the corresponding definition would be predicable of the subject.[2]

These grammatical distinctions of Aristotle's subject-predicate logic find a parallel in his metaphysics as substance-accident. Just as statements are made regarding a subject in a sentence, so, too, attributes are noted of a particular substance. Substance is the principle of inherence for accidents. Consequently, for Aristotle "substance" is the basic ontological unit as "that which is" just as the "subject" is the basic logical unit. The term *subjectum*, then, means logically that of which something is predicated and metaphysically that which receives a perfection, an attribute, an accident.

1.2 The terms within the context of a science.

In the earlier articles of this question (*ST* I 1), Aquinas speaks of science as certain intellectual knowledge drawn from first principles by reasoning, that is, knowledge through causes. In his earlier work, *De*

---

1 Marie-Dominique Chenu, *Toward Understanding Saint Thomas*, translators with authorized corrections and bibliographical additions A.-M Landry and D. Hughes (Chicago: Henry Regnery, 1964), 32. Yet at this time, Aristotle was becoming known in the Christian world as a natural and metaphysical philosopher.

2 Aristotle, *Aristotle's Categories and Propositions (De Interpretatione)*, translated with commentaries and glossary by Hippocrates G. Apostle (Grinnell, Iowa: Peripatetic Press, 1980), 2a20–27. The Greek word for "subject" here is *hypokeimenon*, which means literally, "underlay."

veritate, Aquinas notes that science has as its goal the presence of the perfection of exterior beings (the known) in the mind of the knower. Through science, the human mind seeks to know the subject's essence.[3] He writes:

> ...another kind of perfection is to be found in created things. It consists in this, that the perfection belonging to one thing is found in another. This is the perfection of a knower in so far as he knows; for something is known by a knower by reason of the fact that the thing known is, in some fashion, in the possession of the knower. Hence, it is said in *The Soul* [Aristotle, *De anima,* III, 5 (430a 14)] that the soul is, "in some manner, all things," since its nature is such that it can know all things. In this way it is possible for the perfection of the entire universe to exist in one thing. The ultimate perfection which the soul can attain, therefore, is, according to the philosophers, to have delineated in it the entire order and causes of the universe. This they held to be the ultimate end of man.[4]

These exterior beings possess properties which are metaphysically dependent upon and manifestations of their essences. These properties render the exterior beings intelligible in the mind of the knower and thus constitute the object of science. Due to this understanding of science, Aquinas distinguishes between the subject of the science (the exterior extra-mental being that one seeks to know) and the object of the science (the mental content about that subject).

Aquinas likewise distinguishes between these two notions in the *Summa theologiae's* seventh article of question one. Here Aquinas is intent upon determining the *subjectum* rather than the *objectum* of the sacred science. If one disregards the editor's footnote in the Blackfriar's edition of the text to "neglect here the meaning of 'subject' contrasted with 'object'," one discovers a contrast in Aquinas' mind between the two terms. The key to arriving at the significance of the distinction in this context is the analogy presented in the *responsio*. It is only in this portion of the article that the term *objectum* is used. In

---

3 Aquinas here relies on Aristotle's statement, "for there is knowledge [a science] of each thing only when we know its essence." Aristotle, *Metaphysics,* in *The Basic Works of Aristotle,* edited and with an introduction by Richard McKeon (New York: Random House, 1941), I, ch. 6, 1031b. (Hereafter, referred to as: Aristotle, *Metaph.*)

4 St. Thomas Aquinas, *Truth (De veritate),* translated from the definitive Leonine texts by Robert W. Mulligan (Chicago: Henry Regnery, 1952–1954), q. 2, art. 2. (Hereafter, referred to as *De ver.*)

the remainder of the article, *subjectum* is the only operative term. He writes:

> For a subject is to a science as an object is to a psychological power or train-
> ing. Now that properly is designated the object which expresses the special
> term why anything is related to the power or training in question; thus a
> man or a stone is related to eyesight in that both are coloured, so being col-
> oured is the proper object of the sense of sight. Now all things are dealt with
> in holy teaching in terms of God, either because they are God himself or be-
> cause they are relative to him as their origin and end.[5]

1.3 Aquinas' use of the term *subjectum*

Aquinas' use of *subjectum* here has been defined by his earlier works.
As stated in his *Exposition of the Posterior Analytics* (I, lect. 41), the subject of a science is the end or term of the operation or movement of
that science, thus making it that about which the science is concerned
and comes to know. As every operation proceeds from a certain first
principle and ends at some term, so in the operation of a science, reason proceeds from certain first principles and ends at some term.
Thus, the unity of the subject is considered according to the unity of
its operation or movement. In other words, the fact that science has
one term to which it proceeds is the reason why the science is one.[6]
Aquinas accounts for the diversity of the operations of science not on
account of the subject, for that remains constant, but on account of a
diversity of principles. Various lines of inquiry may consider the single subject under different formalities (i.e., two or more qualitatively
different movements or lines of inquiry [that of veterinary medicine
or that of biology] may converge on a single material subject, a Do-
berman dog, but not on a single science). Thus, the subject of one particular science is that which is considered under a specific formal
principle. It is the term of a particular process of formal inquiry.

5 St. Thomas Aquinas, *Summa Theologiae*, Blackfriars Edition (New York:
   McGraw-Hill, 1964–76), I 1.7. (Hereafter, referred to as *ST*.)
6 St. Thomas Aquinas, *Exposition of the Posterior Analytics of Aristotle*, translated by
   Pierre Conway, revised by William H. Kane, mimeograph by Michel Doyon
   (Quebec: La Librairie Philosophique M. Doyon, 1956), I. lect. 41, n. 6–8. (Hereaf-
   ter, referred to as *Super Post. Anal.*)

In his earlier work, *Scriptum super libros sententiarum magistri Petri Lombardi episcopi Parisiensis,*[7] Aquinas provides further clarification on the nature of the subject of a science when he explains the three following comparisons which the subject has with science. He writes, "The first is that whatever is in the science must be contained under the subject....The second comparison is that knowledge of a subject is principally intended in that science....The third comparison is that science is distinguished by its subject from all other things because sciences are separated just as things are separated."[8] The first comparison mentioned here is that under which the subject is sometimes called the *genus subjectum*. It is simply the genus of things (the subject considered in a general way) which a scientist comes to know progressively through questions and inquiry. It is the interest of a particular science: that which one is questioning or studying. Every aspect of this genus is considered.[9] In this case, the *genus subjectum* is God (the *ens divinum*) and all of creation (*entia creata*) that is related to Him as principle and end.

The second comparison indicates that within this *genus subjectum*, there will be one subject which will be principally studied in the science. This understanding of subject is sometimes called the *subjectum attributionis*. It is that to which all being and intelligibility is attributed, namely, God. God is the subject to which all else that exists and is studied is ultimately referred or attributed.[10]

---

7 Hereafter, referred to as the *Commentary on the Sentences.*

8 St. Thomas Aquinas, *Scriptum super libros sententiarum magistri Petri Lombardi episcopi parisiensis*, ed. R.P. Mandonnet (Paris: Sumptibus P. Leihielleux, 1929), I, prol., q. 1, a. 4, sol. (Hereafter, referred to as *In Sent.*) *Prima est, quod quaecumque sunt in scientia debent, contineri sub subjecto....Secundo comparatio est, quod subjecti cognitio principaliter intenditur in scientia....Tertia comparatio est, quod per subjectum distinguitur scientia ab ominibus aliis; quia secantur scientiae quemadmodum et res....*

9 P. Mariano De Andrea, "Soggetto e oggetto della metafisica secondo S. Tommaso," *Angelicum* 27 (Maggio-Agosto 1950): 176.

10 William A. Wallace, *The Role of Demonstration in Moral Theology: A Study of Methodology in St. Thomas Aquinas*, Texts and Studies, vol. 2 (Washington, D.C.: Thomist Press, 1962), 26. Aquinas explains this understanding of *subjectum attributionis* by giving an example in his commentary on Aristotle's *Posterior Analytics*. There are things which are *per se* principles of the subject triangle (e.g., it consists of three sides and three angles totalling 180 degrees) and principles which are not *per se* principles of the subject but of the subjective parts, such as, isoceles, equilateral, and scalene. While these particular trinagles will be studied by the science, all will ultimately be referred or attributed to the universal concept of triangularity itself (*Super Post. Anal.*, I, lect. 41, n. 9).

The third comparison, which Aquinas had primarily in mind when he spoke regarding the unity and diversity of the sciences, refers to that formality, *ratio*, or aspect of a thing which directly and principally is of interest to a determined science.[11] This understanding of *subjectum* is often referred to as a *genus scibile* which is simply the subject or *genus subjectum* considered under the *ratio formalis* characteristic of scientific demonstration. It is this which specifies and differentiates the sciences. Aquinas begins his identification of the *ratio formalis* in a general way by stating in the *Summa theologiae* that sacred science proceeds *"ex principiis notis lumine superioris scientiae, quae scilicet est Dei et beatorum"* ("from principles known by the light of a higher science, namely, the science of God and the blessed").[12] In a later article, he identifies this *ratio* as considering subjects that are *"divino lumine cognoscibilia"* ("known through divine light").[13] Here the *ratio* is understood from the perspective of the light under which it is known, namely, the *"lumen divinum."* And finally, it may also be understood from the perspective of the subjects illumined by this light (the *ratio formalis objecti*), which another article identifies as the *"divinitus revelabilia"* ("divinely revealed").[14]

1.4 Aquinas' use of the term *objectum*

In the analogy, Aquinas states that the subject is to science as the object is to habit or potency. This comparison is a logical consequence of what he says earlier in the *Summa contra gentiles*, that science is the act by which knowledge is acquired or the habit of mind (the possible intellect) resulting from one or more acts of intellectual consideration.[15] It is reasonable that Aquinas should understand science as a

---

11 De Andrea, 176.

12 *ST* I 1.2, resp.

13 Ibid., I 1.4, resp.

14 Ibid., I 1.3, resp. It also should be stated that just as the material object and the *ratio formalis* (formal subject) specify the sacred science, so, too, does the material object and the *ratio scibilis* (formal object) specify the act and the habit of knowing by which the science is produced. The formal object unifies the body of known statements (the material object) into a substantial science, a *habitus*.

15 St. Thomas Aquinas, *On the Truth of the Catholic Faith (Summa Contra Gentiles)*, translated by James E. Anderson et al., 5 vols. (Garden City, New York: Doubleday, Image, 1955), I ch. 94, [3] and II ch. 60, [12]. (Hereafter, referred to as *SCG*.)

habit since he defines *habitus* as a disposition of a subject which is in a state of potentiality either to form or to operation (i.e., of being in act).[16] Elsewhere he speaks of a habit as a disposition, a capacity readily undertaken to do something well or ill with ease, facility, pleasure, and without further deliberation because it has become connatural.[17] By coherently grasping a body of knowledge, science is indeed a habit for what was potential knowledge about the subject is now actual knowledge; what was previously unknown is now known with facility.

Just as science is correlatively dependent upon the subject for its significance, so, too, is habit correlatively dependent upon the object for its significance. Unless there is a body of knowledge achieved through a gathering of demonstrated conclusions about the subject, there can not be a facility, a disposition in knowing the subject. A habit results when there is a familiarity with a subject achieved through an act of knowing specified by an object.

Aquinas makes a distinction within his understanding of object in its relationship with habit. He says:

> The object of any cognitive habit includes two elements: that which is known, the content, and this stands as the material object; that by which the material object is known, and this is the formal objective. An example: in the science of geometry the content known is the conclusions; the formal objec-

---

16 *ST* I-II 50.1, resp. Two other additional points should be made: 1) since Aquinas correlates an object to a habit which is a disposition of a subject, "object" and "subject" are necessarily distinct in his mind; 2) for Aquinas, whose language has been labelled nominalist at times, a habit need not always be in act: it can exist as a mere possibility or potentiality for act but not yet in act. When it is in act, it is so as an operation or a movement. Aquinas explains, "he who has a habit and is not using it is in a manner in potency, though otherwise than prior to understanding....Now, every habitual intellect understands through some species. For either a habit confers on the intellect a certain ability to receive the intelligible species by which it becomes understanding in act, or else it is the ordered aggregate of the species themselves existing in the intellect, not according to a complete act, but in a way intermediated between potency and act" (*SCG* I ch. 56, [3] and [6]).

17 *De ver.*, q. 20, art. 2, resp., *ST* I-II 49.1, and *SCG* III ch. 160, "...in repentinis signum interioris habitus praecipue accipi potest." Other definitions of "object" are: that which constitutes this habit, the body of truths and conclusions attained in the scientific process; that in which the act of scientific knowing (the habit or the rational assembling of demonstrated truths and conclusions about the subject) terminates.

tive of the science's assent to them is the medium of demonstration through which the conclusions are known.[18]

That which is "thrown against" (the literal meaning of the term *objectum*) is the object which consists of two elements. The material object is the content, the disorganized set of statements. This set comes to cohere into a single understanding by way of the formal object. The formal object is that which causes the science to be a single understanding, a single coherent and integrating grasp of a multitude of discrete elements of knowledge. It is that aspect, that method by which the *scibilia*, the "knowable" elements of a science are coherently united into a formal science in the sense of an accomplished reality, a habit. In his frequent example of sight, the formal object is said to be color or the colored while the material object is said to be the body in which the color is seen.[19] And while he does not use the terms that his later commentators employ, Aquinas does distinguish the formal object further into two aspects: that which is attained by the knowing faculty (*objectum formale quod*) and that by which it is attained (*objectum formale quo*). He writes:

> In some sense light is the object of sight and in another sense not. For, since light is seen by our sight only if through reflection or in some way it is united to a body having a surface, it is not called the essential object of sight. This is, rather, color, which is always in a body having a surface. However, insofar as nothing can be seen except by reason of light, light itself is said to be the first visible thing…[20]

To use the terms of his commentators, the *objectum formale quod* is color, as that which is seen as such, and the *objectum formale quo* is light, as that by which color is made visible and, therefore, able to be attained by the sense of sight.

1.5 Conclusion and section summary

Since science is a habit of the mind, the distinction between subject and object is based on the very nature of the mind's act of knowing. In order to be known, the extra-mental reality (subject) is in the mind by

---

18   *ST* II-II 1.1, corp.
19   Ibid., I 1.7, corp. This example recurs but in slightly different contexts: *De ver.*, q. 24, art. 6 and *ST* I-II 57.2, ad 2.
20   *De ver.*, q. 14, art. 8, ad 4.

means of concepts (object). Since the subject of knowledge is a single indivisible reality, a multitude of concepts, which represent all of its various aspects, render it present, then, in the mind. Aquinas explains:

> The way the known exists in the knower corresponds to the way the knower knows. As shown in the *Prima Pars*, the way of knowing truth proper to the human mind is by an act of combining and separating. For this reason the human mind knows in a composite way things that are themselves simple....To apply this: consider the object of faith from its two perspectives. First, from the perspective of the reality believed in, and then the object of faith is something non-composite, i.e. the very reality about which one has faith. Second, from the perspective of the one believing, and then the object of faith is something composite in the form of a proposition.[21]

Thus, the subject is that single extra-mental reality that is known in the mind through a multitude of concepts or objects. Knowledge of this subject is the goal of the scientific process.[22]

In summary, the subject of a science for Aquinas is that extra-mental reality which is studied under a particular formality as the term or end of a scientific inquiry and as that to which all else is ultimately referred or attributed. The object of a science is the intellectual habit that results in the human mind when otherwise disorganized sets of statements about the subject are integrated and united into a single coherent body of knowledge. "Object" refers to the knowledge act involved in scientifically knowing a knowable reality (the subject).

2 Aquinas' Comparison between the Subject of Sacred Doctrine and the Subject of the Philosophical Disciplines

In establishing the subject of sacred doctrine, Aquinas compares and contrasts it with the subject of the intellectual sciences, the philosophical disciplines. He deals with this issue primarily in four works. They will be considered as chronologically written in order to trace the progression of Aquinas' thought.

---

21 *ST* II-II 1.2.
22 Cf. *Super Post. Anal.*, I, lect. 41, n. 7.

2.1 The comparison as presented in the *Commentary on the Sentences*

In the prologue to his *Commentary* on the first book of Peter Lombard's *Sentences*, Aquinas responds to three objections which state that there is no necessity for any other doctrine (i.e., sacred doctrine) than that of the physical sciences. According to the first objection, philosophy concerns itself with existing things. Since this science is all inclusive, no other science is necessary. "No doctrine is able to be unless it is about existing things, because it is not a science of non-being. Therefore, besides physical disciplines, no doctrine is able to exist."[23] According to the second and third objections, all doctrine is for perfection. Knowledge gained from natural intellect suffices for human perfection. This knowledge is achieved through the demonstrative science of philosophy.[24]

Aquinas situates his counter-response within the context of the pursuit of this perfection. In citing Hebrews 11:6 ("without faith it is impossible to please God"), Aquinas holds that pleasing God is the means of acquiring perfection. It is the highest necessity. For him, philosophy does not concern itself with those things which pertain to faith. Thus, in order to please God, it is proper that some doctrine might proceed from principles of faith. Aquinas acknowledges that philosophy is able to make a recognition of the Creator-God through a reasoning process based on a study of creatures, but "it is proper that some other higher doctrine exists, which proceeds by revelation, and supplements the defect of philosophy."[25] Thus, philosophy does have some knowledge of God, but God is not the proper subject of philosophy since this knowledge is derived from prior principles.

In order to elicit support for this position, Aquinas broadens his scope and cites Aristotle's position in the *Nichomachean Ethics* (X 9) that all philosophical thought is ordained to contemplative happiness which proceeds from the reason of creatures. This type of contemplation is, however, insufficient. Another type is contemplation of God

---

23 *In I Sent.*, prol., q. 1, a. 1. *Sed nulla doctrina potest esse nisi de existentibus, quia non entis non est scientia. Ergo praeter physicas disciplinas nulla doctrina debet esse.* (Whenever there is no published English translation of a text, the original is included in the footnote.)

24 Ibid.

25 Ibid., contra. *Ergo oportet aliquam aliam doctrinam esse altiorem, quae per revelationem procedat, et philosophiae defectum suppleat.*

whereby He is perceived in His own essence which will be perfectly achieved in heaven but is possible now only according to the supposition of faith.[26] The human being "is led by the hand to that contemplation in the state of life by reasoning not taken from creatures but immediately inspired by divine light; and this is the doctrine of theology."[27]

It is interesting to note that Aquinas does not capitalize on a passing remark made by Aristotle in book X, chapter nine of the *Ethics* that some human beings are made good "as a result of some divine causes is [sic] present in those who are truly fortunate." Obviously, Aristotle's paganism does obscure a close connection between his understanding of divinity and Aquinas' but the passage does indicate some similarity.

Thus, philosophy does possess some knowledge of God, but God is not the proper subject of philosophy since this knowledge of God is derived from prior principles. Philosophy acquires this knowledge through a natural reasoning process concerning creatures while theology does so through faith, through divine light.

Aquinas furthers the distinction in *quaesitum* three of article three. Here he adds the issue of highest causes. Both sciences concern themselves with these causes but through different means. Metaphysics considers them by reasoning deduced from creatures; theology through inspiration immediately accepted by God.[28] Aquinas reiterates many of these themes in his prologue to the second book of the *Sentences*, "For philosophers consider creatures, as they consist in their own nature: from this they inquire about their own causes and the passions of things; but the theologian considers creatures, as they exist from the first principle, and are ordered to their final end who is God: from this divine wisdom is correctly called, because it considers the highest cause, which is God."[29]

---

26 Ibid.

27 Ibid., sol. *...homo manuducatur ad illam contemplationem in statu viae per cognitionem non a creaturis sumptam sed immediate ex divino lumine inspiratam; et haec est doctrina theologiae.*

28 Ibid., prol., q. 1, a. 3, qla. 2.

29 *In II Sent.*, prol. *Creaturarum consideratio pertinet ad theologos et ad philosophos, sed diversimode. Philosophi enim creaturas considerant, secundum quod in propria natura consistunt: unde proprias causas et passiones rerum inquirunt; sed theologus considerat creaturas, secundum quod a primo principio exierunt, et in finem ultimum ordinantur*

2.2 The comparison as presented in the *Summa contra gentiles*

Given the purpose and audience of the work (an apologetic presentation of the faith to the non-Christian), it is not surprising that Aquinas
begins his *Summa contra gentiles* as he does. Aquinas discusses the
subject of philosophy and the Christian faith only within the context
of how knowledge of this subject is derived. The subject is discussed
in terms of the method used to know it.

Since many of the non-Christians to be debated were familiar with
Aristotle's thought, Aquinas begins by referring to the thesis presented in the opening sections of the *Nicomachean Ethics* that the wise
person puts things in their right order. This person does so by ordering them according to their end which is something good. The goal of
philosophy, however, is not just ordering something to a particular
good but to the last end of the universe. It is proper to the philosopher then to consider the highest cause.[30] Aquinas continues:

> Now, the end of each thing is that which is intended by its first author or
> mover. But the first author or mover of the universe is an intellect....The ul-
> timate end of the universe must, therefore, be the good of an intellect. This
> good is truth. Truth must consequently be the ultimate end of the whole
> universe, and the consideration of the wise man aims principally at truth. So
> it is that, according to His own statement, divine Wisdom testifies that He
> has assumed flesh and come into the world in order to make the truth
> known....The Philosopher himself establishes that first philosophy is the
> science of truth, not of any truth, but of that truth which is the origin of all
> truth, namely, which belongs to the first principle whereby all things are.
> The truth belonging to such a principle is, clearly, the source of all truth; for
> things have the same disposition in truth as in being.[31]

Obviously, Aristotle did not recognize the incarnate divine Wisdom to
be the manifestation of truth, but he did pursue it implicitly (unthe-
matically) as the origin of all truth. This pursuit is carried out methodologically through the use of natural reason. However, in certain
explicit things of God, natural reason has its failing.[32] Aquinas explains this position with the statement that "the way in which we understand the substance of a thing determines the way in which we

---

30   *SCG* I ch. 1, [1].
31   Ibid., ch. 2, [2].
32   Ibid., ch. 2, [3].

know what belongs to it."[33] The human intellect depends on the senses for the origin of knowledge. Those things that do not fall under the senses can not be grasped by the intellect except insofar as the knowledge of them is gathered indirectly from sensible things. By beginning with sensible things, the intellect can come to the knowledge that God does in fact exist, but it can not go further into the nature of the divine substance itself. That unique knowledge must be divinely revealed for two reasons. First, human understanding is based on the person's ability to perceive the substance of the entity being considered. The human intellect is capable of knowing only that which can be perceived of the divine substance beginning with its natural sense abilities. That which can not be derived in this manner must be revealed to the human intellect.[34] Second, even though an angel is able to know more about God than a human being knows, due to a higher gradation in the hierarchy of intellects, an angel is not able, by means of his natural knowledge, to grasp all the things that God understands in Himself. Here, too, as in the case of human beings, knowledge is limited by the creature's nature. However, the human being, by reason of his lesser status, is not to suspect as false what is divinely revealed through the ministry of angels. Human beings must accept what they can learn about God through the angels, for they are of a higher intellect than they are.[35]

Thus, with regard to the subject of philosophy and theology, Aquinas here is saying that divine Wisdom is the subject of philosophy only insofar as He is reasoned to be the origin and cause of truth. This realization is derived from the consideration of truths known naturally by the human intellect. Divine Wisdom is the subject of theology insofar as the nature of His divine substance is revealed to the intellect.

Throughout this section of book one which deals with how truth about God is achieved (chapters one through nine), Aquinas' use of terms lacks the precision that is evident in his later works. He speaks of the truth(s) of God and the twofold method in which they are arrived at: one to which the inquiry of the reason can reach naturally, the other which surpasses the whole ability of the human reason and

---

33 Ibid., ch. 3, [3].
34 Ibid.
35 Ibid., ch. 3, [4].

thus requires a divine revealing.[36] As was stated in the beginning of this section, Aquinas does not use the term "subject" or "object" but identifies the reality under consideration as the "truth(s) about God," "the truth concerning the divine being." He is not concerned with this truth as the *prius* or prime analogate of theology *per se* but with the method in which these truths are ascertained (namely, through natural and supernatural reasoning). Throughout this discussion, he never uses the terms "sacred doctrine" or "theology" which he uses in his later works. Only once does he speaks of "philosophy" and "metaphysics" (chapter 4, [3]). Thus, in summary, Aquinas identifies the subject of philosophy and theology to be the truth(s) of God but he is primarily interested in how these truths come to be known.

2.3 The comparison as presented in the *Summa theologiae*

Aquinas raises the issue in the first objection of the first article. He asks the question whether sacred doctrine is necessary for the instruction of human beings. Such a question implies the possibility of doubt, for there already exists a science that encompasses the whole realm of human knowledge, namely, the disciplines comprising philosophy. The case for philosophy is continued in the second objection:

> Besides, we can be educated only about what is real; for nothing can be known for certain save what is true, and what is true is identical with what really is. Yet the philosophical sciences deal with all parts of reality, even with God; hence Aristotle refers to one department of philosophy as theology or the divine sciences. That being the case, no need arises from another kind of education to be admitted or entertained.[37]

There appear to be two passages to which Aquinas is referring in Aristotle's *Metaphysics*. The first concerns the characteristics of the scientific pursuit of wisdom (philosophy). Aristotle writes:

> For the most divine science is also most honourable; and this science alone must be, in two ways, most divine. For the science which it would be most meet for God to have is a divine science, and so is any science that deals with divine objects; and this science alone has both these qualities; for (1) God is thought to be among the causes of all things and to be a first principle, and (2) such a science either God alone can have, or God above all oth-

---

36 Ibid., chs. 4 [1] and 9 [1–2].
37 *ST* I 1.1, ad 2.

ers. All the sciences, indeed, are more necessary than this, but none is better.[38]

Thus, for Aristotle, the pursuit of wisdom (philosophy) is a theology, for it is necessarily concerned with divine things. The reason for this is that philosophy is the science of first causes and principles, and deity is, in fact, supreme cause and principle. Consequently, the pursuit of first causes and principles must have deity as its subject; it must then be a theology. The second passage concerns the comparison of the three theoretical sciences. Aristotle writes:

> That physics, then, is a theoretical science, is plain from these considerations. Mathematics also, however, is theoretical; but whether its objects are immovable and separable from matter, is not at present clear; still, it is clear that *some* mathematical theorems *consider* them *qua* immovable and *qua* separable from matter. But if there is something which is eternal and immovable and separable, clearly the knowledge of it belongs to a theoretical science—not, however, to physics (for physics deals with certain movable things) not to mathematics, but to a science prior to both. For physics deals with things which exist separately but are not immovable, and some parts of mathematics deal with things which both exist separately and are immovable. Now all causes must be eternal, but especially these; for they are the causes that operate on so much of the divine as appears to us [i.e., produce the movements of the heavenly bodies (editor's addition)]. There must, then, be three theoretical philosophies, mathematics, physics, and what we may call theology, since it is obvious that if the divine is present anywhere, it is present in things of this sort. And the highest science must deal with the highest genus. Thus, while the theoretical sciences are more to be desired than the other sciences, this is more to be desired than the other theoretical sciences.[39]

Thus, the subject of physics is a sensible material substance considered as sensible and as having a principle of movement. The subject of mathematics is a sensible substance considered as immobile. A higher science with respect to physics and mathematics concerns itself with the immobile, eternal, and separated substance, which is transcendent. Since it is the highest of the theoretical sciences, it is given the names "first philosophy" and "metaphysics" elsewhere in the work. Here it is termed "theology." As such, it not only studies the causes and principles of being, it studies the first cause and principle of being.

---

38 Aristotle, *Metaph.*, I, ch. 2, 983a6–10.
39 Ibid., VI, ch. 1, 1026a6–23; cf. for a parallel passage: XI, ch. 7, 1064a28–1064b5.

According to Aristotle, God is known as cause, as first principle, because being as being is the first and most universal effect of God. (Theology includes the science of being as being [first philosophy, metaphysics] because the science of the cause includes [by unity of consecution] that of its effects.[40]) The knowledge of God derived in this philosophical manner, however, is not totally sufficient for Aquinas because God has destined humanity for an end beyond the grasp of reason. It is expedient that the divine truths surpassing reason should be given to humanity through divine revelation.[41] Besides the philosophical disciplines, a further doctrine is then needed, namely, Scripture. As he says in the *sed contra*, "the second epistle to Timothy says, *All Scripture inspired of God is profitable to teach, to reprove, to correct, to instruct in righteousness.* Divinely inspired Scripture, however, is no part of the branches of philosophy traced by reasoning. Accordingly, it is expedient to have another body of sure knowledge inspired by God."[42] In response to the second objection, Aquinas states that the theology included in sacred doctrine differs in kind from the theology which is part of philosophy. While both can be called divine from the viewpoint of subject, they differ with regard to source and procedure. Just as sciences are differentiated by differing ways of knowing things (e.g., astronomers prove the earth round by means of mathematics and physicists by means of matter itself), so something known by natural reason may also be known by light of divine revelation. Both theologies treat the highest cause, the one on the basis of divine inspiration from God, the other through aspects found in its effects.

2.4 The comparison as presented in the *Commentary on the Metaphysics*

Aquinas deals with the subject of sacred doctrine in comparison with the subject of the philosophical disciplines for a fourth time in his *Commentary on the Metaphysics of Aristotle.* He deals with this issue immediately in the prologue. He first establishes the need for a single

40 Étienne Gilson, *Elements of Christian Philosophy* (Garden City, New York: Doubleday, 1960), 284.
41 *ST* I 1.1, resp.
42 Ibid., I 1.1, sed contra.

ruling science on the grounds that whenever many things are ordered to one end, one must be the ordering element, and the others must be ordered. The science which is most fit to rule and to order will be the most intellectual of the sciences, for to order and to rule is a function of the intellect. Thus, this science is rightfully called "wisdom."

Wisdom concerns itself with the most intelligible things, of which there are three: a) first causes, for they are the sources of intellectual certitude; b) universals, for the intellect comprehends them rather than particulars perceived through the senses; and c) separated substances, for these substances have intellective power by virtue of being free from matter. This science deals then with God and the intellectual substances (which are necessarily the most intellectual since they are totally separated from matter) as well as those things in whose concept matter is not necessarily included such as the concept of being as being.[43]

All three of these considerations are assigned to one and the same science and not to different sciences. Scientific knowledge is precisely knowledge of the cause of a particular subject. In this case, the cause of being as being, of universal or common being (*ens commune*), must be the highest and first cause which has been identified as God. All belong then to the same one science.[44]

Of the three classes of things under discussion (namely, God, the intellectual substances, and being as being), the subject of metaphysics is only one, being as being. Aquinas explains why this is so:

> For the subject of a science is the genus whose causes and properties we seek, and not the causes themselves of the particular genus studied, because a knowledge of the causes of some genus is the goal to which the investigation of a science attains. Now although the subject of this science is being in general, the whole of it is predicated of those things which are separate from matter both in their intelligible constitution and in being (*esse*). For it is not only those things which can never exist in matter which are said to be separate from matter in their intelligible constitution and in being, such as God and the intellectual substances, but also those things which can exist without matter, such as being in general. This could not be the case, however, if their being depended on matter.[45]

In other words, the goal of this science concerning the single subject *ens commune* is knowledge of being's properties. This is achieved

---

43 *Super Metaph.*, prol.
44 Ibid.
45 Ibid.

through knowledge of the first and highest causes of *all* being and not the causes of a *particular* being. However, this "general" knowledge is derived from the compilation of knowledge concerning those particular things which are separated from matter by *esse* (God and intellectual substances) and *ratio* (being as being). The subject is *ens commune* not God, for God is not common being. Rather, God is a concern of metaphysics as the cause of its subject.

Aquinas concludes the prologue by mentioning the three names of this single ruling science or wisdom:

> Therefore in accordance with the three classes of objects mentioned above from which this science derives its perfection, three names arise. It is called *divine science* or *theology* inasmuch as it considers the aforementioned substances [i.e., God and the intellectual substances]. It is called *metaphysics* inasmuch as it considers being and the attributes which naturally accompany being (for things which transcend the physical order are discovered by the process of analysis, as the more common are discovered after the less common). And it is called *first philosophy* inasmuch as it considers the first causes of things. Therefore it is evident what the subject of this science is, and how it is related to the other sciences, and by what names it is designated.[46]

Based on this brief summary of Aquinas' prologue, three general observations can be made. First, Aquinas follows Aristotle very closely here, in that first philosophy or metaphysics is the highest perfection of human intellect. In similarity with Aristotle's "most universal knowledge,"[47] wisdom, for Aquinas, is knowledge of all the intrinsic causes of being derived from the concept of *ens commune*. God then is a consideration of the philosophical sciences only insofar as He is the universal and first cause of being.

Second, in the prologue there is no development similar to that presented in the *Summa theologiae* where "natural theology" is compared to "supernatural theology" with differing sources (in this case, Scripture) and procedures (divine revelation). This prologue is strictly philosophical and does not move into the area of sacred doctrine. Thus, it is simply assumed that the knowledge arrived at by natural theology is so through the use of natural reason alone. There is no contrast made between the procedure or methodology of natural the-

---
46 Ibid.
47 Cf. Aristotle, *Metaph.*, I, ch. 1–2.

ology and that of supernatural theology (reason guided by divine revelation).

Third, Aquinas follows Aristotle by holding that the subject of this science deals with immaterial, immobile, and separated substance.[48] He then augments this position by stating that God indeed is the cause of such a substance due to His constitution as intellectual. God and the intellectual substances are separated from matter by their intelligible constitution and in their being. This emphasis on intellection is more explicit in Aquinas than in Aristotle. Thus, it may be said that the prologue provides a further articulation concerning the subject of the philosophical disciplines as *ens commune* with God as its cause. However, the prologue does not provide an explicit understanding of the subject of supernatural theology except by discussing the subject of the philosophical discipline.[49]

Now attention will be focused on two passages in Aristotle's *Metaphysics* where he deals explicitly with the subject of the philosophical disciplines as divine. To quote the passage again, but in its wider context:

> Hence also the possession of it might be justly regarded as beyond human power; for in many ways human nature is in bondage, so that according to Simonides 'God alone can have this privilege,' and it is unfitting that man should not be content to seek the knowledge that is suited to him. If, then, there is something in what the poets say, and jealously is natural to the divine power, it would probably occur in this case above all, and all who excelled in this knowledge would be unfortunate. But the divine power can not be jealous (nay, according to the proverb, 'bards tell many a lie'), nor should any other science be thought more honourable than one of this sort. For the most divine science is also most honourable; and this science alone must be, in two ways, most divine. For the science which it would be most meet for God to have is a divine science, and so is any science that deals

---

48 Cf. Aristotle, *Metaph.* VI, ch. 1.

49 It should be noted that Aquinas' use of the term *subjectum* here is consistent with its use in the *Summa theologiae*, as explained above. When the term "object" is used in many English translations, it is the rendering of the Latin term *praedictum* and not *objectum*. From the context, "object" is not the best translation if one understands object in the sense defined above. Rather, "essential predicate," that predicate which expresses something essential to the subject (such as God, the intellectual substances, and being in general), seems to be more precise. Cf. Roy J. Deferrari and M. Inviolata Barry, *A Lexicon of St. Thomas Aquinas based on the Summa Theologica*, with the technical collaboration of Ignatius McGuinness (Washington, D.C.: Catholic University of America Press, 1948), 871.

with divine objects; and this science alone has both these qualities; for (1) God is thought to be among the causes of all things and to be a first principle, and (2) such a science either God alone can have, or God above all others. All the sciences, indeed, are more necessary than this, but none is better.[50]

In his commentary on this passage, the science with which Aquinas is concerned is the science of Aristotle's concern, namely, metaphysics or natural theology. Aquinas deals only with this theology and does not venture into supernatural or revealed theology as he did earlier in the *Summa theologiae*. In recognizing the context of Aristotle's discussion (i.e., that metaphysics is: 1] not for any practical end but for its own sake; 2] truly free; 3] divine more than human), Aquinas simply expounds on the two ways in which this science may be called divine. He says:

> The minor premise is proved in this way: a science is said to be divine in two ways, and only this science is said to be divine in both ways. First, the science which God has is said to be divine; and second, the science which is about divine matters is said to be divine. But it is evident that only this science meets both of these requirements, because since this science is about first causes and principle, it must be about God; for God is understood in this way by all inasmuch as He is one of the causes and a principle of things. Again, such a science which is about God and first causes, either God alone has or, if not He alone, at least He has it in the highest degree. Indeed, He alone has it in a perfectly comprehensive way. And He has it in the highest degree inasmuch as it is also had by men in their own way, although it is not had by them as a human possession, but as something borrowed from Him.[51]

When speaking about the subject of sacred doctrine, subject is usually understood as that about which something is said (Aquinas' second way). Thus, the subject of metaphysics is "divine matters," those things which are about God. The source and procedure of this science is on a natural level, and Aquinas leaves it there. As stated above, he does not compare this natural theology to supernatural theology.

It is interesting to recognize, however, that Aquinas appears more intrigued by the first way in which metaphysics is divine, for he returns to it at the end of the paragraph. This science is divine because it properly belongs to God. He possesses this science in a perfectly

---

50 Aristotle, *Metaph.*, I, ch. 2.
51 *Super Metaph.*, I, lect. 3, comm. 64.

comprehensive way, and humanity "borrows" it from Him. It is not had by them as "a human possession" but they do achieve it "in their own way" (i.e., naturally). If one reads no further, this statement could be problematic especially if read in light of what was said earlier in the *Summa theologiae*. There, natural theology could be considered a human possession, for humanity has the capability to acquire knowledge of God through the use of natural reason alone. Supernatural theology, on the other hand, could be more rightfully considered not to be a human possession since it is achieved through divine revelation. The answer comes, however, if one reads further. This science is not a human possession in the sense "that all other sciences are more necessary than this science for use in practical life, for these sciences are sought least of all for themselves."[52]

In conclusion, when metaphysics is spoken of as divine, one must make a distinction, as Aristotle and Aquinas do, between what is usually referred to as the subject (that which a science considers; in this case, divine matters) and the science which God has and in which humanity participates on a most honorable level.

The second passage in Aristotle's *Metaphysics* where he deals with the subject of the philosophical disciplines as divine is the passage that distinguishes theology from physics and mathematics. To quote the passage:

> But if there is something which is eternal and immovable and separable, clearly the knowledge of it belongs to a theoretical science—not, however, to physics (for physics deals with certain movable things) nor to mathematics, but to a science prior to both. For physics deals with things which exist separately but are not immovable, and some parts of mathematics deal with things which are immovable but presumably do not exist separately, but as embodied in matter: while the first science deals with things which both exist separately and are immovable. Now all causes must be eternal, but especially these; for they are the causes that operate on so much of the divine as appears to us. There must, then, be three theoretical philosophies, mathematics, physics, and what we may call theology, since it is obvious that if the divine is present anywhere, it is present in things of this sort. And the highest [most honorable] science must deal with the highest [most honorable] genus.[53]

In his commentary on this passage, Aquinas explicates in more detail why this science is called theology. He writes:

---

52 Ibid., I, lect. 3, comm. 65.
53 Aristotle, *Metaph.*, VI, ch. 1, 1026a15–21.

[Aristotle] concludes that there are three parts of theoretical philosophy: mathematics, the philosophy of nature, and theology, which is first philosophy. Second, he gives two reasons why this science is called theology. The first of these is that "it is obvious that if the divine exists anywhere," i.e., if something divine exists in any class of things, it exists in such a nature, namely, in the class of being which is immobile and separate from matter, which this science studies.

He gives the second reason why this science is called theology; and the reason is this: the most honorable science deals with the most honorable class of beings, and this is the one in which divine beings are contained. Therefore, since this science is the most honorable of the sciences because it is the most honorable of the theoretical sciences, as was shown before—and these are more honorable than the practical sciences, as was stated in Book I—it is evident that this science deals with divine beings; and therefore it is called theology inasmuch as it is a discourse about divine beings.[54]

In other words, this science is called theology because: 1) if the divine exists, it does so under the classification of immobile and immaterial being which is the subject of this science; 2) it deals with the most honorable classification of being and divine beings fall under this classification. However, for Aquinas divine being is among the immobile and immaterial beings which are the proper subject of this science. The subject is then both universally of being as being and determinately of separable and immobile beings. For he says:

...if there is no substance other than those which exist in the way that natural substances do, with which the philosophy of nature deals, the philosophy of nature will be the first science. But if there is some immobile substance, this will be prior to natural substance; and therefore the philosophy of nature, which considers this kind of substance, will be first philosophy. And since it is first, it will be universal; and it will be its function to study being as being, both what being is and what the attributes are which belong to being as being. For the science of the primary kind of being and that of being in general are the same, as has been stated at the beginning of Book IV.[55]

In conclusion, Aquinas, in his commentary on the pertinent passages of Aristotle's *Metaphysics*, does not deviate from Aristotle's understanding that God is related to the subject of metaphysics (*ens commune*) only as an immobile, immaterial, and separable being Who is the highest cause and principle of being. In this discipline He is not the sole subject as He is in supernatural theology. Aquinas does not

---

54 *Super Metaph.*, VI, lect. 1, 1167–68.
55 Ibid., VI, lect. 1, 1170.

attempt to make this distinction except insofar as one may infer it from his brief discussion of the fact that God possesses the science of metaphysics perfectly, and humanity possesses it as "something borrowed from Him," thus possibly implying divine revelation which is proper to supernatural theology.[56]

2.5 Section summary

To summarize this section regarding the subject of philosophy and theology and their interrelationship, several points may be made. First, all four works state that the grounds for the relationship between the two disciplines is that they both seek the highest cause, the first principle of being. This point is fundamental to Aquinas' thought, and it is developed in each of the four works with a different but related emphasis. In his *Commentary on the Sentences*, one pursues this highest cause in order to acquire perfection. Philosophy is capable of some knowledge of God, but a more complete knowledge must proceed from revealed principles of faith. In the *Summa contra gentiles*, Aquinas relates this highest cause to truth. Continuing in the same manner, knowledge of truth is acquired through both natural and supernatural means. He does, however, elaborate on how this truth is methodologically acquired by commenting on how different gradations of intellects are able or not able to comprehend something by perceiving or not perceiving the very substance of that being. In the *Summa theologiae*, Aquinas relies more explicitly on Aristotle and, consequently again, the fundamental concern is the cause of all things, the first principle. God, as the supreme cause and principle, is contrasted in this work, however, with sensible material substance; sensible immaterial substance; and immaterial, immobile, eternal, and sensible substances. Methodologically, there is no major advancement at this point except in that Scripture and its role in divine revelation is spoken of explicitly. Finally in the *Commentary on the Metaphysics*, Aquinas pursues wisdom so as to order the universe. Wisdom is knowledge of all the intrinsic causes of being derived from the concept of *ens commune*. God is considered a subject of philosophy, then, only insofar as He is the universal and first cause of being. The subject of philosophy deals with immaterial, immobile, and separated sub-

---

56 Ibid., I, lect. 3, 64.

stances. God is such a substance due to His intellection. Thus, there is some development with regard to the subject of philosophy and theology; however, in this work, the method in which the subject of each discipline is known does not develop beyond the development achieved in the three earlier works. Rather, it is remarkably more silent on how these subjects are indeed known.

Second, all four works cite Aristotle as an authority by quoting either his *Nicomachean Ethics* or his *Metaphysics*. Aquinas accepts his "natural theology" approach and then augments it with an explanation of the role of divine revelation (Scripture).

Third, Aquinas' use of terms to distinguish and describe philosophy and theology between the four works is varied. His terms for "theology" are rather imprecise in the *Commentary on the Sentences* and the *Summa contra gentiles* (terms such as: "sacred wisdom," "principles of faith," "suppositions of faith," "divine doctrines," "sciences,"and "theology"). In the *Summa theologiae*, these terms, for the most part, drop out and are replaced with a precise use of terms like "sacred doctrine" (which is used in the vast majority of cases) and "theology" (used much less). His terms for "philosophy" are not so varied (consisting of: "first philosophy," "philosophical sciences," "science of truth," and "pursuit of wisdom"). There is no major indication of a pattern of use between the four works.

3 The Identification of the Subject of Sacred Doctrine

3.1 God as the subject of sacred doctrine

In dealing with the subject of sacred doctrine, thus far we have seen that, even though God and separated substances are complete natures as well as principles of being, they are not *per se* the subjects of metaphysics rather *ens commune* is. They are known only as principles within metaphysics. What they are in themselves exceeds human comprehension, not because they lack intelligibility but because they are so full of intelligibility that the human intellect is incapable of comprehension.[57]

God, then, insofar as He is a principle of being or a complete nature in himself, can not be directly known by the human intellect. He is known naturally only through the effects of which He is the principle and cause. It is for this reason that He is considered by metaphysics which deals with the subject of being as being and the principles that pertain to all beings. He may be known, however, if the intellect is "enlightened" by another light which enables the mind to know such principles. If this is the case, as it is with divine revelation and faith, then another science is possible, namely, sacred doctrine. Aquinas explains:

> There is, however, another way of knowing beings of this sort, not as their effects reveal them but as they reveal themselves. The Apostle mentions this way in his *First Epistle to the Corinthians*: "So the things also that are of God no man knoweth, but the Spirit of God. Now we have received not the spirit of this world, but the Spirit that is of God, that we may understand." And again: "But to us God hath revealed them by His Spirit." In this way we know divine things as they subsist in themselves and not only in so far as they are principles of things.
>
> Thus theology or divine science is of two kinds. There is one theology in which we treat of divine things, not as the subject of the science but as the principles of the subject, and this is the sort of theology pursued by the philosophers and which is also called metaphysics. There is another theology,

---

57 Aquinas elaborates on this point: "Even though such first principles are most knowable in themselves, our intellect stands to them as the eye of an owl to the light of the sun, as the *Metaphysics* says; and so we can come to them by the light of natural reason only in so far as we are led to them by their effects. And this is the way the philosophers arrived at them, as is clear from the *Epistle to the Romans*: 'The invisible things of God...are clearly seen, being understood by the things that are made.' So, too, the philosophers study divine things of this sort only insofar as they are the principles of all things; and therefore they are dealt with in that science which studies what is common to all beings, which has as its subject being as being. And the philosophers call this science divine science (*The Division and Methods of the Sciences: Questions V and VI of his Commentary on the De Trinitate*, fourth revised ed., edited by Armand Maurer [Toronto: Pontifical Institute of Medieval Studies, 1953], q. 5, art. 4). (Hereafter, referred to as *Expos. super De Trin.*) He also explains elsewhere: "And certain things which exist of themselves are principles; and these, because they are immaterial, pertain to intelligible knowledge, even though they surpass the comprehension of our intellect" (*Super Metaph.*, XI, lect. 2, 2189).

however, which studies divine things for their own sakes as the subject of
the science; and this is the theology taught in Sacred Scripture.[58]

Thus, the subject of sacred doctrine is God, known supernaturally
through revelation, as He subsists in Himself and not merely as a
principle of being. God, known naturally through reason as a principle of being, is one of many "subjects" of metaphysics.

3.2 Other possible subjects of sacred doctrine

Aquinas first deals with the subject of sacred doctrine, as we have
seen, in his *Commentary on the Sentences*. It is here (prol. q. 1, art. 4)
that he expresses his awareness of other subjects proposed by various
theologians within the tradition. Boethius held that a simple form
(*simplex forma*) is not able to be a subject.[59] God is such a form; therefore, He is not able to be the subject. Hugh of St. Victor held that the
subject should be the works of restoration (*opera restaurantionis*).[60] He
also recognizes Peter Lombard (who was relying on Augustine) by
making a reference to *res et signa*.[61] For Lombard initially, the subject
is "reality and its symbols" or signs. The reference in the "solution," a
few lines later, to the Whole Christ (*totus Christus*), the head and
members (the Mystical Body) acknowledges the position of Robert of
Melun, Robert Grosseteste, and an expanded Peter Lombard.[62] Aquinas makes reference to these opinions again, with the exception of
Boethius', in the *Summa theologiae* (I 1.7, resp.) without mentioning
theologians in particular.

Aquinas most likely was also aware of his mentor's position on
the issue, but he does not mention it explicitly. In his *Commentary on
the Sentences*, Albert the Great says that in general the subject of theology is, as Peter Lombard taught, *res et signa*. Yet, more specifically,
"The special subject is said to be that which is the noblest of all the
topics treated in a science, and hence the subject matter of this science
is God, from whom it receives its name. However, the subject matter

---

58 *Expos. super De Trin.*, q. 5, art. 4.
59 *De Trinitate*, bk. I, ch. II, col. 1250, t. II.
60 *De sacramentis*, bk. I, part I, cap. III, col. 183, t. I; bk. 1, prol. 2.
61 *In I Sent.*, div. text.; d. 1, a. 1 and *De doctrina christiana*, I, 2.
62 *Sententiae*, bk. 1, par. 1, and bk. 2, par. 1; *Hexameron* and *Summa universae theolo-
    giae*, I. lib. I, q. 1, a. 3; *I Sent.*, d. 1, c. 4, respectively.

is not only God as absolutely considered, but also as He is alpha and omega, the beginning and the end."[63] In his *Summa theologiae*, Albert likewise recognizes the *res et signa* and the other three positions (the *opera restaurationis, totus Christus,* and God) as all valid but each according to its own perspective. He writes:

> ...if the subject matter of theology is assigned in accord with the main end of this science and in terms of the truth that has to be known before anything else in it can be treated, God is the subject matter of theology, which also receives its name from Him.
>
> But if subject matter is understood in a second way, as the object of demonstrations and determinations, Christ and the Church are the subject, or the incarnate Word with all the sacraments He administers in the Church. And this is the same as saying that the works of redemption are the subject: for theology shows that these flow from the head and are received in the Church.[64]

Thus, God is the primary subject of theology while Christ is the secondary subject. God is the ultimate subject to which everything in theology is referred; Christ is the integral subject in which everything is recapitulated.[65]

Aquinas adopts a similar position in his *Summa theologiae* (I 1.7) as he did in his *Commentary* (prol. art. 4). Everything discussed in sacred doctrine is discussed *sub ratione Dei*, either because everything pertains to God Himself or is related to Him as principle and end. Thus, the subject of this science is God. Moreover, all the articles of faith pertain directly to God, but these articles are themselves principles of sacred doctrine; therefore, God is the subject of sacred doctrine.

In recognizing that others have proposed other possible subjects, Aquinas does not deny their worth. However, these subjects have been proposed by theologians who were attending to *what* is treated in this science rather than to the aspect *under which* it is treated, namely, *sub ratione Dei*. All of these other worthy subjects relate to God Himself as their principle and end. Even a Christocentric theology is ultimately about God, for "Christ as man is our way of going to

---

63 d. 1, art. 2; as quoted in Emile Mersch, *The Theology of the Mystical Body*, translated by Cyril Vollert (St. Louis: B. Herder, 1951), 64–65.

64 I, tract. 1, q. 3, membr. 1; as quoted in Mersch, 65.

65 *ST* I-II prol.

God."[66] Thus, it may be concluded that sacred doctrine is for Aquinas theocentric. This character is precisely what distinguishes sacred doctrine from any other science. Only sacred doctrine can have God as its proper subject because it is based on revelation and the articles of faith, which are about God, while the best any other human science can do is know God only as the principle or the cause of its subject, never God as its subject.[67]

3.3 The three divisions of *Summa theologiae* I 1 and how article seven relates to them

The primary point of interest in this discussion regarding Aquinas' *prius* or prime analogate of sacred doctrine has been article seven of the *Summa's* first question. This article concerns the subject of sacred doctrine, that which makes sacred doctrine specific in contradistinction to those elements that provide for its generic definition (articles two through six). These articles (two through seven) constitute the second division of the first question; namely, the nature or *quid sit* of the reality being studied. Besides this consideration, the typical scholastic procedure for the study of a particular entity at this time was to concern oneself with the necessity and existence of the entity (the *an sit*) and the method or modality (*de modo*) of that entity. This section of the work will analyze how these divisions of the first question articulate Aquinas' understanding of sacred doctrine and (more importantly) its subject (the *subjectum*).

---

66 Ibid. It is interesting to note, however, that in an isolated case of his *Commentary on the Psalms*, Aquinas notes, "whereas the individual books of the canonical Scriptures have special subject matters, this book treats of the whole of theology." Here Aquinas has in mind the subject of theology. He continues, "Its subject matter is universal, for it includes everything. And since this pertains to Christ, 'because in Him it hath well pleased the Father that all fullness should dwell' (Col. 1:19), the subject matter of this book is Christ and His members" (*Prol.*; as quoted in Mersch, 68).

67 Oliva Blanchette, "Philosophy and Theology in Aquinas: On Being a Disciple in Our Day," *Science et esprit* 28, (Janvier-Avril 1976): 44.

3.3.1 The arrangement of the material

In his *Commentary on the Sentences*, Aquinas arranged his articles concerning the existence and nature of sacred doctrine so that they emulated the standard scholastic procedure. The procedure is as follows:

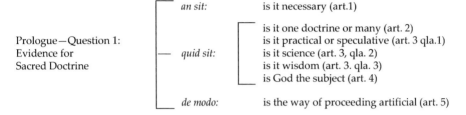

	an sit:	is it necessary (art.1)
Prologue—Question 1: Evidence for Sacred Doctrine	*quid sit:*	is it one doctrine or many (art. 2) is it practical or speculative (art. 3 qla.1) is it science (art. 3, qla. 2) is it wisdom (art. 3. qla. 3) is God the subject (art. 4)
	de modo:	is the way of proceeding artificial (art. 5)

Such an arrangement of the articles is filled with logical deficiencies. James Weisheipl states it succinctly when he writes:

> One can not ask whether *sacra doctrina* is one or many until some logical genus has been established for it, such as "science." Similarly, the question of whether it is practical or speculative does not arise until we know that it is a science of some sort, of a kind that can be divided into practical or speculative. Further, one can not ask whether this doctrine is wisdom until it is compared with all other sciences. Finally, Thomas's consideration of its modality is too narrow, and the "artificiality" of its method is extrinsic to the doctrine. Moreover, Thomas seems to consider *sacra doctrina* in this work as both theology in the mind of the theologian and as revealed doctrine in the heart of the believer.[68]

Aquinas may have recognized these deficiencies for he rearranges the articles more logically in the *Summa theologiae*. The procedure is as follows:

---

68 James A. Weisheipl, "The Meaning of *Sacra doctrina* in *Summa Theologiae* I, q.1," *Thomist* 38 (January 1974): 65.

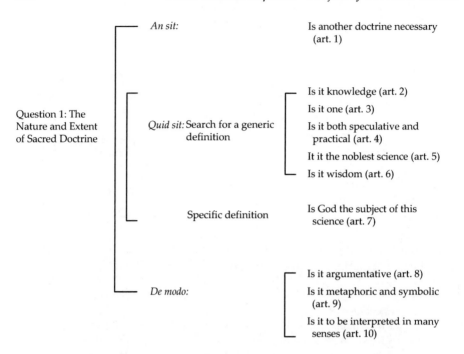

Thus, once it is established that the reality being studied exists necessarily, one may then inquire into its nature. This is done by first seeking a generic definition of the reality and then by narrowing it down to its more specific genus and difference. Finally, the same reality must be examined in regard to its modality, for every science has a modality proper to itself.

3.3.2 The first article

From the prologue of the *Summa theologiae*, we learn of a presupposition that underlies the first article and most of the entire first question. Aquinas' intention in writing this *summa* is to overcome the obstacles that stand in the way of the discipline's beginners (i.e., the swarm of pointless questions, articles, and arguments; essential information is given according to the requirements of textual commentary or academic debates and not to a sound pedagogical order dictated by the discipline; repetitiousness has bred tedium and confusion in the minds of beginning students). The first and last obstacles are commonplace. What is of interest is the second. Aquinas is concerned with leading others to science (*ad sciendum*) over and above an exposition of books or engagement in academic debates. Here is where the presupposition enters. Leading others to science is not in opposition to faith. Rather, faith is an integral part of the enterprise. It is not just faith in divine revelation as such but faith in the entire learning process. In order to learn, to pass from not knowing to knowing, a person must rely on the teacher who is more advanced than the student. Until students are able to know for themselves, they will have to rely in faith on the teacher in order to learn. Faith is operative on the level of human learning.

Moving into the first article, faith is also operative on the level of divine revelation. Why is it that the philosophical disciplines are not sufficient and sacred doctrine is necessary? Sacred doctrine is necessary because human beings are destined by God for an end which exceeds their natural abilities. Thus, if human beings are to direct their actions to this end, they need to be made aware of the truths necessary for this end. These truths must then be revealed. Moreover, even in those things that do not exceed natural human capacity (e.g., human beings can arrive at a natural knowledge that God does indeed exist), truth must be revealed because without it, knowing that end would be something that only a few could attain and only after much time and many errors. Besides the philosophical disciplines which carry on their inquiry by way of human reason, another discipline is necessary, namely sacred doctrine which proceeds by way of revelation. Here Aquinas is not so much arguing for the necessity of a knowledge of divine truths for salvation as he is for the necessity of these divine truths being made known through revelation since it is impossible for all to know them except by being instructed in them through revelation. This instruction in divine truths is called "sacred doctrine."[69] And in the end, faith is present in two ways: on the level of human learning as a kind of trust and on the level of divine revelation as a kind of supernatural enlightenment.

In arriving at this point, it is interesting to note more explicitly the elements that constitute it. In the *responsio*, Aquinas lists three reasons why it is necessary that there be a knowledge revealed by God besides the philosophical science pursued by human reasoning. It was necessary: 1) that divine truths which exceed reason be made known

---

69 Gerald Van Ackeren, *Sacra doctrina* (Rome: Officium Libri Catholici, 1952), 80–81.

to him through divine revelation (*quod ei nota fierent quaedam per reve-lationem divinam quae rationem humanam excedunt*); 2) that human be-ings be taught divine truths through divine revelation (*quod de divinis per divinam revelationem instruantur*); 3) that sacred doctrine be learned through divine revelation (*sacram doctrinam per revelationem haberi*). In the first two reasons, that which is necessary is expressed by the verbs *notum facere* and *instruere*. These verbs connote action. Humanity must receive this knowledge; they must be instructed. *Sacra doctrina* then signifies the action of making known, of instructing human beings in divine things through a kind of natural "faith" or trust in the learning process and a supernatural "faith" on the level of divine revelation. *Sacra doctrina* is not identical with revelation; rather, revelation is the means by which *sacra doctrina* operates. The subject of this *sacra doc-trina* is, then, God and that which is *sub ratione Dei*.

For ease of discussion, the term *sacra doctrina*, has been translated earlier as "theology" and the meaning of the two terms was held as synonymous. A careful reading of the first article and the remaining articles of this first question indicates a demand for more precision in translation and understanding. Aquinas uses the term *sacra doctrina* eighty times in this question compared to only four times for the term *theologia*. The first reference, article one, objection one, states that in the *Metaphysics,* Aristotle called the knowledge of God gained through philosophy, "theology" or "divine science" (which is also called "natural theology").[70] Aquinas expands upon this point further in his reply to the objection (the second reference) by stating that the-ology, included in sacred doctrine, differs in kind (*secundum genus*) from the theology which is part of philosophy. The final reference oc-curs in the *sed contra* of article seven. Here Aquinas, in discussing the etymology of the term, calls *sacra doctrina* "*theologia*" only because it is indeed discourse about God (*sermo de Deo*). However, in all these ref-erences, the discussion revolves around the nature of *sacra doctrina* in contrast to the nature of *theologia*. Consequently, the terms *sacra doc-trina* and *theologia* are not held to be synonymous in Aquinas' mind.

The term *theologia* (with its reference to discourse about God), then, is broader in meaning than *sacra doctrina*. Thus far, *sacra doctrina* has been defined as revealed.[71] It has been shown above that *sacra*

---

70   This issue has been treated above in the discussion surrounding Aquinas' *Com-mentary on the Metaphysics* and his *Commentary on Boethius's De Trinitate*, qq. 5–6.

71   Cf. *In I Sent.*, prol., q. 1, a. 1 and 2; *SCG* I chs. 2 and 3; *ST* I 1.1.

doctrina consists of truths which human beings can not arrive at themselves by merely philosophical argumentation. Rather, they must be revealed by God Himself (Who is the *subjectum* rather than the *objectum*) and accepted by human beings in faith so that they may be saved. These truths are revealed because human beings have a supernatural end. Thus, it follows that the way to that end must be revealed. Aquinas, then, is not trying to demonstrate the existence of revealed truths from rational argumentation (this is more properly ascribed to theology). Rather, he assumes that from the truth that human beings have a supernatural end, it can be demonstrated that revealed truths exist.

3.3.3 The second article

Aquinas holds, as he states in his *Commentary on the Sentences* (prologue, q. 1, art. 1), that *sacra doctrina* is a discipline that proceeds from principles of faith to science and wisdom. Thus, in the second article, Aquinas inquires into *sacra doctrina*, demonstrated to be necessary in article one, as a science. Aquinas developed his understanding of science. "Science" in the strict basic Aristotelian sense is demonstrated knowledge that proceeds from unitary first principles (premises). For Aristotle and Aquinas, understanding the nature of first principles is important, for in this article alone, some form of the phrase *procedere ex principiis* occurs a total of five times. First principles pervade everything that is, and for that reason they are both things and the cognition of a thing. Aquinas accepts this position of Aristotle's as is evident by his commentary on the *Metaphysics*. He writes, "something...is said to be a principle...with reference to a thing's being...or with reference to its coming to be...or with reference to the knowing of it.[72]

Science, then, means to proceed from first principles, from the self-manifestations or revelations (plural in contrast to the single "divine revelation") concerning the subject of inquiry. Consequently, as one proceeds, one comes not only to a demonstrated knowledge but to a knowledge of a thing in its proper cause.[73] It is this causal aspect

---

72 *Super Metaph.*, V, lect. 1, comm. 761.
73 "...we possess scientific knolwedge of a thing only when we know its cause." (Aristotle, *Post. Anal.*, I, ch. 2, 71b30–31); cf. *Metap.*, I, ch. 1.

of which Aquinas is acutely aware in his application of the term "science" to *sacra doctrina*.[74]

One difficulty of such an aspect is expressed in the first objection. Science is knowledge through *per se nota* (self-evident) causes, but none of the causes in divine revelation are *per se nota* since faith is not given to all human beings. Another difficulty is expressed in the second objection. Science, as Aristotle has shown, can not be concerned with individuals as such but only with universals. However, *sacra doctrina* is concerned with salvation history shown in the lives of individuals. Therefore, it is not science.

Aquinas responds by referring to a theory of the subalternation of the sciences which he finds in Aristotle's *Posterior Analytics* (I, ch. 9 and 13) and on which he elaborates in his corresponding *Commentary* (I, lect. 25). Sciences are of two kinds: some are based like arithmetic and geometry on self-evident premises (first principles) known by the innate light of natural intelligence; others are based on premises known by the light of a higher science—for example, optics on geometrical principles. *Sacra doctrina* is of this second kind, for it is based on premises known by the light of a higher science, namely God's own knowledge of Himself which He shares with the blessed in heaven. These premises are the articles of faith revealed by God and taken on faith in the science which God has taught human beings, just as harmony takes on faith the premises which the mathematician teaches (i.e., the revealed article of faith is not known *by* us to be true since we lack a clear understanding of God in Himself. Rather, the article is known *to* God).

Thus, the objections raised are easily met. First, the article of faith, which for human beings is a matter of faith, is directly known to God and the blessed in heaven. Thus, the scientific aspect of *sacra doctrina* is subalternated to the higher knowledge God has of Himself and to the knowledge the blessed in heaven have of Him. *Sacra doctrina* is rightfully called "science," then, for it is founded on divine revelation and, thus, is capable of bestowing causal knowledge (in this case the

74 "Again, if science is the knowledge of a thing through its cause, and if God knows the order of all causes and effects, and thereby knows the proper causes of singulars, as was shown above, it is manifest that in a proper sense there is science in Him. Nevertheless, this is not the science caused by ratiocination [i.e., the process by which one proceeds from the consideration of one thing to another; e.g., syllogistic reasoning], as our science is caused by demonstration." (*SCG*, I ch. 94); cf. *Super Metap.*, I, ch. 1, comm. 35; *Super Post. Anal.*, I, lect. 4.

highest of all causes, God). Second, *sacra doctrina* does concern itself with the individual lives of people, but this is not a primary preoccupation. It does so only in order to provide examples for our own lives and to proclaim the truth of the revelation. Consequently, *sacra doctrina*'s examples and message are indeed universal.

Aquinas' theory of subalternation has influence on his understanding of the subject of theology. This influence is not so evident in the context of the *Summa*, but it is evident in the wider context of his commentaries on Boethius' *De Trinitate* and Lombard's *Sentences*. Even with the assistance of divine revelation, *sacra doctrina* is still a human science in the sense that it is limited to the manner of human knowing. This means that, on the one hand, all human knowledge is gained through sensible objects; for as Aquinas says, "the light of divine Revelation comes to us adapted to our condition. Thus, even though Revelation elevates us to know something of which we should otherwise be ignorant, it does not elevate us to know in any other way than through sensible things."[75]

On the other hand, it is knowledge of a created intellect, which in the state of beatific glory, can know the divine essence, even though it can not completely comprehend it.[76] Yet prior to beatific vision, the same human intellect can not in any way know the essence of an immaterial thing. It is limited to a knowledge that it exists (*an sit*) and a certain confused knowledge of its attributes (technically equivalent to a *quomodo non sit* or *quia* knowledge) ultimately taken from material things.[77] Aquinas explains, "Now knowledge by way of the sensible is inadequate to enable us to know the essences of immaterial substances. So we conclude that we do not know *what* immaterial forms are, but only *that* they are, whether by natural reason based upon created effects or even by Revelation by means of likeness taken from sensible things."[78]

Aquinas draws an analogy comparing this limited science of *sacra doctrina* to a similar situation in human knowledge where a superior science can give a *propter quid* (why) explanation, not exceeding the limits of a created intellect, for something which—otherwise unknown in an inferior science—can be known in a *quia* (that it is such

75 *Expos. super De Trin.*, q. 6, art. 3.
76 Cf. *ST* I 12.1 and 7.
77 Wallace, 39.
78 *Expos. super De Trin.*, q. 6, art. 3, resp.

and so) fashion in that science, provided it accepts on faith principles provided in the superior science.[79] Based on this relationship, Aquinas considers *sacra doctrina* subalternate to the superior science *scientia Dei et beatorum*.

However, in doing so, Aquinas realizes that the subalternation of human sciences is different from the subalternation of a divine science. He explains why he calls the latter "quasi-subalternation" in his *Commentary on the Sentences*:

> One science can be superior to another in two ways: either by reason of subject, as geometry which is concerned with magnitude is superior to optics which is concerned with visual magnitude; or by reason of the manner of knowing, and so theology is inferior to the science which is in God. For we know imperfectly what He knows most perfectly, and just as a subalternated science supposes some things from a superior one, and proceeds from those things as from principles, so theology supposes articles of faith which are infallibly proved in God's science, and believes these, and thus proceeds further to proving those things which follow from the articles. Thus theology is a science quasi-subalternated to divine science, from which it accepts its principles (I, q. 1, prol., a. 3, sol. 2).[80]

The difference between these two types of subalternation, "by reason of subject" and "by reason of the manner of knowing," is of considerable importance and William Wallace, in his work *The Role of Demonstration in Moral Theology*, provides a thorough analysis:

> Optical science, knowing that the rainbow is caused by the reflection and refractions of rays of sunlight through spherical droplets of falling rain, can demonstrate various properties of the bow: for example, that it is always some portion of a circle, that its center is always in a direct line with the sun and the eye of the observer, etc. In these demonstrations, conclusions are taken from the science of geometry: for example, properties of spheres, circles, and lines in various modes of intersection. These are accepted as principles in optical science without question, and are used directly in its proofs. Optical science, however, does not have geometrical lines for its *genus subjectum*, these pertaining to the subject of geometry; rather it considers geometrical lines to which are added an accidental difference—that they are similar to the paths of light rays. Thus its subject is one through addition: it is concerned with the mathematical line *plus* the visibility of a light ray. And because of this composition in its subject, it can use two types of premise in its demonstration: one which is formally mathematical, which applies to the geometrical line, and the other which is formally sensible, which applies to the natural entity—the visible ray and ultimately the rainbow. Therefore, in

---

79   Wallace, 40.
80   Ibid.

the subalternation of optical science to geometry there is subalternation by reason of subject, mathematical form being applied to sensible matter, as well as a corresponding subalternation of speculative principle, insofar as two distinct degrees of abstraction are involved in the judgments of the premises.

Neither of these conditions are found verified in the subalternation of sacred theology to the science of the blessed. The subject of sacred theology is not one through addition, but is exactly the same as that of the science of the blessed: God under the aspect of His divinity. Consequently there is no subalternation of speculative principle: just as the science of the blessed ranges through all of being, without respect to the abstractive differences found in the human speculative sciences, so sacred theology considers all of being, and employs indifferently all types of speculative principles.

The quasi-subalternation of sacred theology, then, is more properly described as a subalternation by reason of the *manner* of knowing "*ratione modi cognoscendi*." Principles which are known to the blessed with the clarity and evidence of vision, *sub lumine gloriae*, are accepted as principles, under the light of faith, in sacred theology. This acceptance and credence of otherwise unknown principles is all that the subalternation of sacred theology has in common with the subalternation of the speculative sciences.[81]

This type of subalternation has influence on the subject of *sacra doctrina*. It neither restricts *sacra doctrina* to *quia* knowledge of divine things nor do the blessed in heaven alone have *propter quid* science, as would be the case if a subalternation by reason of subject were involved. *Sacra doctrina* accepts on faith what is contained in the deposit of revelation, but this does not limit its speculative comprehension of what is revealed. For example, the human intellect is incapable of grasping the quiddity of a separated substance in this life although it can know the essence of God in beatific vision. This means that with regard to the principle subject of *sacra doctrina*, God in Himself, there can be no *propter quid* demonstration in *sacra doctrina*. There are, however, other divine things, not in the order of separated substance, whose quiddities can be sufficiently manifested through the senses and of which *propter quid* science is possible even in this life.[82] Aquinas summarizes:

God is beyond the comprehension of every created intellect, but He is not beyond the uncreated intellect, since in knowing Himself He comprehends Himself. However, He is above the intellect of everyone here on earth as regards knowing *what He is (quid est)*, but not as regards knowing *that He is (an est)*, because they see His essence. Nevertheless divine science is not only

---

81 Ibid., 41.
82 Ibid., 42.

about God. It is concerned with other things as well, which is not beyond
the human intellect even in its present state as regards knowing about them
what they are *(quid est)*.[83]

Thus, the content of divine revelation does not exceed the comprehension of the human intellect such that no *propter quid* demonstration is possible in *sacra doctrina*.[84]

3.3.4 The third article

While it may seem that *sacra doctrina* is not a single unified science
due to the fact that it treats both the Creator and His multitudinous
creation, it is in fact one science. The unifying factor within any science is the formal rational object (*ratio formalis objecti*) and not the material object (as noted above). In this case, the formal object (medium
or method) by which the material object is reached is the fact that
they can be revealed (they are "revealable"; *revelabile*). Everything that
can be divinely revealed shares in the one formal object of this science
and therefore is comprehended as under one science.

   To summarize this article in other words, Aquinas is seeking the
source of unity for this science's task of investigation. Just as in metaphysics "being as being" is the source of unity of all existing things,
so here in *sacra doctrina* the revealed as revealable is the source of
unity of all the revealed (the object). "The revealed" (the subject) consists of God principally and then creatures in relation to Him. (It
should be noted that this article exemplifies the clear distinction between "subject" and "object" in the thought of Aquinas.)

3.3.5 The fourth article

While holding that *sacra doctrina* is primarily a speculative science, it
is indeed both speculative and practical unlike the philosophical disciplines. This is the case because as one, *sacra doctrina* extends to
things which belong to the different philosophical disciplines since it
considers in each the same formality: the fact that they can be known
through divine revelation. *Sacra doctrina* is concerned with all things

---

83   *Expos. super De Trin.*, q. 6, art. 1, sol. 3, ad 2.
84   Wallace, 42–43.

as subject under the formal aspect of revealed. It is, however, concerned mainly with divine things (speculative) and then with human actions (practical) insofar as they direct human beings to perfect eternal knowledge of God.

3.3.6 The fifth article

Aquinas begins to address the relationship between *sacra doctrina* and the other sciences by asking if *sacra doctrina* is more noble than the other sciences. Aquinas presents two objections. The first holds that it is not more noble on grounds that the articles of faith are open to doubt, while the principles of the other sciences can not be doubted since they are *per se nota* principles. Any doubts about the articles of faith arise from the weakness of the human intellect and not from any deficiency in the revelation. The second objection holds that since the lower sciences borrow from the higher sciences, and *sacra doctrina* borrows from philosophy, *sacra doctrina* must therefore be an inferior science. In response, however, the other sciences are to function as handmaids of the divine science. As both speculative and practical, the divine science transcends human sciences under both of these aspects.

As speculative, *sacra doctrina* is more certain than all the other sciences because its certitude comes from the infallible light of divine knowledge. Any doubts about the articles of faith arise from the weakness of the human intellect and not from any deficiency in the revelation.[85] In contrast, the certitude of human speculative science comes from the fallible natural light of human reason. In addition, the subject of *sacra doctrina* is of greater worth than the human sciences because this divine science treats chiefly those things which by their sublimity transcend human reason while the other sciences only consider those things which are within the grasp of reason.

Practical sciences, by their very nature, are to direct one to the final good, the final goal. *Sacra doctrina* is the most noble in this regard,

---

85 This point gives reason to hold that the term *sacra doctrina* should not be translated as "theology" (as argued above) for *sacra doctrina* is certain while theology is hypothethical. Theology is the hypothetical articulation of the faith as revealed. It attempts to take one beyond the revelation as merely given to a not-yet-tried understanding, to a fluid understanding. Theology uses the other human sciences in this exercise of articulation.

because it directs humanity to the highest goal of all, eternal beatitude.

3.3.7 The sixth article

We have seen throughout this question in the *Summa* that the instruction of *sacra doctrina* begins with the imparting of knowledge which is accepted in faith. This faith then leads to science (of which it is the highest) and now in the sixth article Aquinas asks whether it leads even further to wisdom. Aquinas raises this question (as he did in his *Commentary on the Sentences*[86]) after he first established that *sacra doctrina* is indeed a science and after he inquired into the consequential ramifications. Aquinas, though, does deviate in the timing of the question from his next two works: the *Summa contra gentiles* and the *Commentary on Boethius' De trinitate*. In both of these works (I ch. 1 and 2, 1, respectively), wisdom is presented as the general, overarching category under which the question of the relationship between *sacra doctrina* and philosophy had been discussed. There, many of the particulars, such as superiority, have been discussed in terms of wisdom; now these particulars are settled in terms of science and its process. The resorting back in the *Summa* to the earlier structure of the *Commentary on the Sentences* may arise out of a concern for doing what is pedagogically appropriate for beginners who would have more difficulty in handling the notion of wisdom than the more advanced student.[87] This structure, however, does allow one to focus more on the notion that God is the subject of *sacra doctrina* (the nature of the following article), for the process of inquiry is governed by science rather than wisdom. By freeing wisdom from the burdens of process, more emphasis can be placed on the essence of wisdom which has as its ultimate term and resolution the vision of God, the very subject of *sacra doctrina*.

In defining wisdom, Aquinas is dependent upon Aristotle's definition that wisdom is the science of the primary causes and principles, and the ordering to the final end.[88] In this article of the *Summa*, Aqui-

---

86 Cf. outline comparing the *Commentary on the Sentences* (q. 1) with the *Summa theologiae* (I q. 1) presented above.

87 Blanchette, 41–42.

88 Aristotle, *Metaph.*, I, ch. 1.

nas returns to an emphasis that is prevalent in the discussion of wisdom in his commentary on Aristotle's *Metaphysics* (I. lect. 1–3). Here he highlights the fact that this mode of knowledge derives from God Himself and not just from humanity's natural way of knowing. This point is not stressed in the *Summa contra gentiles* (I, ch. 1). Thus, Aquinas' working definition of wisdom in this article may be stated as: that judgment based on knowledge of the highest cause and ordering to the final cause in accordance with a mode that derives from God Himself and not just from humanity's natural way of knowing, which is through creatures. Such a definition, by stressing that *sacra doctrina* essentially treats God viewed as the highest cause—not only so far as He can be known through creatures (*sub ratione Dei*)—but also as He is known to Himself alone and revealed to others, reinforces Aquinas' identification of God and all that relates to Him as the subject of *sacra doctrina*.

Aquinas contests the objections that a doctrine which obtains its principles from elsewhere (i.e., by revelation), that can not prove the principles of other sciences, and that involves rational study and inquiry, deserves not to be called "wisdom." Rather, since this science is derived from God's own wisdom, it does not depend on the principles of the other sciences; it does not seek to prove them but only to judge them according to divine truth. It seeks out its causes through rational inquiry, and it is to be distinguished from the gift of the Holy Spirit, called by the same name, for that gift grasps divine things without inquiry. Thus, *sacra doctrina* is wisdom beyond all human wisdom; not merely in any one order, but absolutely.

3.3.8 The eighth article

Aquinas completes the *quid sit* section of the first question with his explicit treatment of the subject of theology in article seven (which has already been discussed thoroughly). He begins his treatment of the modality section (*de modo*) by asking the question in article eight as to whether or not *sacra doctrina* is argumentative, whether or not it should employ rational inference. On the one hand, it seems not since it is a matter of faith and thus precludes rational argumentation. Likewise, if it advanced arguments, it would do so either from authority or from human reason. Arguments from reason have no merit in matters of faith, because they do not respect its purpose, its end.

Arguments from authority are the weakest form of proof. Rather, for Aquinas, argumentation is used by *sacra doctrina* in two ways. First, it does not prove its premises but argues from one established premise to another just as the other sciences. Second, it uses argumentation to refute those who would resist the faith. If the resistant person admits at least some of the truths of the faith, then the argumentation may proceed either from the authority of Scripture or from another truth of the faith. If the person believes nothing from revelation, all that can be done is to solve the difficulties that inhibit faith, for the contrary of a truth can never be demonstrated. In other words, the *subjectum* must first be accepted under the formality of being revealed (the formal object) in order for argumentation to occur.

3.3.9 The ninth article

In article nine, Aquinas addresses the issue as to whether *sacra doctrina* should use metaphors or symbolic language. The objections hold that such language is more befitting of the least noble of all the sciences (poetry) and not the most noble. Furthermore, this language obscures the truth. In response, Aquinas argues that Scripture uses this language on account of its compatibility to the natural order of humanity. Human beings by nature are sentient beings and thus derive knowledge from bodily sensation. Hence, in Scripture spiritual truths are fittingly taught under metaphors taken from corporality.

Aquinas also presents three more reasons why divine truths should be expounded metaphorically. First, the human mind is better preserved from error, for then it is clear that these expressions are not literal expressions of divine truths. Second, "understatement is more to the point with our present knowledge of God," lest human beings become deceived and think that their language is a clear estimate of Who He indeed is.[89] Third, "thereby divine matters are more effectively screened against those unworthy of them."[90]

---

89 *ST* I 1.9 ad 3.
90 Ibid.

3.3.10 The tenth article

The final article of the question raises the issue of whether or not a word of Sacred Scripture may have several senses. The objections hold that it seems not since many senses would produce confusion and deception and destroy the force of argument which is contrary to Scripture's purpose of articulating truth. Similarly, there is confusion even over what these senses are.

In response, Aquinas argues that Scripture transcends other sciences in that it not only narrates an event but it transmits a mystery as well. On account of this, words not only signify things (as in other sciences), but the things signified by the words also signify something themselves. This first level of signification belongs to the historical or literal sense. The second level of signification, whereby the things signified by the words in turn also signify, presuppose the literal sense and is itself called a spiritual sense. The spiritual sense has a threefold division: the allegorical sense is the sense in which the things of the Old Testament signify those of the New; the moral sense is the sense in which those things done in Christ and in those who prefigured Him are signs of what others should do; the anagogical sense is the sense that refers to things that lie ahead in eternal glory.[91] Since Sacred Scripture is God's word, it is fitting that it should have a spiritual sense to carry one beyond the literal meaning of the text.

In his earlier work *Quaestiones quodlibetales*, Aquinas states that Jesus Christ is the centering point of all four senses.[92] "Even those things which [allegories immanent to the Hebrew scriptures] conceal in truth of the matter [*res*] are ordered to the designation of Christ, as shadow to truth."[93] The passage is even more explicit in relating each of the three spiritual senses to Christ. It states:

> The allegorical sense pertains to Christ not only as regards the head, but also as regards the members....But the moral sense pertains to the members of Christ as agents [*proprios*] of their own acts, and not according as they are considered members....So the allegorical sense pertains to Christ as he is

---

91 Keefe relates the allegorical, moral, and anagogical senses of Scripture with *sacramentum tantum, res et sacramentum*, and *res tantum*.

92 While the Christological section will follow, the material on Christ as the centering point of the four senses of Scripture will be dealt with here since it is obviously connected with this tenth article.

93 *Quaestiones quodlibetales*, n. 7, q. 6, a. 2, ad 1 (hereafter, referred to as *Quod.*); as quoted in Rogers, 58.

head of the church militant, justifying it and infusing grace....Christ's true body itself, and those things which were done in it, are figures of Christ's mystical body, and those things which are done in it, as in it, namely in Christ, we ought to take an example for living. In Christ also the future glory is demonstrated to us in advance [*praemonstrata est*]; whence those things that are said literally of Christ's head itself, are able to be expounded both allegorically, referring to his mystical head; and morally, referring to our acts, which ought to be reformed according to it; and anagogically, in that in Christ the way to glory has been demonstrated to us.[94]

In other words, Christ is the exemplar of the virtues that the moral sense requires: the captain of the Church triumphant that anagogy invokes; and the Head of the Church militant to whom allegory proclaims Him as "justifying it and infusing grace."[95]

These four senses of Scripture are analogous to the four aspects of the Aristotelian first principles. These aspects may be explained as follow: for Aristotle, the demand of the human being for intelligibility (the natural desire to know) is answered by, a) first principles as the end of a program of inquiry; b) the effective structure of the soul that results from such intelligibility consists in first principles as acquired habits of the soul; c) the academic discipline of logical study that embodies that intelligibility derives from first principles as the propositional axioms of deduction in an inquiry that is in good order; and d) the intelligible structure of reality to which that intelligibility corresponds arises from first principles as the forms of natural things.[96] These four aspects of the Aristotelian first principles correspond to the four senses of Scripture as follows: a) anagogical; b) moral; c) allegorical; and d) literal. For Aristotle, form grounds the integrity of the four aspects of first principles; for Aquinas, it has been shown that Jesus Christ grounds the integrity of the four senses of Scripture.[97]

---

94 *Quod.* n. 7, q. 6, a. 2, ad 2–5; as quoted in Rogers, 228.

95 Rogers, 58.

96 Ibid., 34.

97 The following passage discusses the relationship between Aristotelian first principles and form: "Things enjoy an organic development, so that the beginning pushes toward the end, and the end pulls from the beginning. The beginning is a first principle (*arche*), the end is a final principle (*telos*), and the way in between is an inner principle, or form (*morphe*). First principles inhere in actually existing things as their forms, and thingly forms begin in actually existing things as their first principles. Real first principles aim, and forms guide—first principles drive, and forms structure the developement of things, therefore, to secure a fitting or in-itself-intelligible passage of a thing from source to end. As its form, a first principle provides a thing with a track or path or plan along

A broader understanding of this material may be achieved by inquiring into other related passages. In his tract on the Trinity (*ST* I 27–43), the term "Word" is, for Aquinas, the personal and proper name of the Second Person of the Trinity, where it signifies a concept of the intellect and its emanation.[98] This concept is the Form in the mind of God and as such is related to created reality. In knowing Himself in the Son, the Father also knows creatures. "[I]n knowing himself God knows every creature...because by the one act he understands both himself and all else, his single Word expresses not only the Father but creatures as well."[99] Creatures are, then, according to Aquinas, not an afterthought in the mind of God, but they are known eternally as the Father begets the Son.

In addition, "God's knowledge [*Dei scientia*] is purely cognitive with respect to himself, but cognitive and causative with respect to creatures, so also the Word of God is purely expressive of what is in God the Father, but both expressive and causative with respect to creatures."[100] Similarly, in a subsequent article, Aquinas states that the *ratio* by which God creates is like the *ratio* by which the artisan produces his art.[101] In so doing, Aquinas identifies this *ratio* with Aristotelian form and appropriates it to the Son.[102] The mission of the Son is "to render human beings participants in the divine wisdom and knowers of the truth" and to bring human beings teaching.[103] Consequently, Aristotelian science is to form as God's knowledge (*Dei scientia*) is to Christ.

---

which it can run in its passage. On the level of actually existing things, first principles, as forms, are keys to the natures of things; for to have a nature is just to possess an internal principle of change. The inner principles or forms are sources of intelligibility or enjoy intelligibility in themselves, whether anybody notices it or not. The corresponding first principles, therefore, found sciences, whether anybody practices them or not. The first principles of birds, say, manifest themselves in birds' formal structure—wings, feathers, beaks, nests—whether or not the same first principles manage to manifest themselves also in the formal rationales of a developed ornithology. Forms give developing sciences threads to trace; ends give them forms achieved; natures, in short, give sciences something to be *of*" (Rogers, 22–23).

98 *ST* I 34.1 and 2.
99 Ibid., I 34.3, corp.
100 Ibid.
101 Ibid., I-II 93.1.
102 Ibid., Rogers, 59–60.
103 *In Joan.* ch. 14, lect. 6, *ut faciat homines participes divinae sapientiae, et cognitores veritatis*; as quoted in Rogers, 60.

A similar argument is presented by Aquinas in his commentary on Romans 1:20. He states that the human intellect strives to reduce all things to their first principles. This power properly belongs, however, to God; more precisely, it is attributed "to the person of the Son, according to I Cor. 1:24: *Christ the power of God.*"[104] By realizing that the power, according to which a thing proceeds from its first principle, is nothing other than its form, one then is able to conclude (as in the paragraph above) that this commentary also treats the Person of the Son as God's form.

In conclusion, Aquinas does not relate the Word of God in Jesus Christ immediately to the words of God in Scripture; he, rather, relates them mediately through the four senses of Scripture. It has been shown that the Word is the form by which God plans and governs all creation. However, God's plan is just the intention of the author of Scripture, and God's governance is just the providence by which God accommodates the various states of affairs and occurrences to signify what the four senses of Scripture express. These affairs and occurrences that the four senses narrate become *revelabilia* (revealables; those things that contain within themselves the form of revealability) by participating in God's intention. They express and develop what God's knowledge (*Dei scientia*) contemplates and shapes. In so doing, the four senses reflects Aristotle's form and Aquinas' Christ.[105]

Sacred doctrine possesses a revealable rather than an intelligible form for, if this were not the case, the mind of God would be known and God would be seen directly. Some of the *revelabilia* participate more fully or provide better access as the four senses of Scripture attest. These senses have a definite center; chief among the *revelabilia* is the form of God made flesh in the Person of Jesus Christ. The Incarnation, for Aquinas, makes the Word the *ratio* of God. But He is more than *ratio*. As will be seen, He is a rational demonstration of the truth of the divine mysteries, a demonstration, a manifestation, an exemplary cause *par excellence*. He is the *via* to God.[106] This point will be explicated later in the Christology section (chapter four); however, the point has been made initially here in order to indicate that question

---

104 *Ad Rom.*, ch. 1, lect. 6, *persona filii, secundum illud I. Cor. 1:24: Christum Dei virtutem*; as quoted in Rogers, 60.
105 Rogers, 60.
106 *ST* I 2 proem.; III prol.

one does have a Christological component to it, at least fundamentally.

3.3.11 The appropriateness of these last articles

Some scholars have suggested that the last two articles are out of context and are inappropriate places to discuss the senses of Sacred Scripture. They are considered to be not relevant to the issue at hand, namely, the nature and function of *sacra doctrina*. M.-D. Chenu suggests that the internal logic of Aquinas' theory would eventually eliminate these two articles from the consideration of *sacra doctrina*.[107] However, it is the contention of this author that they are appropriately placed in this context for the following reasons. First, question one is structured according to the standard scholastic *questiones: an sit; quid sit; de modo*. It is fitting that the last three articles of the question are presented for they provide an analysis and commentary on the method or modality of the subject. *Sacra doctrina* is an exposition of the word of God (the *subjectum*) and that word is contained in Sacred Scripture. Scripture provides the basic text for instruction which, along with Tradition, is founded upon and articulates divine revelation. It is the sacred writing of this instruction: *Sacra Scriptura huius doctrinae*. Scripture is ordered to *sacra doctrina*; the one implies the other. The two are not identical. If Aquinas had been using the term *sacra doctrina* in the preceding articles for the term *Sacra Scriptura*, why does he stop using it in the tenth? The term does not appear there once, thus indicating a technical distinction in use and essence (the two are essentially distinct, the one being ordered to the other; therefore, this distinction must be reflected in their use).

Second, when Aquinas states that sacred doctrine proceeds from first principles, he is not commenting, except incidentally, on its internal logic.[108] To do so would be to abstract from the first principles in order to evaluate their inner coherence. This is not permissible since sacred doctrine is a subalternated science. Sacred doctrine is founded and dependent on (subalternated to) divine revelation, and from Sacred Scripture one learns that this divine revelation is incar-

107 Marie-Dominique Chenu, *La théologie comme science au XIIIe siecle* (Paris: J. Vrin, 1943), 125, 86.
108 Rogers, 27.

nate in the Person of Jesus Christ. Thus, the first principles may not be reduced to their provisional aspects for the sake of some logic. Sacred Scripture can not be separated from Jesus Christ.

3.3.12 Section summary

In completing this analysis of the first question, one may ask, how then does Aquinas define *sacra doctrina*? *Sacra doctrina* is the exposition of a revealed body of truths necessary for salvation; it is a science more noble than other sciences such that it is called wisdom; it is a science whose subject is God (all things are treated in terms of God, either because they are God Himself or because they relate to Him as their beginning and end); it is more of a speculative than a practical science and as such it is argumentative; it expresses itself through Sacred Scripture which utilizes metaphors, symbolic language, and historical and spiritual senses.

Sacra doctrina is more than *theologia*. It is more than "discourse about God" (*sermo de Deo*), which would include natural theology as practiced philosophically. It is instruction which ought to be accepted and practiced, since it is revealed by a God Who is Truth and thus does not deceive.

Based on this understanding of *sacra doctrina*, the following summary points may be made in reference to the *subjectum* of *sacra doctrina*:

- Article one: *sacra doctrina* is necessary because God is the end for human beings. As such, He exceeds their natural abilities. Therefore, there is a need for revelation.
- Article two: *sacra doctrina* is a science because it is concerned with God, Who is the highest cause.
- Article three: *sacra doctrina* is one science because the *subjectum* is studied under the formality of the *objectum*, "revealed."
- Article four: *sacra doctrina* is speculative insofar as it is concerned with divine things; practical insofar as it is concerned with human actions which are directed toward God.
- Article five: as speculative science, *sacra doctrina* is of greater worth than the human sciences because this science treats chiefly those things which by their sublimity transcend human reason (i.e., God and all that is related to God); *sacra doctrina* is the most

noble in regard to the practical sciences because it directs humanity to the highest goal of all, beatific vision of God Himself.

- Article six: *sacra doctrina* is wisdom, for it contemplates the primary causes and principles, the final end, namely God.
- Article seven: the identification of the *subjectum* itself.
- Article eight: *sacra doctrina* is argumentative because it accepts and does not prove its premises (the articles of faith revealed), but it argues to establish another premise; this argumentation is possible and rational because it is based on God, Who is Truth.
- Article nine: *sacra doctrina* may use metaphor or symbolic language because the subject *per se* is beyond natural human experience but is in fact conveyed through it.
- Article ten: *sacra doctrina* is articulated through Sacred Scripture which is the word of God; the subject, is a mystery therefore, the use of the spiritual senses is fitting and proper.

CHAPTER FOUR

SAINT THOMAS AQUINAS' IDENTIFICATION OF JESUS CHRIST AS THE REVELATION OF GOD

As stated above in the overview, this chapter is an investigation into how Aquinas understands God to be knowable (section 1). Since God is knowable, then by implication there is a relation between the knower and the known (section 2). While these terms will be explained in detail later, Aquinas holds that from the side of the creature, there is a real relation between the creature and God. But from the side of God, there is only a relation of reason. On account of the Incarnation, there is a change that occurs on the side of creation. Jesus Christ is the means by which human creatures come to know and love God.

1 The Knowability of God

As we have seen, the articles of faith, made known by the study of *sacra doctrina*, are concerned with God and all that is related to Him. What distinguishes *sacra doctrina* from natural theology is the special self-disclosure of God which realizes a new relationship of God to humanity because the means and the content of that self-disclosure move beyond humanity's natural ability to grasp a limited portion of the revelation on its own. While this revelation is by nature divinely aided, it is still the human person who comprehends it and does so according to the ordinary capabilities of human nature. All that is known is known according to the nature of the knower; all human knowledge is in terms of humanity's own intellect. Thus, it is instructive to inquire into Aquinas' understanding of how the human person knows God. It is only as the self-disclosure of God reaches humanity in some recognizable manner that it can know God at all.

God in Himself is infinitely knowable because He is supremely actual and nonpossessive of potentiality:

> Since God, being entirely free of all potentiality, is at the extreme of separation from matter, it follows that He is most knowing and most knowable. It follows, too, that the knowability of His nature is directly proportioned to the act of existence which it exercises. Finally, because God is by reason of the fact that He possesses His own nature, it follows that God knows to the extent that He possesses His nature as one most knowing. For this reason Avicenna says: "He Himself knows and apprehends Himself because His own quiddity, being completely stripped (that is, of matter), is that of a thing perfectly identified with Himself.[1]

Since God is the most immaterial, He consequently then is the height of cognition. For Aquinas, it is immateriality that determines the degree of an object's knowability.

Since God is subsistent being for Aquinas, and since His essence and existence are one, there is no possibility of human beings knowing Him properly through a concept distinct from God Himself. The reason for this is that the way in which a thing knows depends on the way it exists. In this life, human souls have their being in corporeal matter. Thus they can not by nature know anything except what has its form in matter or what can be known through matter.[2] The divine essence can not be known through the natures of material things and any knowledge that a human being does have of God obtained through a created likeness is not a knowledge of God's essence.[3] All human knowledge of God must be mediated by the essences of material things. These material things, though effects of God's causality,

---

1 *De ver.*, q. 2, art. 2.; cf. *ST* I 12.1, sed contra and 14.1, sed contra.
2 *ST* I 12.11, resp. and I 12.4, resp.
3 Ibid., I 12.11.

are not effects fully expressing His power, and thus His essence is not perceived. They are, nevertheless, dependent upon Him as their cause, and as such can lead to knowledge that He does exist. They also reveal whatever is true of Him as their first cause.[4] Yet in the end, only God Himself can and does possess proper knowledge of His divine essence, for to know the divine essence is to be that essence, and that is precisely what God alone is. This position is a re-articulation of the position Aquinas put forward earlier in his *Commentary on the Sentences*. There he states, "God is knowable but not to the extent that His essence is comprehended, because every knower has a knowledge of the object known not according to the nature of the object but according to his own nature. However the nature of no creature attains to the height of Divine Majesty. From there it follows, no creature knows God perfectly as He perfectly knows Himself."[5]

In summary, the subject of *sacra doctrina* is infinitely knowable in Himself because He is supremely actual and non-possessive of potentiality. God is knowable by human beings. He is known, however, according to the nature of the knower. Therefore, knowledge of God (Who is the subject of *sacra doctrina*) is mediated by material essences to the human knower.

2 The Category of Relation

2.1 Aquinas' general understanding of relation

Knowledge of God through revelation immediately implies, by definition, a relation of knower and known. The predicamental accident of relation for Aquinas consists of three requisite elements: a being which is referred to another (the subject); a being to which the subject is referred (the term); and that in the subject or in both subject and term on account of which the subject is referred to the term (the foun-

---

4 Ibid., I 12.12, resp.; cf. *De pot.*, q. 7, art. 2, ad 1 and ad 2.
5 *In I Sent.*, d. 3, q. 1, a. 1. *Deus cognoscibilis est; non autem ita est cognoscibilis, ut essentia sua comprehendatur. Quia omne cognoscens habet cognitionem de re cognita, non per modum rei cognitae, sed per modum cognoscentis. Modus autem nullius creaturae attingit ad altitudinem divinae majestatis. Unde oportet quod a nullo perfecte cognoscatur, sicut ipse seipsum cognoscit.*

dation). If all three of the essential elements are real, it is a "real relation." In this case, both the subject and the term are two distinct realities as well as the real distinction that is formed between them (the
foundation). If either the term or the foundation is not real but produced by an act of the mind, then the relation is referred to as a "relation of reason." In the end, a relation of reason is a relation which the
mind constructs between the subject and the term. A real relation is
one that exists independently of the mind.[6] Both have the same intelligibility (i.e., they are understood as involving a subject, term, and
foundation) but only a real relation has *esse*.[7]

While the reality of the requisite elements constitutes either a real
relation or a relation of reason, these relations may also undergo another classification. This classification is the accidental division into
mutual and non-mutual relations. A relation is mutual when the two
terms bear to each other a relation which is of the same order, that is,
when on both sides it is real or on both sides logical (e.g., paternity
and sonship, the relations of genus and species, are mutual relations,
the former is real, the latter logical).[8] The relation is non-mutual when
there is a real relation, properly so called, only on one side.[9] The relation is not the same for each of the terms involved: the foundation is
real on the part of one term and logical on the part of the other term.
Aquinas explains, "the truth about x that it is related to y is due to
something real in x, but the truth about y that it is related to x is not
due to anything real in y."[10] For example, a non-mutual relationship
exists between a person's knowledge and the thing known: since a
person's knowledge depends on the existence of that thing, it is a real
relation; however, since the thing's existence does not depend upon
the person knowing it, the thing known has only a relation of reason

---

6 John F. McCormick, *Scholastic Metaphysics* (Chicago: Loyola University Press,
   1940), 134.
7 *ST* III 2.7, ad 2; *In I Sent.*, d. 20, q. 1, a. 1.
8 *ST* I 28.1 and I 13.7.
9 Cardinal Mercier and Louvain Professors of the Higher Institute of Philosophy,
   Manual of Modern Scholastic Philosophy, translated by T.L. Parker and S.A. Parker
   (London and St. Louis: Kegan, Trench, Trubner and B. Herder, 1932), 503.
10 *ST* I 13.7, resp.

to the person's knowing.[11] This non-mutuality occurs whenever the two terms of the relation are not of the same order.

According to Aquinas, substance *per se* is ordered to itself, relation (as an accident *per se*) must inhere in substance through the medium of another accident which, while being absolute and intrinsic, must in some fashion render its subject capable of reference to another. Only in the quantitative and operative orders does Aquinas find such a foundation, for only quantity and action-passion have the virtual relativity which can cause relation.[12] Aquinas writes, "every relation is based on quantity—for instance, being double or half—or on producing change and being changed [*actionem et passionem*]—for instance the maker or the thing made, master and slave and so forth."[13] In this remark, Aquinas makes reference to Aristotle's *Metaphysics* (XV) which he commented on earlier in his own *Commentary*. He writes:

> These senses are explained as follows: since a real relation consists in the bearing of one thing upon another, there must be as many relations of this kind as there are ways in which one thing can bear upon another. Now one thing bears upon another either in being, inasmuch as the being of one thing depends on another, and then we have the third sense; or according to active or passive power, inasmuch as one thing receives something from another or confers it upon the other, and then we have the second sense; or according as the quantity of one thing can be measured by another, and then we have the first sense.
>
> But the quality as such of a thing pertains only to the subject in which it exists, and therefore from the viewpoint of quality one thing bears upon another only inasmuch as quality has the character of an active or passive power, which is a principle of action or of being acted upon. Or it is related by reason of quantity or of something pertaining to quantity; as one thing is said to be whiter than another, or as that which has the same quality as another is said to be like it. But the other classes of things are a result of relation rather than a cause of it. For the category *when* consists in a relation of time; and the category *where* in a relation to place. And *posture* implies an arrangement of parts; and *having* [*attire*], the relation of the thing having to the things had.[14]

---

11 St. Thomas Aquinas, *On the Power of God (Quaestiones Disputatae De Potentia Dei)*, translated by the English Dominican Fathers (Westminster, Maryland: Newman Press, 1952), q. 7, art. 10. (Hereafter, referred to as *De pot.*)

12 William J. Kane, *The Philosophy of Relation in the Metaphysics of St. Thomas*, Philosophical Studies, vol. 179, no. 30 (Washington, D.C.: Catholic University of America Press, 1958), 18.

13 *ST* I 28.4 corp.

14 *Super Metaph.*, V, lect. 17, comm. 1004–5.

Thus, Aquinas allows these two foundations or grounds for real relations.[15]

2.2 Aquinas' explanation of God's relation to the world as based on this understanding

How then do these two foundations impact on Aquinas' explanation of how God relates to the world? In the *Summa theologiae* (I 28.4), Aquinas states that quantity is not relevant to God's relation to the world since there is no quantity in God. Quantity pertains to material things and God is not material.[16] If this real relation were in the quantitative order, quantity would function as the material cause of the real relation for it is the intrinsic and, in the ontological order, the extrinsic measure of substance. As such, quantity would be the foundation of that relation (the efficient cause in such a quantitative relation is the cause which produced the extremes [subject and term]; the final cause is the term; the formal cause is the reference to one other by the subject and the term).

In the case of a causal relation, the situation is different. Action and passion are the efficient and final causes, respectively, and can not be understood as the material cause of the resultant relation as quantity was above. Aquinas sees this type of foundation (whereby the passion is receptive to the operation of an action) as operative in God's relation to creation and, conversely, creation's relationship to God; however, it is important to notice that Aquinas views this relationship to be *non-mutual* when he speaks of it in the *Summa*. He writes:

> Now since God is altogether outside the order of creatures, since they are ordered to him but not he to them, it is clear that being related to God is a reality in creatures, but being related to creatures is not a reality in God, we say it about him because of the real relation in creatures. So it is that when we speak of his relation to creatures we can apply words implying temporal sequence and change, not because of any change in him but because of a change in the creatures; just as we can say that the pillar has changed from

---

15 Cf. *De pot.*, 7.9 corp.; *Super Metaph.*, V, lect. 17, comm. 1001–5. Aristotle admits a third foundation, that of being measured (*Metaph.*, V, lect. 14, 1020b30).

16 Cf. *ST* I 3.1.

being on my left to being on my right, not through any alteration in the pillar but simply because I have turned around.[17]

This argument is modelled on another non-mutual relation, that of the relations between the knower and the known: the knower-to-known is real, the known-to-knower relation is only of reason (just as the creature-to-God relation is real, the God-to-creature relation is only of reason).

Now, as stated above, non-mutual relations have a foundation only in one extreme which gives rise to a real relation, but in the other extreme, the relation is only logical.[18] Aquinas places the real relation of knower-known, of creature-God in the action-passion category, but action-passion does not always give rise to real relations since "there is not always the same order of movement on both sides."[19] What is caused must always be ordered to the agent since an effect always depends on its cause, but the cause may be completely independent of its effect, unchanged by this effect and outside the order of the *genus* of its effect.[20] In the knower-known relation, the intellect considers something knowable as terminating the relationship of knowledge to it "and thus it imputes to the thing knowable a certain relation to knowledge, [but] such a relation is purely logical."[21]

This order of movement is related to another order, that of nature. In the *Summa* (I 28.1), Aquinas notes that sameness of nature implies sameness of order and for this reason, there is a real relation between a principle and that which issues from that principle.[22] He writes, "But relative terms [relation] by their very meaning indicate only a reference to something. This reference is sometimes in the very nature of things; as, for instance, when certain entities of their nature are connected with and attracted by each other."[23] Later in the same article, he comments on the diversity of order which results from the diversity of natures between God and creatures. "Since creatures come forth from God in diversity of nature, God is beyond the whole world

---

17 Ibid., I 13.7, resp.; cf. *In I Sent.*, d. 30, q. 1, a. 3, sol.
18 Kane, 24.
19 *De pot.*, ch. 7, lect. 10.
20 Kane, 24.
21 *De pot.*, ch. 7, lect. 10.
22 Earl C. Muller, "Real Relations and the Divine: Issues in Thomas's Understanding of God's Relation to the World," *Theological Studies* 56 (December 1995): 677.
23 *ST* I 28.1, corp.

of creatures, nor is being related to them part of his nature. For he does not make creatures because his nature compels him to do so, but by mind and will....That is why in God there is no real relation to creatures. Yet there is in creatures a real relation to him, because they are subordinate to, and in their very nature dependent on him."[24]

This same point is made more analytically by Mark Henninger in his book *Relations*. In his reading of Aquinas, two things can not be mutually really related if the two foundations are incommensurable, that is, if they are radically different in order. "The relations R and R' are real and mutual if and only if there are real extra-mental foundations of the same type [order] in *a* for the relation R to *b* and in *b* for the relation R' to *a*."[25] Henninger returns to Aquinas' analogous example of the relation between knower and known. The knower knows some thing through a spiritual action and this spiritual action is the foundation of the real relation of knowledge in the knower toward the known. There is, however, no foundation of the same order in the thing known; that is, there is no corresponding spiritual passion. The physical order of the thing known is distinguishable from the spiritual order of the knowledge act. These orders are incommensurable, that is, they lack a common basis of comparison. There is no real correlation in the known to the knower because the two do not have foundations of the same type.[26]

In his article entitled, "Real Relations and the Divine," Earl Muller also looks at the relations as presented in the *Summa* (I 28.1) from the explicit perspective of their constitutive elements. He states:

> From the side of God [God's relation to the world] there are these three elements: God and the creature as the subject and term of the relation, and God's creative power (or God's mind or will) as the foundation. But the subject, God, and the foundation, God's creative power, are identically the same, as follows from a consideration of the divine simplicity. Under this formality, therefore, the relationship is not real but only rational (yet still true). There is nothing distinct from God which serves as the foundation of God's relation with the world. From the side of the creature [the creature's relationship to God] there are these three: the creature and God as the subject and term of the relationship, and the creature's dependency on God's creative power as the foundation for the relationship. This dependency is

---

24 Ibid., I 28.1, ad 3.

25 Mark G. Henninger, *Relations: Medieval Theories 1250–1325* (Oxford: Clarendon Press, 1989), 35.

26 Ibid., 36–37.

not to be identified in the same way with the creature as God's power is to be identified with God. Hence the creature's relationship to God is real and not simply rational. We discover, then, that there is a lack of symmetry in the relations.[27]

The crucial point is made as well in this explanation, namely, that the two foundations are incommensurable; they are radically different.

Aquinas articulates elsewhere this point that God is not really related to creation because God and creation are not of the same order (e.g., *ST* I 13.7). He also provides in other written passages various reasons why this is the case. For example, God can not be really related to creation because relations do not exist in God as accidents in a subject, for there can be no accidents in God. Neither can they be identical with the divine substance because relative terms are relative only insofar as they refer to something else. To suppose that the divine substance is essentially relative to something else would violate the fact that God is Being Itself.[28]

In addition, God is the first measure of all things, whereas our knowledge is measured by the things which it knows, since its truth or falsity depends upon its correspondence with reality and the facts. Consequently, God is to be compared to all things as knowable things are to be compared to human knowledge. However, knowledge is really related to its object, while the object, on the contrary, is related to knowledge only by reason. Thus, creatures are really related to God while God is not really related to them.[29]

Furthermore, relations are predicated of God with respect not only to those things that are in act but to those things that are also in potency, for God knows them and, with respect to them, is called the First Being and the Supreme Good. Real relations, however, hold only between actualities; otherwise, a single subject would be involved in an infinite number of real relations. Thus, the sequence of numbers greater than two is potentially infinite, and were the relations between two and these numbers real, they would also be infinite in number. Thus, since God is not involved in change by His very essence, He is clearly not related to things actually existent in any other

---

27 Muller, 677–78.
28 *SCG* I ch. 23, [1–3]; II ch. 12, [1–2].
29 Ibid., II ch. 12, [3].

way than to things potentially existent. Accordingly, He is not referred to creation by a relation really existing in Him.[30]

Lastly, whatever receives something anew must be changed either *per se* or *per accidens*. Relations are indeed predicated of God anew since He is called lord or governor of an entity that begins to exist anew. If such relations were real in God, He would be involved in change, either *per se* or *per accidens*. Thus, these relations can be ones only of reason.[31]

2.3 The significance of the Incarnation

In the Incarnation, God is spoken of as being united with the creature. For Aquinas, it is precisely this union between the divine and human that constitutes God's presence in Christ.[32] He writes, "the presence of God in Christ is by union of human nature with the Divine Person."[33] However, the reality of this hypostatic union subsists wholly in something that belongs to the creaturely realm in that the union refers to the real, unilateral relation to God of Christ's humanity. There is nothing in the divine nature that corresponds to this or any other relation between God and creation. As was specified above, the Incarnation is a non-mutual or mixed relation: it is a relation of reason in the divine nature while it is a real relation in the human nature and, thus, may be spoken of as "something created."[34] Aquinas states:

> The union we speak of is a relation taken to exist between the divine and human nature as they come together in the one person of the Son of God. As noted in the *Prima Pars*, every relation between God and a creature exists really in the creature, for the relation is brought into being by the change of the creature. It does not exist in God really, since it does not arise from any change in God, but only in our way of thinking. Thus we must say that this union is not in God really, but only in our way of thinking. In the human na-

---

30 Ibid., II ch. 12, [4].
31 Ibid., II ch.12, [5]; cf. *In I Sent*. d. 30, q. 1, a. 3, sol.
32 Per Erik Persson, *Sacra doctrina*, trans. Ross Mackenzie (Philadelphia: Fortress Press, 1970), 202.
33 *ST* III 7.13.
34 Ibid.

ture, however, which is something creaturely, it really exists. And thus it is necessary to say that the union is something created.[35]

What are the constitutive elements of the real relation (i.e., from the side of humanity) of the Incarnation? The subject of the real relation is the creature, the created human nature of Christ. More exactly, it is His created human substance since substance is the only medium of real relations.[36] Aquinas states, "the union of which we are speaking is a relation which we consider between the Divine and the human nature, inasmuch as they come together in One Person of the Son of God....the creature is really united to God without any change in Him....this union has its being nowhere save in a created [human] nature."[37]

The term of the real relation, for Aquinas, is the divine nature of Christ while the foundation is the act of assuming a human nature itself. The foundation can not be the Second Person of the Godhead because the Second Person can not be a quantity or an action-passion. There is a created capacity within Christ's humanity which grounds the relation to be so united with God. Yet, that capacity is not identical with human nature as such. He is human but distinct from humanity in general.

From the side of divinity, the relation is one of reason. There is nothing in God that is not identical with the Person of the Son which grounds the act of assuming.[38] That act, which is the action of the Father, Son, and Holy Spirit acting inseparably, is nothing other than the divine nature itself. The foundation and the term coincide; therefore, there is no real relation to Christ's humanity according to Aquinas.

However, Christ's created human substance is really distinct from the Person of the Son. This subject is really distinct from the term, His divine Personhood, and there is a created capacity for such a union between the two. Thus, a real relation exists between Christ's humanity and divinity.

---

35 *ST* III 2.7, corp. Cf. *In III Sent.*, d. 2, q. 2, a. 2, qla. 3, sol. 3; d. 5, q. 1, a. 1, qla. 1; *In Joan.*, 1.7 (1); *Ad Gal.*, 4.2 (204).

36 *In I Sent.*, d. 30, q. 1, a. 2, ad 4. A. Krempel, *La doctrine de la relation chez Saint Thomas: Exposé historique et systématique* (Paris: Librairie Philosophique J. Vrin, 1952), 566.

37 *ST* III 2.7.; cf. *In III Sent.*, d. 5, q. 1, a. 1, qla. 3.

38 *ST* III 2.10 ad 2; *In III Sent.*, d. 5, q. 1, a. 1, qla. 3.

2.4 The change that occurs in creation on account of the Incarnation.

According to Aquinas, when God the Father sent His Son to assume a human nature, this sending was not to be understood as something new occurring to the One Who is sent, but something new occurring to those to whom He was sent.[39] When God acts, something new comes into existence extrinsic to the divine being: something either begins to exist or something that already exists is changed and by being changed is related in a new way to the transcendent cause that effects the change.[40] In the case of the Incarnation, the God-Man exists in time and space through the hypostatic union. This "becoming" does not necessarily imply any change in God for this is a relation of reason between the divine Word and the created human nature. However, there is a change in creation for there is present now a new real relation between the creature and God.

The change that occurs in the creature is that humanity now has personal access to God through the Incarnate Christ. Divine communication is established in the human context and experience. Now we have seen above, in the section dealing specifically with sacred doctrine, that knowledge of God derived from "natural theology" is not totally sufficient because God has destined humanity for an end that is beyond the grasp of reason. It is expedient, then, that the divine truths which surpass reason should be given to humanity through divine revelation. Sacred doctrine is concerned with those truths about God which are necessary for salvation, and so they are made known through revelation, through means beyond the discoveries of natural reason.

What are these necessary truths? Aquinas provides an answer when he states that not only an act of explicit faith is necessary for salvation, but also an explicit faith in Christ (Incarnation, Passion, Resurrection) and the mystery of the Trinity is necessary as well. He writes:

> Faith is concerned chiefly with the realities we hope to contemplate in heaven...and so the matters engaging faith for their own sake are those that

---

39 *In I Sent.*, d. 15, q. 1, a. 1.
40 Persson, 201.

> directly points [sic] us towards eternal life: the three persons in almighty
> God, the mystery of the Incarnation and so on.[41]

> In heaven it will be ours to see two realities: the hidden being of the God-
> head, the vision of which will make us blessed, and the mystery of the hu-
> manity of Christ.[42]

> After sin the mystery of Christ was believed explicitly, not only as compris-
> ing his Incarnation, but also his Passion and Resurrection, which delivered
> mankind from sin and death.[43]

Thus, the necessary truths are those truths which pertain to Christ
and the Trinity. Stated within the context of sacred doctrine, as presented earlier: the subject of sacred doctrine is God, known supernaturally through divine revelation; sacred doctrine is centered on
God, but in and through Christ; sacred doctrine seeks salvation itself,
namely God, and the means to achieve it, Christ. Summarily, sacred
doctrine is the exposition of necessary salvific truths regarding the
Trinity and Christ through the means of divine revelation.

2.5 The union of divinity and humanity

In his discussion of the Incarnation (*ST* III 2–6), Aquinas addresses the
mode of union between the divinity and the humanity of Christ. After
making a distinction between person and nature, he states that the
Person of Christ subsists in two natures, divine and human.[44] In virtue of His divinity, Christ is co-equal with the Father and the Spirit. In
virtue of His humanity, He is like us in all things except sin. This union is a substantial and not an accidental one. The person exists prior
to the union and is not caused by it. Thus, there is only one person,
and that person is the Word of God, the Second Person of the Trinity.[45] The union takes place, then, in the person and not in the nature.[46] This is fitting, for while a divine Person is said to be
incommunicable inasmuch as it can not be predicated of several *supposita*, nothing prevents several things from being predicated of the

---

41 *ST* II-II 1.6, ad 1.
42 Ibid., II-II 1.8, corp.; cf. II-II 2.8, corp.
43 Ibid., II-II 2.7, corp.
44 Ibid., III 2.4.
45 Ibid., III 2.2 and 6.
46 Ibid., III 3.1, corp.

person. Even a created person can possess several natures acciden-tally, as when one person has many qualities. But God in His infinity, without compromising His incommunicability, can possess another nature not accidentally but substantially (i.e., according to which that person exists subsistently).[47]

Aquinas provides further development when he discusses some of the implications of this hypostatic union. In the Incarnation, the two natures are distinct and can not be predicated of each other by using abstract terms. The divine nature is not the human nature; however, they can be predicated in the concrete because they exist in one common subject.[48] Similarly, the statement "a man is God" is both literal and true just as the statement "God is a man" is. He explains, "For the term 'a man' can stand for every subject subsisting in human nature; consequently it can stand for the Person of the Son which we hold to be a subject subsisting in human nature. And it is of course evident that the term 'God' is predicated truly and literally of the per-son of the Son of God. From this it results that the statement, 'A man is God,' is both true and literal."[49]

Furthermore, such an understanding of the hypostatic union is consistent with his insistence that the change occurs in the human na-ture and not in God. According to Aquinas, God made a decision to become incarnate but this decision is eternal. The human body of Je-sus Christ is indeed created, but as a creature it is predestined in the mind of God but not in the essence of God. The change occurs in the creature; that which is predestined in the mind of God comes into created being.

In the tract on the mode of union, the preexistent *Logos* is pre-sented as prehuman. "The Word of God…from all eternity had com-plete being in *hypostasis* or person, but human nature came to be his in time."[50] This statement is typical of Aquinas' position. However, in his tract on the Trinity (*ST* I 27–43), Aquinas makes a statement that is not entirely consistent with this position. He is addressing the ques-tion of whether or not mission is eternal or only temporal. In a reply to an objection, he writes:

---

47 Ibid., III 3.1, ad 2.
48 Ibid., III 16.1, ad 1.
49 Ibid., III 16.2, resp.
50 Ibid., III 2.6, ad 2.

'Mission' conveys not just the coming forth from a principle, but the term in time as well. A mission, therefore, takes place only in time. In other words mission includes an eternal procession, but also adds something else, namely an effect in time; for the relationship of the divine person to a principle is eternal. We speak, therefore, of a twofold procession—the one during eternity, the other during time—in view of the doubling, not of relation to principle, but of the terminations—one in eternity the other in time.[51]

There is, then, a single procession. This procession is the eternal begetting of the Son. There is no change or becoming here, for there is no potency with God. He is Pure Act. There is, however, a temporal term, namely, the Incarnate Christ. Consequently, the created human nature (human race) does change since there is potency within creation.

2.6 Section summary

Knowledge of God through revelation (i.e., the subject of *sacra doctrina*) implies a relation between knower and known. In a real relation, both the subject and the term are two distinct realities as well as the real distinction that is formed as the foundation between them. In a relation of reason, either one of the terms or the foundation is not real but a construct of the mind. These may be accidentally divided into mutual and non-mutual relations. A relation is mutual when the two terms bear to each other a relation which is of the same order. A relation is non-mutual when there is a real relation properly so called only on one side. The relation is real on the part of one term and logical on the part of the other term.

Aquinas holds that relation must inhere in a substance through the medium of another accident. According to Aquinas, quantity and action-passion are the accidents that can serve as a foundation for a relation. In the case of God, quantity does not function as the foundation because there is no potentiality in God. Rather, action-passion serves as the foundation for God's relation to creation and creation's relationship to God but the relationship is non-mutual. This is because there is not the same order of movement on both sides.[52] There is a spiritual action in the relationship between the knower and the object known, but there is no corresponding spiritual passion of the

---

51 Ibid., I 43.2, ad 3.
52 *De Pot.*, ch. 7, lect. 10.

same order between the object known and the knower. In other words, from the side of the creature, the creature and God are distinct and so the foundation of the creature's dependence on God's creative power. Thus, the relation is real. From the side of God, God and the creature are still distinct but God and the foundation, God's creative power, are true and rational but not real. Thus, the relation is one of reason.

In the Incarnation, God (the subject of *sacra doctrina*) is spoken of as being united with the creature, but it is a non-mutual relation. From the side of humanity, the subject of the real relation is the created human substance of Jesus Christ. The term is the divine nature of Christ and the foundation is the act of assuming a human nature itself. From the side of divinity, the subject and the term are the same but since there is nothing in God that is not identical with the Person of the Son, then the act of assuming (the foundation) is nothing other than the term. On account of the Incarnation, there is a change that occurs on the side of creation. This change is the realization that while sacred doctrine is centered on God, it is centered on Him through and in Jesus Christ. Christ is the means by which humanity comes to know God and learns those things that are necessary for salvation.

CHAPTER FIVE

THE ROLES OF JESUS CHRIST IN THE THOUGHT OF SAINT THOMAS AQUINAS

We will now look at the roles Christ assumes in order to establish that He is the Revelation of God and more emphatically, the ultimate, the culmination of all divine revelation. In studying these roles of Christ, we come to a knowledge of the mystery of Christ's Incarnation (one of the two explicit necessary truths of sacred doctrine), and through this knowledge come to some knowledge, however imperfect, of the secret of the Godhead (the other necessary truth). To put this point another way, by inquiring into Christ's roles as prophet, Word of God, teacher, mediator, and priest, we will realize that He is the culmination of revelation. As such, Christ reveals the Godhead. He pulls all things together through His person and action. It will then be argued that Christ, for Aquinas, is the Revelation of God and, as such, is the primary referent of question one of the first part of the *Summa theologiae*. To use Keefe's terminology, He is the prime analogate of sacred doctrine, however implicitly stated in Aquinas.

1 The Revelatory Role of Prophecy

While the ultimate revelation is beatific vision, a less perfect revelation (which receives its specification from the beatific vision) has been bestowed to a limited number of people on earth who must transmit the salvific truths to others. Aquinas identifies these instruments as the apostles and prophets. He writes, "our faith rests on the revelation made to the Prophets and Apostles...not on a revelation, if such there be, made to any other teacher."[1] Apostles and prophets, then, are means through which divinely revealed truths are communicated.

Aquinas is primarily interested in the prophetic aspect of revelation. He speaks of prophecy in the following places: *De veritate*, q. 12 and *Summa theologiae*, II 171–174 provide the extensive treatments while the *Summa contra gentiles*, III, ch. 154; *Commentary on I Cor.*, ch. 14, lect. 1; and *Commentary on Isaiah*, 1,1; 6,1. provide shorter ones which nonetheless deal with the essentials. In his discussion of this aspect, the majority of attention is given to the process of revelation rather than to the content of revelation.

1.1 The general nature of prophecy

Prophecy for Aquinas consists essentially in knowledge, supernaturally imparted by God, of truths exceeding the natural knowledge of a person for the benefit of the community. The prophet is often called a "seer."[2] The prophet's mind is elevated in order to perceive the things it could not understand by its natural ability and in so doing, the prophet not only "speaks from afar" (*procul fans*; i.e., one who announces) but also "sees from afar" (*procul videns*).[3] While prophecy consists first and foremost in knowledge, it involves speech since the content of the prophecy includes truths which are necessary for salva-

---

1   *ST* I 1.8, ad 2.
2   Aquinas relies upon St. Isidore of Seville for the etymology of the term "prophecy," as indicated by his citation of it at the beginning of his commentary on the prophet Isaiah and in the *De Veritate*, 12:1. A prophet is "an interpreter of God." The meaning later attributed to it, "he who foretells the future," is only a derived meaning (Paul Synave and Pierre Benoit, *Prophecy and Inspiration: A Commentary on the Summa Theologica II–II, Questions 171–178*, translated by Avery R. Dulles and Thomas L. Sheridan [New York: Desclée, 1961], 16).
3   *ST* II–II 171.1, corp.; *De ver.*, q. 12, art. 1, resp.

tion.[4] However, knowledge differentiates prophecy from the "gift of tongues" (q. 176), the "gift of speech" (q. 177), and the "gift of miracles" (q. 178), all of them charisms (*gratiae gratis datae*; i.e., graces given gratuitously) which concern speech and action not merely as a result, but as their proper and primary effect.[5] As a result, prophecy pertains to the intellect and not to the will which intervenes after the message has been received and motivates its articulation.[6] The truth of the message can not be confirmed by human reason, since it is divine in origin; however, it may be confirmed by the working of miracles.[7]

Material light manifests material objects; intellectual light manifests intellectual objects. Accordingly, the manifestation is proportionate to the light which causes it. Since prophecy pertains to a knowledge that surpasses natural reason, prophecy, then, requires an intellectual light which surpasses the light of natural reason. Now light may be in a subject in two ways: permanently or transiently. Prophetic light is not in the prophet's mind permanently since he is not able to prophesy at will. If it were in the prophet's mind permanently, the prophet's mind would be perfected to know the principle of all the truths manifested by that light. That principle, in this case, is God Himself, Who in His essence can not be known by the prophets.[8] Thus, the intellectual light of prophecy inheres in the prophet transiently and not as a habit strictly speaking, for a habit is a predicamental quality of the human faculties which may be exercised at one's pleasure, when and as willed.[9]

Since prophetic knowledge comes through divine light,[10] all things, both divine and created, are known. Therefore, prophetic revelation extends to all things in the broad sense. However, in the

---

4 *De ver.*, q. 12, art. 2, corp.
5 Synave and Benoit, 62.
6 Cf. *ST* II–II 172.4, corp. The operation of the will pertains more to the "gift of speech" (Synave and Benoit, 62).
7 *ST* II–II 171.1, corp.
8 *ST* II–II 171.2, corp.
9 Synave and Benoit, 18.
10 In dealing with the causality of prophecy, Aquinas holds that no created intelligence can illumine another by giving it a light of nature, of grace, or of glory. Since prophetic knowledge can not be accounted for by any natural power but rather it is revealed knowledge and not acquired knowledge, God is its cause (*ST* I 106.1, ad 2; II–II 172.1).

narrow sense, prophecy is about things removed from our knowledge; the more remote something is, the more pertinent it is to prophecy. The least remote consists of those things known by some but not by all. Next are those things beyond the knowledge of all, not by any deficiencies in the object of knowledge (i.e., not that they themselves are unknowable) but by the deficiencies of human persons. The most remote consists of those things unknowable in themselves such as future contingencies.[11]

1.2 The conveyance of prophecy

Aquinas first addresses the issue of the conveyance of prophecy by saying that this does not occur by way of a direct (beatific) vision of the divine essence.[12] Those in the heavenly state see, not from afar, but rather as it is, near at hand. Beatitude is perfect knowledge; prophecy is not. When prophets see prophetically, they see only fragmentary images illuminated by the divine light as in a mirror.[13]

In order for prophecy to occur, the human mind is raised above its natural abilities in two respects: the infusion of intellectual light[14] and the representation of things, which is effected by means of certain species.[15] Human teaching is similar to prophecy since a teacher represents certain things to his student with symbols or words, but he can not illumine the student from within as God does. Illumination holds the place of predominance in prophecy, for judgment is the complement and fruit of knowledge.[16]

Three cases are to be considered in this regard: a) representations without light; b) light without representations; c) light and representation. In the first case, no one may be called a prophet without light since knowledge can only be complete when a judgment can be made. Representation of certain realities through imaginative images

---

11 *ST* II–II 172.3, corp.

12 Ibid., II–II 173.1, corp.; II–II 171.2, corp.

13 Ibid., II–II 173.1, corp.

14 I.e., the interior power which illuminates the object and causes one to form a judgment about it (Synave and Benoit, 64).

15 I.e., that which furnishes the subject–matter of the judgment: ideas, and, antecedently, sensations and images from which the ideas are abstracted (Synave and Benoit, 64).

16 *ST* II–II 173.2, corp.; *SCG* III 154, [4].

(as in the case of Pharaoh or Nebuchadnezzar) or through bodily images (as with Belshazzar) are not enough. Light for the sake of judgment is needed for true prophecy.[17] In the second case, if the representations are not granted to the prophet himself but to another who submits them to the judgment of the enlightened man, the latter is a prophet. He is able with his prophetic light to illumine and judge the representations in the other.[18] In the third case, God infuses an intellectual light into the intellect of a man so as to pass judgment in terms of truth on his own representations.[19] Aquinas writes, "if someone has supernatural judgment or judgment and reception [of representations] together, he is called a prophet."[20]

1.3 The excellence of various grades of prophecy

The discussion thus far has shown that prophecy involves grades, according to which it is more or less perfect: conscious or unconscious, accompanied by infused representations or unaccompanied by them, involving intellectual visions, imaginary visions, or even merely sensory visions.[21] The excellence of these various grades of prophecy, however, is measured by how well the end is obtained. The end of prophecy is the manifestation of some truth that surpasses the natural human faculty. The more this manifestation is effective, the more excellent the prophecy.[22] The fullest perfection of divine revelation is realized in the beatific vision. Those who dwell in the presence of the Light are in no need of enlightenment; thus, prophecy has no place in heaven.[23] "[T]he principle of those truths which by God's light are prophetically revealed is the very first Truth itself, whose inner being is hidden from the prophets."[24] Since the perfection of revelation will be in heaven, all other prophecy within this genus of divine revelation

---

17 *ST* II–II 173.2, corp.
18 Ibid.; e.g., the case of Joseph interpreting Pharoah's dreams and Daniel interpreting the writings on the wall.
19 Ibid.; *SCG* III ch. 154, [4].
20 *De ver.*, q. 12, art. 7, corp.
21 Synave and Benoit, 74.
22 *ST* II–II 174.2, corp.
23 Ibid., II–II 174.5.
24 Ibid., II–II 171.4, corp.

will be imperfect.[25] Subsequently, the manifestation of a divine truth that derives from a bare contemplation of the truth itself is more effective than that which derives from images of corporeal things.[26] In the end, the prophet's mind will always be a "defective instrument" by way of its principal cause, the Holy Spirit.[27]

1.4 Aquinas' early thought on Christ's role as prophet

The major issue for Aquinas concerning Christ as a prophet involves reconciling the fact that prophecy gives only imperfect knowledge with the fact that Christ's human knowledge is perfect. Aquinas was fully aware of the scriptural evidence that ties Christ to prophecy[28] but yet he had to deal with the rational question: by virtue of which kind of knowledge is Christ a prophet?[29]

Aquinas' thought on this matter underwent a development throughout his writing career.[30] While the development is rather involved, the focus here will be on the later modified positions he explains towards the end of his career. In the *Summa theologiae*, question 174, article 5 (which is part of his treatise on prophecy II 171–74), he states that there is a distance between beatific vision and prophetic vision in two regards: the truth that is known is not seen in itself (beatific) but in its effects (prophetic) and the knower who is not in the final stage of perfection (beatific) but is remote and on the way (prophetic). The blessed in heaven (corp.) and the angels (ad 2) are not from afar, are not at a distance; therefore, they are not prophets.

---

25 Ibid., II–II 171.4, ad 2.
26 Ibid., II–II 174.2, corp.
27 Ibid., II–II 173.4, corp.
28 Yahweh promised to send a prophet to His People (Deut. 18:15–18), a prophet that the Fathers identified as Christ; Jesus implied that He was a prophet since "A prophet is not without honour except in his native place" (Mt. 13:57; Lk. 4:24; Jn. 4:44); some of His contempariaries took Him for a prophet (Mt. 16:14, 21:11 and 46; Lk. 7:16, 9:8 and 19, 24:19; Jn. 4:19, 6:14, 7:40, 9:17); He showed prophetic knowledge by revealing secret thoughts (Lk. 7:39, 5:22) and foretold the future (Lk. 9:22; Mt. 24:2).
29 C. Cassar, *Revelation in the Incarnate Word: Doctrine of St. Thomas* (Florina, Malta: Empire Press, 1965), 44–45.
30 C. Cassar sets out this development in detail. One of the earliest treatments of this matter is Aquinas' commentary on Matthew's Gospel (specifically 13:57 which reads, "A prophet is not without honor except in his own country") written sometime between 1256 and 1259.

Christ, however, possessed the beatific vision while still being a pilgrim. Christ, then, was a prophet only as a pilgrim but not as a comprehensor. Later in the third part (q. 7, art. 8), he elaborates on this point. Christ is a prophet because He is a pilgrim Who shared our nature. A prophet is one who announces things beyond our knowing whose state he shares. When angels, or God, or the blessed in heaven know and announce what is beyond our knowing, this is not prophecy, for they do not share our state. But Christ shared our state before His death. He was a pilgrim journeying to heaven, as well as one Who was experiencing the beatific vision. So when He knew and announced things beyond our knowing, He was prophesying.[31]

Also in this article, Aquinas for the first time states that enigmatic knowledge is not essential to prophecy. Therefore, while having the most perfect intellectual knowledge, Christ could also be a prophet. Nevertheless, as a pilgrim and a prophet, He had an imagination in which He saw similitudes, reflections of divine things less clearly than in the intellectual mode.[32] Thus, at this stage in his thought, Aquinas teaches that the state of pilgrim, notwithstanding the beatific vision, permitted Christ to be a prophet. By reconciling the beatific knowledge with prophecy, he departs somewhat from his earlier position while still not determining in virtue of which knowledge Christ was a prophet.[33]

The final stage in the development of Aquinas' thought regarding how Christ is a prophet occurs in his discussion concerning Christ's infused knowledge of the *Summa theologiae* and the *Compendium theologiae*. Referring to the extent of Christ's infused knowledge he writes:

> Therefore, it [divinely infused knowledge] allowed [the soul of] Christ to know, firstly, everything that can be known by man through the enlightenment of the active intellect, such as all that comes under the human sciences. Secondly, through this knowledge Christ grasped everything that is made known to men by divine revelation, whether it belongs to the gift of wisdom or prophecy, or to any of the gifts of the Holy Spirit. The soul of Christ knew all these things more exhaustively and more fully than others did. However,

---

31 *ST* III 7.8, corp.
32 Ibid., III 7.8, ad 1.
33 Cassar, 48.

he did not know the essence of God by this knowledge, but only by the knowledge we spoke about earlier.[34]

> Furthermore, since Christ in His human nature was not only the restorer of our nature, but was also the fountainhead of grace, He was endowed with a third knowledge whereby He knew most perfectly all that can pertain to the mysteries of grace, which transcend man's natural knowledge, although they are known by men through the gift of wisdom or through the spirit of prophecy.[35]

Aquinas is saying in both texts that by His infused knowledge, Christ knew most fully all the mysteries of grace, all those things that human beings have learned from revelation whether by the gift of wisdom or, for our present purposes, by the gift of prophecy. It seems then that Christ's prophetic knowledge is no other than His infused knowledge, and that Christ was a prophet in the sense that He spoke supernatural truths to humankind precisely because of this knowledge. The resultant prophetic knowledge is distinct from, inferior to, the beatific knowledge. Apart from the connotations of the state of pilgrim, prophecy is essentially an obscure knowledge of divine realities because the prophet sees these things at a distance from their origin and through a medium other than the divine essence. On account of this, Aquinas holds that Christ was not a prophet by His beatific vision. Indeed, the very presence of this knowledge in Him made it difficult for Aquinas to see how He could be a prophet at all. If Christ was a prophet, it was not by way of His beatific vision but in spite of it.

To summarize, the following points can be made: a) that Christ is indeed a prophet; b) that the presence of the beatific knowledge in Him, even as a pilgrim, neither excluded this nor formally brought it about; c) that Christ knew divine things also from a distance like the prophets, even though much more perfectly and extensively than they; d) that the cognitive medium of the infused species, whereby He knew them in this way, formally constituted Him as a prophet.[36]

---

34 *ST* III 11.1, corp.
35 St. Thomas Aquinas, *Compendium of Theology*, translated by Cyril Vollert (St. Louis and London: B. Herder, 1952), 216. (Hereafter, referred to as *Compend.*)
36 Cassar, 49–51.

1.5 The degree of Christ's role as prophet

In the section above concerning the nature of prophecy, the three aspects of prophecy were discussed in general. To be more specific, they are: a) the reception of revealed knowledge surpassing humanity's natural cognitive power (*acceptio cognitorum*); b) the proclamation of this knowledge by word or deed (*denuntiato verbis aut factis*); c) and the confirmation of the divine origin of the message by the working of miracles.[37] The degree to which Aquinas understood Christ to exercise His prophetic role will be assessed according to these three aspects.

1.5.1 The first aspect: the reception of revealed knowledge

The first aspect in which prophecy may occur is when a prophet receives supernatural instruction (*acceptio cognitorum*) by way of representations, visions which are judged through the power of prophetic intellectual light. The light is not habitual but only temporary, and the visions are occasional and convey a partial knowledge for they are obscure. The visions themselves may be sensible, imaginary, or purely intellectual in kind.

Christ's human mind received supernatural knowledge by both beatific vision and infused knowledge. As stated, the first did not constitute Him as a prophet but the second did. While, theoretically, all three kinds of visions are possible, Aquinas only attributes the highest, the purely intellectual visions, to Christ. The reason intellectual visions are the highest is because they provide the most excellent means of manifesting the divine truth rather than the other two kinds of vision. The other two manifest the truth by means of the similitudes of corporeal things.[38] And according to Aquinas, the intellect can know without phantasms (which are dependent upon sense knowledge), but it can not know without intelligible species.[39] Thus, he holds that Christ, in acting as a comprehensor, can and does know without turning to phantasms.[40]

---

37 Cf. *ST* II–II 171.1, corp.
38 Cf. *ST* II–II 174.2, corp.
39 Ibid., III 11.2, ad 1.
40 Ibid., III 11.2, corp.

Aquinas adds a few details to his conviction that Christ's prophetic knowledge was the most excellent in comparison to that of the other prophets. The first is a metaphysical concern that the intellectual power of the soul be in act, be in a state of ontological perfection. It is unthinkable to have the Incarnate Word of God in the state of potency, for, according to the axiom, "everything in potency is imperfect unless it be reduced to act." The passive intellect of a human being is in potency to all intelligible things, and it is reduced to act, and in so doing, is perfected by intelligible species. Thus, admitted in the soul of Christ are intelligible species which reduce it to the state of act. These intelligible species refer to all existing things, for, if this were not the case, potency would remain to some degree. Thus, Christ knows all those things which, in their proper nature, can be conveyed by intelligible species. It is fitting, then, that the Word Incarnate be in a state of act by knowing all things that can be represented in intelligible species, and be the highest of all these species.[41] If this can be done for the angels, it must be done for One Who is higher than they in the hierarchy of being.[42]

In the initial material on prophecy, it was mentioned that the prophet did not discharge this charism at will. In the *Summa theologiae* (III 11.5), Aquinas uses the point of habit to demonstrate that Christ was the most excellent of the prophets in this regard. In the preceding article he establishes the fact that Christ's infused knowledge is exhaustive in scope and also held as certain. This is because the mode of the knowledge infused suited the subject receiving it; it was received in a manner suited to the recipient. Now, the normal mode of a rational soul is that the intellect is sometimes actual, sometimes poten-

---

41 Aquinas fills this point out even further in q. 11, art. 1 by saying, "it [infused knowledge] allowed Christ to know, firstly, everything that can be known by man through the enlightenment of the active intellect, such as all that comes under the human sciences. Secondly, through this knowledge Christ grasped everything that is made known to men by divine revelation, whether it belongs to the gift of wisdom or prophecy, or to any of the gifts of the Holy Spirit. The soul of Christ knew all these things more exhausively and more fully than others did; however, he did not know the essence of God by this knowledge, but only by the knowledge we spoke about earlier [i.e., beatific knowledge]."

42 Ibid., III 9.3, corp. In III 11.4, corp., Aquinas notes, "the knowledge infused into the soul of Christ by far excelled the knowledge of angels, both in the amount known and in the certainty of knowing. For, the spiritual light which was infused into the soul of Christ is far superior to the light that belongs to angelic natures."

tial. In between full actuality and pure potency stands habit. The normal way for the human soul, then, to receive knowledge is in the form of habit. Thus, the infused knowledge in the soul of Christ was habitual; He could use it whenever He willed, placing Him above all other prophets.[43] It must also be remembered that potency in this context does not undo what Aquinas already established two questions prior; namely, that the passive intellect has been reduced to act by intelligible species. Christ still knows all things that infused knowledge can instill; however, it is potential in the sense that He can act upon this exhaustive scope of knowledge whenever He wills.

To summarize, Christ's reception of revealed knowledge (*acceptio cognitorum*) was superior to that of all other prophets on several grounds. First, its medium was the highest ever used in prophecy; the intellectual visions provided the most excellent means of manifesting the divine truth. Second, it provided an incomparably wider scope of knowledge. In order to achieve a state of ontological perfection, Christ's passive human intellect was reduced to act by the presence of intelligible species which refer to all existing things that can be known through infused knowledge. Thus, Christ's scope of certain knowledge included all things so that no potency would remain. Third, it provided Christ with habitual knowledge that could be used at will, thus distinguishing Him from all other prophets.

1.5.2 The second aspect: the proclamation by word or deed

As mentioned above, God, the principle agent, gives the prophet a divine message and then uses the prophet's inward movement, or speech, or outward action as an instrument.[44] After speaking to the prophet, immediate revelation ends and is followed by the prophet's own mediate communication of it to the people by word or deed (*denuntiatio verbis* or *factis*).[45] In communicating, the prophet chose

---

43 Ibid., III 11.5, corp.

44 Aquinas is using the term "instrument" in regard to prophecy not in its proper but common sense. A "proper" instrument is one in which something is so moved by a principle agent that there is no freedom on its part. A "common" instrument is one that acts through being moved by another even though it possesses the principle of its own activity (*De ver.*, q. 24, art. 1, ad 5; SCG III ch. 149, [2]).

45 *ST* II–II 174.3, ad 3; Cassar, 53.

words and images derived from his own inner temperament and personal experience, thus rendering it a personal act in that sense. Involved in this *denuntiatio verbis* is both proclamation and testimony.

The prophets spoke in God's name and on his behalf. Aquinas
notes that they usually began their proclamations with the phrase,
"Thus says the Lord." Christ, however, does not use this introductory
phrase. Christ taught divine truth not by writing but orally and, when
He spoke, He used the phrase, "I say to you."[46] His speech was that of
the Father, but He and the Father are one in the Spirit. In his commentary on John 3, Aquinas explains:

> Then immediately he [John] adds a commendation of divine truth, saying,
> *For the One whom God sends speaks the words of God.* As if to say: He has given
> this as a sign, namely, that Christ, whose testimony he accepts, *the One whom
> God sends speaks the words of God.* Consequently, one who believes Christ be-
> lieves the Father: "I speak to the world what I have heard from the Father"
> (below 8:26). So he expressed verbally nothing but the Father and the words
> of the Father, because he has been sent by the Father, and because he is the
> Word of the Father. Hence, he says that he even bespeaks the Father.
> Or, if the statement *God is true* refers to Christ, we understand the dis-
> tinction of persons; for since the Father is true God, and Christ is true God,
> it follows that the true God sent the true God, who is distinct from him in
> person, but not in nature.[47]

In the Incarnate Christ, the hypostatic union had given God a human
nature that, unlike the human nature of the other prophets, was God's
joint instrument. In His case, God did not just speak to a prophet and
through a prophet; God Himself had become a prophet and spoke to
human beings in person. In the case of the prophets the doctrine was
from God, but the words were of the human prophetic instrument; in
the case of Christ, the doctrine was from God and the actual words
themselves were of God. The prophets spoke on behalf of God only
when He moved them to do so, but irrespective of whether He used
supernatural knowledge or otherwise, Christ, as the God-Man, spoke
God's words always.[48]

Another aspect of this *denuntiatio verbis* that distinguished Christ
from the other prophets is the testimony that each respectively gave
to the divine truth that He proclaimed. The other prophets testified
that divine truth had been revealed to them, but they could not testify

---

46 *ST* III 42.4, corp.
47 *In Joan.*, ch. 3, lect. 6, 540.
48 Cassar, 54; cf., *In Joan.*, ch. 3, lect. 6 and ch. 14, lect. 2.

to its intrinsic truthfulness since they did not see the divine essence. They instead had faith and not direct vision.[49] Christ, however, was different. He gave testimony to the truth, for this was His mission.[50] In reference to John 3:32a Aquinas writes:

> For Christ, as God, is truth itself; but as man, he is its witness: "For this was I born, and for this I came into the world: to testify to the truth" (below 18:37). Therefore, he gives testimony to himself: "You testify to yourself" (below 8:13). And he testifies to what is certain, because his testimony is about what he has heard with the Father: "I speak to the world what I have heard from my Father" (below 8:26); "What we have seen and heard" (I Jn 1:13).[51]

As God, He was Truth Itself; as Man, He was a witness to the truth. As Man, He was also able to give direct "eye-witness" testimony to the truth itself because Christ was the only prophet with vision rather than faith.[52] "In Christ there was neither faith nor hope, on account of their implying an imperfection. But instead of faith, He had manifest vision, and instead of hope, full comprehension: so that in Him was perfect charity."[53]

Just as Christ's words proclaimed the divinely revealed truths to the people, so too did His deeds (*denuntiatio factis*). The deeds of the prophets signified something divine only occasionally; in contrast, Christ's deeds signified something divine always for by the Incarnation all of Christ's actions were actions of God. Unlike the other prophets, Christ had a permanent spiritual knowledge; thus, His deeds could not but reflect some aspect of it.[54]

In his discussion on the fittingness of the Incarnation, Aquinas states that one of its purposes was for Christ to set an example of right action.[55] He quotes Augustine for support, "Not man, who can be seen, should be followed, but God, who can not be seen. So then, that we might be shown one who would be both seen and followed, God became man."[56] Aquinas then proceeds in later questions of the third part to make statements in regard to Christ as the highest ex-

---

49 Cassar, 55.
50 *In Joan.*, ch. 3, lect. 6, 536.
51 Ibid., ch. 3, lect. 6, 533.
52 Cassar, 55–56.
53 *ST* I–II 65.5, ad 3.
54 Cassar, 61.
55 *ST* III 1.2, corp.; cf. *ST* III 40.1, ad 3.
56 Ibid., III 1.2, corp. (Augustine, *Sermo.* 371, 2. PL 39, 1660).

ample of all virtues, one above the other prophets. He says, "Christ wished to manifest his divinity through his humanity…by preaching and working miracles and by leading among men a blameless and righteous life."[57] "Christ was set before men as an example to all."[58]

In conclusion, Christ's proclamation of the revealed divine truths by word and deed (*denuntiatio verbis et factis*) set Him apart as the greatest of all prophets for several reasons. First, the other prophets spoke in God's name and on His behalf. Christ is distinct in person from the Father, but He and the Father are one in nature with the Holy Spirit. God no longer speaks to a prophet and through him, for He Himself became a prophet so as to speak to human beings in person. Before the Incarnation, God spoke through a prophet only when He moved them to speak. When Christ spoke, His words were always God's words. Second, Christ could testify to the intrinsic truthfulness of what He spoke for God is truth. The other prophets could not. They had faith, He, vision. Third, the deeds of the prophets signified something divine only occasionally. On account of the Incarnation, all of Christ's deeds were deeds of God. Fourth, Christ set an example of right action most perfectly. He is the highest example of all virtues.

1.5.3 The third aspect: the confirmation through miracles

The last aspect of prophecy, although extrinsic to prophecy proper, is the confirmation of the divine origin of the prophetic message by the working of miracles. Both Christ and the prophets worked miracles, but the degree of excellence is exhibited when one compares the miracles with regard to their respective purposes and the manner in which the miracles were worked.

The general purpose of the prophets in working miracles, according to Aquinas, was to confirm their claim that they truly received a divine revelation and, consequently, spoke in the name of God. Christ's purpose was similar, but this was not enough. He also wanted to persuade His listeners that He was, Himself, God. The miracles of the other prophets were intended to confirm the divine origin of the doctrine proclaimed; those worked by Christ were meant to confirm

---

57   Ibid., III 40.1, ad 1.
58   Ibid., III 39.4, ad 3.

both the divine origin of His doctrine and the divine origin of Himself.[59] Aquinas puts this well when he writes:

> Christ wrought miracles in order to confirm his teaching, and in order to demonstrate the divine power that was his. And so, as regards the first, it was not proper for him to work miracles before he began to teach. For it was not proper for him to begin to teach before he had come of age, as stated above, when we discussed his baptism. But as regards the second, it was proper that he should so demonstrate his divinity by miracles that men would believe in the reality of his humanity.[60]

This added purpose thus gave Christ's miracles an excellence above the others.

According to Aquinas, Christ also worked miracles in a manner that set Him above the other prophets. Even apart from their number and variety, which no other prophet could emulate, Christ introduced the distinctive and peculiar element of working them with His own almighty power. It is true that on some occasions He Himself prayed to His Father, as the others did before working miracles, to show that the Father was acting and confirming His actions. But usually, with the greater miracles, He worked them by his own authority so as to show that He, unlike the others, was equal to the Father.[61] Aquinas cites John Chrysostom as his authority on this point:

> As Chrysostom says on Mt 14:19, He took the five loaves and the two fishes, and, looking up to heaven, he blessed and broke: It must be believed concerning Christ, both that he is from the Father and that he is equal to him. And so, in order to demonstrate both, he works miracles now with power, now with prayer. In the lesser things, certainly, he looks up to heaven—for instance, in the multiplication of the loaves—but in the greater, which are proper to God alone, he acts with power; for instance, when he forgave sins and raised the dead.[62]

In addition, Christ worked miracles on Himself which the other prophets did not do. The most notable are the Transfiguration and the Resurrection.[63] Still, like the miracles of the prophets, Christ's miracles did not provide intrinsic evidence of the truth of His doctrine.

---

59 Cassar, 69–70.
60 *ST* III 43.3, corp.
61 Cassar, 70.
62 *ST* III 43.2, ad 2.
63 Cf. *ST* III 45 and 53.

However noble, they furnished only an extrinsic motive for belief in Him and this is why He repeatedly appealed for the virtue of faith.[64]

In summary, the degree to which Christ exercised His prophetic role by carrying out the three aspects of prophecy enables Him to be regarded as the most excellent of prophets. Christ's reception of revealed knowledge (*acceptio cognitorum*) was superior on grounds that its medium (intellectual visions) provided the most excellent means of manifesting the divine truth. It also provided an incomparably wider scope of knowledge and enabled Christ to use this knowledge at will. Christ's proclamation (*denuntiatio*) of the received divine message by word was most excellent in both proclamation and testimony. God no longer speaks to and through a prophet but rather becomes a prophet through the Incarnation. The truthfulness of this speech is supported by the fact that the One Who uttered it is Truth. He sees the divine Essence. The Incarnation is also responsible for the fact that the deeds of Christ are the deeds of God Himself; therefore, He gave a most excellent example of right action, of virtuous living. Christ's miracles confirmed the truthfulness of the revealed message because Christ intended to show that it was God Himself Who performed them. He did so through His own almighty power.[65]

1.6 Christ as the culmination of history

Aquinas not only regarded Christ as the most excellent of prophets but he saw Christ as the culmination of successive and progressive stages in the history of prophecy and salvation. Aquinas based this position on an axiom from Gregory the Great that reads: "knowledge of God went on increasing as time went on" (*Hom. xvi in Ezech.*).[66] This axiom is operative in *Summa theologiae* II-1.7 which deals with the question of whether or not the articles of faith increase over time. He answers that while the number of articles may increase as a result of study, their increase is the result of making explicit what was already implicit. New articles may be written but the substance of the faith remains the same. What is of particular interest is what he says of Christ later in his reply to objection four. He writes:

---

64 Cassar, 70.
65 Cf. *Ad Heb.*, ch. 1, lect.1; *Ad Gal.*, ch. 4, lect. 2; *ST* II–II 1.7.
66 Cf. *Ad Heb.*, ch. 1, lect. 1; *ST* II–II 1.7 and 174.6.

The further away the viewer, the less clear his view. Thus those nearer to Christ's coming had a more detailed awareness of the things to be hoped for....Through Christ grace was given in its final form and so his time is called *the time of fullness*. Those, therefore, who were closer in time to Christ, whether before him, like John the Baptist, or after him, like the Apostles, had a fuller knowledge of the mysteries of faith. It is like human life, where perfection comes at youth and a person is more vigorous the closer he is to his youth, whether before or after.[67]

The closer to Christ, the greater the knowledge: John the Baptist had an advantage over Moses for he pointed Christ out (literally with his finger) in his human presence; the apostles surpass Moses, for they witness a fuller revelation of the mysteries.[68]

Aquinas' identification of the fullness of Christ with the fullness of time is explained even further in his *Commentary on Galatians* where he interprets verse 4:4. He writes:

Hence he [Paul] says: *But, when the fullness of the time was come*, i.e., after the time fixed by God the Father for sending His Son had been accomplished....Two reasons are given why that time was pre-ordained for the coming of Christ. One is taken from His greatness: for since He that was to come was great, it was fitting that men be made ready for His coming by many indications and many preparations....The other is taken from the role of the one coming: for since a physician was to come, it was fitting that before his coming, men should be keenly aware of their infirmity, both as to their lack of knowledge during the Law of nature and as to their lack of virtue during the written Law. Therefore it was fitting that both, namely, the Law of nature and the written Law, precede the coming of Christ.[69]

Thus, time was preordained for the Incarnation so as to highlight Christ's greatness and salvific role. The plenitude is situated in the middle of time: between a "before" and an "after" instead of a perpetual youthfulness.[70]

In conclusion, revelation throughout the history of prophecy and salvation is successive and progressive in that each following stage

---

67 *ST* II–II 1.7, ad 4.

68 Ibid., II–II 174.4, ad 3; II–II 174.6, ad 3; René Latourelle, *Theology of Revelation: Including a Commentary on the Constitution "Dei verbum"* New York: Society of St. Paul, 1966), 161–62.

69 St. Thomas Aquinas, *Commentary on St. Paul's Epistle to the Galatians*, translated by F. R. Larcher, with an introduction by Richard T. A. Murphy, Aquinas Scripture Series, vol. 1 (Albany: Magi Books, 1966), ch. 4, lect. 2. (Hereafter, referred to as *Ad Gal.*)

70 André Hayen, "Le Thomisme et l'histoire," *Revue Thomiste* (Janvier–Mars 1962): 60.

constitutes a greater explicit realization of the implicit articles of faith. The closer one comes to Christ through prophecy and the articles of faith, the closer one comes to the fullness of revelation. For Aquinas, Christ is the culmination of history.

1.7 Section summary

Prophecy, for Aquinas, consists essentially in knowledge, supernaturally imparted by God, of truths exceeding the natural knowledge of a person for the benefit of the community. It requires an intellectual light that surpasses the light of natural reason, inheres transiently in the prophet or the common instrumental agent, and is used by the prophet to make judgments. The excellence of a prophecy is determined by how well it meets its end: the manifestation of some truth that surpasses the natural human faculty. The manifestation is created and imperfect.

Whether or not the title of "prophet" could be applied to Christ was problematic for Aquinas. How could the incarnate Son of God have imperfect infused knowledge? After much development in his thought, Aquinas holds in the end that the term can be applied to Christ because: a) the presence of the beatific knowledge in Christ neither excludes nor formally brings prophetic knowledge about; b) Christ knew divine things also from a distance like the prophets, even though much more perfectly and extensively than they; and c) the cognitive medium of the infused species formally constituted Him as a prophet. Once Aquinas attributes the title of prophet to Christ, he then argues that Christ is the most excellent of all the prophets in the following three areas: a) the reception of revealed knowledge; b) the proclamation of the revealed knowledge; and c) the confirmation of the revealed knowledge's divine origin through miracles. In addition, Christ is the culmination of successive and progressive stages in the history of prophecy.

2 Jesus Christ in the Role of the Word

In dealing with Aquinas' understanding of Christ as prophet, we have seen that Christ teaches humanity divine truths by His created infused knowledge. He does not teach us supernatural truths by created experimental knowledge, for that, by being purely natural, is obviously insufficient. Christ does have experiential knowlegdge and He doubtlessly used it to convey, expound, and illustrate His prophetic truths. Considering the supernatural content of such truths, however, it is clear that experiential knowledge could not have provided Him with the doctrines He taught.[71] He does not teach us by beatific knowledge either because while His human intellect has perfect vision of the divine essence, it can not comprehend or communicate it. Instead Christ reveals divine truths by reason of His created infused knowledge which, while being sufficiently wide in extent, is proportionate to the human intellect and can thus adequately be expressed in human words.[72]

In the human nature which the Word assumed at the Incarnation, God expressed His concept and ordained this expression to His self-revelation.[73] Referring to human speech as an example, Aquinas says that when a human being wishes to express hidden thoughts to another, it is done by means of an external, sensible word.[74] In a similar manner, wishing to reveal Himself to humanity, God clothed His hidden Word in human flesh.[75]

We have looked at the expressed word within the context of prophecy; now mention will be made regarding the unexpressed Word. A contrast needs to be drawn between the expression of the Word in words and the Word itself because Christ (the Word) reveals the Godhead in prophetic words.

---

71 I.e., Christ received the prophetic truths through infused knowledge but conveyed them with the assistance of experiential knowledge. It should also be noted that early in his career Aquinas rejected the idea of experiential knowledge in Christ (cf. *In III Sent.*, d. 14, a. 3, qla. 5, ad 3; d. 18, a. 3, ad 5; *De ver.* q, 20, a. 3, ad 1. Later he reverses himself and accepts the idea (cf. *ST* III 9.4; 12.2; *Compend.*, 216).

72 Cassar, 18, 24–26, 40–44.

73 *Ad Heb.*, ch. 1, lect. 1.

74 *In Joan.*, ch. 1, lect. 1, 25; ch. 14, lect. 2.

75 Ibid., ch. 14, lect. 2 and 4.

2.1 The expression of the Word in words versus the Word Itself

Through prophetic means, God reveals Himself and His plans; however, from the perspective of human involvement, this prophetic knowledge is limited and imperfect. When God wanted to communicate Himself to the fullest and perfect extent, He clothed up His eternally conceived Word with flesh in time.[76] Christ is far superior to the "words" of the prophet (which are nonetheless great due to the action of God) for He is precisely the "Word of the Father." Aquinas explains extensively the differences between human word and the divine Word as follows:

> We should note that this Word differs from our own word in three ways. The first difference…is that our word is formable before being formed….So long as the intellect, in so reasoning, casts about this way and that, the formation is not yet complete. It is only when it has conceived the notion of the thing perfectly that for the first time it has the notion of the complete thing and a word. Thus in our mind there is both a "cognition," meaning the discourse involved in an investigation, and a word, which is formed according to a perfect contemplation of the truth. So our word is first in potency before it is in act. But the Word of God is always in act. In consequence, the term "cognition" does not properly speaking apply to the Word of God….
>
> The second difference is that our word is imperfect, but the divine Word is most perfect. For since we can not express all our conceptions in one word, we must form many imperfect words through which we separately express all that is in our knowledge. But it is not that way with God. For since he understands both himself and everything else through his essence, by one act, the single divine Word is expressive of all that is in God, not only of the Persons but also of creatures; otherwise it would be imperfect….
>
> The third difference is that our word is not of the same nature as we; but the divine Word is of the same nature as God.[77]

Once the Word is sent, no one can expect more from Him because it is not possible to say more. In Christ, God has said everything, has revealed all about Himself and His works, has communicated Himself fully.[78] "All that the Father knows is said with His only Word."[79]

---

76 Ibid., ch. 14, lect. 2.
77 Ibid.., ch. 1, lect. 1, 26–28.
78 Arturo Blanco, "Word and Truth in Divine Revelation: A Study of the Commentary of St. Thomas on John 14, 6," in *La Doctrine de la Révélation Divine de Saint Thomas d'Aquin*, Actes du symposium sur la pensée de Saint Thomas d'Aquin tenu a Rolduc, les 4 et 5 Novembre 1989, edited by Leo Elders, Studi Tomistici, 37 (Vatican City: Libreria Editrice Vaticana, 1990), 31.

Christ's words and deeds as a prophet have been studied. Now the focus will shift to what He has revealed about Himself as the Word of God.

2.2 The Word as truth

Aquinas ascribes the virtue of truth to God on account of His divine essence.[80] Every being is true, and God, as the Supreme Being, is supremely true; in fact, He is Truth Itself, the First Truth.[81] While truth is the essential property of the divine essence, Aquinas argues that it is rightfully appropriated to the Son. This is the case because the Son, as the Word, proceeds by way of the intellect from the Father just as truth follows the conception of the intellect.[82] In this sense then, "truth belongs to him [Christ] *per se*, because he is the Word."[83]

How does this truth impact humanity? In human beings, truth is a possession for intellectual concepts are measured by the respective concepts (since truth is the conformity of the mind with the object known).[84] These concepts (intellectual words) are true, but they are not truth. In God, truth is not measured by other objects; rather, God is the measure of truth. The truth conceived in the divine intellect is the very Truth by essence. Aquinas speaks of this issue in a few places:

> The divine intellect and the divine essence are not, however, made equal to each other in the way in which a measure is related to what is measured, since one is not the source of the other, but are entirely identical. Consequently, the truth resulting from such equality does not involve its having the character of a source, whether it be considered from the standpoint of the essence or from that of the intellect, since both in this case are one and the same. For, just as in God the knower and the thing known are the same, so also in Him the truth of the thing and that of intellect are the same, without any connotation of origin.[85]

---

79 *Quodl. IV*, q. 4 a. 6; as quoted in Blanco, 31, fn. 7.
80 *SCG* I ch. 60, [2–4].
81 *ST* I 16.5, corp.; cf. *SCG* I ch. 61.
82 *ST* I 39.7, corp.; *In Joan.* ch. 18, lect. 6, 11.
83 Ibid.; as quoted in Cassar, 10.
84 Cf. *Super Metaph.*, VI, lect. 4, comm. 1; *ST* I 16.1–3; *De ver.*, q. 1, art. 1–3.
85 *De ver.*, q. 1, art. 7.

> He was also *full of truth,* because the human nature in Christ attained to the divine truth itself, that is, that this man should be the divine Truth itself. In other men we find many participated truths, insofar as the First Truth gleams back into their minds through many likenesses; but Christ is Truth itself. Thus it is said: "In whom all the treasures of wisdom are hidden" (Col. 2:3).[86]

Thus, all human comprehension of truth is dependent upon the Truth. Since this Truth is the Word, all truth has its prime analogate in Christ. Aquinas' position here is significant in light of the search for his theological prime analogate.

2.3 The Word as begotten Wisdom

We have seen, above, in our specific discussion concerning sacred doctrine that wisdom is the knowledge of God, the knowledge of divine things, the knowledge of the Highest Cause.[87] This knowledge obviously belongs to God Himself, and Aquinas even goes so far as to say that God is super-wise.[88] Created wisdom is a participation in the uncreated absolute wisdom of God.[89] In his commentary on John's Gospel, Aquinas makes this point along with the others discussed above:

> I answer that although there are many participated truths, there is just one absolute Truth, which is Truth by its very essence, that is, the divine act of being (*esse*); and by this Truth all words are words. Similarly, there is one absolute Wisdom elevated above all things, that is, the divine Wisdom, by participating in which all wise persons are wise. Further, there is one absolute Word, by participating in which all persons having a word are called speakers. Now this is the divine Word which of itself is the Word elevated above all words.[90]

Aquinas holds that God is wise because He knows Himself. "For if wisdom consists in the knowledge of the highest causes…and if God especially knows Himself, and does not know anything…except by knowing Himself Who is the first cause of all things, it is manifest

---

86   *In Joan.,* ch. 1, lect. 8, 188.
87   *ST* I 1.6, corp.; cf. *ST* I–II 66.5, corp.
88   *De pot.,* q. 7, art. 5.
89   *ST* I 41.3, ad 2; *ST* II–II 23.2, ad 1; *SCG* III ch. 163.
90   *In Joan.,* ch. 1, lect. 1, 33.

that wisdom must most especially be attributed to Him."[91] God's act of understanding is His essence.[92] Wisdom along with truth is part of that understanding and, due to the identity, part of the essence. "By natural knowledge...only God sees himself, because essence and intellect in God are the same thing and so God's essence is present to his intellect."[93]

By being identical with the divine essence, it follows that divine wisdom is attributed to God only essentially.[94] Wisdom, therefore, is held equally by the three divine Persons, Who are one wisdom as they are one essence.[95] "In the godhead 'to be wise' or 'to be knowing' do not have any but an essential sense; this is why we can not say that the Father is wise or knowing by the Son."[96] Nevertheless, like truth, and for the same reason, wisdom is appropriated to the Son for being intellectual, wisdom resembles the Son's origin, that of proceeding from the Father as the Word of His mind.[97] Aquinas writes:

> [A]ppropriation may be made on the grounds that what is common nevertheless has a greater resemblance to what is proper to one person than it has to what is proper to another....Similarly, wisdom is appropriated to the Son, because it resembles what is proper to the Son, since the Son proceeds from the Father as His Word, and *word* describes an intellectual procession. Consequently, because the book of life pertains to knowledge, it should be appropriated to the Son.[98]

Augustine, knowing that the Word is generated by the Father, speaks of the wisdom appropriated by the Word as "Begotten Wisdom" in his book, *De Trinitate*.[99] Aquinas picks this term up and adds that the Father is wise in conceiving and the Son is His conceived Word. He speaks of this in *De potential:*

> As the Father is God begetting and the Son God begotten, so must we say that the Father is wise and conceiving, while the Son is wise and conceived. Because the Son in that he is the Word is a conception of a wise being. But since whatsoever is in God is God it follows that the very conception of a

---

91 *SCG* I ch. 94, [2].
92 *ST* III 9.1, ad 1.
93 *I ad Cor.*, ch. 13, lect. 4; as quoted in Cassar, 12.
94 *In I Sent.*, d. 27, q. 2, a. 2, qla. 2, sol. 1, ad 1.
95 Ibid., *prol.*
96 *ST* I 37.2, ad 1.
97 *In I Sent.*, d. 34, q. 2, a. 1; as quoted in Cassar, 12.
98 *De ver.*, q. 7, art. 3, corp.
99 Bk. 7, ch. 2: PL 42, 936.

wise God is God, is wise, is powerful and whatsoever is appropriate to God.[100]

Since the Son is the Begotten Wisdom of the Father, He then is the supreme perfection of His wisdom. This same conclusion may be arrived at using the principle, which Aquinas does in fact use, that whatever proceeds from another bears some resemblance to the principle from which it proceeds.[101] The aspect being dealt with here concerns intelligence by which the lesser can know its principle. Now the closer their resemblance to God, the more perfect is their resulting knowledge of Him. The Son, however, has the most perfect resemblance to the Father since He has the same essence and power as the Father does, and so He knows the Father most perfectly. The reasons for the Son's perfect knowledge of the Father is due to the Son's eternal generation through which He is consubstantial with the Father. By begetting the Son as the perfect image of Himself, the Father gave Him the whole perfection of His own wisdom.[102] Thus, Christ, the Incarnate Word, was the highest sending of God's Wisdom to humankind.[103]

2.4 Section summary

In summarizing Aquinas' doctrine of uncreated truth and wisdom, both belong to God and are said of Him by way of essence, simply and absolutely. The Word, as indistinct from the divine essence, is identified with both of them. Since, however, the Word proceeds from the Father by way of intelligence, and since truth and wisdom are intellectual, they are appropriated to the Son as Begotten Truth and Wisdom. Consequently, the Son is the Father's Wisdom.[104] He is the "Doctrine of the Father."[105] As sent, He reveals the Godhead in the highest form of truth and wisdom, for He is such by reason of His existence as divine essence. He is the culmination of revelation in that He reveals the Father perfectly as Truth and Wisdom.

---

100   *De pot.*, q. 9, art. 9, ad 6.
101   Cassar, 14.
102   *In Joan.*, ch. 7, lect. 3, 1065; cf. *In Joan.*, ch. 7, lect. 2, 1037.
103   Cassar, 15.
104   Ibid.
105   *In Joan.*, ch. 7, lect. 3.

With regard to created truth and wisdom, Christ, as man, had the fullness of truth and wisdom. He possessed acquired knowledge more perfectly than any other human being. He enjoyed the beatific vision and thus knew the divine essence. He had infused species whereby He knew all natural things and all divine mysteries, with the exception of the divine essence, and revealed this knowledge perfectly as a prophet. As a prophet, He revealed the uncreated Truth and Wisdom through created truth and wisdom. In Jesus Christ, God sent humanity His own uncreated Wisdom in human flesh; in Him, God also sent humanity a prophet possessing the fullness of created truth and wisdom. Christ is the fullness of revelation.[106]

3 Jesus Christ in the Role of Teacher

As presented above, Christ proclaimed divine truth by virtue of His infused knowledge which constituted Him as a prophet. He was the most excellent of all the prophets by the dignity of His divine Person, by the extent of His knowledge, and by the testimony He gave to its truthfulness.[107] Now attention will be focused on the related performance of His teaching mission as the most excellent teacher of the faith. In this role, it will be discovered that, for Aquinas, He is again the fullness of revelation.

In His widely diverse teaching and preaching ministry, Christ spoke of truths that both could be and could not be known without explicit revelation. The content of His teaching revealed a new conception of God and of His Kingdom, a content rooted in His being the Word of God. By being the Word of God, He could identify Himself as the Way, the Truth, and the Life. He is the Way, the means through which all must pass in order to know God and enter into His Kingdom. He is the Truth because He is the Word conceived in the divine intellect.[108] He is the Life because as Word, He proceeds in God according to His intellectual operation and has the ability to act of Himself without being moved by others.[109] By preaching as such, Aquinas

---

106 Cassar, 25–26.
107 Ibid., 56.
108 Cf. *In Joan.*, ch. 1, lect. 8; ch. 14, lect. 2.
109 Cf. *ST* I 18.4; *SCG* I ch. 97; *De pot.*, q. 10 art. 1; *De ver.*, q. 4, art. 8.

grants Him the titles: "the first and principal Doctor of the faith";[110] the "most excellent Doctor";[111] and "Doctor of wisdom."[112]

These titles are befitting of Christ because He was uniquely gifted for this teaching mission. First, as noted above, He possessed uncreated and created truth and wisdom. Second, Aquinas attributes to Him the gifts of the Holy Spirit because of the fact that His soul was perfectly subject to the movement of the Holy Spirit; therefore, He was endowed with these gifts.[113] Third, Christ was endowed with charisms (*gratiae gratis datae*). He explains:

> The charisms are designed to help present the faith and spiritual teaching....A teacher must have the means to present his doctrine; otherwise his doctrine will be useless. Now Christ is the first and most authoritative doctor of the faith and of spiritual teaching. As Hebrews says, *It was declared at first by the Lord, and it was attested to us by those who heard him, while God also bore witness by signs and wonders.* It is clear then that Christ had all the charisms in a surpassing degree, as befits the first and original teacher of the faith.[114]

These charisms were given to other preachers and prophets as need be for their mission, often in a temporary fashion. Christ, however, possessed all of them permanently because of the full and perfect union of the human nature with the divine nature. He elaborates in his commentary on John's Gospel:

> But in Christ, in whom human nature is united to the divinity in the unity of a *suppositum*, we find a full and perfect union with God. The reason for this is that this union was such that all the acts not only of his divine nature but also of his human nature were acts of the *suppositum* [or person]....He was also *full of truth*, because the human nature in Christ attained to the divine truth itself, that is, that this man should be the divine Truth itself. In other men we find many participated truths, insofar as the First Truth gleams back into their minds through many likenesses; but Christ is Truth itself. Thus it is said: "In whom all the treasures of wisdom are hidden" (Col 2:3).
>
> ...these words [*full of grace and truth*] can be applied in relation to the perfection of his soul. Then he is said to be *full of grace and truth* inasmuch as in his soul there was the fullness of all graces without measure: "God does not bestow the Spirit in fractions," as we read below (3:34). Yet it was given in fractions to all rational creatures, both angels and men. For according to

---

110 *ST* III 7.7, corp.
111 Ibid., III 42.4, corp.
112 *In Joan.* ch. 1, lect. 14.
113 *ST* III 7.5, corp.
114 Ibid., III 7.7, corp.

Augustine, just as there is one sense common to all the parts of the body, namely, the sense of touch, while all the senses are found in the head, so in Christ, who is the head of every rational creature (and in a special way of the saints who are united to him by faith and charity), all virtues and graces and gifts are found superabundantly; but in others, i.e., the saints, we find participations of the graces and gifts, although there is a gift common to all the saints, and that is charity.

Further, Christ was also *full of truth* because his precious and blessed soul knew every truth, human and divine, from the instant of his conception.[115]

The gifts possessed by Christ influenced His teaching methods which were superior as well. Jesus taught not only in a manner that was persuasive, with authority, and confirmed by miracles, but also His manner itself was set apart by His righteousness demonstrated in His sinless lifestyle.[116] Christ taught nothing immoral. He taught not to the few but to all who would hear Him. He did speak to the crowds in parable about spiritual mysteries that were obscure. This was due to the crowd's inability or unworthiness to grasp the mysteries. It was, however, better for them to be instructed in this subtle manner than not to be instructed at all. To the few who were able and worthy (namely, his disciples), He spoke clearly and openly about these mysteries.[117] He always spoke and did not commit anything to writing. This is due to the fact that it was fitting for the most excellent of teachers to use the most excellent means of teaching, namely, imprinting his doctrine on the heart by speaking and not by writing. In the end, writing is ordered to the same end—the imprinting of doctrine in the hearts of the listeners.[118] In so doing, Christ also had the power to illuminate one's mind to ensure the effect of His external words.[119]

Thus, Christ is the most excellent of teachers since the content of His teaching is based on His existence as the Word of God. In addition, He was uniquely gifted with special gifts for His teaching mission which enabled Him to carry it out in a manner far superior to any other teachers. Since the purpose of His teaching was to communicate truths concerning the Godhead, and He did so in a most excel-

---

115 *In Joan.*, ch. 1, lect. 8, 188–89; cf. *ST* III 7.1.
116 *ST* III 42.2, ad 2.
117 Ibid., III 42.3, corp.
118 Ibid., III 43.4, corp.
119 Cf. *ST* III 13.2; *In Joan.* ch. 15, lect. 5, 4; Cassar, 58–59.

lent manner, here is yet another manifestation of His role as the Revelation of God, the culmination of all divine revelation. It is fitting that Aquinas should say of Christ, He "is the first and original teacher of the faith."[120]

4 Jesus Christ in the Role of Mediator

Jesus Christ's role as prophet and teacher are closely associated in Aquinas because they are both functions of a mediator.

4.1 The nature of a mediator

According to Aquinas, a mediator possesses two properties. First, a mediator is to be a middle term; second, a mediator is to bring together and unite the two extremes. A mediator communicates to the one something that belongs to the other so as to establish some sort of connection.[121] It acts on behalf of both.

The title of mediator is attributed to various rational persons such as angels, demons, priests, and prophets.[122] According to Aquinas, they, however, are secondary and imperfect mediators since they are dependent upon Christ as the principal and perfect mediator. Christ is a mediator because He possesses the two properties of such a role not as God but as man. Aquinas explains:

> For as God he is distinct in nature and lordship from the Father and the Holy Spirit; nor do the Father and the Holy Spirit possess anything which the Son does not possess and which, as belonging to them and not to himself, he might bear to others.
>
> But both elements are realized in Christ as man. For a man he is set apart from God in nature and from men in the eminence of his grace and glory. Likewise as man his office is to unite men with God, which he does by setting before men the divine commandments and gifts and by atoning and interceding for men with God. It is, therefore, as man that he is, in the truest sense of the word, mediator.[123]

---

120   *ST* III 7.7, corp.
121   *In III Sent.*, d. 19, a. 5, qla. 3, sol. 2;
122   *ST* III 26.2, ad 2.
123   Ibid.

In other words, Christ is a mediator as man for his human nature is a created nature. On the one hand, it remains distinct from the divine nature; on the other, in the same human nature, Christ has a fullness of grace which distinguishes Him from all other human beings.[124] It is as human that Christ unites human beings to God by transmitting to them divine precepts and gifts and by offering God satisfaction and prayers for human beings. On account of the importance of two natures in uniting the two extremes, it is obvious that the role of mediator can not apply to either the Father or the Holy Spirit.

It is also important to point out that the above quotation makes mention of the reason why the Son of God became incarnate. He did so "to unite men with God, which he does…by atoning and interceding for men with God."[125] The God-Man is the perfect mediator insofar as His death brought about something that no other human being could do; namely, He reconciled the human race with God by removing the obstacles of sin and death. He united humanity to God by communicating to human beings precepts and gifts and by offering perfect satisfaction and prayers to God for sinful humanity.[126]

4.2 The excellence of Christ as mediator due to grace

To return to the theme of Christ's excellence as a mediator, such a perfection is also due to "the eminence of his grace and glory" which is given as a result of the hypostatic union.[127] Aquinas identifies two types of grace in Christ. The first is the grace of union. It is the personal existence that is freely and divinely given to the human nature of Christ in the Person of the Word as a result of the Word assuming a human nature.[128] The second type of grace, habitual grace, pertains to the spiritual holiness of the person and is derived from the grace of union which precedes it in the order of nature.[129] That Christ is full of grace and truth derives from the fact that He is the Only-Begotten Son of the Father which belongs to Him through the union. Other human

---

124 Cl. Chopin, *Le Verbe Incarné et Rédempteur*, Le Mystère Chrétien: Théologie Dogmatique, vol. 8 (Tournai, Belgium: Desclée, 1963), 115.
125 *ST* III 26.2, corp.
126 Ibid.
127 *ST* III 26.2, corp.; III 7.13, corp.
128 Ibid., III 6.6, corp.
129 Ibid., III 7.13, corp.; cf. *De ver.*, q. 29, art. 1.

beings are in union with God by the activities of knowing and loving Him, and such a union presupposes habitual grace perfecting these activities.[130] In contrast, the union of human nature with the Word of God is a union of personal existence and that depends on no habit but rather on the nature itself.[131]

According to Aquinas, Christ indeed possessed this habitual grace for three reasons. First, His human soul was in union with the Word of God. God is the source of grace and the closer any recipient is to its source or cause, the more it is influenced by it. So it is most fitting that His soul receive that grace. Second, the dignity of Christ's soul requires that He know and love God in the most intimate way. This is accomplished by the bestowal of grace upon the human soul. Third, His position in the human race as mediator between God and humanity requires that He have grace to such an extent that it overflows to others. As God's Son by nature, Christ is entitled to His eternal inheritance, uncreated happiness in the uncreated act of knowing and loving God. Due to the fact that it is of a human nature, Christ's soul is not capable of such an activity. Thus, it must attain God by a created act of bliss that can only be derived from habitual grace.[132]

According to Aquinas, habitual grace has two different aspects. As personal to Christ, justifying His soul, habitual grace is called personal grace. As coming from Christ and extending to others, members of His Church, it is called capital grace. Aquinas writes, "the personal grace, which justifies the soul of Christ, is in reality the same thing as the grace which makes him the head of the Church, justifying others. It has, however, a different meaning."[133] There is simply a distinction of reason between them.[134]

Habitual grace, for Aquinas, reached its fullness and perfection in Christ both intensively and extensively. Grace existed in Him intensively because, as stated above, His soul was closest to the source of grace and as mediator He was the means by which grace flowed to others. His grace also extended to every activity and effect that grace can produce. The reason for this is that grace was given to Him as a

---

130 The grace of union is not designed for activity but personal existence. Habitual grace is designed for some type of activity (*ST* III 8.5, ad 3).
131 *ST* III 6.6.
132 Ibid., III 7.1.
133 Ibid., III 8.5, corp.
134 Ibid.

universal principle of an order which extends itself to all the effects of that order. Thus, the absolute fullness of grace is proper to Christ alone.[135]

Christ also possesses all the virtues which are in Him as a natural outpouring of His fullness of grace. Grace pertains to the essence of the soul while virtues pertain to its powers. As powers flow from the essence of the soul, the virtues flow from grace. Since grace is perfect and complete in Christ, the virtues that flow from it must likewise be complete. In Christ, then, the fullness of grace unfolds itself into a fullness of virtue.[136]

For Aquinas, with this in mind, Christ is the most excellent of all mediators because He possesses the fullness of grace and all the virtues. As such, "of His fullness we all have received, grace for grace" (Jn 1:16) and through this grace, reconciliation between God and humanity has been achieved. Humanity is now able to participate in divine life as originally intended by God.

4.3 The excellence of Christ as mediator due to glory

As stated above, Aquinas holds that the excellence of Christ as mediator is due not only to the eminence of His grace but also to the eminence of His glory. Aquinas does not spell out the significance of His glory as directly and systematically as he does with Christ's grace. Its significance can be elucidated, however. Aquinas accepts Cicero's, Ambrose's, and Augustine's definition of glory as clear knowledge with praise of a person's displayed goodness.[137] It consists in being clearly known, not necessarily by many but by a few, as a person with good qualities that are worthy of praise and admiration.[138]

The reason for God's glory intrinsically is His infinite goodness and excellence in all attributes; extrinsically, all His works are excellent as well.[139] The reciprocal act of glorification is God's knowledge, love, and praise of Himself and creation's knowledge, love, and praise of Him and His works.[140] It was stated above, however, that the Word

---

135 Ibid., III 7.9.
136 Ibid., III 7.2, corp.
137 Ibid., II–II 132.1; *SCG* III ch. 29, [2].
138 *ST* I–II 2.3; II–II 145.3.
139 Ibid., I–II 114.1, ad 2.
140 Ibid., I–II 114.1; II–II 81.7.

Incarnate is mediator in His humanity. It is the hypostatic union that is the foundation of such mediation and of its perfection. In effect, it is in consequence of this union that there is in Christ the fullness of grace.[141] Now grace is a disposition for glory. All things pertaining to glory are first in Christ, the fullness of grace. As the fullness of grace, He is the author of glory.[142] The life of grace is directed to glory.[143]

The reason for Christ's glory intrinsically is the dignity afforded to His human nature which is most excellent by virtue of the hypostatic union and the fullness of grace.[144] Extrinsically, the resulting accomplishments (in word and deed as prophet, teacher, miracle worker, etc.) are most excellent and worthy of honor and praise. The reciprocal acts of glorification are His own self-respect and His high public regard and reputation. In other words, because Christ's human nature was full of grace, the glory due Him was set far above the glory due to any other human being. The greatness of His glory was shown forth in His Resurrection from the dead. It was fitting to manifest the excellence of Christ's power that He rise from the dead and so inaugurate the third epoch of salvation history, the eternity of glory.[145]

4.4 Section summary

To conclude, Christ, in His role as mediator, unifies God and humanity as the middle term by communicating reconciliation between the two. In so doing, He reveals the mystery of His Incarnation (Who He is) and the secret of the Godhead which was previously withheld from irreconciled humanity. That is, Christ, as God and man, unites the Creator with creation through the Incarnation. Then He incorporated into His very essence (the Godhead), through His act of reconciliation, all those who would desire to become the children of God. Such an accomplishment sets Him above all other mediators. This is due to the eminence of His grace and glory which is given as a consequence of the hypostatic union. In this role as mediator, Christ is, for Aquinas, the Revelation of God.

---

141 Ibid., III 26.2.
142 Ibid., III 53.3, ad 3.
143 Ibid., III 24.2, ad 3.
144 *De ver.*, q. 29, art. 7, ad 1.
145 *ST* III 53.2.

5 Jesus Christ in the Role of Priest

In the *Summa theologiae*, Aquinas' treatment of the priesthood of Christ (III 22) actually precedes his treatment of the mediatorship of Christ (III 26). The latter treatment summarizes his prior discussions concerning both prophet (II-II 171–178) and priest as mediators. The treatment of the priesthood in the *Summa theologiae* systematically and concisely presents many of the more random points that Aquinas makes earlier especially in his commentary on the letter to the Hebrews. Here, as well as in the *Summa*, the focus is on the mediator as priest rather than as prophet. Aquinas comments, "every priest is a mediator."[146] The role of the priest is to mediate reconciliation and harmony through a pact between God and His people.[147]

5.1 The definition of priest

The priest, for Aquinas, functions uniquely as a mediator by communicating the things of God to the people. The priest is defined by Isidore as "the one who gives holy things."[148] The holy things of the Old Covenant are temporal goods which prefigure the perfect, heavenly, and spiritual goods dispensed by Christ in the establishment of the New Covenant.[149] The priest also functions uniquely as a reconciler by making reparation or satisfaction for the sins of the people and by offering the prayers of the people to God. Both of these functions specify the office of the priest. They also help achieve the ends for which Christ became incarnate, namely: to manifest the truth (i.e., to reveal holy things); to free humanity from sin (i.e., to make reparation or satisfaction for sin); and to enable access to God (i.e., to provide the medium for communication).[150]

These two functions of the priesthood are present, as stated above, in Aquinas' *Commentary on the Letter to the Hebrews*. In his study of chapters seven through ten, discussions regarding these functions are scattered but numerous. Aquinas states that the holy things which a

---

146 *Ad Heb.*, ch. 8, lect. 2, *Omnis enim sacerdos mediator est.*
147 Ibid., ch. 7, lect. 4.
148 *ST* III 22.1, corp.
149 *Ad Heb.*, ch. 9, lect. 3.
150 *ST* III 40.1, corp.

priest of the New Covenant dispenses (the first function) are the perfect, stable, heavenly, and spiritual goods established by Christ. They are prefigured by the imperfect, temporal, earthly goods of the Old Covenant.[151] These spiritual goods of the New Covenant are superior on several counts. First, these gifts are distributed by the priest who ministers at the tabernacle where holy things are reserved ("...a minister of the sanctuary and of the true tabernacle that the Lord, not man, set up. Now every high priest is appointed to offer gifts and sacrifices..." [Heb. 2–3a]). Christ exercises this ministry most excellently due to the hypostatic union; in Aquinas' words, Christ is a minister "not only inasmuch as he is God, because he is thus the author, but inasmuch as he is man."[152] As a result, the spiritual goods derive their excellence based on the excellence of their priest. Second, all spiritual goods that are dispensed through Him are true. (Truth is superior since it is a transcendental.) They are true on two counts: first, that which is prefigured by another contains the truth; second, the truths of the New Covenant have their origin in God, thus indicating their excellence. Third, the goods of the Old Covenant were multiplied by their priests, for they were corruptible. Christ, as the Incarnate Word of God, however, is incorruptible and eternal; therefore, His good is not multiple, for it is likewise incorruptible and eternal.[153] Fourth, when perfection is present, all imperfection ceases. Christ is full of grace and truth. He is not made from human seed and is, therefore, free of original sin. Consequently, the goods that are bestowed through Him are perfect in comparison to those made by human hands.[154] Fifth, the goods of the Old Covenant are cleansed by the blood of animals sacrificed; the goods of the New Covenant are cleansed by the blood of the more noble Jesus Christ, offered in perfect sacrifice.[155] And finally, the weakness of the Old Covenant consists in its mention of the promise of the Law's fulfillment; the strength of the New Covenant consists in charity, which is the fulfillment of the Law. Thus, the goods of the Old Covenant are images of the future goods expressed in charity. But in the end, while these

---

151 *Ad Heb.*, ch. 7, lect. 4; ch. 8, lect. 3.
152 Ibid., ch. 8, prol., *non quidem inquantum Deus, quia sic est auctor, sed inquantum homo.*
153 Ibid., ch. 7, lect. 4.
154 Ibid., ch. 9, lect. 3.
155 Ibid., ch. 9, lect. 5.

goods are superior to those of the Old Covenant, privation of future goods happens on account of sin.[156]

The *Summa theologiae's* treatment of the second priestly function is very concise and to the point. Christ reconciled the human race to God by making satisfaction for humankind's sins.[157] Due to the nature of a commentary on an epistle, Aquinas' treatment of the same function is quite diffuse and extensive in his commentary on the letter to the Hebrews. Here Aquinas does not mention the fact that satisfaction for sin removes the punishment due to sin, as he does in the *Summa*,[158] but he does dwell on the major works and accomplishments of Christ's act of reconciliation more thoroughly than in the *Summa*.[159]

In this commentary, Aquinas elaborates on Christ as the mediator of the New Covenant. This Covenant is established by the shedding of His blood and, thus, Aquinas speaks of this action's efficacy. First, Christ poured out His blood through the movement and instinct of the Holy Spirit. The sacrifice is a result, then, of the charity of God. Second, the action is efficacious because Christ is immaculate. As a result, He is able to cleanse humanity from sinfulness because He Himself is free from stain. In addition, the blood of Christ cleanses the conscience through His gift of faith which purifies the recipient's heart. In contrast, the blood of animals in the Old Covenant cleansed only from an exterior stain.[160] Third, this Covenant is given efficacy as a result of the death of Christ the covenantor or testator. Prior to death, a testament or will is open to change. After death, the testament is made firm and strong, for the wishes of the testament are enforced and bestowed upon the inheritors.[161] Finally, the New Covenant is efficacious because Christ wills it by moving beyond the Old Covenant which was not able to abolish guilt and sin. As a result, sin deprived the bestowal of the heavenly goods until the New Cove-

---

156 Ibid., ch. 10, prol.
157 *ST* III 22.1, corp.
158 Ibid., III 22.3, corp.
159 The accomplishments Aquinas mentions may be stated as follows: Christ remits sins and overcomes the consequences of sin, including death, by shedding His blood and by dying on the Cross ; as a result, Christ sanctifies and redeems humanity for all eternity (*Ad Heb.*, ch. 9, lect. 3–5; ch. 10, lect. 1).
160 *Ad Heb.*, ch. 9, lect. 3.
161 Ibid., ch. 9, lect. 4.

nant was indeed established by Christ.[162] Thus, the New Covenant is efficacious by reason of the excellence of its Priest. That is, the efficacy is due to the work of the Holy Spirit in Christ, the purity and redeeming character of Christ's blood, and the sealing of the testament by His death.

5.2 The excellence of Christ as priest

The excellence of Christ as priest has been indirectly referenced in this discussion concerning the spiritual goods offered and the efficacy of the Covenant established by the shedding of His blood. To be consistent, however, with the material presented on Christ's excellence as a prophet and mediator, a direct reference is needed.

In the *Summa theologiae*, Aquinas ties Christ's excellence to His victimhood. The fact that Christ's humanity was holy does not prevent the same humanity, offered to God in the Passion, from being sanctified in a new way. As a victim actually offered, Christ's humanity acquired then the actual holiness of a victim from the charity which it possessed from the beginning of its Incarnation and from the grace of union sanctifying it absolutely.[163]

In his *Commentary on the Letter to the Hebrews,* Aquinas speaks of the excellence of Christ as priest by speaking of its preferability to that of the Levitical priesthood. The context for this discussion is Hebrews 7:20–28 where the eternal priesthood of the order of Melchisedech was confirmed by Christ's oath as promised to Abraham (6:13) but not to the Levitical priesthood. Aquinas explains, "that which is established without an oath is less valid than that which is established with an oath; however, the priesthood of Christ has been established with an oath, as is evident, because he says: the Lord swore."[164] In addition, Christ's priesthood is eternal because Christ, rising from the dead, no longer dies. He then "can save unto eternity."[165]

Within the same lecture, Aquinas then begins to speak of Christ's excellence as priest from the perspective of sacerdotal character. The first character is holiness. Christ from the beginning of His conception

---

162 Ibid., ch. 10, lect. 1.
163 *ST* III 22.2, ad 3.
164 *Ad Heb.*, ch. 7, lect. 4.
165 Ibid.

was consecrated to God. This consecration fosters holiness. Second, Christ is most innocent for He committed no sin. Third, Christ is unpolluted. While He is indeed a descendent of Adam, He is not stained by the sin of Adam. And finally, Christ did not mix with the defiled, not as in the sense of avoiding conversation with them but in avoiding a life of sin. By being segregated in this sense, He raised human nature in Himself and now sits at the Father's right hand.[166] Thus, Christ is the most excellent of all priests just as He is the most excellent of all prophets and mediators.

5.3 The Passion operates as an efficient means

The reconciliation between God and humanity was achieved through Christ's Passion. Discussion regarding this reconciliation is long, involved, and scattered throughout Aquinas' writings. At times Aquinas presents the leading New Testament means by which salvation was achieved: merit by representation, satisfaction, sacrifice, and Redemption.[167] At other times he states that humanity is liberated from sin through Christ's Passion either formally or efficiently.[168] If efficiently, there are three kinds of this cause: 1) *perficiens effectum*; 2) *disponens materiam*; and 3) *agens instrumentale*.

In the *Commentary on the Sentences*, God alone is the *perficiens effectum* since He alone completes or perfects by infusing grace into the soul. Aquinas reaffirms this in the *Summa theologiae* by saying that Christ's Passion derives its infinite power from the Godhead. Yet Aquinas goes even further by relating this perfective causality to Christ's humanity. He writes, "since Christ's humanity is the instrument of his divinity, all Christ's acts and sufferings work instrumentally in virtue of his divinity in bringing about man's salvation."[169] Thus, not only is Christ's divinity a perfective cause of grace (as affirmed by both the *Commentary* and the *Summa*) but His humanity is as well.

---

166 Ibid., ch. 7, lect. 4.
167 *ST* III 48.1–4, respectively. These means distinguish the Passion from the Resurrection of Christ which can not be a meritorous cause. Rather, it is an exemplar and an instrumental efficient cause.
168 *In III Sent.*, d. 19, a. 1, qla. 1–2; *In IV Sent.*, d. 1, q. 1, a. 4.
169 *ST* III 48.6.

Through His merits, Christ as a human being, is *disponens materiam*, since His merits dispose or prepare humanity to receive grace which leads to perfection. He acts as a dispositive cause in a variety of ways: a) by making human nature more acceptable to God through His own assumption of this nature in the Incarnation; b) by making it possible for human beings to have faith in Him; c) by removing the obstacles of sin; d) by meriting grace and glory for humanity; and e) by praying for all persons.[170]

The sacraments, for Aquinas, are instrumental agents (*agens instrumentale*) of divine mercy (i.e., they act by the power of their principal cause [a principal cause is that which acts by its own power]).[171] Aquinas argues for the causality of the sacraments from the causality of Christ's humanity. Here it is assumed that Christ's humanity, operating as an instrument of the divinity, can produce supernatural effects not only in performing miracles but also in causing humanity's Redemption. From this premise, it is supposed that the sacraments likewise must be true causes since they have been instituted to apply the redemptive work of Christ to human souls and, therefore, participate in His sanctifying power.[172] Aquinas writes:

> We must therefore say that neither a sacrament nor any other creature can give grace as a principal agent, because this is proper to the divine power exclusively....But the sacraments work instrumentally toward the production of grace. This is explained as follows.
>
> Damascene says that in Christ His human nature was like a tool of His divinity, and thus His human nature shared somewhat in the working of the divine power. By touching a leper, for instance, Christ made him clean. The very touch of Christ thus caused the health of the leper instrumentally.
>
> It was not merely in corporeal effects that Christ's human nature shared instrumentally in the effect of the divine power but also in spiritual effects. Thus Christ's blood poured out for us had the ability to wash away sins....
>
> Thus the humanity of Christ is the instrumental cause of justification. This cause is applied to us spiritually through faith and bodily through the sacraments, because Christ's humanity is both spirit and body. This is done to the end that we may receive within ourselves the effect of sanctification, which is had through Christ. As a consequence the most perfect sacrament is that in which the body of Christ is really contained, the Eucharist; and it is the consummation of all the others, as Dionysius says. But the other sacra-

---

170 *De ver.*, q. 27, art. 3, ad 6; q. 29, art. 4, ad 9; *In III Sent.*, d. 13, q. 2, a. 2, sol. 1.

171 *In III Sent.*, d. 19, a. 1, qla. 1–2; Cf. ST I–II 112.1 ad 1.

172 William D. Lynn, *Christ's Redemptive Merit: The Nature of Its Causality According to St. Thomas*, Analecta Gregoriana, vol. 115 (Rome: Gregorian University Press, 1962), 128.

ments also share some of the efficacy by which Christ's humanity works instrumentally for our justification. By reason of it a person sanctified by baptism is said by the Apostle in the Epistle to the Hebrews (10:10–21) to be sanctified by the blood of Christ. Christ's passion is accordingly said to work in the sacraments of the New Law. Thus the sacraments of the New Law are causes of grace working in some sense instrumentally to produce it.[173]

Thus, sacraments are dispositive and perfective causes of grace.

5.4 Worship is revelatory

It has been shown above that the role of a priest is to act as mediator between God and His people, to hand on the things of God to the people, to offer the prayers of the people to God, and to make satisfaction to God for the people's sins. This role is befitting of Christ, for He shared with humanity the divine nature and reconciled it to God.[174] Aquinas points out, however, that Christ was not only a priest in offering sacrifice; He was Himself the victim offering in sacrifice. Sacrifice, the offering of one's contrite spirit to God, is needed for three reasons: a) to forgive the sin by which human beings turn away from God (sin-offering); b) to preserve humanity in God's grace where peace and salvation lie (peace-offering); and c) to unite the human spirit perfectly to God (burnt-offering). Christ, through His human nature, conferred on humanity these three effects by being the most perfect of victims: freely offering Himself at once as a sacrifice for sin, a peace-offering, and a burnt-offering.[175] By His function as priest and victim, Christ then enables communication to exist between God and humanity. Christ unites the two by communicating one to the other that which belongs to the other.[176]

Aquinas continues by saying that it is through His Passion that Christ, as priest and victim, offers authentic worship to the Father, a worship otherwise not possible to human beings on account of sin. He writes, "Likewise by His Passion He inaugurated the rites of the Christian religion by offering *Himself—an oblation and a sacrifice to God*

---

173   *De ver.*, q. 27, art. 4, resp.
174   *ST* III 22.1, corp.
175   Ibid., III 22.2, corp.
176   Ibid., III 26.2, corp.

[Eph. V.2]."[177] It is through these rites that the faithful are able to enter into Christ's sacrifice and, consequently, worship the Father through Him. Christian worship is derived from the most perfect act of worship, Christ's Passion.[178]

Worship, for Aquinas, is revelatory. It is not only rooted in the salvific actions of Jesus Christ, Who is the Word (i.e., the Revelation of the Father), but the rite itself contains a word. Every aspect of authentic worship has intellectual and sense components to it. Worship is not simply symbols and actions but an action with words that announce something of God.[179] The human intellect hears a word, is instructed, comprehends it, and the will responds by giving reverence and honor to God. Worship is then a two way encounter: human beings are taught by God through revelation and they respond to the revelation in faith. "Through revelation" refers to Christ and the response "to the revelation" is a response to Christ for He is the Word of God, the Revelation of the Father.

Besides offering worship directly, the priest also functions then indirectly as a "revealer" through and in the power of the One High Priest, Jesus Christ. He does so because worship has a word attached to it and conveys some truth about God. This worship conveys divine revelation. Keeping this in mind is important since one purpose of this section is to substantiate the claim that Christ is the Revelation of God.[180]

5.5 Section summary.

According to Aquinas, a priest has two main functions: a) he is a mediator who communicates the things of God to the people; b) he is one who reconciles by making reparation or satisfaction for the sins of the people and by offering the prayers of the people to God. The spiritual goods that the priest mediates are superior because they flow from the New Covenant, which has Jesus Christ as its Priest and Victim, rather than from the imperfect Old Covenant. The reconciliation

---

177   Ibid., III 62.5, corp.

178   Ibid., III 63.3, corp.; *In IV Sent.*, d. 15, q. 3, a. 1, qla. 1.

179   *ST* III 60.6.

180   As such, it appears that Jesus Christ is becoming the primary referent of *ST* I 1 (regarding the subject of *sacra doctrina*). According to Keefe, being a primary referent is a function of a theological *prius*.

that the priest mediates is contingent upon the death of Jesus Christ by Whose blood the stain of sin has been washed away. With regard to both of these functions, Aquinas holds that Christ is the most excellenct of priests because: a) His priesthood was established by an oath to Abraham that the levitical priesthood did not have; b) His character, holiness, and innocent was unblemished. As perfect priest and victim, Christ offers authentic worship to the Father. The worship is revelatory because it is rooted in the Word of God and it has His word attached to the rituals and actions.

CHAPTER SIX

JESUS CHRIST AND HIS RELATIONSHIP TO THE CHURCH IN THE THOUGHT OF SAINT THOMAS AQUINAS

1 Jesus Christ's Grace of Headship

Thus far, the roles of Christ have been considered insofar as they are revelatory of God. Within these roles (as prophet, mediator, priest, etc.) Christ is presented by Aquinas as the culmination of that particular role because He is the most excellent of all those who share in the same role. This excellence is due to the fullness of grace which He possessed substantially as an individual man by virtue of the hypostatic union. Christ also possessed an accidental holiness by reason of sanctifying grace as an effect of the hypostatic union. Consequently, due to the grace of union (*gratia unionis*), Christ received personally the fullness of grace (*gratia habitualis* or *gratia sanctificans*) which He freely bestowed upon rational creatures thus exhibiting His grace of headship (*gratia capitis*). Focus will now be on Christ as the recipient of the fullness of grace as an individual man, Who then bestows grace upon the Mystical Body as its Head. As Head, He provides the organizational structure of the Mystical Body.[1]

1.1 The grace Christ possesses as an human being

According to Aquinas, Christ possesses a substantial holiness by reason of the hypostatic union whereby His human nature is sanctified through union with the Person of the Word.[2] Christ also possesses an accidental holiness by reason of sanctifying grace as an effect of the union. That Christ is full of grace and truth (sanctifying grace) derives from the fact that He is the only-begotten Son of the Father, and that follows upon the hypostatic union (grace of union).[3] The human soul of Christ possesses sanctifying grace then for three reasons: a) the soul is in union with the Word of God; b) the soul is to attain knowledge and love of God in a most dignified manner; in order to achieve these operations, grace is necessary; c) His role as mediator between God and humanity requires Him to have grace which then overflows to all others.[4] This grace exists most completely in Christ because His soul is nearest to the source of grace, God, and because He is the channel of grace to all other human beings. His grace, as cause, extends then to all effects. In Christ, there is the fullness of grace in intensity and in power.[5] Through the hypostatic union (*gratia unionis*), Christ receives personally the fullness of grace (*gratia sanctificans* or *gratia habitualis*) which enables Him to acquire the grace of headship (*gratia capitis*). Consideration will now be made with regard to how the personal grace of Christ as Head flows to the members of His Mystical Body.[6]

---

1 Keefe has identified the ability to supply an organizational structure to the entire content of divine revelation a function of a theological *prius*.
2 Cf. prior section on Christ as mediator.
3 *ST* III 6.6, corp.
4 Ibid., III 7.1.
5 Ibid., III 7.9.
6 Ibid., III 8.1, corp.

1.2 The grace Christ possesses as head

According to Aquinas, Jesus Christ possesses a grace of headship. It is instructive to analyze Aquinas' understanding of this specific grace.

1.2.1 The nature of this grace

Aquinas assigns the role of head to Christ and the role of heart to the Spirit, saying that the head has a preeminence over the other exterior members of the body while the heart vivifies and unifies the body.[7] In the *Commentary on the Sentences*, he states that Christ, in His humanity, is properly called the Head of the Church by similarity with a natural head (*"per similitudinem capitis naturalis"*). He then outlines four conditions which are proper to the head and one that is common to all members of a body.[8] First, the head excels in: *dignity*, for it is the highest place on the human body; *nobility*, for it contains the noblest powers such as memory and imagination; *perfection*, for all the senses are found in the head while the other members of the body enjoy merely the sense of touch. Second, the head is the principle of the other members since it grants them sense and motion. Third, the head directs the other members of the body through the imagination and the senses which are found formally in it. Fourth, all members of the body share in a common property, namely conformity in one nature.[9]

Aquinas develops his treatment of headship in *De veritate* where he takes many of the ideas from the *Commentary on the Sentences* and advances a twofold relationship of distinction and conformity between the head and the body. He writes:

> There is distinction in three respects: (1) in point of dignity, because the head fully possesses all the senses, but the other members do not; (2) in point of government, because the head governs and regulates all the other members in their acts by means of both the external and internal senses, which have their seat in the head; (3) in point of causality, for the head causes sensation and motion in all the members....The conformity of the head to the members is also found to be threefold: (1) in nature, for the head

---

7 Ibid., III 8.1, ad 3.
8 Thomas R. Potvin, *The Theology of the Primacy of Christ According to St. Thomas Aquinas and Its Scriptural Foundations*, Studia Friburgensia, nouvelle séri, 50 (Fribourg, Switzerland: University Press, 1973), 32–33.
9 *In III Sent.*, d. 13, q. 2, a. 1; cf. Potvin, 32–33.

and the rest of the members are parts of one nature; (2) in order, for there is
a union of order between the head and the members inasmuch as the members are of service to each other....(3) in continuity, for the head is continu-
ous with the other members in a physical body.[10]

Aquinas continues by noting that the term "head" may be attributed metaphorically to a variety of different beings in different contexts. Some things are called head because of their conformity of
nature. Headship is attributed to them because of their eminence or
dignity. Thus, a lion is called the head of the animal kingdom, or a
certain city is called a capital of a nation. Some things are called head
because of their conformity in a unity of order, being ordained to one
end. Thus, the term is applied to government since its purpose is to
lead all to the common good.[11]

In the *Summa*, Aquinas lists three meanings to the term head. Order is attributed to the head because organization of a body begins
from the higher part and moves to the lower parts ("from the head
down"). Perfection is attributed to the head because in it dwell all the
senses while only touch resides in the members. Power is attributed
to the head since its sensitive and motive power directs the power
and motion of the other members.[12]

While these meanings for the term "head" are not exactly the
same as the meanings Aquinas used in his *Commentary on the Sentences* and in *De veritate*, the ideas being conveyed are very similar. In
addition, even though he does not speak of conformity of nature and
conformity based on the unity of order, they are at least implicit in
this writing. For example, conformity of nature may be seen underlying Aquinas' quotation of Romans 8:29, "that He might be the first-
born amongst many brethren" and in the reply to the third objection
where he says that Christ may be compared to the head since, as man,
He possesses a preeminence over other human beings. Conformity
based on the unity of order may be seen underlying his discussion of
power. There he mentions that the head provides direction in their
actions, thus ordaining their end. In conclusion, then, the term "head"
for Aquinas is rich in meaning. Aside from its literal designation as a
part of the human or animal body, it can be used to designate "a
leader," "a source or cause," "an organizing principle," or "the sum-

---

10 *De ver.*, q. 29, art. 4, resp.
11 Ibid.
12 *ST* III 8.1, corp.

mit or culmination point."[13] All of these are operative in Aquinas' treatment of Christ's Headship.

1.2.2 The manner and mode of this grace's bestowal

After establishing that Christ indeed possesses the nature of headship,[14] Aquinas addresses the issue of how Christ the Head bestows His grace upon the members of His Body in terms of causality. Above, in the section on Christ's priesthood, we have seen how, through the Passion, the God-Man acts as an efficient cause in a three-fold manner: as a *perficiens effectum*, a *disponens materiam*, and an *agens instrumentale*. In addition to having a physical influence on the bestowal of grace as an efficient cause, Christ also has a moral influence as a meritorious cause.[15] Merit is the right to a reward due for a morally good action. Supernatural merit is that which arises from an action performed under the influence of divine grace (merit's principle of action) and, thus, is in a relationship with a supernatural end. In order to be supernaturally meritorious, a human action must arise from a deliberate free will and from a divinely bestowed principle raising it to the supernatural level, namely, sanctifying grace. Christ's humanity was given the fullness of grace, the supernatural source of merit.[16] All His actions and passions were accepted then freely through love and obedience. Christ's actions, however, were not intended to sanctify only His humanity but also His fellow human beings. Every action of Christ merited infinite grace and glory for others: merited, because grace was a principle of each action; infinitely, because each was the human action of a divine Person and so it had an infinite value.[17] In addition, these actions merited for others not congruously but condignly.[18]

After Christ's earthly existence, Aquinas holds that since His humanity is the instrument of the Godhead, all Christ's actions and passions operate instrumentally in virtue of the Godhead for the

---

13 Potvin, 35.
14 *ST* III 8.1.
15 *ST* III 8.1, ad 1.
16 Ibid., III 19.3–4, corp.
17 Ibid., III 19.4; David A. O'Connell, *The Union Between Head and Body in the Mystical Body*, PhD. diss. (Washington, D.C.: Dominican House of Studies, 1941), 23.
18 *ST* I-II 14.6, corp.

salvation of humanity.[19] No limit is imposed on this instrumental operation; the humanity of Christ is united to the divinity so that God can bestow grace and effect salvation.[20] He writes:

> But the human nature in Christ is assumed with the result that instrumentally He performs the things which are the proper operation of God alone: to wash away sin, for example, to enlighten minds by grace, to lead into the perfection of eternal life. The human nature of Christ, then, is compared to God as a proper and conjoined instrument is compared, as the hand is compared to the soul.[21]

Salvation, then, is a human operation of Christ Who produces His effect by way of merit and Who produces grace as an instrument of the Godhead. These two aspects, of merit and instrumentality, are related to the human action of Christ[22] for as Aquinas explains:

> A thing is termed an instrument because it is moved by a principal agent; but apart from this it may possess a native activity corresponding to its own form, as in the example already used of fire. Accordingly, the action of an instrument precisely as instrument is not distinct from the action of the principal agent. Yet, as a reality with its own nature, it may also possess another activity. Applying this to the case of Christ: the activity of his human nature, insofar as that nature is the instrument of the divinity, is not distinct from the activity of the divinity; for it is one and the same saving action by which his humanity and his divinity save us. At the same time Christ's human nature, as a nature, possesses its own activity distinct from the divine activity, as has already been noted.[23]

More will be said later regarding efficient and meritorious causality in the context of the nature of the union between Christ the Head and the Church, the Body.

Finally, the humanity of Christ is the exemplary cause of grace for other human beings. He is an exemplary cause not in the sense that mental ideas influence and direct the action of agent but in the less proper sense that extra-mental reality serves as a model for a similar object to be produced.[24] This is particularly true when the object to be

---

19 Ibid., III 48.6, corp.
20 Bernard Catao, *Salut et Rédemption chez S. Thomas D'Aquin: l'acte Sauveur du Christ*, in *Théologie*, Études Publiées sous la Direction de la Faculté de Théologie S.J. de Lyon-Fourvière, vol. 62 (Paris: Aubier Éditions Montaigne, 1965), 146.
21 *SCG* IV ch. 41, [11].
22 Catao, 149.
23 *ST* III 19.1, ad 2.
24 Ibid., I 44.3; O'Connell, 13.

imitated is the first and most perfect of its kind, for Aquinas holds that the most perfect being is always the exemplar and model upon which the less perfect are based.[25] Christ's humanity is such an exemplary cause, for He is the first-born and the most perfect of the children of God (this has been demonstrated above in the discussion of how Christ is the "most excellent" of the prophets, mediators, priests, teachers, etc.). Christ was predestined to be the natural Son of God whereas human beings are predestined to participate by adoption.[26] Obtaining this status as children of God is accomplished by grace. Aquinas explains that this status is most manifest in Christ because human nature in Him, without any antecedent merits, was united to the Son of God.[27]

Christ's humanity, however, is the exemplar only to a certain point. Human beings need not conform to Christ's example in every detail because Aquinas notes, "The exemplate need not be conformed to the exemplar in all respects: it is sufficient that it imitate it in some."[28] Since Aquinas holds grace to be an accident, it is essentially the same in Christ as it is in us. It is an accident in the essence of His human soul as it is in any human soul. However, grace came to the soul of Christ immediately from the divine nature, whereas it comes to others through the instrumentality of Christ's humanity or that of the sacraments (efficient causality).[29] In terms of final causality, grace is given to Christ for His own sanctification and the sanctification of others while it is given to other human beings through Him for their own personal sanctification.[30]

Finally, the activity of Christ as Head, in bestowing grace, extends to all members of the Mystical Body. With regard to human beings, He is Head over them in varying degrees depending upon their status: first, to the actual members who are associated with Him actually by glory, by charity, or by faith and, second, to the potential members who are either destined to be members in eternity by glory or in time by faith and charity, or who are not destined to be because

---

25 *ST* III 56.1, ad 3.
26 Ibid., III 24.3, corp.
27 Ibid.
28 Ibid., III 24.3, ad 3.
29 Ibid., I-II 112.1.
30 Ibid., III 7.1, 9, and 11; III 8.1; O'Connell, 13–14.

of some personal sin. Christ, then, is head of all human beings either actually or potentially.[31]

1.3 Section summary

According to Aquinas, Christ possesses a substantial holiness by rea- son of the hypostatic union whereby His human nature is sanctified through union with the Person of the Word. On account of this hypo- static union (*gratia unionis*), Christ personally receives the fullness of grace (*gratia sanctificans* or *gratia habitualis*) which enables Him to ac- quire the grace of headship (*gratia capitis*).

Since the head has preeminence, Aquinas assigns the role of the head to Christ and the role of the heart to the Holy Spirit. Once this is established, attention is then focused on how Christ as Head bestows His grace upon His Body in terms of causality. First, Christ is an effi- cient cause in a three-fold manner.[32] Second, Christ has a moral influ- ence as a meritorious cause. His human actions are supernaturally meritorious because they arise from a deliberate free will act and from a gift of sanctifying grace which elevates the actions to the supernatu- ral level. These actions are intended for the grace and glorification of others. Third, Christ is an instrumental cause in that all His human actions and passions are at the service of the principal agent, the Godhead, for the salvation of humanity. Fourth, Christ is an exem- plary cause not because He is an exemplary cause in the sense that mental ideas influence and direct the actor but because the extra- mental reality serves as a model for a similar object to be produced. Fifth, Christ's own sanctification and the sanctification of others are given by grace, which constitutes the final cause. As Head, Christ then extends grace to all members of the Mystical Body depending upon their status as actual or potential members.

---

31 *ST* III 8.3.
32 Cf. part I, chapter 3, section 5.3 for the three points.

2 The Nature of the Union in the Mystical Body

Above the nature of Christ's headship, the manner and mode of the exercise of this headship, and the bestowal of grace which constitutes and sustains the members of the Body of Christ have been discussed. It is now important to study the nature of this union between Christ, the Head, and the Church, the Body. How does Aquinas understand this union?

2.1 A Christomonism.

One understanding that can be immediately dismissed is that of a Christomonism. A strict Christomonism reduces all to Christ through the submersion or annihilation of the personhood of the members of Christ's Body. Aquinas eliminates this possibility in the *Summa theologiae*. By quoting John Damascene's passage from *De fide orthodoxa* that the Son of God "did not assume human nature as a species, nor did He assume all its hypostases" (iii. 11), Aquinas explains:

> It was not appropriate for human nature to be assumed in all its supposits. First of all, because this would take away the multitude of individuals human nature requires. Since we ought not affirm any other supposit in the assumed nature than the person assuming, as noted above, if there were no human nature that was not assumed, it would follow that there would be only one person having human nature, namely the person assuming.
>
> Secondly, because this would take away from the dignity of the incarnate Son of God, who is *the firstborn among many brethren* according to his human nature, just as he is *the firstborn of all creatures* according to the divine. In the hypothesis raised all men would be his equal in dignity.[33]

Thus, it is not fitting that the Son of God should become incarnate in all human persons (*supposita*) because that would reduce the whole human species into one divine Person; it would destroy all other persons of the human nature (thus, a Christomonism). Such a position would likewise undermine Christ's rank and dignity as the first-born of all creatures which Aquinas can not allow.

This position is a corollary to the argument presented three articles earlier in article two. Here it is not fitting that the Son of God should become incarnate by assuming a single human person (a pre-

---

33 Ibid., III 4.5, corp.

existing personal hypostasis). Aquinas writes that a human person is not presupposed to assumption. For if it were presupposed, it must either have been corrupted, in which case it was useless, or it remains after the union. Thus, there would be two persons, one assuming and the other assumed and this is false (i.e., Nestorianism).[34] It seems that a solution to this problem would be the annihilation of a human person presumed to have been assumed by the Son. Yet this is unacceptable, as well, on grounds that it violates the doctrine of the Incarnation. The union that exists between Christ and the members of His Body is one that is established with uncorrupted, unannihilated, unabsorbed, distinct human persons.

This understanding needs to be kept in mind when one reads texts of Aquinas that deal with *una mystice persona*. One is tempted to conclude that he understands the union to be reduced to a monism because he speaks of a oneness. The phrase *una mystice persona* may give this impression in the following two classic and then two related texts:

> [G]race was in Christ...not simply as in an individual man, but as in the Head of the whole Church, to whom all are united as members to the head, forming a single mystic person [*mystice una persona*].[35]

> The head and members form as it were a single mystical person [*una mystica persona*]; Christ's satisfaction therefore extends to all the faithful as to his members.[36]

> For the natural body, though made up of different members is one, and the whole Church which is Christ's mystical body, is deemed to be one person [*una persona*] with its head, Christ.[37]

> The members and the Head are but one person [*una persona*]. Therefore, since Christ is our Head by reason of His divinity and His superabundant fullness of grace, and since we are His members, His merit is not something outside us, but it is communicated to us or flows into us (*influit*) on account of the unity of the Mystical Body [*unitatem corporis mystici*].[38]

---

34 Ibid., III 4.2, corp.
35 Ibid., III 19.4, corp.
36 Ibid., III 48.2, ad 1.
37 Ibid., III 49.1, corp.
38 *In III Sent.*, d. 18, a. 6, sol. 1; as quoted in M. Eugene Boylan, *The Mystical Body: The Foundation of the Spiritual Life* (Westminster, Maryland: Newman Bookshop, 1948), 50.

One must resist this temptation in light of the underlying principles regarding whether the Son of God assumed a person or a human nature in all individuals set out in the *Summa theologiae* III 4.2 and 5 as indicated above. The phrase needs to be interpreted in this context. Aquinas' *una mystice persona* can only be a "person" that contains, or is composed of, unabsorbed, unannihilated, uncorrupted, distinct persons. To put it conversely, it can not be interpreted as implying any such thing.

This conclusion finds support, though expressed less specifically, in Aquinas' earlier discussion of whether Christ is capable of having dowries in his *Commentary on IV Sentences* (d. 49, q. 4, a. 3). There he makes reference to a triple union in Christ. One is said to be consonant, by which He is joined to God by a connection of love [i.e., Trinitarian union]; another regards dignity by which the human nature is united to the divine [i.e., hypostatic union]; and the third is that by which Christ Himself is united to the Church. After defining a dowry as that which is given to the bride in regard to ownership and dominion and that which is given to the groom for use, Aquinas explains that it does not seem proper to apply the term to Christ in the context of His being united to the Father through a consensus of love. Since He is God, no marriage is possible because there is no subjection within the Godhead, which should be the bride's to the groom. Then Aquinas proceeds to explain that the term can not apply to the hypostatic union, but it does apply to the union between Christ and the Church for those same three reasons. First, because there is required a *conformity of nature* between the groom and the bride in that marriage where dowries are given; and this is absent in the joining of human nature with the divine. Second, because here there is required a *distinction of persons*; the human nature however is not distinct personally from the Word. Third, because a dowry is given when the bride is introduced for the first time into the home of the groom and so it seems to pertain to the bride, that *from being not-joined she becomes joined*; the human nature, however, which is assumed into a unity of person by the Word, never was anything but perfectly joined.[39] Thus, for our purposes, the union between Christ and the members of the Church is one of: conformity of nature, a distinction of persons, from being not-joined to becoming joined. Since there is a distinction of

---

39 *In IV Sent.*, d. 49, q. 4, a. 3.

persons in unity, a Christomonism is not feasible according to Aquinas.[40]

2.2. An organic view

Having dismissed a Christomonism, Aquinas, under the force of I Cor. 12 and other comparable Scriptural texts, develops a related but different understanding of the union between the Head and the Body. He outlines an organic view. As a cursory survey of his texts demonstrates, Aquinas understands the term "organic" to refer to an organism, a body supplied with diverse organs.[41] Even more specifically, the term refers to "any body equipped with the various organs required by a living body in consequence of the life-principle's various vital activities."[42] Scripture applies this term to the union of the head and body only under the form of a comparison, yet Aquinas recognizes that the Mystical Body is more than an abstraction; it is a reality wherein God dwells.

The union between Christ and the members of the Church, between the Head and the Body, is unique. For Aquinas, there are certain parallels with "organic bodies" as presented in I Cor.12 (cf. Rom. 12:4–8). However, under the force of Eph. 5 and other comparable Scriptural texts, he is aware of certain parallels with "marital bodies." Thus, Aquinas relies on both analogies, draws from one or the other but usually gives some indications (though they may be slight) that

---

40 It is interesting to note that in discussing the distinction between *faith* as applied to the reality believed in (what must be believed) and *faith* as applied to that by which an individual believes in his heart, Aquinas holds that in the more subjective second use of the term, "*one faith* designates the unity of the habit of faith by which all believe. I mean that it is specifically one — not numerically one — since the same faith is present in each one's heart; just as when many persons want the same thing, they are said to be of one will" (*Ad Eph.*, ch. 4, lect. 2). In the Mystical Body, the head and members are one in faith since each person believes in his own heart. Thus, they are not "numerically one"; there is no Christomonism.

41 Cf. *ST* I 76.4, 5, 8; III 76.3; Suppl. 79.3 and 80.2; *De spiritualibus creaturis* art. 4, resp. 13; *De anima* q. 8, resp. 14; q. 10, corp.; *Sententia super De anima*, II, lect. 1, n. 231.

42 St. Thomas Aquinas, *Aristotle's De Anima in the Version of William of Moerbeke and the Commentary of St. Thomas Aquinas*, translated by K. Foster and S. Humphries (New Haven, Connecticut: Yale University Press, 1951), II, lect. 1, n. 230.

he is also aware of the other, and, in the end, holds both views simultaneously though not to an extent that ambiguities did not arise.

2.2.1 Characteristics of the organic view

In dealing with the organic view, Aquinas delineates the proper functions of the head and attributes these to Christ as well. Following are several texts that relay an organic understanding. In *Summa theologiae* III 8.1 (as seen above), he lists the functions of the head as: a) *order*, since the head is the higher first part of man from which all else proceeds; b) *perfection*, since the head possesses all the senses (both interior and exterior) whereas in the other parts of the body there is only the sense of touch; and c) *power*, since the head controls the power and movement of every part of the body by means of its sensory and motor faculties. These functions, then, apply to Christ as Head of the Church because: a) His grace is of the highest and first *order* on account of His closeness to God; b) He has *perfection* due to the fullness of grace; and c) He has the *power* to bestow grace on all members of the Church.

This list in the *Summa theologiae* (III 8.1) is comparable to Aquinas' earlier list in the *Commentary on Ephesians* (1:22–23; ch. 1, lect. 8; the second text). There he lists the functions of order and perfection, but power in the *Summa* replaces the fact that the head is of the same *nature* as the rest of the members of the body.[43] Later in the same commentary (4: 14–16; ch. 4, lect. 5; the third text), Aquinas discusses the three ways in which the members of such an organic body are composed and how a rapport is established: a) its organs are interrelated; b) they are bound together by tendons; and c) each member serves the rest.[44] He elaborates:

> Therefore, one body is composed of many members in these three ways: through its structured whole or unity, through its connective bindings, and through its reciprocal actions and assistance. Just as all these actions of interrelating organs, the connection of tendons, and movements take their initiative from the body's head, so the spiritual counterparts of these flow from Christ, our head, into his body, the Church.[45]

---

43 *Ad Eph..*, ch. 1, lect. 8.
44 Ibid., ch. 4, lect. 5.
45 Ibid.

In his *Commentary on Romans* (12:4–6; ch. 12, lect. 2), Aquinas provides a slightly different list. He writes:

> With warning, here the Apostle assigns the reason assumed from the likeness of the mystical body to the natural body. And first he treats of three things concerning the natural body. First, indeed the unity of the body, when he says, *For just as in one body*; second, the plurality of members, when he says, *We have many members*; for the human body is an organism constituted from a diversity of members; third, the diversity of functions, when he says, *However all the members do not have the same act*. For in vain would there be a diversity of members unless they would be ordered to diverse acts. Then he adapts these three things to the mystical body of Christ, which is the Church.[46]

Aquinas speaks of this unity, plurality, and functionality in the context of I Cor. 12:12 (*I Ad Cor.*, ch. 12, lect. 3). He states:

> Having distinguished the gifts, he now shows it by a likeness to the natural body. First he makes the similitude in general, second he exemplifies each one in particular, *For the body, etc.* Concerning the first he does two things. First, he states the likeness, second, the adaptation of the similitude, *So also Christ, etc.* About the first it must be considered that, as in the first book of the *Metaphysics*, anything one *per se* is said in three ways. In one mode by indivisibility, as unity and a point, according to which unity totally excludes multiplicity, not only actual but even potential. In another mode the one is said by continuity, as a line and a surface, which excludes actual but not potential multiplicity. In a third mode by integrity, which does not exclude multiplicity, neither potential nor actual, just as a house is one which is constructed by different stones and wood. And in the same mode the body of man or of any animal is one, because its perfection is integrated from diverse members, just as [the perfection] of the soul from diverse instruments. Hence, the soul is said to be the act of an organic body, that is constituted from diverse organs. Therefore, the Apostle first proposes that the unity of a body does not exclude a multiplicity of members, saying that *Just as the body is one and has many members*. Hence, in Rom. XII it is said, *In one body we have many members*. Likewise he states that the multiplicity of members does not take away the unity of the body, and so adds, *All the members of the body, although they are many*, still are *one body*, which is perfected by all. Hence, in

---

46 *Praemissa admonitione, hic Apostolus rationem assignat sumptam ex similitudine corporis mystici ad corpus naturale. Et primo in corpore naturali tangit tria. Primo quidem corporis unitatem, cum dicit:* Sicut enim in uno corpore; *secundo, membrorum pluralitatem, cum dicit:* Multa membra habemus; *est enim corpus humanum organicum ex diversitate membrorum constitutum; tertio officiorum diversitatem, cum dicit:* Omnia autem membra non eumdem actum habent. *Frustra enim esset membrorum diversitas, nisi ad diversos actus ordinarentur. Deinde aptat haec tria ad corpus Christi mysticum, quod est Ecclesia.*

Job X it is said, *You have clothed me with skin and flesh, you have composed me from bones and nerves.*[47]

Earlier, Aquinas spoke of this unity in more organic terms when he commented on I Cor. 10:16–17. There he writes:

Then he [Paul] says: *Because one bread, etc.,* he shows that we all are one in his mystical body. Where he first proposes a unity, secondly he gives the rationale for the unity, there: *All who are from one, etc.* In the first one, he treats a double unity. The first is of incorporation, by which we are transformed into Christ, when he says: *One bread, etc.* The other is of life and sense, which we receive from the head, Christ, when he says: *And one body, etc.*[48]

2.2.2 The wider context also contains a marital view

However, within these seemingly model organic texts, their wider contexts also portray at least a slight understanding and reliance upon a marital view. In the *corpus* of *Summa theologiae* III 8.1 (the first text), Aquinas references Rom. 12 and I Cor. 12 which tend toward an organic portrayal of the union. However, at least four of the texts that

---

47   *Posita distinctione gratiarum, hic manifestat eam per similitudinem corporis naturalis. Et primo ponit similitudinem in generali; secundo exemplificat eam in speciali, ibi: Nam et corpus, etc. Circa primum duo facit. Primo ponitur similitudo; secundo similtudinis adaptatio, ibi: Ita et Christus, etc. Circa primum considerandum est, quod sicut in quinto Metaphysicae tripliciter dicitur aliquid unum per se. Uno modo indivisibilitate, ut unitas et punctum, secundum quem modum unitas excludit totaliter multitudinem, non solum actualem, sed etiam potentialem; alio modo dicitur unum continuitate, ut linea et superficies, quae quidem unitas excludit multitudinem actualem, sed non potentialem; tertio modo integritate, quae non excludit multitudinem neque potentialem, neque actualem; sicut domus est una quae constituitur ex diversis lapidibus et lignis. Et eodem modo corpus hominis aut cujuslibet animalis est unum, quia ejus perfectio integratur ex diversis membris, sicut ex diversis animae instrumentis. Unde et anima dicitur esse actus corporis organici, id est, ex diversis organis constituti. Proponit ergo primo Apostolus quod unitas corporis membrorum multitudinem non excludit, dicens quod sicut corpus unum est, et multa membra habet. Unde et Rom. XII dicitur: In uno corpore multa membra habemus. Item proponit quod multitudo membrorum non tollit corporis unitatem; unde subdit: Omnia autem membra corporis cum sint multa, nihilominus unum corpus sunt, quod ex omnibus perficitur. Unde et Job X: Pelle et carne vestisti me, ossibus et nervis compegisti me.*

48   *Deinde cum dicit:* Quoniam unus panis, etc., *ostendit, quod omnes sumus unum in corpore ejus mystico. Ubi proponit primo unitatem, secundo subdit unitatis rationem, ibi: Omnes qui de uno, etc. In primo tangit duplicem unitatem. Primam incorporationis, qua in Christum transformamur, cum dicit:* Unus panis, etc. *Aliam viate et sensus, quam a Christo capite accipimus, cum addit:* Et unum corpus, etc.

he directly quotes have marital or familial overtones. The passage Ezech. 16:25, "At every head of the way, thou hast set up a sign of their prostitution," implies a comparison between prostitution and marriage. The passages from Is. 9:15, "The aged and honorable, he is the head"; I Kings 15:17, "When thou wast a little one in thy own eyes, was thou not made the head of the tribes of Israel"; and Rom. 8:29, "For whom He foreknew, He also predestinated to be made conformable to the image of His Son; that He might be the first-born amongst many brethren" all refer to Christ as the first among His many brethren in the familial tribe which is the result of marriage. In the reply to objection two, Aquinas states that the father is the head of the "domestic multitude" (the tribe, the family) which is ordered to one end (a result of marriage). In the reply to objection one, Christ provides power and movement to the members of the body while the sensitive and motive power is identified preeminently with the Holy Spirit. This gift of the Holy Spirit involves free reception which can occur only within a free person and not some organic (irrational) part of the body. Freedom and the free appropriation of the gift of the Holy Spirit is possible only within a rational, willing person. An organic understanding does not permit this freedom while a marital understanding does and even presupposes it.[49] Thus, a marital relationship exists between the Godhead and the Mystical Body.

In his wider discussion regarding the relationship between the head and the other members of the body due to the sameness of nature (*Comm. on Eph.*, ch. 1, lect. 8; the second text), Aquinas states that Christ is not the head of angels but of humans, "for nowhere doth he take hold of the angels, but of the seed of Abraham he taketh hold" (Heb. 2:16).[50] Then in commenting on the manner in which Christ is the head of humans only, the Song of Songs is quoted, "'Thou hast wounded my heart, my sister,' through nature, 'and my spouse,' through grace (Cant. 4:9)."[51] Grace renders the body as the bride or spouse of Christ, Who is the Bridegroom.

In his wider discussion on how one body is composed of many members and the rapport that results (*Comm. on Eph.*, ch. 4, lect. 5; the

---

49 To refer back to the discussion regarding Christomonism, if members of the body are simply subsumed to the one person of Christ, then they are not free to resist grace or to freely appropriate the gift.

50 *Ad Eph.*, ch. 1, lect. 8.

51 Ibid.

third text), Aquinas states that one way in which this unity is achieved is through faith. The role of faith is crucial here for a marital understanding of the union since the passage and supporting quotes can give the impression of an organic union, or, even worse, an aggregate. It reads as follows:

> First, there is a structured unity through faith. Whence he says *from* Christ who is our head, as was already mentioned, *the whole body, being compacted* is joined together in a unity. "He will gather together the dispersed of Israel" (Ps. 146:2). "He will gather together unto him all nations, and heap together unto him all people" (Hab. 2:5). Christ is "the head, from which the whole body, by joints and bands, being supplied with nourishment and compacted, groweth unto the increase of God" (Col. 2:19).[52]

If a structured unity is achieved through faith, this unity must be marital and not organic since faith involves an operation of the intellect and will. It is a *rationabile obsequium* (a free submission of human reason) and a theological virtue according to Aquinas. A free person then is entering into this union.

Charity also plays a role in achieving this unity and both faith and charity are infused through the grace of Christ. They are given gratuitously "according to the measure and competency of each member" so that "they [the members] may grow spiritually" and serve others.[53] Faith, charity, and spiritual growth require freedom on the part of the recipient; thus, a more marital understanding.

In the *Summa theologiae* II-23.1, Aquinas' analysis of charity is in terms of an interpersonal friendship between God and humanity. Any interpersonal relationship is based on the awareness by both individuals that he himself is a person who is in union with another person. Friendship "requires a mutual loving; it is only with a friend that a friend is friendly....Friendship goes out to another in two ways: when he is loved in himself, and such friendship is only for a friend; and when he is loved because of another person, as when for the sake of a friend you love those belonging to him."[54] By definition then, the mutual recognition of personhood in charity necessitates a marital rather than an organic understanding of the union.

Unity achieved through faith and charity is also a part of the wider context for Aquinas' *Commentary on Romans* (ch. 12, lect. 2; the

---

52 Ibid., ch. 4, lect. 5.
53 Ibid.
54 *ST* II-II 23.1 corp. and ad 2.

fourth text); however, he goes further by stating that this unity is achieved through Christ's spirit which incorporates the Mystical Body into the Godhead. He writes:

> Second he [Paul] treats the unity of the mystical body when he says: *We are one body—So that he may reconcile both in one body, etc.* (Eph.II). However, the unity of this mystical body is spiritual, through which we are united to God by faith and the working of charity, according to Eph. IV: *One body, and one spirit.* And since the spirit of unity is derived in us from Christ (*If anyone does not have the spirit of Christ, this man is not of him* (Eph. VIII)), he adds: *In Christ,* who unites us through his spirit, which he gives to us, and in turn unites us as well to God. *So that they be one in us, just as we are one* (John XVII).[55]

This spirit of unity is identified as the Holy Spirit in the paragraph following the one cited above from the *Commentary on I Corinthians* (ch. 12, lect. 3; the fifth text). The benefit of the gift of the Holy Spirit is regeneration and salvation, which is a theme that is presented more fully in Aquinas' *Commentary on Ephesians* (ch. 5), as will be presented shortly. He explains:

> One reason for the unity is the Holy Spirit, according to Eph. IV: *One body and one spirit.* But we obtain a two-fold benefit through the power of the Holy Spirit. First, because we are regenerated through him, according to John III: *Unless one be reborn by water and the Holy Spirit.* Hence he says: *Indeed in one spirit,* namely, by the power of the Holy Spirit, *we are all,* that is, we who are members of Christ, *baptized in one body,* that is, in the unity of the Church which is the body of Christ, according to Eph. I: *He has given him as head over the whole Church, which is his body,* and Gal. III: *All you who have been baptized in Christ, have put on Christ.* Secondly, through the Holy Spirit we are renewed for salvation, and he adds, *And all drink in the one spirit,* that is, through the power of the one Holy Spirit.[56]

---

55 *Secundo tangit corporis mystici unitatem, cum dicit:* Unum corpus sumus. –Ut reconciliet ambos in uno corpore, etc. *Hujus autem corporis mystici est unitas spiritualis, per quam fide et affectu charitatis invicem unimur Deo, secundum illud Ephes. IV:* Unum corpus, et unums spiritus. *Et quia spiritus unitatis a Christo in nos derivatur* (Si quis spiritum Christi non habet, his non est ejus), *ideo subdit:* In Christo, qui per spiritum suum, quem dat nobis, nos invicem unit et Deo. Ut sint unum in nobis, sicut et nos unum sumus.

56 *Una quidem ratio unitatis est Spiritus Sanctus, secundum illud Ephes. IV:* Unum corpus et unus spiritus. *Sed per virtutem Spiritus Sancti duplex beneficium consequimur. Primo quidem, quia per ipsum regeneramur, secundum illud Joan. III:* Nisi quis renatus fuerit ex aqua et Spiritu Sancto. *Unde dicit:* Etenim in uno spiritu, sc. per virtutem unius Spiritus Sancti, omnes nos, qui sumus membra Christi, summus baptizati in unum corpus, *id est, in unitatem Ecclesiae, quae est corpus Christi, secun-*

In his *Commentary on I Corinthians* (10:16–17; ch. 10, lect. 4), Aquinas adds hope to the virtues of faith and charity and then speaks of the sacramental aspect of this union. He writes:

> Therefore he says: *Because one, etc.*; as if he would say: Through this it is clear that we are one with Christ, because there is one bread in the union of faith, hope, and charity; and although many we are one body in the good works of charity. It is the body, namely of that head who is Christ. *Many*, I say, namely all, *who from one bread*, that is the body of Christ, *and from one cup*, that is the blood, *we share*, in a worthy participation, namely spiritual, not only sacramental. As Augustine says, "Understand that the Church of Christ is called one bread and one body, therefore, as one bread is from many grains, and one body is composed from many members, thus the Church of Christ is connected by the many faithful joined together in charity" (Ch. 3).[57]

In conclusion, this discussion of the theological virtues and the role of the sacraments in fostering the union between Christ and His Church in the Holy Spirit moves in the direction of a marital understanding of that union. While it is not explicit, it is implicit, for this activity is possible only with a free person.

2.3 A marital view

Aquinas' marital view of the union is expressed in his *Commentary on Ephesians*.

---

dum illud Ephes. I: Ipsum dedit caput super omnem Ecclesiam, quae est corpus ejus; et Gal. III: Omnes qui in Christo batpizati estis, Chrisum induistis. *Secundo per Spiritum Sanctum reficimur ad salutem. Unde subdit:* Et omnes potati sumus in uno spiritu, *id est, per virtutem unius Spiritus Sancti.*

57 *Dicit ergo:* quoniam unus, etc.; *quasi dicat: Per hoc patet, quod unum sumus cum Christo, quoniam unus panis unione fidei, spei et charitatis, et unum corpus multi sumus per subministrationem operum charitatis. Corpus sc. illius capitis, qui est Christus.* Multi, *dico sc.* omnes, *qui de uno pane, id est corporis Christi, et de uno calice, id est sanguine, participamus, digna participatione, sc. spirituali, non tantum sacramentali. Augustinus: Accipite, quia unus panis et unum corpus Ecclesia Christi dicitur, pro eo quod sicut unus panis ex multis granis, et unum corpus ex multis membris componitur, sic Ecclesia Christi ex multis fidelibus charitate copulatis connectitur.*

2.3.1 Ephesians 5

As stated above, Eph. 5 is a key Scriptural passage for Aquinas. It is here that he primarily develops his marital understanding of the union between Christ and the Church. Lecture eight contains his commentary on Eph. 5:22–28a where he recognizes Paul's warning about subjection. In quoting Ecclesiasticus 25 [30], "a woman, if she have superiority, is contrary to her husband," points out that the woman's role is patterned after the man's role. While Paul is understood to maintain an androcentric structure, Aquinas recognizes and comments on Paul's extensive refocusing of that structure.[58] Aquinas explains:

> So he [Paul] especially warns them about subjection. This is *as to a lord* since the relation of a husband to his wife is, in a certain way, like that of a master to his servant, insofar as the latter ought to be governed by the commands of his master. The difference between these two relationships is that the master employs his servants in whatever is profitable to himself; but a husband treats his wife and children in reference to the common good. Thus he mentions *as to a lord*; the husband is not really a lord, but is *as* a lord. "Let wives be subject to their husbands" (I Pet. 3:1).[59]

Thus, one characteristic of this refocusing of the structure is that the husband is not to relate to his wife and children in a way that is advantageous to himself but to the common good. Second, he is not a lord but is to act *as* a lord. He himself is subject to *the* Lord.[60] Aquinas continues, "The reason for this subjection is that the husband is the head of the wife, and the sense of sight is localized in the head—'The eyes of a wise man are in his head' (Eccl. 2:14)—and hence a husband ought to govern his wife as her head. 'The head of the woman is the man' (I Cor. 11:3)."[61] Here the motive for this subjection gives the impression of being organic. The head, through sight, is exerting an external influence on the body. It is reacting to a perceived external object and directing the body accordingly. But Aquinas does not leave his analogy there. He mentions "the eyes of a wise man." Thus, the head not only exerts an external influence but an interior influence as

---

58 Stephen F. Miletic, *"One Flesh", Ephesians 5:22–24, 5:31, Marriage, and the New Creation*. Analecta Biblica, vol. 115 (Rome: Pontificio Istituto Biblico, 1988), 115–16.

59 *Ad Eph.*, ch. 5, lect. 8.

60 Miletic, 100.

61 *Ad Eph.*, ch. 5, lect. 8.

well. Figuratively speaking, "sight," which is an activity centered in the head, directs the members of the body not only externally, but internally. It provides wisdom; thus, it is good that the body be subjected to the head. Consequently, the relationship between the head and the body is not so much organic as it is marital since wisdom, as knowledge put to good use, appeals to the intellect and will of a person. Aquinas develops this marital understanding further by stating:

> Then he [Paul] brings in his example when he says: *as Christ is the head of the church.* God "hath made him head over all the church, which is his body" (Eph. 1:22–23). This is not for his own utility, but for that of the Church since *he is the saviour of his body.* "For there is no other name under heaven given to men, whereby we must be saved" (Acts. 4:12). "Behold, God is my saviour; I will deal confidently and will not fear" (Is. 12:2).[62]

By referring to "utility," Aquinas is returning to his recent point that the head is not to act in a way that is "profitable to himself" but for the common good. The head does so by acting as "saviour of his body." With this remark, a soteriological element has been introduced into the union. The body is to "deal confidently" and "not fear" by entering into a relationship with the head who acts so as to remove that which prohibits the establishment of the union, namely, sin. Aquinas, however, is careful to note that not everything that is said of Christ applies to the husband as well. Only Christ, as God, assumes the role of saviour. The husband's role as head is modelled on that of Christ's. He is to possess an other-centered love which is directed to the salvation of all those involved in the union and for the common good. The object of the wife's subjection, the headship of her husband, is rooted in the headship of Jesus Christ.[63]

Aquinas then comments on the conclusion that Paul intended:

> *Therefore, as the church is subject of Christ.* As though he [Paul] said: It is not proper for an organ to rebel against its head in any situation; but as Christ is head of the church in his own way, so a husband is the head of his wife; therefore, the wife must be obedient to her husband *as the church is subject to Christ.* "Shall not my soul be subject to God?" (Ps. 61:2), *so also let the wives be to their husbands.* "And thou shalt be under thy husband's power" (Gen. 3:16), *in all things* which are not contrary to God, for Acts 5 (29) affirms: "We ought to obey God rather than men."[64]

---

62 Ibid.
63 Miletic, 104.
64 *Ad Eph.,* ch. 5, lect. 8.

Here the paradigm for the wife's subjection is the Church's subjection to Christ. Just as it is unnatural for a bodily organ to rebel against its head, so, too, is it unnatural for the Church to rebel against Christ or the wife to rebel against her husband. The wife, as a free rational person in marital union with her husband, is to exercise her freedom in obedience to her husband just as the Church is freely obedient to Christ. Marital love has no room for rebellion since that implies coercion and subordination to a despot.[65]

Since this is a union between two people, Aquinas comments on the reciprocal side of the relationship, that of the husband. He writes:

> *Husbands, love your wives.* For certainly it is from the love he has for his wife that he will live more chastely and both of them will enjoy a peaceful relationship. If he should love another more than his own wife, he exposes both himself and his wife to the possibility of sin. "Husbands, love your wives and be not bitter towards them" (Col. 3:19)....
>
> Thus he [Paul] says: *as Christ also loved the church*; "Be ye therefore followers of God, as most dear children; and walk in love, as Christ also hath loved us and hath delivered himself for us" (Eph. 5:1–2). The sign of Christ's love for the church is that *he delivered himself up for it.* "The Son of God who loved me and delivered himself for me" (Gal. 2:20). "He hath delivered his soul unto death" (Is. 53:12). And for what? *That he might sanctify it*: "Wherefore Jesus also, that he might sanctify the people by his own blood, suffered without the gate" (Heb. 13:12). "Sanctify them in truth" (Jn. 17:17); that is the effect of Christ's death.
>
> As a result of this sanctification he cleanses it from the stains of sin. Hence he adds *cleansing it by the laver of water.* This washing has a power from the passion of Christ....
>
> The goal of this sanctifying action is the Church's purity. Thus he states *that he might present it to himself, a glorious church*; as if the Apostle said: It would be highly improper for the immaculate bridegroom to wed a soiled bride. This is why he presents her to himself in an immaculate state, now through grace and in the future through glory....
>
> From the above he [Paul]...draws the conclusion he intended by affirming: *So also ought men to love their wives as their own bodies.*[66]

The marital understanding of this union is evident in this section. The command that the husband love his wife more than another woman so as to avoid sin and the fact that Christ sacrificed Himself for the sake of purifying her from sin both deal with the moral issue of sin. Only free rational persons may sin. An organic understand of this un-

---

65 Miletic, 117.
66 *Ad Eph.*, ch. 5, lect. 8.

ion would render the present discussion invalid since it is not predicated on two autonomous rational persons.

Aquinas also discusses what the husband's love for his wife should entail. His love is sacrificial. He must be willing to deny himself and give himself completely to her, even to the point of death. By this self-sacrifice and self-gift, the husband enters into and gives witness to Christ's saving love in the Passion. The wife gives herself over to and accepts his love, thus entering into salvation and sanctification. Now purified, the bridegroom presents her to himself and weds her.

Lecture eight discussed the two roles of a marital relationship: the wife is to be subject and the husband is to love. These roles serve as the means by which one achieves unity. This goal of unity is the subject of lecture ten. Aquinas delineates a threefold union between a husband and wife:

> The first union is through the devotion of their love, for it is strong enough in each that they both left their fathers behind....But this is natural, for natural desires fit in harmoniously with actions that must be performed. It is evident that a desire exists in all higher agents that they administer to, and communicate with, lower agents. Thus a natural love for the lower is present in them. Now a man is an inferior in relation to his father and mother, he is not higher than they; hence he is naturally more drawn towards his wife and children, to whom he is superior, than to his parents. And also because his wife is intimately united to him in the act of procreation.
>
> The second union is through living together. Thus he says *and he shall cleave to his wife.* "With three things my spirit is pleased, which are approved before God and man: the concord of brethren, and the love of neighbors, and man and wife that agree well together" (Si. 25:1–2).
>
> The third is their carnal union—*and they shall be two in one flesh,* that is, in their carnal intercourse. For in any act of generation there is an active and a passive power. In plants both powers are in the same [plant], but in the perfect animals they are distinguished. And hence in the act of generation among animals the male and female become, as in plants, only one and the same body.[67]

This entire discussion is impossible if it is based on an organic understanding of the union. In the first union, the man, as her head, is drawn to the woman. The two leave their families of origin, cleave to each another, and live "together" (the second union). "Two" are "gathered" as one.[68] They are together to such an extent that they become "one flesh" through carnal intercourse (the third union). Notice

---

67 Ibid., ch. 5, lect. 10.
68 Cf. Ibid. ch. 2, lect. 5.

that in this act of procreation, the two remain two yet come together as one. For Aquinas, the male (the active power) and the female (the passive power) are not commingled so that they lose their distinct identity.[69] Rather, the two persons share a oneness.[70]

Aquinas continues by noting that this marital union is to be interpreted mystically. It is a sign, a sacrament of the union between Christ and the Church and as such it is to be called a great sacrament. In reference to Eph. 5:32 which reads, "This is a great sacrament; but I speak in Christ and in the church," he says:

> Notice here that four Sacraments are termed great. Baptism by reason of its effect, since it blots out sin and opens the gate of paradise; Confirmation by reason of its minister, it is conferred only by bishops and not by others; the Eucharist because of what it contains, the Whole Christ; the Matrimony by

---

69 From a similar passage on the perfection of humanity at the final Resurrection (*Ad Eph.*, ch. 4, lect. 5), one could deduce another argument against a Christomonism. Aquinas writes, "He relates first of all the perfection itself when he says *unto a perfect man* [Eph. 4:13]. This should not be understood as though women will be changed into men at the Resurrection—some have misread it in such a fashion. Both sexes will remain, though sexual intercourse will not longer occur, as our Lord indicates in Matthew 22 (30): 'For in the Resurrection they shall neither marry nor be married, but shall be as the angels of God in heaven.'"

70 Many of these marital themes are prevelant in Aquinas' commentary on John 3:29: "…we should note that on the human level it is the groom who regulates, governs and has the bride. Hence he says, *It is the groom who has the bride.* Now the groom is Christ: 'Like a bridegroom coming out of his bridal chamber' (Ps 18:6). His bride is the Church, which is joined to him by faith: 'I will espouse you to myself in faith' (Hos 2:20). In keeping with this figure, Zipporah said to Moses: 'You are a spouse of blood for me' (Ex 4:25). We read of marriage: 'The marriage of the Lamb has come' (Rv 19:7). So, because Christ is the groom, he has the bride, that is, the Church; but my part is only to rejoice in the fact that he has the bride" (*In Joan.*, ch. 3, lect. 5, 518). It is interesting to note not only the Christ-Church, Bridegroom-Bride motif, but the action of Moses' wife, Zipporah, the daughter of Jethro (a priest of Midian). She saves Moses from the danger of death by taking a piece of flint, cutting off her son's foreskin, and touching his person says, "You are a spouse of blood to me" (Ex 4:25). This phrase does not appear elsewhere. In touching Moses' person, she is recognizing his dignity, freedom, and autonomy as a person, as her husband. The two have brought forth through their marital covenant and marital intercourse this son, a free person with dignity who is a reflection of their one flesh union. The blood, as the principle of life, seals the covenant. Circumcision initiates one into this covenant with Yahweh and is a necessary qualification for participation in the Passover sacrifice This is an important reference to the Eucharist, as will be pointed out shortly.

reason of its signification, for it symbolizes the union of Christ and the Church. If, therefore, the text is mystically interpreted, the preceding passage should be explained as follows: *For this cause shall a man*, namely, Christ, *leave his father and mother*. I say *leave his father*, because he was sent into the world and became incarnate—"I came forth from the Father and am come into the world: (Jn. 16:28)—*and his mother* who was the synagogue—"I have forsaken my house, I have left my inheritance, I have given my dear soul into the hand of her enemies" (Jer. 12:7). *And he shall cleave to his wife*, the Church. "Behold, I am with you all days, even to the consummation of the world" (Mt. 28:20).[71]

Aquinas quotes Eph. 5:32 and refers to 5:31 by citing the parallel text of Gen. 2:23–24 in his discussion of the woman's creation. What he says in this context is instructive here because it argues against a strict Christomonistic view of the union. He writes:

When all things were first formed, it was more suitable for the woman to be made from man than (for the female to be made from the male) in other animals. First, in order thus to give the first man a certain dignity consisting in this, that as God is the principle of the whole universe, so the first man, in likeness to God, was the principle of the whole human race. Wherefore Paul says that *God made the whole human race from one* (Acts 17:26). Secondly, that man might love woman all the more, and cleave to her more closely, knowing her to be fashioned from himself. Hence it is written (Gen. 2:23, 24): *She was taken out of man, wherefore a man shall leave father and mother, and shall cleave to his wife*. This was most necessary as regards the human race, in which the male and female live together for life; which is not the case with other animals. Thirdly, because, as the Philosopher says (Ethic. 8:12), the human male and female are united, not only for generation, as with other animals, but also for the purpose of domestic life, in which each has his or her particular duty, and in which the man is the head of the woman. Wherefore it was suitable for the woman to be made out of man, as out of her principle. Fourthly, there is a sacramental reason for this. For by this is signified that the Church takes her origin from Christ. Wherefore the Apostle says (Eph. 5:32): *This is a great sacrament; but I speak in Christ and in the Church.*[72]

In this passage there are many points that are made which support a marital view of the union. First, the woman is made from man for the sake of his dignity. Individual persons are distinct, autonomous, and have dignity. Second, a motive for the man's love of the woman is that she has been fashioned from him. Love always consists of a mutual relationship between two separate individuals. Third, man and woman have their own particular duty. They could not fulfill their

---

71 *Ad Eph.*, ch. 5, lect. 10.
72 *ST* I 92.2, corp.

respective duties if they were only one organism. Fourth, a sacrament, by definition, is the means of mediation between two individuals: God and human beings.

Furthermore, since marriage is a sign of the reality of the bond between Christ and His Church, the indissolubility of that bond is derived from that bond as well. Aquinas explains:

> Now, the union of Christ and the Church is a union of one to one to be held forever. For there is one Church, as the Canticle (6:8) says: "One is My dove, My perfect one." And Christ will never by separated from His Church, for He Himself says: "Behold I am with you all days even to the consummation of the world" (Mt. 28:20); and, further: "we shall be always with the Lord (I Thess. 4:16), as the Apostle says. Necessarily, then, matrimony as a sacrament of the Church is a union of one man to one woman to be held indivisibly, and this is included in the faithfulness by which the man and wife are bound to one another.[73]

It is also important to point out rejection of a Christomonism with such phrases as, "a union of one to one" and "a union of one man to one woman."

In conclusion, Aquinas understands Paul's notion of marital union to be androcentric (i.e., the wife is subordinate to the husband) but that Paul refocused the dynamics within that structure. The wife's role is to be subordinate in the sense that she freely and responsibly enters into the relationship with her husband. She accepts her husband's Christ-like love and gift of himself. The husband, as subject to the Lord, is willing to deny what is advantageous to himself and give himself completely over to her even to the point of death. By doing so, witness is given to Christ's saving love in the Passion. Purification, sanctification, salvation are actualized so that the goal of mystical union is achieved. They become one flesh.[74]

2.3.2 A marital understanding of the four previously quoted *una mystice persona* passages

With this marital understanding of the union in place, it is now advantageous to return to the two classic and two related *una mystice persona* texts listed above and interpret them in this light. Above it

---

73 *SCG* IV ch. 78, [5]; cf. III ch. 123, [7].
74 Miletic, 111–12, 117.

was argued that this phrase was not to be understood in a monistic sense due to the fact that Aquinas argues in this tract on the Incarnation that it was not fitting that the Son of God should become incarnate in all human persons (*supposita*), for that would reduce the whole human species into one divine person; it would destroy all other persons of the human nature (thus, a Christomonism).[75] For the sake of convenience, these four texts will be cited again in expanded form:

> Grace was in Christ…not simply as in an individual man, but as in the Head of the whole Church, to whom all are united as members to the head, forming a single mystical person. In consequence, the merit of Christ extends to others in so far as they are his members.[76]

> The head and members form as it were a single mystical person. Christ's satisfaction therefore extends to all the faithful as to his members. When two men are united in charity, one can satisfy for the other.…But it is not the same where confession and contrition are concerned; satisfaction has to do with the exterior act, and here one can make use of instruments, a category under which friends are included.[77]

> Christ's passion causes forgiveness of sins by way of ransom. He is our head and has, by his passion—endured out of love and obedience—freed us, his members, from our sins, the passion being as it were the ransom. It is as if, by performing some meritorious work with his hands, a man might redeem himself from a sin he had committed with his feet. For the natural body, though made up of different members, is one, and the whole Church which is Christ's mystical body, is deemed to be one person with its head, Christ.[78]

> The members and the Head are but one person. Therefore, since Christ is our Head by reason of His divinity and His superabundant fullness of grace, and since we are His members, His merit is not something outside us, but it is communicated to us or flows into us (*influit*) on account of the unity of the Mystical Body.[79]

All four texts are concerned with the merit Christ achieved for the Body. As stated above, this is the role of the Head, to be willing to deny Himself and give Himself completely for the Body, even to the point of death. In so doing, He conquers that which inhibited the establishment of the union, namely, sin. The objection is raised that one person can not merit for another person. Aquinas resolves this di-

---

75 *ST* III 4.5, corp.
76 Ibid., III 19.4, corp.
77 Ibid., III 48.2, ad 1.
78 Ibid., III 49.1, corp.
79 *In III Sent.*, d. 18, a. 6, sol. 1; as quoted in Boylan, 50.

lemma by positing only a single person here: Christ merits for Himself, but this "Himself" is "mystical." In commenting on Eph. 5:28b–30 ("He that loveth his wife loveth himself. For no man ever hated his own flesh, but nourisheth and cherisheth it, as also Christ doth the church; Because we are members of his body, of his flesh and of his bones"), Aquinas writes, "Then he [Paul] indicates that a man must love his wife through an example. Thus he says, *Christ also loves the Church* as something of his very self *because we are members of his body.* 'For we are members one of another' (Eph. 4:25)....he says this mystically so that *of his flesh* refers to the weak who are of the flesh, and *of his bones* would refer to the strong who are hard as bone."[80] Aquinas here is applying his marital understanding of the union between Christ and the Church. He holds this love or merit for "oneself" as including a maritally structured love, a "mystical person" (*una mystice persona*) as including maritally ordered persons. The husband is not to relate to his wife and children in a way that is advantageous to himself but to the common good.[81]

In the end, salvation involves more than substitution or even vicarious satisfaction. It involves a marital union, the vital intimacy of the One Flesh between Christ and the members of His Church. Instead of one person meriting for another, it is rather as if one person were meriting for himself.[82] Aquinas explains further, "grace was bestowed upon Christ, not only as an individual, but inasmuch as He is the Head of the Church, so that it might overflow into His members; and therefore Christ's works are referred to Himself and to His members in the same way as the works of any other man in a state of grace are referred to himself."[83] Thus, the individual members are not absorbed in Christ to form one physical person with the loss of their own personal identity. It is not a union which results from annihilation but rather it is a union that is creative. It is marital; it is mystical.[84] Through this union, individual and unique persons, not organisms, experience the salvific merits of Jesus Christ.

---

80   *Ad Eph.*, ch. 5, lect. 9; cf. St. Thomas Aquinas, "Letter to Archbishop of Palermo on Articles of Faith, Art. 10" in *An Aquinas Reader*, ed. Mary T. Clark (Garden City, New York: Image Books, 1972), 493–94.

81   *Ad Eph.*, ch. 5, lect. 8.

82   Boylan, 50.

83   *ST* III 48.1, corp.

84   Boylan, 51–52. Joseph Cardinal Ratzinger, in this book, *Called to Communion: Understanding the Church Today* (San Francisco: Ignatius Press, 1996) puts it in

2.3.3 The marital understanding expressed in terms of causality

Aquinas also conveys this point by using at times the language of causality. He states that an efficient cause is twofold: principal and instrumental. He explains:

> The principal cause produces its effect in virtue of its form, to which that effect is assimilated, as fire warms in virtue of its own heat. Now it belongs to God alone to produce grace in this way as its principal cause. For grace is nothing else than a certain shared similitude to the divine nature....An instrumental cause, on the other hand, acts not in virtue of its own form, but solely in virtue of the impetus imparted to it by the principal agent. Hence the effect has a likeness not to the instrument, but rather to that principal agent, as a bed does not resemble the axe which carves it but rather the design in the mind of the carpenter.[85]

> It is by nature of an instrument as instrument to move something else when moved itself. The motion by which the instrument is moved by the principal agent is therefore related to the instrument as a complete form is related to an agent acting of itself. It is in this way, for instance, that a saw works upon a bench. Now although the saw has an action which attaches to it in accordance with its own form, that is, to divide, nevertheless it has an effect which does not attach to it except in so far as it is moved by a craftsman, namely, to make a straight cut agreeing with the pattern. Thus an instrument has two operations, one which belongs to it according to its own form, and another which belongs to it in so far as it is moved by the principal agent and which rises above the ability of its own form.[86]

---

these terms, "the Church is the Body, not by virtue of an identity without distinction, but rather by means of the pneumatic-real act of spousal love. Expressed in yet another way, this means that Christ and the Church are one body in the sense in which man and woman are one flesh, that is, in such a way that in their indissoluble spiritual-bodily union, they nonetheless remain unconfused and unmingled. The Church does not simply become Christ, she is ever the handmaid whom he lovingly raises to be his Bride and who seeks his face throughout these latter days" (39). Pius Parsch, in his book, *We are Christ's Body* (Notre Dame, Indiana: Fides, 1962), states it this way, "The members are not identical, but have differing functions and a due subordination to each other" (39). Pius XII in *Mystici Corporis Christi* (NCWN, 1943 ed.) writes, "In the natural body the principle of unity unites the parts in such a manner that each lacks its own individual subsistence (that is, the bodily members do not exist by and of themselves); on the contrary, in the Mystical Body the mutual union, though intrinsic, links the members by a bond that leaves to each complete enjoyment of his own personality" (60).

85 *ST* III 61.2, corp.
86 *De ver.*, q. 27, art. 4.

Aquinas holds that the principal efficient cause of human salvation is God.[87] Since, however, Christ's humanity is the instrument of the Godhead, all Christ's action and suffering operate instrumentally due to His divinity for effecting the salvation of humanity.[88] Consequently, Christ's Passion, by the power of the Godhead, accomplishes salvation, causes grace in humanity both meritoriously and efficiently.[89] In other words, Christ's humanity was the means, the instrument by which grace was merited for all of humanity, but in so meriting, He was a created principal cause.[90]

According to the second quotation above from *De veritate*, an instrument, however, is that which is raised by the power of a principal cause to produce an effect of a higher order than itself and is proportionate to the power of the principal cause. With this in mind, Christ, in exercising meritorious causality, can not be an instrument in the strict sense because He can not be at one and the same time a principal cause and instrument properly defined. However, in a broad sense, any cause employed by God, the principal and first cause of all, may be spoken of as His instrument in producing a particular effect, even though that instrument by itself, in its own order, is a principal cause of the effect.[91] It is in this sense that Christ in His humanity is God's instrument in meriting grace; but, in meriting, Christ was a created principal cause. On the other hand, Christ's humanity is an instrument as strictly defined above in the actual production of grace in the race. To put it differently, a creature can be no more than an instrument in the production of grace. Meriting is one thing; producing grace is something else. A creature can do the first as a principal cause but the second only as an instrumental cause.[92]

Thus, Christ the Head in His humanity is an instrument in its strict understanding, concurring with divine action in the production of grace in the Mystical Body.[93] He, in His humanity, is not an instrument existing apart from the Godhead. The principal efficient cause of grace is God Himself, and due to the fact that Christ's humanity is

---

87   *ST* III 8.1, ad 1; 48.6, corp.
88   Ibid., III 13.3, corp; 43.2, corp.; 48.6, corp.
89   Ibid., III 8.1, ad 1; III 48.6, corp.
90   O'Connell, 27. A creature can merit as a principal cause but can only produce grace as an instrumental cause.
91   *ST* I-II 21.4, ad 2.
92   O'Connell, 27.
93   Ibid., 28.

united with His divinity, He is a united (conjoined) instrument in contrast to a separated instrument (e.g., a distinct tool).[94] In the supernatural order, the humanity of Christ is the chief instrument of grace. As was stated above in the discussion on the excellence of Christ, He has the fullness of grace extensively and intensively, for it not only exists in His soul in the most perfect manner, but also it extends to all the effects of grace (e.g., in being poured out upon others).[95]

Christ as Head pours forth His grace upon the members of the Mystical Body. Aquinas writes, "Other men have certain graces distributed among them: but Christ, as being the Head of all, has the perfection of all graces. Wherefore, as to others, one is a lawgiver, another is a priest, another is a king; but all these concur in Christ, as the fount of all grace."[96] By bestowing grace, Christ chooses these members as instruments in manifesting salvation. Aquinas writes, in his tract on the grace of Christ's headship, "Hence, the entire humanity of Christ, body and soul, acts upon men, on their bodies as well as on their souls—although it acts primarily on their souls and only secondarily on their bodies. This happens when we follow the exhortation of Paul in *Romans, yield your members…to God as instruments of righteousness*—a righteousness which has come to our souls from Christ."[97] Aquinas applies his distinction between separated and united instruments in this context as well as before. In the preceding question he responds:

> Sanctifying grace is meant to produce meritorious actions, internal and external. Charismatic grace, for its part, is meant to produce certain external actions—miracle-working and the like—which serve to present the faith. Christ had both kinds of grace in full. Because his soul was united to the divinity it was fully empowered to do all the things that have just been mentioned. Other saints, because they are moved by God, not as built-in but as detached instruments, receive a partial power to do this or that particular action. And so these graces are shared out among the saints; but it was not so with Christ.[98]

Such a position moves in the direction of supporting a marital rather than simply an organic understanding of the union in the Mystical Body. The members of the Body are divided, separated instruments

---

94 *ST* III 62.5, corp.
95 Ibid., III 7.9, corp.
96 Ibid., III 22.2, ad 3.
97 Ibid., III 8.2, corp.
98 Ibid., III 7.7, ad 1.

and, thus, remain free and autonomous. As such, they are capable, then, of entering into a marital union, although Aquinas does not state that here. If they were united instruments, they would be understood as part of Christ's own personal humanity, which is a position that moves in the direction of an organic and/or Christomonistic understanding. Thus, when Aquinas regards the members of the Church as separated instruments, his understanding of the union between those members and their head is not merely organic.

2.4 Section summary

In addressing the nature of the union between Christ the Head and the Body, the Church, Aquinas dismisses the possibility of a Christomonism. First, it is not fitting that the Son of God become incarnate in all human persons on grounds that it would: a) reduce the whole human species into one divine Person and destroy all other persons of the human nature and; b) undermine Christ's rank and dignity as the first-born of all creatures because all persons would be His equal. Second, it is not fitting that the Son of God become incarnate by assuming a single human person on grounds that it would either result in two persons remaining after the union (which is Nestorianism) or the person assumed would be annihilated by the Son of God (which is a violation of the doctrine of the Incarnation). Instead of a monism, the union of persons between Christ and His Church is one of: a) conformity of nature; b) distinction of unabsorbed, unannihilated, uncorrupted persons; c) being not-joined to becoming joined.

Aquinas relies on Sacred Scripture to derive two views in order to understand this mystical union between persons. The first view is organic. The head in an organic body possesses order, perfection, and power. Christ possesses these characteristics, and so it is fitting that He is called the head. The various parts of the body have a rapport in such a way that they are interrelated, bound together in a continuity, and are of service to the whole.

The second view is marital. The role of the wife is to be subordinate to her husband in the sense that she freely and responsibly enters into the spousal relationship. She accepts her husband's Christ-like love and gift of himself. The husband, as subject to the Lord, is willing to deny what is advantageous to himself and give himself over to her completely. When both act accordingly, they form a mystical union through which they experience the salvific merits of Jesus Christ.

Aquinas explains how this marital union is achieved and sanctified in terms of causality. In His humanity, Christ the Head is an instrumental cause Who concurs with divinity in the production of grace in the Mystical Body.[99] The principal efficient cause of grace is God Himself and, due to the fact that Christ's humanity is united with His divinity, He is a united (conjoined) instrument in contrast to a separated instrument. The members of the Mystical Body are the separated instruments and, as free and autonomous, they are capable of choosing to enter into the graced marital union with Christ or not.

3 The Primacy of the Mystical Body

It has been shown above that Aquinas understands the union in the Mystical Body to be both organic and marital. This section will demonstrate that the Mystical Body is of fundamental importance to Aquinas because he uses it as the underlying basis for building his theological structure.[100] The discussion will begin with Redemption and how its fruits are applied to the Mystical Body.

The realization of the work of Redemption (i.e., "objective redemption" or "redemption effected") is explained by the fact that Christ is the Head of humanity and, as such, is endowed with capital grace.[101] The Redemption was effected, according to Aquinas, by a five-fold method: the way of merit, atonement, Redemption, sacrifice, and efficiency.[102] It has been demonstrated, above, that for Aquinas, Christ was able to merit, atone, and sacrifice for human beings and to

---

99 O'Connell, 28.

100 This is a significant point because one of the main functions of a theological *prius* is to provide an organizational structure to the content of divine revelation.

101 Emilio Sauras, "Thomistic Soteriology and the Mystical Body," *The Thomist* XV (October 1952): 544–45.

102 *ST* III 48 prol.

redeem humanity and accomplish salvation efficiently because He is indeed the Head of the race and possesses capital grace.[103]

Now in the third part of the *Summa theologiae*, Aquinas addresses how the fruits of objective Redemption are applied so that human beings are initiated and incorporated into the Mystical Body of Christ. Their life in union with Christ is fostered by the sacraments, of which the Eucharist is primary for Aquinas. This application of Redemption to the members of the Body has been called "applied redemption" or "subjective redemption."[104]

For Aquinas, the doctrines of grace and redemption are predicated upon the mystical union between Christ as Head and the Church as Body. He gives an indication of this in his prologue to his commentaries on the epistles of St. Paul. He writes:

> For this is the entire doctrine concerning the grace of Christ: which indeed is able to be considered in three ways. In the first way according to that which is in the head, namely Christ; and so he comments in the Epistle to the Hebrews. In another way, according to that which is in the principal members of the mystical body; as so he comments in the Epistles which are for the prelates. In a third way, according to that which is in the mystical body itself which is the Church; and so he comments in the Epistles which are sent to the Gentiles: this is their distinction. For the very grace of Christ is able to be considered in three ways. In one way according to itself; and so he comments in the Epistle to the Romans. In another way, according to that which is in the sacraments of grace; and so he comments in the two Epistles to the Corinthians; in the first one of these he discusses the sacraments themselves, in the second, he talks about the worthiness of the ministers; and in the Epistle to the Galatians, in which the superfluous sacraments [Old Testament] are excluded contrary to those who are wishing to join the old sacraments to the new. In the third way, the grace of Christ is considered according to the effect of unity which it makes in the Church. Therefore, the Apostle [Paul] first indeed discusses the institution of ecclesiastical unity in the Epistle to the Ephesians; in the second way, he speaks about its strengthening and progress in the Epistle to the Philippians; and in a third way, he discusses its defense, indeed contrary to errors in the Epistle of the Colossians, he speaks about it contrary to the persecution to be sure in the first Epistle to the Thessalonians, and about future persecutions to be sure, especially in the time of the anti-Christ in the second letter. He instructs to

---

103 Sauras, 545. Concerning merit, cf. *ST* III 19.4; 48.1; concerning satisfaction, cf. III 48.2, ad 1; concerning liberation, cf. III 49.1; concerning sacrifice, cf. 22.1, ad 3; and concerning efficiency, cf. III 8.1, ad 1.

104 Sauras, 544–45. In speaking of sufficient and efficient causality, Aquinas expresses the distinction between objective and subjective redemption for the first of many times in his *In III Sent.*, d. 19, a. 1, qla. 2, sol. 1, ad 4.

be sure the prelates of the Church—both the spiritual ones and temporal ones. Indeed the spiritual ones concerning instruction and governance of ecclesiastical unity in the first Epistle to Timothy; about its strength against persecutions in the second; and in a third way about its defense against heretics in the Epistle to Titus. To be sure he instructs temporal masters in the Epistle to Philemon. And so the rationale of distinction and order of all the letters is clear.[105]

Consequently, the grace of Christ is considered in three ways: first, in the Head itself, that is in Christ, as described in the Epistle to the Hebrews; second, in the principal members of the Mystical Body, as described in the Pastoral Epistles; third, in the Mystical Body, which is the Church itself, as described in the epistles addressed to the Gentiles. This last group is subdivided into the study of grace as conferred by the sacraments or grace in the effect of unity which it produces in the Church.[106] In the end, all of the Pauline epistles, according to Aquinas, may be grouped around this fundamental ideal: the grace of Christ as it is in the Head Himself, in the members of the Mystical Body, and the Mystical Body itself.[107] With this point in place, it seems reasonable to assume, as many other scholars have,[108]

---

105 *Est enim haec doctrina tota de gratia Christi, quae quidem potest tripliciter considerari. Uno modo, secundum quod est in ipso capite, sc. Christo, et sic commendatur in epist. ad Hebr. Alio modo, secundum quod est in membris principalibus corporis mystici, et sic commendatur in epistolis quae sunt ad praelatos. Tertio modo, secundum quod in ipso corpore mystico, quod est ecclesia; et sic commendatur in epistolis quae mittuntur ad gentiles: quarum haec est distinctio. Nam ipsa gratia Christi tripliciter potest condierari. Uno modo, secundum se, et sic commendatur in epistola ad Romanos. Alio modo, secundum quod est in sacramentis gratiae, et sic commendatur in duabus epistolis ad Cor., in quarum prima agitur de ipsis sacramentis; in secunda de dignitate ministrorum. Et in epist. ad Gal., in qua excluduntur superflua sacramenta, contra illos qui volebant vertera sacramenta novis adjungere. Tertio consideratur gratia Christi secundum affectum unitatis, quem in ecclesia fecit. Agit ergo Apostolus primo quidem de institutione ecclesiasticae unitatis in epistola ad Ephesios. Secundo, de ejus confirmatione et profectu in epist. ad Phil. Tertio, de ejus defensione contra errores quidem in epist. ad Col., contra persecutiones vero praesentes in I. ad Thess., contra futuras vero, et praecipue tempore antichristi, in II. Praelatos vero ecclesiarum instruit et spirituales et temporales. Spirituales quidem de institutione, instructione et gubernatione ecclesiasticae unitatis in prima ad Tim.; de firmitate contra persecutores in secunda. Tertio, de defensione contra haereticos in epistola ad Titum. Dominos vero temporales instruxit in epistola ad Philemonem. Et sic patet ratio distinctionis et ordinis omnium epistolarum* (*In omnes S. Pauli Apostoli Epistolas*, prol.).

106 Abbé Anger, *The Doctrine of the Mystical Body of Christ: According to the Principles of the Theology of St. Thomas Aquinas* (London: Longmans, Green, 1932), xvii.

107 John T. Dittoe, "Sacramental Incorporation into the Mystical Body," *The Thomist* 9 (October, 1946): 472–73.

108 Several scholars argue this position: E. Mersch (*The Whole Christ*, Milwaukee: 1938, passim) and J. Dittoe ("Sacramental Incorporation into the Mystical

that the Mystical Body may have been seen to be the fundamental principle underlying the building of his theological structure (at least in the third part of the *Summa theologiae*).

The prologue may be outlined, as adapted from the article by John Dittoe, as follows:[109]

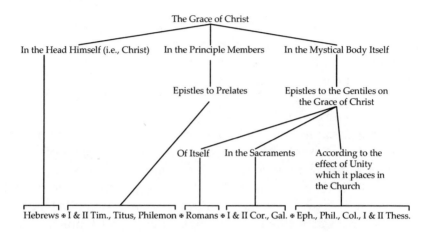

In the mind of Aquinas, the two natures of Christ, sanctifying grace, redemption, the Mystical Body, and the sacraments are inextricably linked. Each one implies the others. The Mystical Body of Christ was established by the God-Man so that humanity could be redeemed through the grace of Christ. It is through the means of the sacraments that one is initiated and incorporated into the Mystical Body of Christ. Unless one is nourished and sustained through the sacraments as a member of this Body, one can not be saved. The Mystical Body is utterly essential.[110]

Body," *The Thomist*, IX [October, 1946]: 473) cite Cyprian, Cyril of Alexandria, John Chrysostom, and Augustine, in addition to Aquinas, as holding that the Mystical Body was a central idea and a unifying viewpoint in building a theological structure; Abbé Anger (10) holds that the doctrine of the Mystical Body is "the central dogma of all his [Aquinas'] theology" and it "dominates and unifies everthing in the work of the Angelic Doctor."

109   Dittoe, 473.
110   Cf. *SCG* IV ch. 56, [1]; *ST* III 60.3, 62.1, and 79.2, ad 1.

4 The Primacy of the Eucharist

The preceding section argued that the Mystical Body is a fundamental principal underlying the theological structure of Aquinas' work. It is instructive to note that Aquinas becomes even more narrowly focused when he turns to the relationship between the Mystical Body and the sacraments. The sacraments were instituted for the unity and well-being of the Mystical Body. Through them the restorative, salvific, life-giving, and unitive influences of the Head are given to members of the Body. One sacrament, however, is "the sacrament of ecclesiastical unity, which requires that many be one in Christ"[111] and has as its reality (*res*) "the unity of the Mystical Body of Christ"[112] or "Christ's Mystical Body, which is the fellowship of the saints."[113] The Eucharist is "spiritual nourishment through the union with Christ and his members, as food becomes one with the person fed."[114] It is the ultimate sign of what people are meant to be, for it contains the source (the life of God) of its effect (the life of grace).[115] By it, people are "brought to spiritual perfection in being closely united to Christ who suffered for us."[116] So the Eucharist is also that by which people *are* what they are meant to be. Aquinas explains:

> The effect of this sacrament should be looked at first and foremost from what the sacrament holds, and this is Christ. Just as by coming visibly into the world he brought the life of grace into it, according to John, *Grace and truth came through Jesus Christ*, so by coming to men sacramentally he causes the life of grace; *He who eats me also shall live because of me.* Accordingly Cyril writes, *The life-giving Word of God by uniting himself with his own flesh made it also life-giving. And so it was right that he should be united with our bodies through his sacred flesh and precious blood, which we receive as a life-giving blessing in the bread and wine.*[117]

It has been discussed, above, that Aquinas held this union to be physical in the sense that through the hypostatic union, the divine

---

111 Ibid., III 82.2, ad 3; cf. III 67.2.
112 Ibid., III 73.3, corp.
113 Ibid., III 80.4, corp.
114 Ibid., III 79.5, corp. Note that Aquinas has identified the Eucharist as the primary sacrament. This is Keefe's theological *prius*.
115 Brian Davies, *The Thought of Thomas Aquinas* (Oxford: Clarendon Press, 1992), 362.
116 *ST* III 73.3, ad 3.
117 Ibid., III 79.1, corp.

Word assumed a human nature. By this hypostatic union, and in it, the whole Church came to be united with the divine Person of the Word in an ineffable manner.[118] Now this union is physical in the sense that through the sacrament of the Eucharist, Jesus Christ comes to communicate and unite Himself to all the faithful sacramentally by feeding them with His body, blood, soul, and divinity which is truly, really, and substantially present. The unity of the Mystical Body is the reality of the sacrament.[119] Thus, with the Incarnation, the body of the divine Word appeared in history as the source of a wholly new eucharistically centered system which gives rise to the perfect body of the faithful.[120]

4.1 The primacy of the Eucharist by reason of the *res et sacramentum*[121]

By way of an introduction, the following subsections (i.e., 4.1, 4.2, and 4.3) will analyze why Aquinas holds the Eucharist to be primary among the sacraments. They will do so by dividing the sacrament into the three constitutive principles of the traditional sacramental *ordo*: *sacramentum tantum*, *res et sacramentum*, and *res tantum*. The following is a brief overview of this sacramental *ordo* which will assist the broader analysis.

The *sacramentum tantum* is the sign or sacramental rite which consists of the form and matter. The *res et sacramentum* is the *ex opere operato* effect (*res* or sacramental reality) of the placing of the sign, the *sacramentum tantum*. The *res et sacramentum* is not only (*tantum*) an ef-

---

118 Roger Freddi, *Jesus Christ the Word Incarnate*, translated by F. J. Sullivan (St. Louis: B. Herder, 1904), 127.
119 *ST* III 73.3, corp.
120 Coleman O'Neil, "St. Thomas on the Membership of the Church," *The Thomist* 27 (April, July, and October 1963): 107.
121 The roots of the formula *"sacramentum tantum, res et sacramentum, res tantum"* may be traced back to St. Augustine and his debate with the Donatists. The formula is present implicitly but substantially in Hugh of St. Victor's treatise on the Eucharist, *De Sacramentis christianae fidei* (L. II, p. 8, c. 7). It is decidedly explicit a few years later in Peter Lombard's *Sententia* (IV, d. 8, d. 22). By the time of St. Thomas Aquinas, it is commonplace as is evident from his commentary on *IV Sent.* (d. 1 and d. 4) and the *Summa theologiae* (e.g., III 63.6, 66.1, 73.1 ad 3, 84.1 ad 3) (Toshiyuki Miyakawa, "St. Thomas on the Relation between *Res et Sacramentum* and *Res Tantum*," *Euntes Docete: Commentaria Urbaniana* XVIII [1965]: 61–65).

fect, but it is also itself a sign and cause of another effect, the *res tantum*. This effect is brought about *ex opere operantis* and yet it is entirely dependent upon the prior reality (*res et sacramentum*). In itself it will never be a sign. All three elements are essential constitutive elements of this sacramental *ordo*. Since Aquinas makes use of this *ordo* in his sacramental theology, the primacy of the Eucharist will be discussed in light of each of these constitutive elements.

4.1.1 The excellence, perfection, end, and consummation of the Eucharist by reason of its *res et sacramentum*

Aquinas indicates the excellence, dignity, and nobility of the Eucharist by calling it "the sacrament of sacraments,"[122] "the chief sacrament,"[123] "the greatest sacrament,"[124] and "the most noble...sacrament."[125] While the contexts of these expressions do not clearly indicate that it is by reason of the *res et sacramentum* that the Eucharist is of such excellence, they do suggest that this is indeed the reason.[126]

Other passages indicate this excellence more clearly and why it is so. In discussing the appropriateness of giving the Eucharist various names, Aquinas has this to say about the term *eucharistia*, "it is called 'desirable gift', because *the free gift of God is eternal life*, as we read in *Romans*, or because it really contains Christ, who is full of grace."[127] In the second objection Aquinas makes the following point, "What is common to all the sacraments is attributed antonomastically [*antonomastice*] to this one on account of its excellence." Thus, Aquinas' point seems to be that this sacrament can be antonomastically called *eucharistia* because it contains Christ. How is this term *antonomastice* to be understood? *A Lexicon of St. Thomas Aquinas* provides the following definition, "a figure of speech which is used when a name appropri-

---

122 *In IV Sent.*, d. 24, q. 2, a. 2, qla. 2, resp.
123 ST II-II 83.9 corp.
124 *In IV Sent.*, d. 24, q. 2, a. 1, qla, 2, ad 1; d. 25, q. 1, a. 1 ad 4.
125 *SCG* IV ch. 74, [6].
126 James W. Kinn, *The Pre-Eminence of the Eucharsit Among the Sacraments According to Alexander of Hales, St. Albert the Great, St. Bonaventure and St. Thomas Aquinas*, Dissertationes ad Lauream, 31 (Mundelein, Illinois: Saint Mary of the Lake Seminary, 1960), 92.
127 *ST* III 73.4, corp.

ate to several different things is applied to that of one of them to which it is preeminently suitable."[128] The term refers to some sort of pre-eminence. Thus, the Eucharist is excellent because it contains Christ.[129]

Aquinas explains this at length in his *Commentary on the Sentences* (IV d. 8, q. 1, a. 1, qla. 3, sol. 1). This explanation may be summarized in the following way: a sacrament is that which sanctifies; but something can be sanctified or holy in itself or in its effect; the other sacraments are holy only in their effects whereas the Eucharist is holy in itself because it contains Christ; therefore, the Eucharist is truly a sacrament and is of greater dignity than the others because it is holy in itself. The Eucharist is holy because it is Christ.[130]

Earlier in the *Commentary on the Sentences*, Aquinas outlines five ways in which one sacrament may be more worthy than another. In the end, he concludes that the Eucharist is simply the most worthy, it is the most perfect sacrament, and it is the perfection of the other six sacraments because it in fact contains Christ.[131]

Elsewhere he has reached the same conclusion but on slightly different grounds. In *De veritate*, he writes:

> Thus the humanity of Christ is the instrumental cause of justification. This cause is applied to us spiritually through faith and bodily through the sacraments, because Christ's humanity is both spirit and body. This is done to the end that we may receive within ourselves the effect of sanctification, which is had through Christ. As a consequence the most perfect sacrament is that in which the body of Christ is really contained, the Eucharist; and it is the consummation of all the others....But the other sacraments also share some of the efficacy by which Christ's humanity works instrumentally for our justification.[132]

In other words, the humanity of Christ is the instrumental cause of justification, but the Eucharist contains Christ Himself while the other sacraments simply share in the power of Christ's humanity; therefore, the Eucharist contains the instrumental cause of justification in a

---

128 Deferrari and Berry, *Lexicon of St. Thomas Aquinas*, 79.
129 This conclusion is also supported by the Blackfriars translation of this second object. It reads as follows: "That which is common to all the sacraments is attributed *par excellence* to this one; it is supreme" (Kinn, 93).
130 *In IV Sent.*, d. 8, q. 1, a. 1, qla. 3, sol. 1 (Kinn, 94).
131 Ibid., d. 7, q. 1, a. 1, qla. 3, resp.
132 *De ver.*, q. 27, art. 4.

more perfect way than the other sacraments and is the most perfect sacrament.[133]

The presupposition in this argument seems to be that which contains something substantially is greater than that which contains something virtually. Aquinas, in the following statements, again argues that the Eucharist is the perfection of the other sacraments not only because it contains Christ substantially but because all the others participate in it:

> ...that sacrament [the Eucharist] is the end and perfection of all the sacraments. And this is the reason, because "being" which is by its essence, is the end and perfection of those things which exist by participation: for other sacraments contain Christ by participation; in this very one, however, it is Christ according to substance: therefore, as Dionysius says, there is no sacrament which is not made complete in the Eucharist.[134]

> ...in this sacrament [the Eucharist] Christ is present substantially. Now it is a universal rule that that which is of a certain kind by its very essence is greater than that which is so by participation.[135]

In other words, in any genus that which exists or possesses a certain quality by itself is the perfection of that genus and of all others in that genus since these exist or possess that quality merely by participation.[136]

Aquinas also states that the Eucharist is the end[137] and the consummation of all the sacraments.[138] Underlying these two assertions is the same presupposition with the appropriate variations: that which contains something substantially is the end or the consummation of that which contains it merely virtually. The Eucharist is the end and the consummation of all the sacraments because it contains Christ (n.b., the end and consummation is not technically Christ Himself but the sacrament). The other sacraments contain Christ through

---

133 Kinn, 98.
134 *In Matt.*, ch. 26, 3. *Unde illud sacramentum finis et perfectio omnium est sacramentorum; et ratio est, quia esse quod est per essentiam, est finis et perfectio eorum quae per participationem: alia enim sacramenta Christum continent per participationem; in isto autem est Christus secundum substantiam: ideo dicit Dionysius quod nullum est sacramentum quod non perficiatur in Eucharistia.*
135 *ST* III 65.3, corp.
136 Kinn, 98.
137 *In IV Sent.*, d. 7, q. 1, a. 1, qla. 3, resp.; *ST* III 63.6, corp.; 65.3, corp.; *In Matt.*, ch. 26, 3.
138 *SCG* IV ch. 74, [6]; *ST* III 63.6, corp.; *De ver.*, q. 27, art. 5, resp.

participation; they symbolize Christ and contain a certain instrumental virtue or power flowing to them from His humanity. The Eucharist contains not merely a participation of this humanity, but the Body of Christ Himself. He is substantially present in the sacrament; the other sacraments possess a certain instrumental power which is a share in Christ's power.[139]

4.1.2 The problem of sacramental presence

Two modes of presence are, thus, possible: the Eucharist makes substantially present the Body of Christ; the other sacraments make present the activity of this Body. This does not mean that Christ is at all limited in His activity. Through either presence, His humanity, as an instrument of the divinity, is equally efficient.[140] Why, then, is there need for the presence of the Body of Christ when His power is sufficient for the effect? Why is there a need for a sacrament containing Christ Himself when He can bring about the same effect by a virtual contact?[141]

Just as there was need for the Body of Christ in the Incarnation, there is a need for it as well in the Eucharist. Christ wished to draw near to the human race by taking flesh so that He might encourage the race to know Him.[142] While Aquinas holds that God could have found other ways to redeem, the way He did act was most fitting for the present condition of fallen humanity. There is a similar fittingness that characterizes the presence of Christ in the Eucharist. Christ's presence in the Eucharist is fitting as: a) a demonstration of the greatest charity in the fact that He gives Himself as food; b) an elevation of hope from so familiar a union with Him; c) an opportunity for the greatest merit of faith in that many things are believed in this sacrament which are not only beyond reason, but are also contrary to the senses.[143]

---

139 Sr. Francis Assisi, *The Eucharist: The End of All the Sacraments According to St. Thomas Aquinas and His Contemporaries*, Ph. D. Diss. (Sinsinawa, Wisconsin: Saint Clare Convent, 1972), 246–47.
140 *ST* III 56.1, ad 3.
141 Loughery, 247–48.
142 *ST* III 1.2, ad 3.
143 *In IV Sent.*, d. 10, a. 1.

In the *Summa theologiae*, Aquinas provides three reasons for the fittingness of Christ's Real Presence in the Eucharist. In so doing, he ties it into the broader soteriological and sacramental theme that the humanity of Christ is our way to God.[144] The first reason emphasizes the importance of Christ's sacrificial death in the plan of salvation. He writes:

> This [the presence of Christ's body and blood in the sacrament] is entirely in keeping, first of all with the perfection of the New Law. The sacrifices of the Old Law contained that true sacrifice which was the passion of Christ, only in a figurative way.
> ....It was only right that the sacrifice of the New Law instituted by Christ should have something more, that it should contain Christ himself who suffered for us, and contain him, not merely as by a sign or figure, but in actual reality as well. So it is that this sacrament which really contains Christ himself is, as Dionysius says, the *fulfillment of all the other sacraments*, in which a share of Christ's power is to be found.[145]

The perfection of the New Law demands something more than the figure of Christ's Passion signified by the sacrifices of the Old Law. There is need for a sacrifice which contains the crucified Christ not merely in figure but in truth. This is due to the fact that the Church needs access to the sacrifice of Christ so that she may appropriate the merit won by that sacrifice. The sacraments obtain their effect through the power of Christ's Passion and His Passion is applied to humanity through the sacraments.[146] This application takes place primarily through the sacramental representation of the sacrifice of Christ whereby the Church has access not only spiritually but corporeally to the very victim Who offers Himself on the Cross.[147] The body that was slain on the Cross is now sacramentally present; the merit gained by that slaying is now sacramentally accessible.[148]

The second reason for the fittingness of Christ's Real Presence in the Eucharist is closely related to sacrifice: fellowship with Christ in the mystery of His Passion and death is a precursor to fellowship with Him in glory. He explains:

---

144 *ST* I 2, prol.
145 Ibid., III 75.1, corp.
146 Ibid., III 61.1, ad 3; cf. 49.1.
147 Ibid., III 70.5 and 7.
148 Loughery, 251–55.

> Secondly, it [the presence of Christ's body and blood in the sacrament] fits in perfectly with that charity of Christ which led him to take a real body having human nature and unite it to himself in order to save us. And because it is the very law of friendship that *friends should live together*, as Aristotle teaches, he promises us his bodily presence as a reward, in the text of Matthew, *wherever the body is, there the eagles will be gathered together*. In the meantime, however, he has not left us without this sacrament in the reality of his body and blood. For this reason he says, *he who eats my flesh and drinks my blood abides in me and I in him*. Hence this sacrament, because it joins Christ so closely to us, is the sign of the extreme of his love and lifts our hope on high.[149]

As a general tendency, friends seek to live together. So it is with Christ and His disciples. His bodily presence is an accomplishment of this desire; however, this accomplishment is not given merely as an event in time. Christ's bodily presence will also be in heaven as a reward of friendship. Aquinas makes this point evident in his quoting of the eschatological passage from Matthew, "wherever the body is, there the eagles will be gathered together" (24:28). Christ's body will be the center of convergence for calling together the faithful of God. Membership in His Body on earth is a necessary condition for this heavenly assemblage.[150]

Those who are earthly members of His Mystical Body feed on His body sacramentally until that time when they will be in His presence eternally. Christ desires to live together with His faithful friends until they are called to live with Him in heaven; thus, the Eucharist is given as a sign of His love and a source of their eternal hope.

The third reason for the fittingness of Christ's Real Presence in the Eucharist lies within the context of faith. Aquinas writes:

> Thirdly, this real presence is just what is right for the perfection of our faith, which bears not only on the divinity of Christ, but also on his humanity; as he has said, *believe in God, believe also in me*. Now faith has to do with unseen realities, and just as he offers his divinity to our acceptance as something that we do not see, so in this sacrament he offers his very flesh to us in like manner.[151]

Christ's bodily presence in the Eucharist perfects the person's faith in the unseen: Christ offered His divinity to each person invisibly in His human nature and now His flesh (along with His divinity) is offered

---

149   *ST* III 75.1, corp.
150   Loughery, 255–57.
151   *ST* III 75.1, corp.

invisibly in this sacrament. By encountering His divinity and flesh in an invisible manner, each person will hopefully come to know more familiarly, in faith, Christ Who will be the object of the beatific vision. Such a position is consistent with his earlier discussion of faith in the *Compendium of Theology*. There he says:

> Faith is a certain foretaste of that knowledge which is to make us happy in the life to come....Our Lord taught us that this beatific knowledge has to do with two truths, namely, the divinity of the Blessed Trinity and the humanity of Christ. That is why, addressing the Father, He says: "This is eternal life: that they may know Thee, the only true God, and Jesus Christ, whom Thou hast sent" (John 17:3). All the knowledge imparted by faith turns about these two points, the divinity of the Trinity and the humanity of Christ. This should cause us no surprise: the humanity of Christ is the way by which we come to the divinity. Therefore, while we are still wayfarers, we ought to know the road leading to our goal.[152]

Through faith, one encounters the humanity and divinity of Christ Who is present sacramentally in the Eucharist. The Eucharist anticipates the beatific vision which is the reward for those who believe in Christ.

To summarize from his early *Commentary on the Sentences* to his closing reflection in the *Summa theologiae*, Aquinas presents three fundamental ideas concerning the fittingness of a sacrament containing the Body and Blood of Christ. They are: 1) for a perfect union of Christ the Head with His members there is need for a sacrament which contains Him, not only participatively, but also essentially; 2) for a manifestation of the greatest charity and for an elevation of human hope, there is need of a friend (i.e., Christ) to live with friends; 3) for the perfection of faith, there is need for persons to believe in the humanity of Christ as well as His divinity.

In the *Summa*, Aquinas adds that the fittingness of Christ's Real Presence in the Eucharist is understood only with the realization that the humanity of Christ must be met: 1) in sacrifice, because it is humanity's personal entry into the event of Calvary which is the measure of participation in its redemptive grace; 2) in glory, because humanity's consummation depends upon Christ Who is the illumination of His friends, the saints of God; 3) in faith, because human beings are pilgrims who travel in the realm of the invisible towards the beatific vision in heaven. This explains the need for contact with

---

152 *Compend.*, 2.

Christ's humanity. The entire sacramental system is designed for this purpose: in the other six sacraments there is contact with Christ's sanctifying power; in the Eucharist this contact reaches a peak of intensity through the presence of the sanctifying Christ Himself incorporating humanity fully into the mystery of His saving love.[153]

4.1.3 Subsection summary

To summarize this section on the primacy of the Eucharist by reason of the *res et sacramentum*, Aquinas argues that the Eucharist holds the place of primacy (i.e., it is excellent, perfect, the end, and consummation) in regard to all of the sacraments by reason of its content: it contains the Real Presence of Christ Himself. The other sacraments contain a certain instrumental power which is a participation in Christ's power. The Gospels testify, however, that Christ is equally efficient whether He is present to an object by bodily contact or by the mere contact of His power (the servant of the centurion; Mt 8:5–13). This raises the question: Why is there a need for a sacrament containing Christ Himself when He can bring about the same effect by a virtual contact? Aquinas explains that there is no absolute need for a sacrament of the Real Presence; however, there is a profound fittingness which is akin to the fittingness of the Incarnation. In the end, it comes down to four reasons: 1) there is need for a sacrament which contains Christ not only participatively, but through essence, in order that there might be a perfect union of Head and members of the Body (this reason is also why the Eucharist has primacy); 2) this presence belongs to the charity of Christ Who desires to live among His people as a friend; 3) this presence stirs up the faithful's hope by so familiar an intimate relationship with Christ; 4) this presence belongs to the perfection of faith which regards the humanity of Christ as well as His divinity.[154]

---

153 Loughery, 262–65.
154 Ibid., 271–72.

4.2 The primacy of the Eucharist by reason of the *sacramentum tantum*

Aquinas identifies the *sacramentum tantum* as the sacramental rite which consists of the form and matter.[155] Attention now will focus on the *sacramentum tantum* of the Eucharist and the primacy which is attributed to the sacrament because of it. According to Aquinas, the *sacramentum tantum* is the "bread and wine"[156] or the "species of bread and wine."[157] Yet none of the sacraments are perfect signs merely by means of the matter; they require the form or specific words which perfects the signification of the sacraments.[158]

The primacy by reason of this element of the sacramental *ordo* is not as much a concern for Aquinas as the other two elements: the *res et sacramentum* and the *res tantum*. He does, however, treat it briefly. The *corpus* of *Summa theologiae* III 73.4 deals with the signification of the sacrament and even though objection two and its response deals with the effects, the *corpus* of any article should at least contain the solution to the objections. Thus, the article teaches something about signification in light of its effects. The objection, *corpus*, and response to the objection reads as follows:

> [obj. 2] Moreover, a species is not suitably signified by a name that belongs to the genus. Now the Eucharist is a sacrament of the New Law. All the sacraments of the New Law have this in common, they confer grace. But the word 'Eucharist', which is translated 'good grace', means just this. Also, all the sacraments act as restoratives as we journey through this present life, and this is precisely what a 'viaticum' does. Likewise, in all the sacraments something sacred is made: so they have the nature of 'sacrifice'. Finally, in all the sacraments the faithful enter into union with one another; this is signified by the name '*synaxis*' in Greek or '*communio*' in Latin. Therefore, it is not right to restrict these names to this sacrament.

> [resp.] This sacrament signifies three things. It looks back to the past: in this sense it commemorates the passion of our Lord, which was the true sacrifice, as we saw earlier. Because of this it is called 'sacrifice.' In regard to the present, there is another thing to which it points. This is the unity of the Church, into which men are drawn together through this sacrament....It has

---

155 Cf. *ST* III 60.6, ad 2; 66.1, corp.; 66.5, corp.; 73.1, ad 1; 84.1, ad 3; *De articulis fidei et ecclesiae sacramentis ad Archiepiscopum Panormitarum*, in *Opuscula Theologica*, vol. 1, edited by Raymundi A. Verardo (Romae: Marietti, 1954): n. 614.
156 *ST* III 73.6, corp.
157 *In IV Sent.*, d. 10, divisio textus; *In Matt.*, ch. 26, 4.
158 *ST* III 60.6.

a third significance with regard to the future. It prefigures that enjoyment of God which will be ours in heaven. That is why it is called *'viaticum'*, because it keeps us on the way to heaven....

[reply to obj. 2] That which is common to all the sacraments is attributed *par excellence* to this one; it is supreme.[159]

The argument may be outlined as follows: that which is common to all the sacraments in their effects can be attributed antonomastically to the Eucharist, but the sacraments affect the very reality they signify; therefore, in the order of the signification of the sacraments, that which is common to all the sacraments can be attributed antonomastically to the Eucharist.[160]

Another passage from the *Commentary on the Sentences* implies that the Eucharist is more noble than the other sacraments by reason of its signification. The following is the objection and response:

To the degree...that something is more simple, it is more noble....But this sacrament [the Eucharist] is more noble than the others....Since therefore the other sacraments have only one matter...its seems that there ought not to be a double matter of this sacrament....[we must say that] the significance of the sacrament is from the effect by causing it to appear by a sacrament, because the sacraments effect what they signify. And so, when this sacrament is taken for the salvation of the body and soul, it is proper that under the species of bread to signify the salvation of the body and under the species of wine to signify the salvation of the soul, this sacrament is brought to perfection....To [that objection] we must say that simplicity by itself is not the cause of nobility, but perfection...and therefore this sacrament although it might be more composite by reason of matter, nevertheless it is more noble, because it is more perfect.[161]

If the phrase "the signification of the sacrament is from the effect" (*"significatio sacramenti est de effectu"*) is taken to refer to each of the

---

159   Ibid., III 73.4.

160   Kinn, 104–5.

161   *In IV Sent.*, d. 11, q. 2, a. 1. *Quanto...aliquid est simplicius, tanto nobilius....Sed hoc sacramentum [eucharistiae] est nobilius aliis....Cum ergo alia sacramenta unam tantum materiam habeant...videtur quod non debeat esse duplex materia hujus sacramenti....[dicendum quod] significatio sacramenti est de effectu per sacramentum inducendo, quia sacramenta efficiunt quod figurant. Et sic, cum hoc sacramentum ad salutem corporis et animae sumatur, oportet quod sub specie panis ad signficandum salutem corporis, et sub specie vini ad significandum salutem animae, hoc sacramentum perficitur....Ad [illam objectionem] dicendum quod simplicitas per se non est causa nobilitatis, sed perfectio....Et ideo hoc sacramentum quamvis sit magis compositum ratione materiae, est tamen nobilius, quia est magis perfectum.*

sacraments and not only the Eucharist, then the argument may be summarized as follows: the main element in determining the nobility of anything is not its simplicity but its perfection; but the Eucharist is more perfect among the sacraments by reason of its signification, for it signifies the sanctification of both the soul and the body; therefore, the Eucharist is the more noble sacrament.[162]

The primacy of the sacrament has been considered from the perspective of the matter; however, it may be considered from the perspective of the form as well. In his answer to the question regarding whether the words of consecration are the form of the sacrament, Aquinas writes:

> There are two respects in which this sacrament differs from the others. First, this sacrament is fully established when the matter is consecrated; the other sacraments are brought to completion only when the consecrated matter is being used. Second, in the other sacraments the consecration of the matter consists merely in a certain blessing, as a result of which the consecrated matter receives an instrumental spiritual power; this derives from the minister who is a living instrument able to reach inanimate objects. But in this sacrament the consecration of the matter consists in a miraculous change of the substance, which only God can bring about. So it is that the minister has no other act in effecting this sacrament than to pronounce the words.
>
> Now since the form of a thing ought to be in accordance with its nature, it follows that the form of this sacrament differs from the forms of the other sacraments in two respects. First of all, the forms of the other sacraments imply that the matter is actually being used, as, for example, Baptism and Confirmation; but the form of this sacrament implies only that the matter is being consecrated, and this is the transubstantiation which takes place when the priest says the words, 'This is my body', or 'This is the chalice of my blood'. Secondly, the forms of the other sacraments are pronounced by the minister speaking in his own person, either as exercising some action, as when he says, 'I baptize you', or 'I confirm you'....But in this sacrament the form is pronounced as in the person of Christ himself speaking; by this we are to understand that the part played by the minister in the effecting of this sacrament is the mere utterance of the words of Christ.[163]

Aquinas is arguing for the uniqueness of the Eucharist in two points: it consists in the consecration of its matter whereas the other sacraments consist in use of matter already consecrated; when in the other sacraments the matter is consecrated, a blessing is bestowed by which the matter derives a spiritual power whereas in the Eucharist, the consecration involves a change of substance. Since the sacramental

---

162 Kinn, 105.
163 *ST* III 78.1, corp.

form must reflect these two points regarding its nature, the form of the Eucharist refers only to the transubstantiation of the matter (a distinctive occurrence) whereas in the other sacraments, the form refers to action or use of the matter. Likewise, with the Eucharist, the minister speaks in the person of Christ whereas in the other sacrament, he speaks in his own person. Thus, the form of the Eucharist is also indicative of its primacy since it stands out as unique from all the other sacramental forms.

4.3 The primacy of the Eucharist by reason of the *res tantum*

Aquinas identifies the *res tantum* of the Eucharist by saying, "the thing signified [*res sacramenti*] is the unity of the mystical body of Christ."[164] Its principal effect is the union of Christ to humanity, Head to Body.[165] Union with God is the human person's ultimate perfection in this life:

> Final perfection for men in their present life is their cleaving to God....[166]

> Still it is true that when the sacrament [the Eucharist] itself is really received grace is increased and the life of the spirit perfected....In this sacrament, however, grace is increased and the life of the spirit perfected and made whole by union with God.[167]

> ...this sacrament [the Eucharist], which fulfills a man in himself by union with Christ.[168]

The Eucharist then brings about a perfect incorporation into Christ, the Head, and in so doing, the person's spiritual life is perfected.

Besides effecting this unity, the Eucharist also causes an outpouring of the virtue of charity. By giving an increase of charity, it unites a person more closely to the Mystical Body. Aquinas explains, "Through the power of the sacrament [the Eucharist] it produces directly that effect for which it was instituted. Now this was not for the satisfaction of sins but for spiritual nourishment through union with

---

164 Ibid., III 73.3, corp.; cf. III 73.2, corp.
165 *In IV Sent.*, d, 12, q. 1, a. 1, qla. 3, sol. 2; q. 2, a. 2, qla. 3, sol. 3.
166 *ST* I-II 3.2, ad 4.
167 Ibid., III 79.1, ad 1.
168 Ibid., III 82.3, ad 3.

Christ and his members, as food becomes one with the person fed. However,…this union is through charity."[169]

With this in mind, the following questions may be raised: How does the Eucharist bring about this perfect incorporation? How does it actually effect a perfect union of Christ the Head with His members? An answer to these questions starts with an inquiry into Aquinas' understanding about the nature of eucharistic perfection in general.[170]

4.3.1 The general nature of eucharistic perfection

Besides the Eucharist, Baptism, Confirmation, Holy Orders, and Extreme Unction perfect the Christian. In order to explain how each of these sacraments perfects and how the Eucharist is the "perfection of perfections," Aquinas distinguishes between various kinds of perfection. Perfection may be divided generally into perfection in the reality itself (perfection *in re*) and perfection outside of the reality (perfection *extra rem*). Within the division of perfection *in re* are two subgroups: first and second perfection. First perfection refers to the perfection of a reality in the reality itself by the actualization according to what the reality is (*secundum quid*—according to something; in a certain respect). The principle of this actualization is the substantial form (or that by which a thing is what it is), and the possession of this form by a reality means that the reality is perfect in *esse*. It is this first perfection (substantial), a perfection in spiritual being, which the sacrament of Baptism confers.[171]

Second perfection refers to the perfection of a reality in the reality itself when the reality has the operation of its form. Such a reality is said to be perfect *simpliciter* (i.e., in a simply, straightforward manner). This second perfection (operational) has two sacramental manifestations. It is the perfection which Confirmation confers since it makes a *private* individual fearless in the confession and practice of the faith. It is the perfection which Holy Orders confers since it makes an individual a *public* minister in the Church.

---

169   Ibid., III 79.5, corp.
170   Loughery, 272–73.
171   Ibid., 275.

Third perfection refers to the perfection of a reality outside of the reality itself when the reality is capable of attaining the final end or purpose for which it was created. Such a reality is said to be perfect *complens*. This third perfection (final) has two sacramental manifestations. Extreme Unction prepares for the participation of union with God in heaven. The Eucharist prepares for the participation of union with God on earth.[172]

The diagram below, adapted from James Kinn[173], summarizes this explanation as follows:

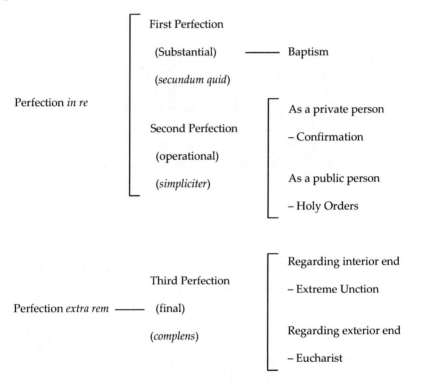

First Perfection

(Substantial) ——— Baptism

(*secundum quid*)

Perfection *in re*

Second Perfection

(operational)

(*simpliciter*)

As a private person

– Confirmation

As a public person

– Holy Orders

Third Perfection

Perfection *extra rem* ——— (final)

(*complens*)

Regarding interior end

– Extreme Unction

Regarding exterior end

– Eucharist

4.3.2 The specific nature of eucharistic perfection

Aquinas explains that God's love for His creation is eternal and unchanging. However, the effect of that love, which is grace, may be interrupted and, indeed, was by sin. Yet God did not let the sin of

---

172   *ST* I 6.3, corp.; *In Sent. IV*, d. 8, q. 1, a. 1.
173   Kinn, 116–17.

human beings thwart His divine plan. Thus, through the infusion of grace, sin is remitted and humanity is united to God.[174] Christ, Who became incarnate, is the embodiment of that love. God pours out the gift of divine love not from a realm of intangible reality but from the tangible nearness of His Word made flesh.[175] After His earthly life, this tangible self-gift of God Himself is perpetuated sacramentally in the Eucharist. God provides for humanity according to the conditions it requires by nature[176]; thus, God vests Himself in what appears to be bread and wine so as to make His presence known to creatures who know through corporeal and sensible reality.[177] Under the sign of eucharistic food, Christ puts His own Body and Blood in contact with His members to pour out upon them the fullness of His charity and grace so that they may achieve their perfection by being one with Him in heaven.

Both effects of the Eucharist (i.e., incorporation into Christ and an increase in charity) are conveyed fittingly by the nature of the Eucharist as a sacrament of food. Through reception of this eucharistic food, the one nourishing and the nourishment become one. It is fitting and proper that the purpose and effects of a sacrament are conveyed through the sacrament's matter. There is a natural affinity between the sacrament and its sensible, material signs. But unlike corporeal food, this particular sacrament goes further, and the eucharistic food changes the recipient into itself (i.e., into Christ Himself). He explains:

> And therefore every sacrament ought to be proposed in figure of its sensible realities, it is proper that the sacrament in which the Incarnate Word ought to be joined with us...in the figure of food, not so much as food being converted to us through some joining but rather by this joining we might be converted into itself according to what Augustine says about the Incarnate Word, "you do not change me into the food of your flesh but you are changed into me."[178]

---

174 *ST* I-II 113.2.

175 Ibid., I-II 108.1.

176 This is an variation of the philosophical dictum of "one receives according to one's own mode of reception" (*quidquid recipitur ad modum recipientis recipitur*). Cf. SCG IV ch. 56.

177 Ibid., III 61.1.

178 *In IV Sent.*, d. 8, a. 3, qla. 3, sol. 1. *Et ideo cum omne sacramentum, in figura alicujus rei sensibilis proponi debeat, convenienter sacramentum in quo ipsum Verbum incarnatum nobis conjungendum continetur, proponitur nobis in figura cibi, non quidem convertendi in nos per suam conjunctionem ad nos, sed potius sua conjunctione nos in ipsum convertens, secundum quod Augustinus ex persona Verbi incarnati dicit (lib. 7*

Now, bodily life needs material nourishment, not only to increase in quantity, but to maintain the nature of the body as well...in the same way it was necessary to have spiritual nourishment for the spiritual life that the reborn may both be conversed in virtues and grow in them.

Spiritual effects were fittingly given under the likeness of things visible...therefore, spiritual nourishment of this kind is given to us under the appearances of the things which men rather commonly use for bodily nourishment. Bread and wine are of this sort. Accordingly, this sacrament [the Eucharist] is given under the appearances of bread and wine.

But consider this: He who begets is joined to the begotten in one way, and nourishment is joined to the nourished in another way in bodily things. For the one who begets need not be conjoined to the begotten in substance, but in likeness and in power only. But nutriment must be conjoined to the one nourished in substance. Wherefore, that the spiritual effects may answer the bodily signs, the mystery of the incarnate Word is joined to us in one way in baptism which is a spiritual rebirth, and in another way in this sacrament of the Eucharist which is a spiritual nourishment. In baptism the Word incarnate is contained in His power only, but we hold that in the sacrament of the Eucharist He is contained in His substance.[179]

The signs of many of the other sacraments (e.g., the water of Baptism, the chrism of Confirmation) are appropriated by the sense of touch, but they do not signify incorporation. Eating food does express incorporation and, in this case, the recipient is joined to Christ and is "changed" into Him.

Elsewhere Aquinas distinguishes between ordinary and eucharistic food. In his commentary on chapter 6 of John's Gospel, he compares the two with regard to their life-giving qualities. He says:

He [Jesus] said, *I am the living bread*; consequently, I can give life. Material bread does not give life forever, because it does not have life in itself; but it gives life by being changed and converted into nourishment by the energy of a living organism. *That has come down from heaven*: it was explained before [3:13; ch. 3 lect. 2] how the Word came down. This refuted those heresies which taught that Christ was a mere man, because according to them, he would not have come down from heaven.

He has the power to give eternal life; thus he says, *If anyone eats of this bread*, i.e., spiritually, *he will live*, not only in the present through faith and justice, but *forever*.[180]

Confess., cap. 10): Non tu me mutabis in te, sicut cibum carnis tuae; sed tu mutaberis in me.

179   *SCG* IV ch. 61, [1–3].

180   *In Joan.*, ch. 6, lect. 6, 957–58.

Ordinary food gives life only in the sense that it provides nourishment necessary for a living organism. The Eucharist gives eternal life because it contains Christ Who has the very power to give life itself. Through Him all living things were created.

Besides increasing life under the sign of food, the Eucharist likewise increases the other virtues in a similar fashion to food. The Eucharist, however, does not increase a virtue in the same way that the other sacraments do, but in a unique way. The other sacraments find grace already present in the recipient. They then add to the grace already there and so increase the virtue—an increase akin to an increase by addition. The Eucharist increases virtue in its own proper manner by converting the recipient into Christ according to the manner of spiritual food.[181] Such an augmentation results from eating; a thing increases when it is in the living being through the assimilation of food.[182] Of all the virtues, charity is the one most closely associated with food in its unifying and transforming effects.[183] The Eucharist is the sacramental food that increases virtue by a transformation or conversion into Christ. For this reason, Aquinas attributes the increase of charity to the Eucharist more than to the other sacraments.[184]

The Eucharist transforms human beings into Christ through love.[185] Contact with the physical Body of Christ is now brought to a transcendent perfection in that His human flesh, an instrument of the Godhead, converts into the Body of Christ those who sacramentally feed upon Him in love.[186] Just as Christ entered visibly into the world to bestow on it the life of grace, now He enters sacramentally into His members of the Mystical Body to communicate to them His life-giving virtue under the species of bread and wine.[187] This point is an application of another point, stated before, regarding the causality of Christ's humanity: His flesh and the mysteries accompanying that flesh are instrumental causes in the process of giving life to the

---

181   *In IV Sent.*, d. 12, q. 2, a. 1, qla. 1, ad 1.
182   Kinn, 122; Loughery, 284.
183   Cf. the following references for Aquinas' discussion on charity's role in effecting union, conversion, or transformation: *In III Sent.*, d. 27, q. 1, a. 1, resp.; ad 2 and ad 5; *De Caritate*, q. unica, a. 1, ad 3; *Quodl. III*, q. 6, a. 3, resp.; *ST* I-II 28.1, corp.
184   *In IV Sent.*, d. 12, q. 2, a. 1, qla. 1, ad 1.
185   Ibid., d. 12, q. 2, a. 2, qla. 3, sol. 1.
186   Ibid., d. 11, q. 3, a. 3, ad 3.
187   Loughery, 284–85.

soul.[188] This life-producing flesh is the same flesh that is present sacramentally in the Eucharist.

Thus, for Aquinas this effect is to be considered principally from what is contained in the sacrament, namely, Jesus Christ Who is God's Word come into the world. Just as He bestowed grace and charity by becoming one with humanity during His life on earth, now He continues to do the same by becoming one with humanity sacramentally. As a result, secondary effects precipitate, namely: 1) the remission of sin; 2) the sustaining, increasing, rousing, restoring, and giving delight to the spiritual life just as material food does for the body; 3) the bringing about of unity out of multiplicity.[189] Since charity is an effect of the Eucharist, Aquinas holds that this sacrament is the principal cause of the Church's unity and often refers to it as "the sacrament of ecclesiastical unity" (or some variant thereof).[190] Reception of the Eucharist not only unites the individual person with Christ, but it unites the person as well with others. Aquinas elaborates:

> In regard to the present [the here and now], there is another thing to which it [the Eucharist] points. This is the unity of the Church, into which men are drawn together through this sacrament. Because of this it is called 'communio' or 'synaxis'. As Damascene says, *it is called 'communion' because by it we are joined to Christ and because we share his flesh and his godhead, and because we are joined and united to one another through that.*[191]

> Now the reality of this sacrament [the Eucharist] is twofold...one which is signified and contained, namely Christ himself, the other which is signified yet not contained, namely Christ's mystical body, which is the fellowship of the saints. Whoever, then, receives the sacrament by that very fact signifies that he is joined with Christ and incorporated in his members.[192]

It is through this sacrament that the divine will is achieved: God willed to bestow His salvific grace upon human beings not as separate individuals without a mutual bond but, rather, He willed to make them united in one Mystical Body through the reception of His sacramental Body.[193] By feeding on His Body, He unites us through

---

188   *ST* III 62.5, ad 1.
189   Ibid., III.79.1.
190   Ibid., III 67.2, corp.; 73.2, sed contra; 73.4, corp.; 80.5, ad 2; 82.2, ad 3; 83.4, ad 3; *In IV Sent.* d. 12, q. 1, a. 3, qla. 3, obj. 2; *In Joan.*, ch. 6, lect. 6; *I ad Cor.*, ch. 11, lect. 7.
191   *ST* III 73.4, corp.
192   Ibid., III 80.4, corp.
193   Cf. *I ad Cor.*, ch. 12, lect. 3; *Ad Rom.*, ch. 12, lect. 2.

His Spirit into one Mystic Person. This Mystic Person is then offered and united to God the Father.[194] It acknowledges the Father in truth and serves Him in holiness.[195] It is this holiness which Christ the Head purchased for His Body on Calvary and which He now bestows on His Church in the gift of Himself.[196]

In the end, the Eucharist effects a union with Christ, the Head, and a union between members of the Mystical Body through the causality of charity. The Eucharist is the sacrament of unity because charity transforms the communicant into Christ according to the manner of spiritual food (i.e., through conversion). It brings this unity about more than any other sacrament because it is the most excellent of them all.

4.4 Section summary

According to Aquinas, the Eucharist has primacy by reason of the *res et sacramentum* since it contains the Real Presence of Jesus Christ Himself. Real Presence is more fitting than a virtual presence, for by it a perfect union between the Head and members is established not only through participation but through essence as well. This presence belongs to the perfection of faith, hope, and charity. The Eucharist has primacy by reason of the *sacramentum tantum* since its signifies the sanctification and perfection of both the body and soul. Its matter also consists in the consecration of the bread and wine, whereas the other sacraments consist in using matter already consecrated. The form refers only to the transubstantiation of the matter, whereas in the other sacraments, the form refers to action or use of the matter. The Eucharist has primacy by reason of the *res tantum* since it effects a perfect union between Christ and the members of His Mystical Body through the causality of charity. Thus, the Eucharist is the perfection, the end, and the consummation of all the sacraments because: a) it mediately contains Christ substantially; b) immediately, it is the sacrament of perfect incorporation into Christ through grace and worship; c) it ultimately leads to a perfect union with Christ in eternal life.

---

194 *Ad Rom.*, ch. 12, lect. 2.
195 Loughery, 292–93.
196 *Ad Eph.*, ch 5, lect. 8; *In IV Sent.*, d. 8, q. 1, a. 1, qla. 3, sol. 1.

5 Transubstantiation

The primacy of the Eucharist is essentially metaphysically dependent upon the Event of the conversion of the bread and wine into the Body and Blood of Jesus Christ.[197] In the sacramental *ordo*, discussed above, this is the *res et sacramentum*. By the saying of the proper form over the proper matter (the *sacramentum tantum*), the bread and wine are changed into the Body and Blood of Jesus Christ, Who is really, truly, and substantially present (the *res et sacramentum*). This is the Event of transubstantiation and, since it grounds the primacy and centrality of the Eucharist, it is advantageous to investigate Aquinas' understanding of it. It is the means by which the faithful enter into mystical union with God (the *res tantum*).

5.1 Significant general points regarding the eucharistic conversion

It is through faith and not the senses that human beings know that the Body and Blood of Christ is truly present in the sacrament of the Eucharist. It is fitting that this sacrifice contains Christ Himself, "not merely as by a sign or figure, but in actual reality as well."[198] He recognizes a spiritual presence in the sacrament since an invisible reality is visibly signed; however, he rejects as heretical the position that it is only a symbolic presence. Yet, it is a presence not in the way a body is in a place (i.e., corresponding with the dimensions of a place), but rather in a way that is unique to this sacrament (i.e., *per modum substantiae* not *per modum accidens*, which would account for a local presence).[199]

This sacramental presence of Christ's true Body and Blood can not occur unless the substance of bread and wine is converted into it. This conversion is an instantaneous and not a gradual change. The reason is that between that last instant of the bread and the first instant of the body would be another instant in which neither is present. This intervening instant would be a void with nothing present. Consequently,

---

197 It must be remembered that metaphysical priority is independent of temporal priority. In this case, the consecration is metaphysically prior in relationship to the offertory even though the offertory is temporally prior.

198 *ST* III 75.1, corp.

199 Ibid., III 75.1, ad 3.

no conversion is possible. Thus, the last instant of the pronunciation of the words of consecration (i.e., when the meaning of the words is complete) coincides with the first instant of the presence of the body. The end of the substance of bread and the beginning of the substance of body are one and the same moment.[200]

The whole Christ is present in this sacrament, not merely His divinity or His body or His soul. This whole presence is accomplished in two ways. First, as the result of or by the force of the sacramental sign (*vi sacramenti*)—meaning that when the words, "This is my body" are pronounced, the body of Christ is truly present. The words of consecration are efficacious. Whatever else is present (i.e., His blood, soul, and divinity), is there not as a result of the sacramental sign (*vi sacramenti*) but by natural concomitance (the second way). When the words, "This is my blood" are pronounced, the blood of Christ is present as a result of the sacramental sign, and the body, soul, and divinity are present by natural concomitance.[201] The divinity and the humanity are never laid aside, for they are held in a hypostatic union. It is interesting to note that Aquinas does not apply this understanding of concomitance to the One Flesh of the second Adam and the second Eve in the eucharistic *res et sacramentum*.

In answering the question whether or not the whole Christ is present under each and every part of the species, Aquinas says, "the whole nature of any substance is under any part of the dimensions that contain it."[202] This means that the whole Christ is present not in a manner that is proper to dimensions (i.e., the whole only in the whole and a part only in a part) but in a manner that is proper to a substance (i.e., the whole in the whole and also in each part).

The entire dimensive quantity of Christ's body is present under the sacrament because it is inseparable from the substance of the body. The dimensions are not the result of the efficacy of the sacramental sign (*vi sacramenti*) but of concomitance. Consequently, the dimensions, as well as all the other accidents of Christ's body, are there according to the manner of substance (*per modum substantiae*) and not according to the manner of accidents (*per modum accidens*). For example, Christ's body is not in this sacrament locally, as in a

---

200   Ibid., III 75.7.; it is interesting to note that in this article on the accidents, there is no mention of their sign-function.
201   Ibid., III 76.1 and 2; *SCG* IV ch. 64.
202   *ST* III 76.3 corp.

place. His body is present in the way a substance is present, not in the way the accident of dimensive quantity is—that is, with its particular dimensions coinciding with the dimensions of a particular place.[203]

After the consecration, the accidents of bread and wine are miraculously sustained in being in the absence of a substance. These are without a substance in which to inhere, yet they do exist. The consecrated host can be fractured, measured, and corrupted. They need to be predicated of something, but this something can not be Jesus Christ, Who is indeed sacramentally present because His body is now glorious and immune from change. In observing that dimensive quantity is the more fundamental accident than the other less fundamental accidents of quality, Aquinas then predicates these qualitative accidents to quantitative dimension. This inherence in dimension accounts for their continued perceptibility, divisibility, and unity.[204]

5.2 The theological understanding of matter and form

The matter of the Eucharist is bread and wine as required by Scripture. Bread and wine are the most common human food for natural nourishment and are fitting to symbolize spiritual nourishment. They are generally available in all places, at least by being transported to them. The bread must be of wheat and not some other grain. It may be leavened, but it should not be. The wine must be grape wine.[205]

Regarding the proper form of the sacrament, Aquinas holds that it does not include, "take, eat" or any mention of the minister or of his action (e.g., as analogous to Baptism's "I baptize you...."). The primary reason for this is the distinction between the Eucharist and the other sacraments: the Eucharist is directed to a reality; the other sacraments are directed to an action. This distinction is expressed in two ways: first, the consecrated species in contrast to Baptism's, "I baptize you...," which is directed to the use of the water; second, unlike Baptism, the consecration is the action of Christ, not of a minister speaking in his own name. The priest speaks in the name—and with the

---

203 Ibid., III 76.4 and 5.
204 Ibid., III 77.1; *SCG* IV ch. 63 and 65.
205 *ST* III 74.1, 3–5; *SCG* IV ch. 69.

authority—of Jesus Christ. In the end, the form consists in, "This is my body....This is the chalice of my blood."[206]

In answering objections that challenge the truth of the words of consecration, Aquinas simply states that the words are indeed true because Jesus said, "I am the truth" (Jn 14:6). The words are not to be interpreted in the merely subjective sense of, "what is signified by this is my body." The words are efficacious; what is signified is actually brought about. This efficacy is derived from the power of Jesus Christ Himself.[207]

5.3 The philosophical understanding of form and matter and the eucharistic conversion

Aquinas is true to his Aristotelian system in the sense that he understands the eucharistic conversion and the form and matter in terms of act and potency. This conversion is a change and, according to Aristotelianism, change occurs when a potency (that which has the capacity for a perfection) is actualized (act; that which is perfected). Both substantial and accidental change are ontologically possible only when a medium is recognized between potency and act. This medium is in potency or movement. It is a passage from potency to act, a movement from relative non-being to being.

Before movement begins, the term to be acquired or perfected is only in a state of potency with regard to the subject of movement. Once movement has reached its point of destination and the perfection has been actualized, movement may be referred to as an accomplished fact.[208] However, in the interim, Aquinas calls this movement an imperfect act (*actus imperfectus*) in the sense that it is through movement that the subject is realizing a perfection not yet fully actualized or possessed. This movement terminates in the perfect and complete act to which the potency was ordered.[209]

---

206 *ST* III 78.1.

207 Ibid., III 78.5.

208 Salvatore Bonano, *The Concept of Substance and the Development of Eucharistic Theology to the Thirteenth Century*, an abstract of a dissertation, The Catholic University of America Studies in Sacred Theology (Second Series), no. 121 (Washington, D.C.: Catholic University of America Press, 1960), 144.

209 *Super Metaph.*, 11, lect. 9, comm. 2305.

Change, then for Aquinas, consists of three elements: a) a *terminus a quo*—the end from which, the point of departure; b) a *terminus ad quem*—the end to which, the point of destination; and c) a *commune tertium*—the common third, inner connection, the passage of one to the other. To have a real change, to have the subject pass from one to the other, the opposition between the two terms must be such that the attainment of the one excludes the continuance of the other. This opposition may be considered as either contradiction or contrariety. Hence, there are two kinds of change. If the terms are contradictory, as in the case of being and relative non-being, the one is necessarily the formal negation of the other. There can not exist between the two terms an inner connection (a *commune tertium*) which comprises part of the one and part of the other. This change is not conversion. Conversion occurs when the terms are in contrariety. Both terms are positive: conversion neither starts from nothing nor ends at nothing. Neither annihilation or creation can be strictly called conversion for this reason. Conversion means the transition of the *terminus a quo* into the *terminus ad quem* under some aspect of being (the *commune tertium*).[210]

Aquinas identifies two types of conversion. In an accidental conversion, the same subject persists while one accident succeeds another. In a substantial conversion either one substantial form succeeds another in the same prime matter[211] or both the substantial form and prime matter of one subject succeed the substantial form and prime matter of a different subject.[212] This latter case is a total substantial conversion since both the substantial form and prime matter are converted. The former case is a partial conversion since the prime matter remains constant.

---

210 Bonano, 146.
211 Bonano points out that for Aquinas, "form is not *id quod*, or the thing converted, but the *id quo* or that according to which or due to whose removal, the whole is converted" (148–49). He cites *ST* III 75.3, ad 2 to substantiate this position.
212 *SCG* IV ch. 63, [6–7]. If the substantial form itself is not considered but the composite of substantial form and prime matter is, then there is a third option for substantial conversion. It is one in which the substantial form remains constant and the prime matter is changed. This change could be called "transmateriation." Aquinas rejects this but at least he raises this possibility in *ST* III 75.6 when he states that some theologians hold that after the consecration substantial form and the accidents remain, but the matter is changed into the Body of Christ.

Transubstantiation is a total substantial conversion. It is unique in that ordinarily, when a substantial conversion occurs naturally, the accompanying accidents also change accordingly. Transubstantiation is then a supernatural conversion unlike all other natural conversions. The entire substance of the *terminus a quo* (i.e., bread and wine) is converted into the entire substance of the *terminus ad quem* (i.e., the body, blood, soul, and divinity of Jesus Christ) while the accidents of bread and wine remain (the *commune tertium*).[213] There is no annihilation involved. Annihilation of the bread and wine is rejected on grounds that it does not account for the presence of Christ's body. The reduction of the substance to prime matter is dismissed as metaphysically impossible: pure potency does not exist *per se* without form. The substance is not removed by local motion either because if it were, the sense of sight would perceive it. The substance is not seen departing. The only other feasible option is the supernatural substantial conversion of one substance into another substance: transubstantiation.[214]

The accidents of bread and wine that remain after the consecration do not have the substance of bread and wine as their subject of inherence for that subject no longer exists. Neither do they inhere in the subject of Christ's body because the human body does not have these accidental qualities. In this case, accidents are existing without a subject of inherence not by virtue of their own nature but by the power of God. The other accidents which remain in this sacrament exist in the dimensive qualities of bread and wine as if in their subject.[215]

Transubstantiation is realized when the proper form (i.e., the words of consecration) are said over the proper matter (i.e., bread and wine). The words are efficacious and bring about the Real Presence *ex opere operato*. Consequently, Aquinas views the relationship between the form and the matter also in terms of act and potency. The words come from the divine power of Christ and are uttered in His name. Through the instrumentality of a duly ordained priest, the pronounced words actualize the transubstantiation of the bread and wine into the Body and Blood of Jesus Christ. The bread and wine stand in potency to these words which accomplish what they say.[216] The bread

---

213 *ST* III 75.4–6.
214 Ibid., III 75.3 and 4; *SCG* IV ch. 63.
215 *ST* III 77.1 and 2.
216 Ibid., III 78.4–5.

and wine do not possess this potency in and of themselves. They receive it by being separated from all other food stuffs with the Church's intention that they be used for the sacrament. This designation of potency occurs at the offertory. The potency is then actualized at the consecration.

5.4 Section summary

Aquinas understands the Eucharist, Real Presence, and transubstantiation in terms of his Aristotelian act-potency system. The particular circumstances that revolve around this eucharistic presence are primarily rooted in the fact that Christ is present *per modum substantiae* and not *per modum accidens*. Where this becomes problematic, however, is over the issue of whether the accidents of bread and wine that remain after the consecration inhere in a substance or not.

6 Chapter Summary

We have seen that the subject of a science for Aquinas is that extramental reality which is studied under a particular formality as the term or end of a scientific inquiry. The subject of sacred doctrine is identified to be God, known supernaturally through revelation as He subsists in Himself and not merely as a principle of being. This distinction between subsistence and the principality of being is a comparison made between sacred doctrine and the philosophical sciences (e.g., [natural] theology, metaphysics, first philosophy). The distinction is made even more obvious in that, for sacred doctrine, God is the subject of the science and not the cause or principle of the subject of a science such as metaphysics.

While God then is the subject of sacred doctrine (*genus subjectum*), all that is related, attributed to Him (*sub ratione Dei*), is included as *subjectum attributionis*. This science attends not only to *what* is treated as subject but also to that formality *under which* the subject is treated (i.e., the object). This formality is that of being revealed. Divine revelation, then, provides the science of sacred doctrine with its first principles.

As subject, God is knowable to creatures, and by definition, then, there is a relationship between known and knower. For Aquinas, there is a real relationship between creatures and God because the foundation of the relationship between the subject and the term is real and distinct. The foundation is the creature's dependence on God's creative power expressed in the person of Jesus Christ. In contrast, the relationship between God and creatures is one of reason because the foundation, God's creative power (the act of assuming a human nature), is identical with the subject, God. Yet, God is knowable under the formality of being revealed. Jesus Christ, the God-Man, serves as the revelation of God; to use Aquinas' words, "Christ as man is our way to going to God."[217]

Jesus Christ is known to be the revelation of God by virtue of the various roles He assumes. In exercising these roles, He is realized to be the culmination and the most excellent of all those who share in these roles. Due to this primacy, He is implicitly identified as the primary referent of the first question of the *Summa theologiae* regarding the nature of *sacra doctrina* and its subject. This Christ, Who is the primary referent, is also substantially present in the Eucharist through the miracle of transubstantiation. It is through the Eucharist, then, that human beings have access to Christ, and access to Christ enables one to enter into His revelation of the Father, of God. This revelation is intimately tied to—and consequently furthered by—the ultimate effect (*res tantum*) of the Eucharist, namely, mystical union with God. By reception of communion, one fosters the individual's union with God and, in so doing, deepens one's knowledge and appreciation of the revelation. The Eucharist, because it contains Jesus Christ, the Revealer (*res et sacramentum*), is the means by which God reveals Himself to His creation and enters into relationship with it. It is the means by which one experiences God and all that is related to God, the subject of *sacra doctrina*. To summarize it in one sentence, "Jesus Christ is that to which sacred doctrine returns and attends as to its first principle."[218]

---

217 Ibid., I-II prol.
218 Rogers, 66.

SYNTHESIS

1 Purpose and Structure of the Chapter

The previous two parts have investigated the identification and nature of a theological *prius* or prime analogate in the theologies of Donald Keefe and Thomas Aquinas. The purpose of this chapter is to put Keefe and Aquinas into "conversation." This will be done by comparing and contrasting the two theologians on the essential points regarding a theological *prius*. In light of the advancements in contemporary systematic theology and theological methodology, Keefe's work will provide the questions that are asked of Aquinas' theology. As a result, a "testing dialogue"[1] will ensue in order to establish the possibility of a limited convergence. "Convergence" in this context is to be understood as "a movement towards" and not "an arrival at." It does not mean a complete consensus or agreement but rather that previously perceived oppositions or tensions are relocated as being no longer at the center.[2] Recent work by other contemporary theologians will also be referred to and utilized in order to substantiate the claim that such a relocation is feasible and faithful to the texts of Aquinas. As a result, this work will also develop Aquinas' theology in its own right.

It is important to realize, as part one indicates, that Keefe has provided an "idealized" interpretation of Aquinas, meaning that he has read Aquinas with the Aristotelian metamethodological principles so much to the fore that he himself concludes that Aquinas' use of the Aristotelian act-potency system in particular cases will not permit him to hold a particular theological position. In many of these situations, Keefe holds that the system is moving in one direction set by the principles and yet Aquinas will deviate from this direction in a

---

1   This phrase was suggested by D. Thomas Hughson, S.J.
2   Buckley, 324, following Rogers' usage in *Thomas Aquinas and Karl Barth*, passim.

desire to remain loyal to the faith. Consequently, an inconsistency develops. Such an idealized reading (and the often oppositional conclusions) on the part of Keefe then has necessitated a more "textual" reading of Aquinas' work. This means that the relevant passages of his writings have been read more on their own terms (i.e., literally) to test whether or not there is some evidence for a convergence on the issues which Keefe raises. It then can be asked, did Aquinas hold such an oppositional position in his actual writing, or has Keefe concluded to this position by following the logic of Aquinas' brand of Aristotelianism to its reasonable end? In light of the systematic and methodological questions Keefe raises, are there indeed points of convergence between the two theologians that can be discovered by reading Aquinas with Keefe's questions and issues in mind? Is there evidence in Aquinas' writing that would support Keefe's position but which was overlooked by an idealized rather than a textual reading of Aquinas?

This chapter will follow the general description of procedure already stated above in section three of the introductory chapter. Since the function of philosophy is to articulate the faith whose entire content has been structured by a *prius* (a prime analogate), the issue of philosophy's methodological role is addressed first, followed by the second issue, the identification of a theological *prius*. It is here that the possibility of a Christocentric prime analogate in Aquinas is discussed. A Christocentric prime analogate is not yet a covenantal prime analogate. In order to be covenantal, Keefe points out that Jesus Christ must not be understood "as the contingent static and impersonal relation between the Son's divinity and humanity (the hypostatic union which is the central issue of the classic Thomist Christology), or in terms of the "Christomonism" which absorbs the Church into the personal unity of Christ."[3] Consequently, the issues of how Aquinas avoids a Christomonism and converges upon a covenantal notion that respects the personhood and proper roles of the Body and the Head are discussed before the caution regarding the hypostatic union is addressed. One obstacle in this movement toward a covenantal prime analogate for Aquinas is his position that God is not in a real relationship with His creation. This problem has been addressed by several contemporary theologians, two of whom suggest possible alternatives. The climax is achieved at the end of the

---

3 Keefe, *Covenantal Theology*, 433.

chapter when Keefe's explicit understanding of a eucharistic prime analogate is compared with Aquinas' less explicit movement in that same direction. In the end, Aquinas' use of the act-potency philosophical system will inhibit him from affirming all that needs to be affirmed by a eucharistic prime analogate. Keefe advocates a deeper transformation of the system, not its abandonment.

2 The Issues

2.1 One or two systems

Within revelation, Keefe has identified the New Covenant, or its sacramental manifestation of the Eucharist, as the *prius* or prime analogate of theology. Since Catholic theology is fundamentally a metaphysics, the metaphysics provides then a methodological structure to articulate coherently the revelation which is structured analogically by the prime analogate. Keefe holds that there are two basic and equally valid metaphysical systems or methods which, when in correlation, can serve to articulate the prime analogate. These systems are the discursive-analytical interpretation based in Aristotelianism and the intuitive-dialectical interpretation based in Platonism. Each system is the logical alternative to the other and both alternatives exhaust the number of other possibilities since methodological contradictories can not be reconciled. One can inquire into the revelation either by a phenomenology of subjective consciousness or by an objective analysis of its intrinsic coherence. There are no other options for the logic is binary. The two systems disagree on the relation between form and matter; consequently, the contradictories can not be reconciled. When either one of these philosophical systems is correlated to the Christian revelation, there is a movement from philosophy to theology.[4]

For Keefe, this correlation is free and, as such, the method is freely subordinate to the revelation, the prime analogate, as its prior truth and reality. If this were not the case, the prime analogate would be subordinate to a methodological *a priori*. This can not be since Chris-

---

4 Keefe, *Thomism and Tillich*, 2–6.

tian theology is *ex nihilo sui et subjecti*. Consequently, Keefe holds that each of these systems must undergo a theological conversion so that they themselves are transformed by the prime analogate. Without such a conversion, revelation will be dictated to and expressed by some sort of natural unfree reason derived from the intrinsic necessity of the system. For Keefe, this position is intolerable. Rather, theological systems are adequate only insofar as they are understood to be hypothetical rational constructs that attempt to frame the *quaerens intellectum* which is inseparable from the affirmations of the faith. Thus, the system's rationality is entirely subordinate to the revelation.[5]

In the case of this work's focus, Keefe holds that the fundamental principle operative in Aquinas' work is the Aristotelian act-potency relationship (with its correlates, substantial form-prime matter and accidents-substance) rather than the Platonic universal hylomorphism. Keefe argues that Aquinas began a transformation of the Aristotelian method by introducing another act-potency relationship, that of *esse*-essence. Such a transformation was needed, for according to the Christian revelation, reality is created and free rather than eternal and necessary. However, according to Keefe, Aquinas started the transformation but he did not fully grasp its significance and ramifications or completely work it out. If he had, he presumably would have recognized that the transformation of Aristotelianism need be Christocentric methodologically inasmuch as it proceeds on the basis of an intrinsic rather than an extrinsic analysis of the real world. The union of God and humanity can not be reduced to a notion of human participation in divinity which invokes an extrinsic cosmological source (i.e., God as Being Itself; *Deus Unus*), but rather, Christ must be recognized as the immanent source of union and significance in creation. The participation of humanity in divinity must be regarded as a mediated participation in Christ, the God-Man, Who is in covenantal relation with His creation.[6]

Thus, to summarize, Keefe holds that there are two basic and equally valid metaphysical systems which can articulate and interpret the revelation in general or the prime analogate in particular: the discursive-analytical interpretation (Aristotelianism) and the intuitive-dialectical interpretation (Platonism). The correlation between the

---

5   Ibid., 38–40; Keefe, *Covenantal Theology*, 13–15.
6   Keefe, *Covenantal Theology*, 14; Keefe, *Thomism and Tillich*, 5–6, 12–13, 40.

methodological system and that of revelation is one of freedom whereby the system is subordinate to the revelation.

Both Keefe and Aquinas hold that sacred doctrine (theology) is a single unified science predicated on a single prime analogate. However, the identification of this prime analogate differs, as earlier stated, between the two theologians. Once this is identified, Keefe then proceeds by holding that the articulation of the prime analogate can be by means of the two metaphysical systems. Aquinas, on the other hand, does not deny the validity of the Augustinian tradition (the intuitive-dialectical interpretation based in Platonism); however he does not use it as his system. Aquinas himself intended to react to much of the Augustinian-Franciscan tradition and so he used the discursive-analytical interpretation. As a result, his *corpus* will be limited to an Aristotelian articulation and it will not contain the intricacies and emphases of which a Platonic articulation is capable. It will not highlight that basic inquiry of the human mind regarding one's own personal subjectivity, the experience of suffering, the experience of being at once a sinner and just. This is the standard two-loves doctrine which is a phenomenology of consciousness. It will, rather, seek to understand analytically the doctrinal worship of the Church by striving to understand it in terms of its intrinsic coherence without putting its truth into question. The Church's doctrine is a straightforward statement of objective truth; truth is not a paradox, as it is for the Augustinian tradition.

2.2 The identification of a *prius*

For Keefe, theology is concerned throughout with a free subject matter: its subject is revelation, a free gift of a truth available only by the free reception of that gift. As free and historical, revelation is the event of Jesus Christ, anticipated in the Old Testament; given in His conception, life, and death; fulfilled in His Resurrection and Ascension. From Keefe's vantage point, this fact is often mitigated by Aquinas' concern that revelation also be a practical necessity: not a strict necessity, but one which permits feeble human minds to know things which, in principle, are rationally available but, in fact, are known by few people at that level. This provision presupposes that in fact the strictly necessary revelation (e.g., of the Trinity, of the Incarnation, of those truths that are mysteries) is somehow coincident with a revelation of truths which is quite dissociated in being from those mysteries (e.g., the knowledge that is called "natural theology" or the knowledge of the "natural law"). Thus, according to Keefe, Aquinas supposes that in fact there is an ungraced knowledge bearing upon an ungraced creation, which is yet somehow so indispensable to salvation that it is required to be revealed to those people who are unlikely to come to it on their own. For Aquinas, this natural knowledge of God is to revealed knowledge (i.e., faith) as nature is to grace. This position, according to Keefe, presents little sense in the end.

One reason for this assessment is that, for Keefe, revelation is not information. The revelation rather is free and historical: it is the *Event* of Jesus Christ. No part of this revelation is nature. It is all *gratia capitis* and its free acceptance in faith is equally of grace. There is no reason to suppose—and every reason to deny—that there is a prerequisite of faith to be provided by natural reason as the necessary precondition of free assent to the revelation. The faith is *ex nihilo*; it has no pre-condition.

A second reason for this assessment is that a necessary created order is a contradiction in terms: a free creation is implicit in the freedom of the Creator. A free act by a free agent excludes necessity.

It is evident to Keefe, then, that Thomistic metaphysics, which he understands to be the conversion of Aristotle's act-potency analysis of being and its transcedentals to the historical truth of the faith, requires a free, historical, and revealed prime analogate. The only possible analogate is the sacramental, eucharistic representation of the New Covenant, the One Flesh of Christ and His Church. The revelation in its fullness is the gift of the prime reality, that is the prime analogate, the prime substance, for the analogy of being concerns the analogous predication of substance.

In chapter three, it has been demonstrated that Aquinas does hold that God is the subject of sacred doctrine. God is, however, related to the subject of metaphysics, which is *ens commune*, only insofar as He is an immobile, immaterial, and separable being Who is the highest cause and principle of being. The subject of metaphysics deals with the being of separated substances, and God is such a substance. But God is of interest to metaphysics only to the degree that He is a being and, thus, can be studied under the formality of being.

To repeat, for Aquinas, God is the highest cause of being and as a separated substance, He is complete nature as well as a principle of being. Due to this existence, He can not be known directly by the human intellect, not because He lacks intelligibility, but because He is so full of intelligibility that the human intellect is incapable of comprehending Him. He is known deductively and naturally then only through the effects of which He is the principle and the cause. God may be known, however, if the human intellect is enlightened by another light which enables the mind to know such principles. If this is the case, as it is with divine revelation and faith, then another science is possible. This science is sacred doctrine, and God, as He subsists in Himself and not merely as a principle of being, is its subject.

Aquinas, however, recognizes that other possible subjects have been proposed by theologians who have preceded him historically in the tradition. It has been shown that he is not closed to their likelihood, but he does point out that by and large these theologians were attending to *what* is treated in this sacred science and not *under which* aspect it is treated (i.e., God and all that is related to God [*sub ratione Dei*]). God is known under the formality of being revealed. Sacred doctrine possesses a revealable rather than an intelligible formality. This means that first principles (i.e., the *revelabilia*) provide access to God as the subject of sacred doctrine rather than access to the mind of God or God known in the beatific vision.

In the above discussion on the tenth article of question one from the *Summa theologiae*, which pertains to the role of the four senses of Scripture in sacred doctrine, it was suggested that there is a strong indication that Jesus Christ is the centering point of these four senses. If this is the case, then chief among the first principles (the *revelabilia*) is the form of God made flesh in the person of Jesus Christ. Thus, this author holds that divine revelation for Aquinas should be understood more broadly than merely information, as Keefe suggests. It should include the person of Jesus Christ. Sacred doctrine, as a science, attends to first principles, and it takes them from divine revelation. Aquinas does not immediately locate revelation *in* sacred Scripture but he refers to a revelation *upon which* sacred Scripture is founded.[7] The fullness of revelation, upon which sacred Scripture is founded, is Jesus Christ. Thus, this author holds that there is evidence that Aquinas does move in this direction. While Aquinas does in fact identify God as the subject of sacred doctrine (the *Deus Unus* as Keefe points

---

7 *ST* I 1.2, ad 2; Rogers, 19.

out), there is a strong indication that Aquinas studies God under a Christocentric formality.[8] Christ is the primary referent of the first question of the *Summa theologiae*. Christ is the revelation that grounds sacred doctrine and the explication that constitutes it, that provides its content. He grounds sacred doctrine by being the Word which is the form in the mind of God and, as such, is related to creation. In knowing Himself in the Son, the Father also knows creatures. The mission of the Word is to "render human beings participants in the divine wisdom and knowers of the truth" and to bring them teaching.[9] He does so by grounding, for example, the four senses of Scripture. Christ constitutes sacred doctrine through the various roles He assumes in order to be the way (the *via*) by which we are led to know and serve God. In assuming these roles (prophet, Word, teacher, mediator, priest), He is recognized with special primacy because He is the most excellent and the culmination of all those who share in these roles. To use the words of Aquinas, "Christ as man is our way [*via*] to God."[10] The fundamental aspect of this journey, this "way," is covenantal union with God which is realized sacramentally in the Eucharist. It is here that the members of Christ's Body are One Flesh with their Head.

Thus, it appears that the need for a Christocentric prime analogate, as emphasized by Keefe, is at least not foreign to the thought of Aquinas. Part II has outlined the indications and development in Aquinas' thought with regard to this matter. Other theologians have proposed similar theses that tend to support a Christocentric prime analogate, and these theses will now be considered.

---

8 This position is close to that of Aquinas' Master, Albert the Great, as noted above.

9 *In Joan.* ch. 14, lect. 6, #1958.

10 *ST* I-II, prologue.

2.2.1 Scholars who likewise recognize a Christocentric prime analogate in Aquinas[11]

In his book, *Thomas Aquinas and Karl Barth*, Eugene Rogers, Jr. presents a three-part argument to contend that the commonly held position that Aquinas and Barth are irreconcilably opposed to each other on the issue that a natural knowledge of God is wrong. Rogers challenges the standard view of Aquinas which holds that natural knowledge provides the foundation for a supernatural knowledge of God, that nature and grace are autonomous and extrinsic to each other. He also challenges the standard view of Barth which holds that a natural knowledge of God is impossible; rather, God reveals Himself solely through Jesus Christ Who is the one and only means of communication with humanity. Rogers argues that a more accurate reading of Aquinas is one in which:

> ...the natural cognition of God functions properly...only in the presence of *grace*. Natural cognition of God *without grace* is an anomaly, a residual, defective "cognition," so called only by courtesy that proves irrelevant to salvation except negatively, in increasing human fault, in showing our cognition of God to be as has-been. Natural cognition of God without grace is a self-consuming artifact, *un*natural, *de*natured, a paradox.[12]

In substantiating this argument, Rogers makes two points that are of interest to this work. First, he holds that Aquinas parses the *scientia* of sacred doctrine (in *ST* I 1, 2, 9–10) so that: 1) the more Aristotelian it is, the more scriptural it is; and 2) the more Aristotelian it is, the more Christoform it is.[13] If this is indeed the case, Rogers addresses the possible objection as to why this Christoformity does not appear again in the *Summa theologiae* at any great length until the third part. Rogers writes:

> Why would Thomas leave a crucial christological presupposition to be recalled for long stretches without repetition? Because he thinks more like a mathematician and less like an after-dinner speaker: the christological presupposition can very well go without saying when Thomas programmatically announces it, like a negative sign before a parenthesis, and therefore

---

11 In addition to the scholars discussed below, André Hayen ("Le Thomisme et l'historie," *Revue Thomiste* 62 [Janvier-Mars 1962], 51–82) and, more recently, John I. Jenkins (*Knowledge and Faith in Thomas Aquinas* [Cambridge: Cambridge University Press, 1997]) could be included.

12 Rogers, 183.

13 Ibid., 17.

constantly implies it. By programmatic remarks I have in mind two that en-
close all that lies between them under the sign of Christ. The opening parenthesis is the remark that "Christ, as a human being, is the way that has been
stretched out for us into God" (*via nobis tendendi in Deum*, I.2 proem.). That is
so, objectively, whether readers recognize it or not. Thomas does not cease
to lead the reader on that way, just because he does not often look down at
his feet. The closing parenthesis refers to that same *via*, "the way of truth for
us, [which Jesus Christ] has demonstrated to us in himself" (*viam veritatis
nobis in seipso demonstravit*, III prol.). The great parenthesis opens immediately after Thomas considers the scientific character of theology in Question
1, and closes only at the beginning of christology proper. It encloses everything in the *Summa*. It encloses everything after Question 1 that is not itself
explicit christology. Everything in the *Summa* is either christology, or
marked by a christological sign. Everything that is not christology follows a
road that Christ has stretched out, and everything that is not christology
leads to the christology that stands at the road's end. For Jesus Christ is also
"the consummation of the whole theological enterprise" (III prol.).[14]

With this objection answered, Rogers returns to the immediate
point at hand. For Aquinas, a science is more Aristotelian the more it
proceeds from first principles. First principles take propositional and
real forms. For sacred doctrine, those first principles are respectively
Scripture and Jesus Christ.[15] Thus, sacred doctrine and natural theology are radically Christocentric for Aquinas. Neither can be separated
from the primacy and centrality of God's revealed Word.

Rogers relies on the work of Michel Corbin, who, in his book *Le
Chemin de la théologie chez Thomas d'Aquin*, concentrates on four basic
texts where Aquinas develops his understanding of the scientific nature of sacred doctrine. Corbin's treatment of Aquinas' understanding
is not simply an historical or a theological but a speculative reading.
Aquinas' texts can not be treated in an immediately historical fashion,
for that focuses on what Corbin calls the "conditioned presence" of
the text, and it magnifies the distance between the reader and the author. Nor is it a purely theological reading, for that focuses only on
what he calls the "unconditional aim" of the works, that is, to answer
propositions put to the faith. Corbin rather proposes a speculative
reading which is bound by the realization that no human exegesis can
be purely historical or theological. History and theology are instead
axes approached asymptotically in the uninterrupted act of reading,

---

14 Ibid., 17–18.
15 Ibid., 18.

as the partial unity of the two, in the hope of constructing a reading that is lucid about its own fundamental presuppositions.[16]

According to Corbin, the writings of Aquinas contain various systems of sacred doctrine. These systems can be compared by the appearances of new elements that appear within them.[17] In the commentary on the *Sentences*, there is a structured parallelism between theology and philosophy. Theology is the traditional notion of *intellectus fidei* (the understanding of the faith). The commentary on Boethius' *De trinitate* is characterized by the preambles of faith. Reason helps to establish the preambles of the faith and furnish the similitudes used to illustrate the mysteries of the faith.[18] However, Corbin thinks that this understanding does not mesh well with the *intellectus fidei*. In the *Summa contra gentiles*, Aquinas' understanding of sacred doctrine's structure may be characterized as a doubling within the *intellectus fidei*. That is, there is a doubling between necessary reasons and all others; between *rationes demonstrativae* and *rationes persuasoriae*; between reasons and similitudes.[19] However, since the truth of the faith images the one simple God, any doubling within it can not stand.[20] Thus, by the end of the work, Aquinas moves away from an understanding of faith as natural and supernatural towards a unified integration that is carried over and developed in the *Summa theologiae*. Faith and reason, theology and philosophy are not related extrinsically but intrinsically; as Rogers puts it, "Thomas does not use *scientia* primarily to relate biblical and extra-biblical knowledge....Rather, in Question 1 Thomas is working *within* sacred doctrine to specify a relation internal to it, a relation within sacred doctrine between the revelation that founds it and the explication that constitutes it."[21] In the *Summa theologiae*, this integration is carried out in the person of Jesus Christ. The necessary philosophical reasons are integrated under the reasons of faith in the person of Jesus Christ.

---

16 Michel Corbin, 50, 53 as in Mark D. Jordan, "The Modes of Thomistic Discourse: Questions for Corbin's *Le Chemin de la théologie chez Thomas d'Aquin*," *The Thomist* 45 (January 1981), 82–83.

17 Michel Corbin, *Le Chemin de la théologie chez Thomas D'Aquin*, Bibliothèque des Archives de Philosophie (Paris: Beauchesne, 1974), 65.

18 Joseph De Finance, review of *Le Chemin de la théologie chez Thomas D'Aquin,* by Michel Corbin, *Gregorianum* 57, fasc. 1 (1976): 164.

19 Corbin, 630–31 as in Jordan, 84–85.

20 Jordan, 85.

21 Rogers, 20.

Theology is not the superimposition of a philosophy on the faith. Rather, it is the interpretation of the finite course (i.e., a philosophical expression) of the revealed (thus, requiring faith) Word of God expressed in Jesus Christ. Thus, the structure of the *Summa theologiae* does not, according to Corbin, follow the double mode of *exitus-reditus* but the integrated structure of God, man, God-Man.[22] It has a Christological structure which would be a move in the right direction according to Keefe.

Rogers also agrees with Corbin's thesis that in the *Summa theologiae* Aquinas came to replace an emphasis on *scientia's* reflexive (discursive or logical) aspect with an emphasis on its principled (real, virtual, or elaborated) aspect.[23] Corbin argues that Aquinas in his earlier writing held that *sacra doctrina* depended on God for its first principles and, thus, is a subalternated science. The reason for this is that in the past, Aquinas had thought that a discipline was scientific in that it proceeded from its reflexive aspect, from its deployment of categories, syllogisms, and judgments. However, Aquinas came to realize that to take a science's first principles from another that one can not, in principle, ever seize for oneself, precisely breaks the discursive aspect upon which the definition of *scientia* was based. That the first principles of *sacra doctrina* are true is a judgment that human beings can not make, so in the end subalternation is not subalternation at all but rather it is rupture. With that the scientific character that needed to be established is not established at all but ruined.[24]

Corbin continues then that Aquinas moved out of this bind by holding to the Aristotelian position that real first principles can relate to each other without their relation depending on human knowledge of it. In the *Summa theologiae* the scientific character of a discipline now proceeds from first principles not on account of the discursive linkages they have with a higher science but on account of the principal light they shed even if that light lies in the beyond. A science is distinct not due to the fact that it has a logic (which is common to all sciences) but that it has a specific revelation, specific first principles. According to Rogers, the *Summa*, then, is not to be read in a discursive, logical mode. "Discursive" has a technical meaning for Aquinas. It refers to the process by which the finite mind proceeds from one

22 De Fínance, 164.
23 Corbin, 717; as quoted in Rogers, 26.
24 This summary is based on Roger's summary of Corbin, 26.

conclusion to another, one at a time, in order, rather than all at once. Logic studies this process which assures that a proper sequencing results in one fitting conclusion. Unlike a real form, logic's reflexive work is not itself a new source of light; logic studies the process in and of itself, the sequence of finite thinking. Logic secures the necessary, not the conditions of truth. The revealed first principles, not logic, give rise to a properly scientific (i.e., its particular form-governed) character. Thus, when Aquinas states that a science proceeds from first principles, he is not referring to its discursivity or logic. He is stating that science is deeply connected with a concrete object that gives it rise. As Corbin writes, "Briefly, in strict Aristotelianism sacred doctrine is not founded as a science by the fact of drawing its conclusions from first principles, but by the first principles' very *existence*."[25] This concrete object is the revelation of God, Jesus Christ.

If Corbin and Rogers are correct, the prime analogate for Aquinas is Jesus Christ, the revelation of God.[26] Their position then is in agreement with Keefe's, at least on the identification of Christ's role which is revelation as event and not as mere information. They do not indicate whether or not they fill His role out in the covenantal sense as Keefe would like. In other words, they do not indicate or elaborate on how the Church is part of the Mystical Body of Christ.[27]

2.2.2 A covenantal prime analogate in Aquinas?

Keefe has argued for a prime analogate that is Christocentric and covenantal.[28] The immediate discussion above indicates that, while

---

25 Corbin, 718 as in Rogers, 25.

26 It should be noted that Rogers also cites a passage from Victor Preller's book, *Divine Science and the Science of God: A Reformulation of Thomas Aquinas* (Princeton: Princeton University Press, 1967), to support further his position. The wider passage reads, "*Sacra doctrine* [for Aquinas] is the action of God who makes himself known. The prime locus of God's act of self-communication is God himself—the eternal and immanent expression of his personal intentional state, terminating in the eternal Word (the Image of God, or the second 'Person' of the Trinity)....The central historical locus of the temporal mission of the Word of God is the sacred humanity of Christ. Therefore, the prime locus of 'speech about God' is *sacra scriptura*, the primary subject of which is Christ" (232).

27 Rogers, 25–27.

28 Keefe, *Covenantal Theology*, 17.

Keefe understands Aquinas' prime analogate to be the *Deus Unus*, there is some textual evidence to conclude that at least the notion of a Christocentric prime analogate is not foreign to Aquinas' thought. However, a Christocentric prime analogate for Keefe must be more than that; it must be covenantal as well.[29] Keefe explains:

> For the object of the creative mission of the Son is not simply the Christ, whether understood as the contingent static and impersonal relation between the Son's divinity and humanity (the hypostatic union which is the central interest of the classic Thomist Christology), or in terms of the "Christomonism" which absorbs the Church into the personal unity of Christ; it is rather the One Flesh of the New Covenant that terminates the Son's mission, and consequently the New Covenant is also the object of the divine creative will, which as divine is Trinitarian: the sending of the Son by the Father to give the Spirit.[30]

2.2.2.1 The latter point (from the above quote [2.2.2]) regarding a Christomonism

In light of this position, has Aquinas avoided a Christomonism? (Keefe's first point in the above quote regarding the hypostatic union will be dealt with later [cf. 2.2.2.2].) This author would answer yes. As concluded above, since the annihilation of a human person presumed to have been assumed by the Son is unacceptable on the fundamental level of the Incarnation, a similar solution on the level of the association between members of the Mystical Body and Christ is likewise unacceptable. The union that exists between Christ and the members of His body is one that is established with uncorrupted, unannihilated, unabsorbed, distinct human persons. Thus, there is no Christomonism.

2.2.2.1.1 A covenantal understanding in Aquinas?

Does Aquinas have a covenantal understanding of the union between Christ and the Church, as Keefe desires? The answer for this author is conditionally yes. There is textual evidence to suggest again that the idea is not foreign to Aquinas' thought. The evidence suggests that

---

29 Ibid., 178, 433.
30 Ibid., 433.

Aquinas oscillates between an organic and a marital understanding of the union depending on the context and the point needing to be made. In both cases, the union is, for Aquinas, more than an abstraction. It is a reality. It is unique.

Even in the classic texts presented above that relay an organic view, there are implicit indications of a marital understanding in their respective wider contexts. These contexts often have marital-familial overtones. They speak of grace and virtues being bestowed upon human beings. They speak of persons recognizing each other mutually in charity. In the end, all of these activities are possible only with a free moral agent which implies by definition a marital understanding.

In addition to these texts, this author has indicated above that Aquinas' commentary on Ephesians 5 presents a more explicit indication of a marital understanding. Here Aquinas recognizes a refocusing that occurs within the androcentric structure of the pericope 5:22–33. The refocusing by Paul is modelled on the relationship between Christ and the Church. This relationship is based on a profound love whereby the unique personhood and dignity of both individuals is recognized. Since love is the motivating force, all dispositions and actions are intended: a) to recognize the goodness of the other; b) to possess a spirit of self-donation and free reception; c) to strive for sanctification, eternal salvation, and mystical union with the Lord. Such a union could not take place unless the persons were free and autonomous to recognize and affirm the other.[31] Constitutive elements or parts of an organic union are incapable of doing so. In the end, there are indications that Aquinas did have some awareness of a marital understanding of the mystical union. However, this understanding is not as extensive as Keefe would have preferred, since Aquinas is also willing to entertain an organic understanding as well.

---

31 Freedom and autonomy are also important elements when Aquinas discusses this union in the texts above that employ more of a language of causality. The prinicipal cause of grace is God Himself and due to the fact that Christ's humanity is united with His divinity, He is a united (conjoined) instrument. Christ as Head pours forth His grace upon the members of the Mystical Body and by doing so, they are instruments in manifesting salvation to the world. However, in order to do so, they must be divided, separated instruments, who, through the exercise of their freedom, autonomy, and will enter into the mystical union. Thus, the union is marital and not organic. Organic unions do not require freedom, autonomy, and will.

2.2.2.1.2 The Church as a person and the Mystical Body

The discussion above raises the issue of how Keefe and Aquinas understand the Church. While both men view the Church as a community, as the Mystical Body which culminates in the individual person of Mary, Keefe is more acutely aware and articulate of Mary's importance. He is rooted in the Pauline and patristic tradition which speaks of Mary as the second Eve who proceeds from the second Adam as a glory from a head, a source. It has been shown above that he expands upon this tradition by saying that the term of her sinless procession is existence in a nuptial union with the second Adam. The Church has no other existence than this; to consider the Church in abstraction from that union is to misunderstand her entirely. The Church is not autonomous; nevertheless, she is free. Her union with Christ, as nuptial, can not be other than free, not in the fallen sense of freedom, as the choice of one alternative over another, but in the transcendent sense by which rational beings are free in heaven. According to Keefe, this is the sense of sinlessness, which does not consider turning away from the good, the true, the beautiful to which the sinless person can not but be freely committed, without reservation. This is the freedom of the sinless Church, as it was the freedom of the sinless Mother of God in her conception of her Son. To put it briefly, it is the freedom by which the sinless second Eve turns to her Lord in worship.

Baptism into the Church, for Keefe, relates the faithful to Mary as their mother (*ecclesia mater*). She is the mother of every Christian, as the Church is. The faithful enter into that relationship by baptism into the Church who, as Keefe will stress, is primordial, metaphysically prior to her members. That is to say, the Church is not caused by baptism, as though she were made up of the total number of the baptized. Her cause, her source, is the second Adam, so that they depend on her, not she upon them.

It has been shown above that for Aquinas, Christ's grace of headship is not a matter of grace simply being present in Him. It is that by which others are united to Him as head is to body. Christ and the Church are taken as one mystical person (*una mystica persona*). Unlike Keefe's clear distinction and explicit preference, Aquinas understands this union primarily as organic and yet there are instances when a marital understanding is also operative. It is the opinion of this author that Aquinas does not see the systematic ramifications of a marital understanding of this union with regards to the *prius* of theology. He simply recognizes that there are both interpretations present in Scripture. The organic view is rooted in I Cor.12 and the marital view is rooted in Ephesians 5. Either one, however, may be invoked depending upon the context and the points needing to be made. Keefe, as already noted, has a preference for the marital understanding since it is essential to the understanding of a free Covenant and a eucharistic prime analogate. Understanding the Church as a person, a concrete entity, a second Eve is essential for a nuptial symbolism (a sacramental realism) which is always an assertion of the covenantal freedom of the Church in her relation to her Head. An organic understanding does not support such an assertion.

2.2.2.1.3 The primacy of Christ in His various roles

Recall that a prime analogate provides the metaphysical basis for an analogy with secondary analogates and for their participation in the prime analogate's perfection.[32] Keefe is acutely aware of this fact and is consistent in applying it in reference to the New Covenant. Chapter five uses a deductive process to locate the prime analogate in Aquinas' case. By looking at the way in which Aquinas deals with the various spiritual roles (i.e., secondary analogates) that God uses to reveal Himself to His creatures, one is able to deduce and to identify the prime analogate of his theological system. Of all the prophets, preachers, teachers, mediators, and priests throughout history, Jesus Christ is the most excellent, according to Aquinas. He is not only this but He is the culmination of successive and progressive stages in the history of prophecy and salvation. This is due to the fact that the Incarnation was preordained to be the center point of history; between a "before" and an "after" is the perpetual youthfulness of the Incarnation. If one takes the Eucharist as the prolongation of the Incarnation, as Keefe does, this point may be read as supporting the premise that the Eucharist is the prime analogate of salvation history.

This deductive reasoning provides a Christocentric prime analogate, but does it provide a covenantal one for Aquinas, as Keefe requires? Yes, but the evidence is not as explicit as it is for a Christocentric prime. For Aquinas, all of the spiritual roles are revela-

---

32 Keefe, *Covenantal Theology*, 394, 450.

tory of God, Who is the subject of theology. However, Jesus Christ, by possessing these roles in the most excellent of manners, is the Revelation of God. The ground for this degree of possession is the hypostatic union. Christ possesses a substantial holiness as an individual human being by reason of the hypostatic union (grace of union) whereby His human nature is sanctified through the bond with the person of the Word. He also possesses an accidental holiness by reason of sanctifying grace as an effect of the union. This grace exists most completely in Christ because His soul is nearest to the source of grace, God. Consequently, He also possesses the grace of headship. As head, He excels over the other members of the body because: a) the head is the highest place on the body; b) it contains both the highest intellectual powers and all the senses; and c) it orders, governs, and causes motion in the other members.

For Aquinas, however, this grace of headship is intended for the members of Christ's Mystical Body. So it is bestowed upon the Body through the power of God. As God, Christ is the principal cause of grace. As a human being, Christ is the efficient, meritorious, instrumental, and to a certain extent, the exemplary and final causes of grace. As cause, then, He is greater than the effects which are dependent upon that cause (for there is no effect without a cause). And yet, the divine intention, is to establish a covenantal relationship, a One Flesh union. It is in this sense that the deductive reasoning provides for a covenantal prime analogate.

2.2.2.1.4 A comparison

In the end, Keefe's acknowledgment of the prime analogate is much more direct and explicit. The prime analogate is the New Covenant. It is the Event of Jesus Christ. Revelation is free and historical; it is all *gratia capitis* and its free acceptance in faith is equally of grace. Aquinas' acknowledgment of the prime analogate is on the surface direct and explicit as well. The prime analogate is God and all that is related to God.[33] However, this acknowledgment becomes more involved with the qualification that God is known under the formality of being revealed. Beginning in articles nine and ten of the first question in the *Summa theologiae*, one begins to pick up the indication that revelation

---

33 *ST* I 1.7.

is not immediately located *in* sacred Scripture but revelation is that *upon which* sacred Scripture is founded. The revelation upon which Scripture is founded is Christ, or at least this appears to be the direction Aquinas is headed. Thus, the subject of sacred doctrine for him is God studied under the formality of the revealable, under a Christocentric formality. If one follows the argument made by Rogers, then, this Christocentricity is put in a "parenthesis" until the third part of the *Summa theologiae*.[34]

Notice must be drawn, however, to the fact that this conclusion is the result of a sequential and deductive reasoning process. It is not so explicit and obvious as Keefe's identification and analysis of the prime analogate (but it is definitely a move in the direction Keefe would desire). Yet, in fairness to a Doctor of the Church, Aquinas did not have the advantage of working within a theological context where methodological principles and concerns were explicit and to the fore. Rather, his work made later theological methodology possible.

In addition, Keefe strives to build a theological system that is coherently, consistently, and completely structured around a free and historical prime analogate. Keefe has provided great insight into theological methodology by pointing out that Aquinas is not always coherent, consistent, and complete in his system. This author agrees with Keefe that, at times, Aquinas recognizes that truth is historical because the revelation is historical in Jesus Christ, but his system will not permit him to make this point in regard to method. His system has not been converted enough from its pagan cosmology, for in such a system, truth is determinant and not free. However, if one prescinds from a strict idealized reading of Aquinas and reads his texts more literally, there is evidence for the positions Keefe wants. We have seen this above and the following is another good example.

2.2.2.2 The former point (from the quote above [2.2.2]) regarding the hypostatic union

In the passage quoted above, Keefe states that the object of the creative mission of the Son is not simply the Christ, whether understood as a Christomonism (which has just been discussed) or understood as

---

34 Corbin would disagree with this imagery. Christ, for him, pervades and shapes the entire structure of the *Summa theologiae*.

a contingent static and impersonal relation between the Son's divinity
and humanity, the hypostatic union. According to Keefe, Aquinas' acceptance of Aristotle's dictum that the Absolute Being can not be related to anything without ceasing to be absolute, leads him in the first
part of the *Summa theologiae* to hold that things can be related to God
without His being related to them (a one-sided relationship). In the
third part this dictum is expressed by the position that the *Logos* is not
related to His humanity, but His humanity is related to Him. If the
prius is cosmological rather than historical and covenantal, one is
faced with the impossible problem of relating God to humanity, cosmos to history, according to Keefe.[35]

Keefe believes that such an interpretation of Aquinas leads to at
least two problems. First, if Aquinas is correct in holding that the *Logos* uses His human nature as an instrument (in this case an instrumental cause of the economy of salvation), then can an agent use an
instrument without relation to it? According to Keefe, Aquinas would
answer yes. An agent is not related to the object upon which it acts.
The effect of the action is in its object and not in the agent. If God is
unrelated from the outset, He stays unrelated to the creation He
causes. Keefe finds this problematic.

Second, if Aquinas is correct in holding (as Keefe understands
him) that the "Self" of Christ is the *Logos* and not the man, then Jesus'
"ego eimi" statements in the Gospels are those of the *Logos* simply and
not of the man Who is Jesus Christ. If this is the case, then Keefe argues that it can only be because Jesus is not the *Logos*, not God, not
the Son of the Eternal Father. If He is not, then Mary is not the Mother
of God. Consequently, Nestorianism appears on the horizon, for there
is no personal union of humanity and divinity in Christ despite Aquinas' efforts to account for the hypostatic union. The *Logos* is not immanent in salvation history. His humanity is, but He is not personally
identified with His humanity because being so would destroy His ab-
soluteness as divine. If, on the other hand, the Chalcedonian Creed is
followed and Jesus Christ is accepted as "one and the same," the One
Son of the Father and of Mary, then a personal or "hypostatic union"
is upheld. It is no longer supposed that the "Self" of the Incarnate *Logos* is not the "Self" of the Son of Mary.[36]

35 Keefe, *Covenantal Theology*, 408–09.
36 Ibid., 324, 447–48, 611–12.

To use Keefe's language of historicity, Aquinas holds that the immanent Second Person, the eternal Son is the subject of the Incarnation. However, such a subject is nonhistorical because it is preexistent. Keefe holds that the Incarnate Word, the Christ, subsists in a triune divine substance, which is triune by His subsistence in it. He subsists in a human substance, which is covenantal, nuptially unified as the One Flesh of the New Covenant, by His subsistence in it. By such subsistence, the Incarnation is historical. It is the event of freely being One Flesh with the second Eve, whether it be in His conception by Mary or in the institution of the New Covenant with His Bride the Church on the Cross (thus, a historical prime analogate).

Keefe's interpretation of Aquinas on the issue of the hypostatic union is shared by many other theologians. Keefe, however, is unaware of the caveat presented in the response to the third objection of *Summa theologiae* I 43.2. As was noted above, here Aquinas is stating that there really is only a single procession which is at once eternal and temporal. This is at least one way to state what Keefe is arguing for and desires. The issue of whether or not this understanding of the procession is coherent and consistent with Aquinas' wider systematic presentation is another matter. Second, the caveat presented in I 16.2 above whereby the two natures of Christ can be predicated in the concrete but not in the abstract because they exist in one common subject, namely, the Son of God, seems to weaken Keefe's suggestion that Aquinas has a Nestorian leaning. Based on this passage, Aquinas does have a preexistent Logos in the sense that the Son existed before He assumed humanity and that humanity takes its origin at a particular time and place. What Aquinas does not reflect much on, and Keefe does, is the primordial character of the earthly Jesus Christ. Still, what Aquinas does state does not rule out the primordial character of Jesus.

2.2.2.3 Modern criticisms of Aquinas' explanation

Many contemporary theologians, within this current highly psychological and anthropological age, have criticized Aquinas' theory of relations especially as it pertains to Trinitarian theology.[37] Aquinas'

---

37 There is a host of other theologians who take another approach, such as Michael Dodds who says, "If we were to ask what sort of relation to the world should be affirmed in God when this kind of relation [a real relation] is denied, our answer must be simply, 'We

position that God does not have a real relation with creation is often understood (rightly or wrongly) to contribute to the theological tendency that Karl Rahner argued against, namely, to say that the immanent Trinity is not the economic Trinity.[38] As Catherine LaCugna puts it, "The doctrine of the Trinity is ultimately therefore a teaching not about the abstract nature of God, not about God in isolation from everything other than God, but a teaching about God's life with us and our life with each other."[39] Such an emphasis on relationship, a communion of divine and human persons, is not fostered by the *Summa's* structural distinction between *de Deo Uno*, which holds that the nature of God is To-Be, and *de Deo Trino*, which holds that the nature of God is To-Be-Related.[40] While this does not mean that Aquinas sees no fundamental relationship between God and His creation, it is oftentimes perceived in this manner.

This perception is exacerbated by both an existential perspective and a causal perspective as well. Existentially, a relation of reason is preferred less than a real relation because a relation of reason is caused by and depends upon an activity of the mind for its existence. In contrast, a real relation is caused by and depends upon some *real* extra-mental foundation in the subject of the relation for its existence. All three constitutive principles of a real relation are indeed real.[41]

---

don't know." With this answer, we are at once back at the starting point of our discussion and at the ultimate exteme of our knowledge of God: to know God as unknown. We know from creatures that God is truly involved in them, sustaining their existence at each moment, but we do not know the mode of God's involvement or intimacy in creation since we do not know the being of God" (Michael J. Dodds, "Ultimacy and Intimacy: Aquinas on the Relation Between God and the World," in *Ordo Sapientiae et Amoris: Image et Message de Saint Thomas D'Aquin à travers les récentes études historiques, herméneutiques et doctrinales*, edited by Carlos-Josaphat Pinto de Oliveira, Studia Friburgensia, nouvelle séri, 78 [Fribourg, Switzerland: Éditions Universitaires Fribourg Suisse, 1993], 226.)

38 Karl Rahner, *The Trinity*, translated by J. Donceel (New York: Herder and Herder, 1970).

39 Catherine Mowry LaCugna, *God for Us: The Trinity and Christian Life* (San Francisco: HarperSanFrancisco, 1991), 1.

40 Ibid., 152–53.

41 It is informative to note that the reality of a relation had been questioned even in the time of Aquinas. While constantly affirming its reality, he equally affirms that relation has a *debilissimum esse*. In spite of this weakness of being, he uses relation for two important revealed truths. He uses the metaphyically strongest of the three types to explain the Trinity (the *actio-passio* relation) and the metaphysically weakest (the *aliud ad ipsum* relation) to explain that creation is only linked to God by the accident of relation and thus is entirely dependent on God.

Causally, real relations may have their foundation in action-passion. A foundation in action-passion by definition obviously is an order that results from cause and effect. Now order may be the product of one's own thought (a relation of reason) but there is a more fundamental order that results from the terms and the foundations which are anterior to thought (a real relation). Sense data and intellectual activity must admit a real dependence on the extra-mental and the real. Without real relations there can be no real adaptation of means to ends, and no real dependence of effect on cause; real adaptation, interdependence, coordination, etc., all then demand real relations.[42] Thus, for these existential and causal reasons, there is a desire for a real relation between God and creation in the contemporary theological context.

Constantine Cavarnos offers a critique of Aquinas' theory by inquiring into how relations affect the essence of God and the attribute of immutability. Cavaronos begins by comparing God's relation to His creation with the process of knowing. In knowing, the thing known is not really related to the knower because knowing posits something in the intellect but nothing in the object known. God, though, is said not to be really related to His creatures, even though He acts. The relation of being an effect, a creature, posits an action in God, but this action does not add a relation to Him. The implication in the case of knowing was that if knowing *did* posit change in its term, the converse relation *would* be a real relation. This view seems inconsistent.[43]

Cavarnos recognizes that Aquinas took this position out of a need to maintain the immutability of God and he found precedence in Aristotle. However, the relation of Aristotle's God to the things of the universe could with greater plausibility, according to Cavarnos, be regarded as a logical relation because God for Aristotle is not a creator. He does not act and moves only in the sense that things move towards Him as their goal. On the other hand, God, for Aquinas, is a

Cf. *In Meta.*, V, lect. 17, n. 1004; *In Phys.*, 1.3, lect. 1; *De Pot.*, q. 7, art. 11, corp. (Norbert D. Ginsburg, "Metaphysical Relations and St. Thomas Aquinas," *The New Scholasticism* XV (July 1941): 247–49).

42 William J. Kane, *The Philosophy of Relation in the Metaphysics of St. Thomas*, Philosophical studies, vol. 179, no. 30 (Washington, D.C.: Catholic University of America Press, 1958), 34.

43 Constantine Cavarnos, *The Classical Theory of Relations: A Study in the Metaphysics of Plato, Aristotle and Thomism* (Belmont, Massachusetts: Institute for Byzantine and Modern Greek Studies, 1975), 94.

Creator, and to say that He creates His creatures, but is not really related to them, seems, for Cavarnos, to be saying that He creates creatures but *does not really create* them; which is absurd.[44]

The case is not that simple, however. Aquinas does not deny that
God *acts* and *is* the Creator. What he does deny is that God's actions
produce relations in God. While this position saves the immutability
of God so far as *relations* are concerned, it does not save it so far as
actions are concerned, for how can God act, without in some way
changing? If the view that God is immutable has to be abandoned so
far as *actions* are concerned, Cavarnos does not see any good reason
why the view that God is immutable so far as *relations* are concerned
should be insisted upon. Admissions of such changes in God is not
tantamount to a denial of His immutability since these do not affect
the divine essence to which the doctrine strictly pertains.[45]

Earl Muller, in his critique, proposes that the relation be located
not in the nature of God but rather in the person, the subsistent relationality, which distinguishes the persons of the Godhead.[46] Such a
shift, he argues, can avoid the problematic positions taken by Aquinas
in speaking of Jesus' relation with His mother while still respecting
the fundamental methodological and theological principles.[47]

Muller explains that Aquinas, in arguing that there is only a relation of reason between God and creation, is thinking first and foremost of the divine essence. The subject is God, the term is creation,
and the foundation is God's creative power; but since the subject and
the foundation are identical, the relation is one of reason and not a
real relation. God is God's power.[48]

Difficulties arise with the incarnate Jesus Christ. Persons, who are
human, are in real relations with temporal created realities. The perfection of human nature (the mission of Jesus Christ) requires that the
members of the species be in real relations with one other. If Jesus
Christ possesses human nature fully and perfectly, then He is in real

---

44 Ibid.

45 Ibid., 94–95.

46 Earl C. Muller, "Real Relations and the Divine: Issues in Thomas's Understand-
    ing of God's Relation to the World," *Theological Studies* 56 (December 1995): 673–
    95.

47 Cf. *ST* III 35.5, corp.; *In III Sent.*, d. 8, q. 1, a. 5. Aquinas needs to reconcile the
    Incarnation with his positions that there is no real relation between God and
    creation and that Jesus did not have a real relation with His mother.

48 Muller, 678, 686.

relations with other human beings.[49] He must have a real relation
with His mother. How so?

Muller sees this as possible by considering the relation in terms of
person rather than in terms of nature, of subsistent relationality rather
than of accident-substance. The subject is Jesus Christ and the term is
creation. However, the foundation is not God's creative power but
that which distinguishes the person of the Son from the person of the
Father, namely, the generativity of the Father and the filiability of the
Son. The subject and the term are not identical. If they were, the Trinity would collapse. Thus, each of the three elements is real and there
is then a real relation. This shift to subsistent relationality has provided the metaphysical grounding for real relations.[50]

Muller points out that the immutability of God, which was a key
concern for Aquinas, is maintained in the shift as well. According to
Muller, Aquinas holds that if you become equal in height to me, I,
without really changing, become related to you. In no way am I
changed since the relation of equality to you already exists in me "as
in its root" (*in sua radice*) before you changed size.[51] In other words,
there was already in me, before you grew up, the root of that real relation, namely, the measure. You changed and when you reached that
measure, what had been a root in me becomes a real relation. This is
said with regard to categorical relations, but there is no clear reason
why it can not be applicable to divine relations.[52] What changes is not
the Son, but creation. At the Incarnation, Mary becomes Christ's
mother. His filiation is met reciprocally with maternity, thus constituting a real relation with His mother, with creation.

Muller focuses on *Summa theologiae* I 45.6 to argue that Aquinas
provides some grounding for the metaphysical position on subsistent
relationality that he suggests. Muller writes:

> Thomas addresses the question whether creation is proper to any Person in
> *ST* 1, q. 45, a. 6 by noting that creative action is common to the three Per-
> sons. This much will yield the philosophical judgment that there is no real
> relation between the world and God. Thomas goes on to note that "the cau-
> sality concerning the creation of things answers to the respective meaning of

49 Ibid., 687–88.
50 Ibid., 690–91.
51 Ibid., 684. Muller is relying on Mark Henninger, *Relations: Medieval Theories
    1250–1325* (Oxford: Clarendon Press, 1989), 20. He cites *In V Physica*, lect. 3 (ed.
    Leonine, vol 2, 237b, n. 8) (ed. Pirotta, 1292).
52 Ibid.

the coming forth each Person implies." What he has in mind is God's action through His mind and will. But here also there is no real relation between God and the world....However, Thomas is preparing us for a shift: "In like manner God the Father wrought the creature through His Word, the Son, and through his Love, the Holy Spirit. And from this point of view, keeping in mind the essential attributes of knowing and willing, the coming forth of the divine Persons can be seen as types for the comings forth of creatures."

Although Thomas does not take notice of the differences this makes, the shift he has executed produces significant results when one reformulates the elements of the relation now, not in terms of God and the world, but in terms of the Father and the world. The Father is related to the world through the Son and in the Spirit. The Father and the world are the subject and term of the relationship; the Word of God serves as the foundation. As long as one considers the issue in terms of God's mind, one does not have a distinct foundation, because God and God's mind are identically the same. But the Son is not the same Person as the Father even if He is the same God, and thus the relationship between the Father and the world can be understood as having a distinct foundation.

It is clear, of course, that Thomas would not consider this to be a legitimate argument. The chief objection he would raise is that the Father and the world are of different ontological orders. God's causality in creating us through our parents is not a paternal causality. There would seem to be no real relation between the Father and the individual human on this basis. The issue becomes less clear-cut when one turns to our divinization in Christ and in the Holy Spirit. One way to underscore that our adoption as children of God involves truly being given divine life would be to develop some way of speaking of the Father's real relation to us as "our Father." In any case, it is clear that one can not understand God as having a real relation to the world apart from understanding that relation as a Person-to-person relationship, and that relationship can not be understood as multiplying the Trinity though it is real in God only as "rooted" in the real relations that do multiply the Trinity.[53]

Thus, while Aquinas does not explicitly state it, there is room in his thought for concluding that there is a real relationship between creation and God if the ground is taken to be person understood as a subsistent relationality.

2.2.3 The prime analogate: the Eucharist and transubstantiation

Keefe is very explicit in identifying his prime analogate as the Eucharist: the event of the One Sacrifice of the Cross, the event of transubstantiation. The Eucharist is the radical presence of God in the world

---

53 Muller, 691–92.

and, as such, it can not but be normative of all unity, goodness, truth, and beauty in the world. As the prime analogate, it is the source of all metaphysical explanation for all that is.

Keefe holds that Aquinas' prime analogate, the *Deus Unus* Who can not have a real relationship with creation, is cosmological. That means there is an effort to explain the historical Catholic faith in terms of a nonhistorical notion of truth derived from Aristotle. He tries to explain the Eucharist on the basis of this radically nonhistorical truth. This Keefe flatly rejects.

Again, a rereading of Aquinas' writing, in light of the questions Keefe brings to it, indicates that Aquinas is more congruous with Keefe's line of thought than Keefe himself perhaps realizes. Chapter six has shown that Aquinas considered the Mystical Body to be the fundamental principal underlying his theological structure. His teachings on grace, Redemption, the Incarnation, and the sacraments are all inextricably linked to the Mystical Body. Aquinas' insistence on the importance of the mystical union between the Head and the Body (especially as indicated in his prologue to his commentaries on Paul's epistles) could be exploited more by Keefe.

Chapter six then goes on to demonstrate that the sacraments were instituted for the unity and well-being of the Mystical Body. Of these sacraments, Aquinas identifies the Eucharist as the most excellent of all the sacraments, as the primary sacrament. However, Keefe is perceptive in stating that Aquinas' act-potency system, as he has structured it, does not accurately articulate this position. There is indeed an inconsistency or incongruity between the logic of Aquinas' system and what he states theologically. Several points may be made in this regard.

Aquinas does relate the sacramental form and matter in terms of Aristotle's act-potency analysis. The form, the words of consecration, are true and efficacious for Aquinas, and when they are spoken over the matter, the bread and wine do become the Body and Blood of Christ. Aquinas understands this relationship between form and matter in terms of change (potency moving to act; a *terminus a quo* proceeding in terms of a *commune tertium* to a *terminus ad quem*). The words of consecration are indeed instrumental in changing the *terminus a quo* into the *terminus ad quem*. The inner connection (the *commune tertium*) between the two *termini* is the remaining appearances of bread and wine. However (and this is the point of controversy), these appearances or species are considered by Aquinas to be accidents without a subject of inherence (i.e., the original subject of inherence, bread and wine, no longer exists and they do not inhere in the subject of Jesus Christ; rather they are suspended by "dimensive quantity").

Thus, the matter-form analysis, as Aquinas uses it,[54] places all sacramental efficacy in the words of consecration. It is only by the consecratory form that the bread and the wine signify and cause what they signify. Keefe concedes that Aquinas recognizes that bread and wine are indispensable to this efficacy. They alone, and no other food stuffs, are to be used by authority of Scripture and Tradition. However, Keefe observes that Aquinas does not provide an act-potency explanation for their indispensability. If, as Aquinas holds, the words of consecration truly provide the formal content of the sacramental sign, then the matter upon which the form gives meaning must be formally insignificant. They do no more than individuate the sign in space and time. Thus, any material whatsoever would suffice in providing this purpose. In other words, Aquinas is saying that the sign value of the matter, the bread and wine, is not contained in the form. Keefe holds this to be inadequate. There is more to the sign content of the sacrament than the mere words, which is the only form Aquinas provides through his metaphysics. Elsewhere, as Keefe points out, Aquinas recognizes the sign character of the bread and wine (for the Eucharist is indeed real food and drink) but when he does, he is relying on the faith tradition of the Church and not his metaphysics. Thus, this is one example where Aquinas' philosophical system does not accurately articulate his theological belief.[55]

In a second example, Keefe also observes that Aquinas' form-matter analysis of the eucharistic sign places the full significance of the Eucharist (i.e., the whole of the sacramental sign and, therefore, its full efficacy) in the moment in which the words of consecration are pronounced. He agrees with Aquinas that the words are indispensable and that they effect the *res et sacramentum*, but if they are taken in isolation, they exhaust the formal significance, the sign quality, and come close to conceding the efficacy of the sacrament. Keefe is aware that Aquinas knows this: he recognizes that Aquinas does distinguish between the *sacramentum tantum* and the *res et sacramentum* of the Eucharist. Yet, his argument that the words "take ye and eat" or

---

54   Cf. *ST* III 78.1.
55   Keefe, *Covenantal Theology*, 422.

"drink ye all of this" of the institution formula are not part of the form risks isolating the canon of the Mass from the offertory and the communion.[56] Keefe indicates that Aquinas is aware that the offertory and communion are integral to the Eucharist, even though they are not consecratory, but again, his form-matter analysis does not account for it.[57] Metaphysical distinctions between form and matter, offertory, canon, and communion draw one into necessity and the quagmire of cosmology. This is why Keefe does not use the language of form-matter but the patristic formula of *sacramentum tantum, res et sacramentum*, and *res tantum* instead. The relationship between these three elements is free; they are distinguished historically as past, present, and future.

In another example, Keefe points out that Aquinas does not have an efficacious eucharistic signing of the Real Presence of the Body and Blood of Christ by the bread and wine as true food and drink. As accidents without a subject of inherence, they are simply irrelevant to the Eucharist as food and drink, as they are to every other historical reality. Signs are causes only to the extent that they are transcendentally related to some substance in which they inhere. If there is no substance in which they have their existence, then they have no power to effect anything.[58] Transubstantiation must then be accounted for on some other basis than the truth of the words of conse-

---

56 These references to the Church are secondary for Aquinas. This results in isolating the Head from the Body. The focus is primarily on the Real Presence and not on the Sacrifice which is covenantal; "...for this is my Body which is given for you." Keefe puts it another way, Aquinas removes the Church from the *res et sacramentum* of the Eucharist: he makes the Church to be the *res sacramenti*, the final and invisible effect of the *res et sacramentum*. This means that the Church is invisible; thereby it is deshistoricized, made to be simply eschatological, which is untrue. The Church's presence in history is sacarmental, i.e., liturgical. Her visibility is her worship, which is radically Eucharistic.

57 Keefe, *Covenantal Theology*, 422–23.

58 According to Keefe, a visible sign's primary function is to render present sensibly a metaphysical reality. The reality signs itself to us through our sense organs. Thus, we know it is there. Otherwise, nothing is present except possibly an illusion. For example, when a person sees fire, fire inheres in an object that burns and it is indicating that it is burning. Fire without anything to burn is not fire anymore. Applied to the Eucharist, bread and wine cause the presence of Christ in the sense that He is present as true food and drink. This can not be unless the bread and wine sign His presence as food and drink. When they cease to sign (e.g., bread becomes moldy or wine is diluted with water), there is no presence of Christ.

cration (upon which Aquinas relies), for, according to his account of transubstantiation, that event so dissociates the appearances of bread and wine from the Eucharist as food and drink that their identification by the words of consecration with the Body and Blood of Christ, simply is not true.[59]

In the end, Keefe is saying that an impasse is ultimately reached with Aquinas' act-potency analysis of the Eucharist and transubstantiation. At certain points Aquinas does not apply the analysis and concludes to an essentialist, nominalist account of the accidents that remain, according to Keefe. He abandons his metaphysics when he asserts that after the consecration, accidents have no substance in which to inhere. Keefe rejects here Aquinas' theology and his metaphysics as it stands and instead proposes a cure that transforms both. The cure is based on a new prime analogate: the eucharistic Event celebrated by the Church. This prime analogate is covenantal and nuptial: the union of Christ and His Church. This "substance," this prime analogate, rather than some cosmological notion of substance, is the source of all metaphysical explanation. The Eucharist does the "defining" rather than having it be defined by some nonhistorical notions of necessary intelligibility. This author agrees.

Central to Keefe's theology is the insistence that the Eucharist is an event. It is imperative that this be understood since it defines Keefe's understanding of transubstantiation. It is a dynamic event that integrates past, present, and future. It does not entail "things": the static transformation of one thing into another thing. For Keefe, the past is a potency which has a free potentiality toward the future. The present can not be deduced from the past. It is a free event and, as such, the event in the here and now derives from the past, but it is not a necessary derivation. Rather it is a free derivation.

Potency and act are in a free relationship for Keefe. Act is analogous to the present and is thus dependent upon potency in the past but freely dependent. The fullness of their relationship is the future. This fullness is substance: existential, plenary, being. Thus, the past, present, and future are analogous to potency, act, and (plenary) substance.

These triads are also analogous to the sacramental *ordo* of *sacramentum tantum, res et sacramentum,* and *res tantum* and the liturgical

---

59 Keefe, *Covenantal Theology,* 422–23.

ordo of offertory, canon (consecration), and communion. The bread and wine of the offertory (the *sacramentum tantum*) are not simply ordinary foodstuffs. They receive their meaning within the liturgy of Christ's One Sacrifice. Their reality is not indifferent and apart, but historical. Their reality is already referred to God in a moment of thanksgiving recalling the manna and quail that sustained the Israelites during the Exodus and representing all the Old Testament sacrifices which culminate in Mary's sacrificial *fiat mihi*. The bread and wine now become the subject of transubstantiation when they, representing the Church's sacrifice of praise, are transformed and identified by the words of consecration as the Bread of Life and the Cup of Eternal Salvation in the present. They become the historical concreteness, the personal and covenantal actuality, in fallen history, of the risen Lord.[60] According to Keefe, the actualization of the present does not annul the past. In this sense then, it is perfectly all right and indeed necessary to speak of the species or the appearances as remaining. They are not canceled by transubstantiation. If they were, there would be no relationship whatsoever between the present and the past. There would be no perfection of all the failed Old Testament sacrifices. Rather, it is an offering of all that the Church has received from Christ in Whom she has her source and which, in free obedience to His command, she offers under the signs of bread and wine. By His work and power, the Church's gift of herself (*per Ipsum et cum Ipso et in Ipso ad Deum Patrem omnipotentem*) becomes His oblation, the One Sacrifice of His Body and Blood (the *res et sacramentum*) at the consecration. But it does so only in the union of One Flesh with her whose offering is thus transubstantiated by His obedience to the Father to become *sarx* so as to institute the *mia sarx* of the New Covenant.[61]

The Church is not herself transformed into Christ; rather, she is created primordially by the mission of the Son which terminates in the New Covenant.[62] Thus, the species of the bread and wine remain to sign freely the transformation of the Church's sacrifice of praise into the Lord's One Sacrifice. They have no significance of their own except that they sign the Body and Blood of Christ. The term "sacrifice of praise," strictly speaking, is not used after the consecration. However, the Church's presence continues to be signed not so much

---

60 Ibid., 437.
61 Ibid., 436.
62 Ibid.

through the species but through her ongoing visibility in her worship, which is radically eucharistic. The Church's presence in history is sacramental, which is to say, liturgical.

Through this offering of Christ (the *res et sacramentum*), the Holy Spirit is poured forth upon creation. It is in the Holy Spirit then that individuals are drawn into communion with Jesus Christ and formed into His Mystical Body. This communion of the Church with the Risen Christ in the Holy Spirit is the *res tantum*. The covenant between the Church and Christ may be sacramentally represented only because it is eschatologically achieved in the Resurrection, in the Ascension, and in the giving of the Holy Spirit.[63]

To summarize, Keefe treats transubstantation as an event, the Event of Christ's One Sacrifice for His Church. He proceeds to understand this Event through the following historical metaphysical analysis: a) the offering of bread and wine, the subject of transubstantiation, as the *sacramentum tantum*; b) the sacrificial presence of the Christ to His Church as the *res et sacramentum*; c) the plenary communion of the Church with the risen Lord as the *res tantum*.[64] Aquinas treats transubstantiation as an object and proceeds to understand its intrinsic intelligibility as act to potency. The *terminus a quo* consists of the accidents and the substance of bread and wine. The *terminus ad quem* consists of the accidents of bread and wine miraculously inhering in dimensive quantity and the substance of the Body and Blood of Jesus Christ. The *tertium commune* between the two *termini* is likewise the accidents of bread and wine.

2.3 The act-potency relations of being

By proposing an historical covenantal understanding of being, it has been shown that Keefe fundamentally changes the act-potency analysis of that being. Keefe proposes, and then follows, what may be termed a multi-dimensional model rather than the classic Thomistic hierarchical model. In the hierarchical model, *ens* (a being of a certain kind which is) consists of two constitutive principles: *esse* (that by which a being actually exists) and essence (that by which a being is what it is). *Essence* in turn consists of two constitutive principles: acci-

---

63   Ibid.
64   Ibid., 437.

dents (that by which the beings exists in another and not in itself as a subject of inherence) and substance (that by which the being exists in itself and does not inhere in another). Substance likewise consists of two constitutive principles: substantial form (that by which the substance has an inner unity and is constituted as a specific nature or kind) and prime matter (that by which the substance is material and by which the composite can undergo changes while remaining material). Each principle within a paired relationship is proportional to the other: act to potency. Also each principle will be related to other principles and each paired relationship will be related to the others according to the principles of analogy. Since the principles are constitutive of each other, the analogy is hierarchically structured.

In Keefe's multi-dimensional model, the same reality, the same historical existential substance, namely, the New Covenant, is considered—only different questions are asked of it by the different act-potency relations.[65] In the hierarchical model, the subject of consideration may vary.

Since this existential substance is historical, and freedom is one of the fundamental categories of the historical, Keefe has given a historical meaning to all of the act-potency relations which raise questions of the same historical existential substance (i.e., the prime analogate). Thus, the *esse*-essence relation concerns itself with the free (i.e., the contingent character of creation is not randomness but is intrinsically intelligible only as free [creation *ex nihilo sui et subjecti*]) immanence of the existential cause of contingent existence (i.e., of the Creator). How is the New Covenant immanent freely in creation? How is it the formal cause of humanity and the world?[66]

The accident-substance relation concerns itself with history, with the temporal sequence. How is history integrated by and in the *ordo* of the sacramental Event that has been designated "transubstantiation" by the doctrinal tradition of the Church? This analysis is focused on providing a theology of history.[67]

The substantial form-prime matter relation concerns itself with the existential substance as intrinsically relational (covenantal) and free. How is form intelligibly immanent in matter? More specifically, how is God immanent in humanity, in the world? How is it that the

---

65 Ibid., 431–32, 441–42.
66 Ibid., 431.
67 Ibid., 454–55.

New Covenant (i.e., the nuptial *ordo* of the Christ-Church relation that is concrete and historically actual in the Event of the Sacrifice of the Mass) is the means by which God is present to His creation?[68]

In the end, freedom for Keefe is operative in all three act-potency relations. For Aquinas, freedom (contingency) is present in the *esse-*essence relation but not with the other two relations. Rather, for them, necessity is present.

3 Chapter Conclusion

Both Keefe and Aquinas hold that sacred doctrine (theology) is a single unified science predicated on a single prime analogate. Keefe holds that the articulation of the prime analogate can be by means of two metaphysical systems: the discursive-analytical interpretation (Aristotelianism) and the intuitive-dialectical interpretation (Platonism). The correlation between the systems and the prime analogate is one of freedom whereby the systems are subordinate to the prime analogate (and, consequently, converted or recast from their necessitarianism by the free prime analogate). Aquinas, on the other hand, does not deny the validity of the intuitive-dialectical interpretation but he does not use it as the foundation for his system. Rather, his system is based on the discursive-analytical interpretation. The correlation between this single system and the prime analogate is not totally free, for the prime analogate is not recognized to be free and, thus, is not permitted to rid the system of its necessitarian presuppositions that are rooted in the logic of paganism.

In Aquinas' system, whatever is intelligible is so in terms of an act-potency causality and is, thus, intrinsically necessary. It is said to be "nature" or "natural." For Aquinas then, the order of creation is natural: although its being is contingent, it is intelligible only in terms of intrinsically necessary causes and, therefore, is not free. His system is not able to relate an inherently free creation with an inherently free God; it seeks intrinsically necessary reasons for that which is not intrinsically necessary. The system, according to Keefe, is not adequate for theological purposes, for theology is concerned throughout with a

---

68 Ibid., 452.

free subject matter: its subject is revelation, a free gift of a truth available only by the free reception of that gift. For this reason, Keefe rejects Aquinas' prime analogate (*Deus Unus, Ipsum Esse Subsistens*) for it is known without revelation and without faith.

Keefe believes that to maintain such a theological position would be finally to reject the revelation in favor of a philosophical system that operates in terms of intrinsic necessity. Consequently, Keefe converts rather than rejects Aquinas' metaphysics by seeking to discover the intrinsic intelligibility of free substance and not of necessary substance. In sum: all reality is free; all truth is free; no necessary truth, no necessary being is actual anywhere in the created or uncreated order. This creation is a free order since it is an image of the free unity of the Trinity. This trinitarian image is also reflected in the One Sacrifice of Christ for his Bridal Church, which is the institution of the New Covenant, the One Flesh of the Second Adam and the Second Eve. This Sacrifice, this One Flesh, this Covenant, is the prime creative act of the Trinity: the Father sending the Son to give the Holy Spirit. Its actuality in history is only as a free graced event, only as eucharistic. Thus, Keefe's prime analogate is the Eucharist and not *de Deo uno*.

With that said, Aquinas is aware of other possibilities for the prime analogate. He is not closed to these possibilities and he even gives indication of some movement towards a more relational prime analogate. In the discussion above, it has been shown that Jesus Christ is the prime referent in the first question of the *Summa theologiae*. Christ is the revelation of God. He is the revelation that grounds sacred doctrine and the explication that constitutes it, that provides its content. He grounds sacred doctrine by being the Word which is the Form in the mind of God and, as such, is related to creation. In knowing Himself in the Son (filiability), the Father (paternability) also knows and relates to creatures. The Son of the Father relates to creatures and constitutes sacred doctrine through the various roles He assumes. In so doing, He is the way by which creatures are led to know and serve God. While He is the most excellent and the culmination of all these roles, it is as Head of the Mystical Body that the union between the Creator and creatures takes on its covenantal aspect. While this union is at times considered to be organic, Aquinas does consider it to be covenantal, marital, nuptial, as Keefe would insist.

The sacraments, according to Aquinas and Keefe, were instituted for the unity and well-being of the Mystical Body. Both men maintain that the Eucharist holds the place of primacy among the sacraments. In holding such a position, Aquinas has given some indication that his prime analogate has not only shifted from the *Deus Unus* to Jesus Christ as the Revelation of God, but to Jesus Christ as sacramentally present in the Eucharist. However, for the reasons outlined above, Keefe is accurate in stating that Aquinas' act-potency system, as he has structured it, can not accurately articulate this position. Aquinas does not have an efficacious eucharistic signing of the Real Presence of the Body and Blood of Christ by the bread and wine as true food and drink. As accidents without a subject of inherence, they are simply irrelevant to the Eucharist, as they are to every other historical reality. Transubstantiation is then accounted for on some other basis than the truth of the words of consecration, for, according to his account of transubstantiation, that event so dissociates the appearances of bread and wine from the Eucharist as real food and drink that their identification, by the words of consecration, with the Body and Blood of Christ, simply are not true. In the end, an impasse is ultimately reached with Aquinas' act-potency analysis of the Eucharist and transubstantiation. Instead of abandoning the system, Keefe suggests recasting it with a new prime analogate: the free eucharistic Event of the New Covenant between Christ and His Church.

This author agrees with Keefe that continuing the work of recasting this system depends upon a renewal of interest in systematic theology and, more particularly, in theological methodology. To do so would require the enlistment of the current generation of Catholic intellectuals in the metaphysics of Aquinas. Yet the major exponents of Thomism today are so unaware of, or confined by, the limits of the system (as it is so structured by Aquinas) that they say little of any real theological interest. The desire to move beyond this confinement (started forty or fifty years ago by men like Rahner, Lonergan, Schillebeeckx) needs to be refostered with the conviction that the Catholic tradition is tenable under the scrutiny of the modern mind. The system can faithfully and coherently articulate the faith, but it must be recast and set free from the methodological confines of the past. Keefe asks if there is anyone willing to consider his suggestions on how and where to begin. While this work does not agree with all that Keefe has said and it has tried to point out that there is more in Aquinas that provides support for what Keefe intends than Keefe himself recognizes, it is an effort to show serious interest and to take him up on the challenge.

BIBLIOGRAPHY

Alvira, Tomas, Luis Clavell, and Tomas Melendo. *Metaphysics*. Translated by Luis Supan and M. Guzman. Philosophy Book Series. Manila, Philippines: Sinag-Tala Publishers, 1991.

Anger, Abbé. The Doctrine of the Mystical Body of Christ: According to the Principles of the Theology of St. Thomas Aquinas. London: Longmans, Green, 1932.

Aquinas, St. Thomas. *Aristotle's De Anima and Commentary*. In *Past Masters [Humanities Databases]*. [CD title: The Collected Works of Thomas Aquinas]. Charlottesville, Virginia: InteLex, 1992.

————. Aristotle's De Anima in the Version of William of Moerbeke and the Commentary of St. Thomas Aquinas. Translated by K. Foster and S. Humphries. New Haven, Conn.: Yale University Press, 1951.

————. *Commentary on Saint Paul's Epistle to the Galatians*. Translated by F. R. Larcher, with an introduction by Richard T. A. Murphy. Aquinas Scripture Series, vol. 1. Albany, New York: Magi Books, 1966.

————. *Commentary on Saint Paul's Epistle to the Ephesians*. Translation and introduction by Matthew L. Lamb. Aquinas Scripture Series, vol. 2. Albany, New York: Magi Books, 1966.

————. *Commentary on the Gospel of St. John*. Translated by James A. Weisheipl with Fabian R. Larcher. Aquinas Scripture Series, vol. 4. Albany, New York: Magi Books, 1980.

————. *Commentary on the Metaphysics of Aristotle*. Translated by John P. Rowan. Chicago: Henry Regnery, 1961.

————. *Compendium of Theology*. Translated by Cyril Vollert. St. Louis and London: B. Herder, 1952.

————. De *articulis fidei et ecclesiae sacramentis ad Archiepiscopum Panormitarum*. In *Opuscula Theologica*. Vol. 1. Edited by Raymundi A. Verardo. Rome: Marietti, 1954.

Aquinas, St. Thomas. *The Division and Methods of the Sciences: Questions V and VI of His Commentary on the De Trinitate of Boethius Translated with Introduction and Notes.* Fourth revised ed. Edited by Armand Maurer. Toronto, Canada: Pontifical Institute of Mediaeval Studies, 1953.

———. *Evangelia S. Mattaei et S. Joannis Commentaria.* Taurini, Italy: Marietti, 1925.

———. *Exposition of the Posterior Analytics of Aristotle.* Translated by Pierre Conway, revised by William H. Kane, mimeograph by Michel Doyon. Quebec: La Librairie Philosophique M. Doyon, 1956.

———. "Letter to the Archbishop of Palermo on Faith, Article 10." In *An Aquinas Reader.* Edited by Mary T. Clark. Garden City, New York: Image Books, 1972.

———. *On the Power of God (Quaestiones disputatae de potentia Dei).* Translated by the English Dominican Fathers. Westminster, Maryland: Newman Press, 1952.

———. *On the Truth of the Catholic Faith (Summa Contra Gentiles).* Translated by James E. Anderson, Vernon J. Bourke, Charles O'Neil, and Anton Pegis. 5 vols. Garden City, New York: Doubleday, Image Books, 1955–1957.

———. *Scriptum super libros sententiarum magistri Petri Lombardi episcopi Parisiensis.* Edited by R.P. Mandonnet. Paris: Sumptibus P. Lethielleux, 1929.

———. *Summa Theologiae: A Concise Translation.* Edited by Timothy McDermott. Westminster, Maryland: Christian Classics, 1989.

———. *Summa Theologiae.* Blackfriars Edition. New York: McGraw-Hill, 1964–1976.

———. *Super epistolam S. Pauli apostoli ad Hebraeos.* Vol. 2 of *In omnes S. Pauli apostoli epistolas: commentaria.* Taurini, Italy: Marietti, 1820.

———. *The Trinity and the Unicity of the Intellect.* St. Louis: B. Herder, 1946.

———. *Truth (De veritate).* Translated from the definitive Leonine texts by Robert W. Mulligan. Chicago: Henry Regnery, 1952–1954.

Aristotle. *Aristotle's Categories and Propositions (De Interpretatione).* Translated with commentaries and glossary by Hippocrates G. Apostle. Grinnell, Iowa: Peripatetic Press, 1980.

————. *Aristotle's Metaphysics*. Translated with commentaries and glossary by Hippocrates G. Apostle. Bloomington, Indiana and London: Indiana University Press, 1966.

————. *Metaphysics*. In *The Basic Works of Aristotle*. Edited and with an introduction by Richard McKeon. New York: Random House, 1941.

Augustine. *De civitate Dei*. Vol. 47 of *Corpus Christianorum Latinorum*. Serie Latina. Turnholt 1, 1953 ff.

Barth, Karl. *Church Dogmatics*. Vol. I/1: The Doctrine of the Word of God. Translation by G.T. Thomson. Edinburgh: T & T Clark, 1963.

————. *Dogmatics in Outline*. New York: Harper Brothers, 1959.

Billot, Ludovico. *De Ecclesiae Sacramentalis: Commentarius in Tertiam Partem S. Thomae*. 2 vols. Rome: Gregorian University Press, 1931.

Blanchette, Oliva. "Philosophy and Theology in Aquinas: On Being a Disciple in Our Day." *Science et Esprit* 28 (Janvier-Avril 1976): 23–53.

Blanco, Arturo. "Word and Truth in Divine Revelation: A Study of the Commentary of St. Thomas on John 14, 6." In *La doctrine de la révélation divine de saint Thomas d'Aquin*. Actes du symposium sur la pensee de Saint Thomas d'Aquin tenu a Rolduc, les 4 et 5 Novembre 1989, edited by Leo Elders. Studi Tomistici, vol 37. Vatican City: Libreria Editrice Vaticana, 1990.

Bonano, Salvatore. *The Concept of Substance and the Development of Eucharistic Theology to the Thirteenth Century*. An abstract of a dissertation. Catholic University of America Studies in Sacred Theology (second series), no. 121. Washington, D.C.: Catholic University of America Press, 1960.

Boylan, M. Eugene. *The Mystical Body: The Foundation of the Spiritual Life*. Westminster, Maryland: Newman Bookshop, 1948.

Boyle, Leonard E. *The Setting of the Summa theologiae of Saint Thomas*. The Etiene Gilson Series, vol. 5. Toronto: Pontifical Institute of Medieval Studies, 1982.

Brinkman, B.R. "Allargando Poco a Poco: An Essay Review." Review of *Covenantal Theology: The Eucharistic Order of History*, by Donald J. Keefe. *Heythrop Journal* 36 (January 1995): 65–72.

Buckley, James J. Review of *Thomas Aquinas and Karl Barth: Sacred Doctrine and the Natural Knowledge of God,* by Eugene F. Rogers, Jr. *The Thomist* 61 (April 1997): 320–25.

Burrell, David B. *Aquinas: God and Action.* Notre Dame, Indiana: University of Notre Dame Press, 1979.

Carter, Gerald Emmett Cardinal, Archbishop of Toronto. *"Do This in Remembrance of Me:" A Pastoral Letter on the Sacrament of Priestly Orders.* Toronto: Mission Press, 1983.

Casel, Odo. *Le Mystère Du Culte dans le Christianisme.* Lex Orandi, vol. 6. Paris: Les Éditions du Cerf, 1946.

———. *The Mystery of Christian Worship and Other Writings.* Edited by Burkhard Neunheuser. London: Darton, Longman and Todd, 1962.

Cassar, C. *Revelation in the Incarnate Word: Doctrine of St. Thomas.* Florina, Malta: Empire Press, 1965.

Catao, Bernard. *Salut et Rédemption chez S. Thomas D'Aquin: l'Acte Sauveur du Christ.* In *Théologie.* Études Publiées sous la Direction de la Faculté de Théologie S.J. de Lyon-Fourviére, vol 62. Paris: Aubier/Éditions Montaigne, 1965.

Cavarnos, Constantine. *The Classical Theory of Relations: A Study in the Metaphysics of Plato, Aristotle and Thomism.* Belmont, Massachusetts: Institute for Byzantine and Modern Greek Studies, 1975.

Chenu, Marie-Dominique. *Is Theology a Science?* Translated by A.H.M. Green-Armytage. Twentieth Century Encyclopedia of Catholicism Series. New York: Hawthorn, 1959.

———. *La Theologie comme Science au XIIIe Siecle.* Paris: J. Vrin, 1943.

———. *Toward Understaning Saint Thomas.* Translators with authorized corrections and bibliographical additions A.-M Landry and D. Hughes. Chicago: Henry Regnery, 1964.

Chopin, Cl. *Le Verbe Incarné et Rédempteur.* Le Mystère Chrétien: Théologie Dogmatique, vol. 8. Tournai, Belgium: Desclée, 1963.

Corbin, Michel. *Le Chemin de la théologie chez Thomas D'Aquin.* Bibliothèque des archives de philosophie, nouvelle séri, 16. Paris: Beauchesne, 1974.

Crownfield, David. "The Seminal Trace: Presence, Difference, and Transubstantiation." *Journal of the American Academy of Religion* 59 (Summer 1991): 361–71.

Davies, Brian. "Is *Sacra Doctrina* Theology?" *New Blackfriars* 71 (March 1990): 141–47.

————. *The Thought of Thomas Aquinas.* Oxford: Clarendon Press, 1992.

De Andrea, P. Mariano. "Soggetto e oggetto della metafisica secondo S. Tommaso." *Angelicum* 27 (Maggio-Agosto 1950): 165–95.

De Finance, Joseph. Review of *"Le Chemin de la théologie chez Thomas D'Aquin,"* by Michel Corbin. *Gregorianum* 57, fasc. 1 (1976): 163–66.

de la Taille, Maurice. *Mysterium Fidae.* Paris: Gabriel Beauchesne, 1921.

Deferrari, Roy J. and M. Inviolata Barry. *A Lexicon of St. Thomas Aquinas based on the Summa Theologica.* With the technical collaboration of Ignatius McGuinness. Washington, D.C.: Catholic University of America Press, 1948.

Dittoe, John T. "Sacramental Incorporation Into the Mystical Body." *The Thomist* 9 (October 1946): 469–514.

Dodds, Michael J. "Ultimacy and Intimacy: Aquinas on the Relation Between God and the World." In *Ordo Sapientiae et Amoris: Image et Message de Saint Thomas D'Aquin à travers les récentes études historiques, herméneutiques et doctrinales: hommage au professeur Jean-Pierre Torrell.* Edited by Carlos-Josaphat Pinto de Oliveira. Studia Friburgensia, nouvelle séri, 78. Fribourg, Switzerland: Éditions Universitaires Fribourg Suisse, 1993.

Doronzo, Emmaneul. *De Eucharistia.* 2 vols. Milwaukee: Bruce Publishing, 1947.

Filograssi, Giuseppe. *De Sanctissima Eucharistia: Quaestiones Dogmaticae Selectae.* 6th ed. Rome: Gregorian Univeristy Press, 1957.

Freddi, Roger. *Jesus Christ the Word Incarnate.* Translated by F. J. Sullivan. St. Louis: B. Herder, 1904.

Gagnebet, P. Rosarius. "Dieu Sujet de la Theologie selon Saint Thomas D'Aquin." In *Problemi Scelti di Teologia Contemporanea.* Analecta Gregoriana, vol. 68. Rome: Gregorian University Press, 1954.

Galloway, A. D. Review of *Thomism and the Ontological Theology of Paul Tillich: A Comparison of Systems,* by Donald J. Keefe. *The Expository Times* 83 (July 1972): 313.

Garrigou-Langrange, Reginald. *Christ the Savior: A Commentary on the Third Part of St. Thomas' Theological Summa.* St. Louis: B. Herder, 1950.

————. *La Synthèse Thomiste*. Paris: Desclée de Brouwer, 1946.

Geiselmann, Josef. *Die Eucharistielehre der Vorscholastik*. Padenborn: Druck und Verlag von Ferdinand Schoningh, 1926.

Gerken, A., "Dogmengeschichtliche Reflexion uber die heutige Wende in der Eucharistielehre." *Zeitschrift für katholische Theologie* 94 (1972): 199–226.

————. *Theologie der Eucharistie*. München: Kösel-Verlag, 1973.

Gilson, Étienne. *Elements of Christian Philosophy*. Garden City, New York: Doubleday, 1960.

Ginsburg, Norbert D. "Metaphysical Relations and St. Thomas Aquinas." *The New Scholasticism* XV (July 1941): 238–54.

Guéranger, Prosper L.P. *Institutions Liturgiques*. 4 vols. Paris: Société Générale de Librairie Catholique, 1880.

Hankey, W. J. *God in Himself: Aquinas' Doctrine of God as Expounded in the Summa Theologiae*. Oxford: Oxford University Press, 1987.

————. "Theology as System and as Science: Proclus and Thomas Aquinas." *Dionysius* 6 (December 1982): 83–93.

Hayen, André. "Le Thomisme et l'histoire." *Revue Thomiste* 62 (Janvier-Mars 1962): 51–82.

Heiser, W. Charles. Review of *Covenantal Theology: The Eucharistic Order of History*, by Donald J. Keefe. *Theology Digest* 38 (Winter 1991): 364.

Henninger, Mark G. *Relations: Medieval Theories 1250–1325*. Oxford: Clarendon Press, 1989.

Hervé, J.M. *Manuale Theologiae Dogmatiae*. 4 vols. Westminster, Maryland: Newman Bookshop, 1946.

Hughson, Thomas. "Dulles and Aquinas on Revelation." *The Thomist* 52 (July 1988): 445–471.

Jelly, Frederick M. Review of *Thomism and the Ontological Theology of Paul Tillich: A Comparison of Systems*, by Donald J. Keefe. *The American Ecclesiastical Review* 167 (June 1973): 423–24.

————. Review of *Thomism and the Ontological Theology of Paul Tillich: A Comparison of Systems*, by Donald J. Keefe. *The Thomist* 36 (January 1972): 166–73.

Jenkins, John I. *Knowledge and Faith in Thomas Aquinas*. Cambridge: Cambridge University Press, 1997.

Jones, Paul H. *Christ's Eucharistic Presence: A History of the Doctrine*. American University Studies, series 7, Theology and Religion, vol. 157. New York: Peter Lang, 1994.

Jordan, Mark D. "The Modes of Thomistic Discourse: Questions for Corbin's *Le Chemin de la Theologie chez Thomas D'Aquin.*" *The Thomist* 45 (January 1981): 80–98.

Kane, William J. *The Philosophy of Relation in the Metaphysics of St. Thomas.* Philosophical Studies, vol. 179, no. 30. Washington, D.C.: Catholic University of America Press, 1958.

Keefe, Donald J. *Covenantal Theology: The Eucharistic Order of History.* Revised edition with an appendix. Novato, California: Presidio Press, 1996.

———. "Mary as Created Wisdom: The Splendor of the New Creation." *The Thomist* 47 (July 1983): 395–420.

———. "The Present Situation of Eucharistic Theology." *Faith & Reason* 14 (Fall 1988): 255–322.

———. "Sacramental Sexuality and the Ordination of Women." *Communio* 5 (Summer 1978): 228–51.

———. "The Sacrament of the Good Creation: Prolegomena to the Discussion of the Ordination of Women." *Faith & Reason* 9 (Summer 1983): 143–54.

———. *Thomism and the Ontological Theology of Paul Tillich.* Leiden, Netherlands: E. J. Brill, 1971.

———. "Toward a Renewal of Sacramental Theology." *The Thomist* 44 (July 1980): 357–71.

———. "La 'Veritatis splendor' e il fondamento eucaristico della morale." *Rivista di Teologia Morale* 110, no. 2 (Aprile-Giugno 1996): 209–20.

Kilmartin, Edward. *Christian Liturgy: Theology and Practice.* Kansas City: Sheed and Ward, 1988.

Kinn, James W. *The Pre-Eminence of the Eucharist Among the Sacraments According to Alexander of Hales, St. Albert the Great, St. Bonaventure and St. Thomas Aquinas.* Dissertationes ad Lauream, 31. Mundelein, Illinois: Saint Mary of the Lake Seminary, 1960.

Klubertanz, George P. *Introduction to the Philosophy of Being.* New York: Meredith, 1963.

Krempel, A. *La Doctrine de la Relation chez Saint Thomas: Exposé Historique et Systématique.* Paris: Librairie Philosophique J. Vrin, 1952.

Kreyche, Robert J. *First Philosophy: An Introductory Text in Metaphysics.* New York: Henry Holt, 1959.

LaCugna, Catherine Mowry. *God for Us: The Trinity and Christian Life.* San Francisco: HarperSanFrancisco, 1991.

Latourelle, René. *Theology of Revelation: Including a Commentary on the Constitution "Dei verbum."* New York: Society of St. Paul, 1966.

Leenhardt, Franz J. "This is My Body." In *Essays on the Lord's Supper.* General editors George Davies and A. Raymond. *Ecumenical Studies in Worship*, vol. 1. Richmond, Virginia: John Knox Press, 1958.

Le Roy, Edouard. *Dogme et Critique.* Paris: Bloud, 1907.

Little, Joyce A. *Toward a Thomist Methodology.* Toronto Studies in Theology, vol. 34. Lewiston/Queenston: Edwin Mellon Press, 1988.

Loughery, Sr. Francis Assisi. *The Eucharist: The End of All the Sacraments According to Saint Thomas Aquinas and His Contemporaries.* Ph.D. Diss. Sinsinawa, Wisconsin: Saint Clara Convent, 1972.

Lynn, William D. *Christ's Redemptive Merit: The Nature of Its Causality According to St. Thomas.* Analecta Gregoriana, vol. 115. Rome: Gregorian University Press, 1962.

Macy, Gary. *The Banquet's Wisdom.* Mahweh, New Jersey: Paulist Press, 1992.

———. "The Development of the Notion of Eucharistic Change in the Writings of Thomas Aquinas." Unpublished M.A. thesis, Marquette Unversity, Milwaukee, 1973.

———. *The Theologies of the Eucharist in the Early Scholastic Period: A Study of the Salvific Function of the Sacrament According to the Theologians c. 1080–c.1220.* Oxford: Clarendon Press, 1984.

Martin, Francis. *The Feminist Question: Feminist Theology in the Light of Christian Tradition.* Grand Rapids, Michigan: William B. Eerdmans, 1994.

McCormick, John F. *Scholastic Metaphysics.* Chicago: Loyola University Press, 1940.

Mercier, Désiré Joseph Cardinal and Professors of the Higher Institute of Philosophy, Louvain. *Manual of Modern Scholastic Philosophy.* Translated by T.L. Parker and S.A. Parker. 2 vols. London and St. Louis: Kegan Paul, Trench, Trubner and B. Herder, 1932.

Mersch, Emile. *The Theology of the Mystical Body.* Translated by Cyril Vollert. St. Louis: B. Herder, 1951.

Miletic, Stephen F. *"One Flesh", Ephesians 5:22–24, 5:31, Marriage, and the New Creation.* Analecta Biblica, vol. 115. Rome: Pontificio Istituto Biblico, 1988.

Miyakawa, Toshiyuki. "St. Thomas on the Relation Between *Res et Sacramentum* and *Res Tantum.*" *Euntes Docete: Commentaria Urbaniana* XVIII (1965): 61–108.

Muller, Earl C. "Real Relations and the Divine: Issues in Thomas's Understanding of God's Relation to the World." *Theological Studies* 56 (December 1995): 673–95.

O'Brien, T.C. "'Sacra Doctrina' Revisited: The Context of Medieval Education." *The Thomist* 41 (October 1977): 475–509.

O'Connell, David A. *The Union Between Head and Body in the Mystical Body.* Ph.D. Diss. Washington, D.C.: Dominican House of Studies, 1941.

O'Connor, James T. *The Hidden Manna: A Theology of the Eucharist.* San Francisco: Ignatius Press, 1988.

O'Donnell, John J. *The Mystery of the Triune God.* Mahwah, New Jersey: Paulist Press, 1989.

O'Donoghue, Noel D. Review of *Thomism and the Ontological Theology of Paul Tillich: A Comparison of Systems,* by Donald J. Keefe. *The Scottish Journal of Theology* 25 (August 1972): 354–56.

O'Neil, Colman. "St. Thomas on the Membership of the Church." *The Thomist* 27 (April, July, and October 1963): 88–140.

Parsch, Pius. *We Are Christ's Body.* Translated and adapted by Clifford Howell. Notre Dame, Indiana: Fides, 1962.

Pegis, Anton C. "*Sub Ratione Dei*: A Reply to Professor Anderson. *The New Scholasticism* 39 (1965): 141–57.

Persson, Per Erik. *Sacra doctrina.* Translated by Ross Mackenzie. Philadelphia: Fortress Press, 1970.

Phillips, R. P. *Modern Thomistic Philosophy.* London: Burns Oates & Washbourne, 1935.

Piolanti, Antonius. *De Sacramentis.* 3d ed. Rome: Marietti, 1951.

Potter, Vincent G. Review of *Thomism and the Ontological Theology of Paul Tillich: A Comparison of Systems,* by Donald J. Keefe. *Theological Studies* 34 (December 1973): 731–35.

Potvin, Thomas R. *The Theology of the Primacy of Christ According to St. Thomas Aquinas and Its Scriptural Foundations.* Studia Friburgensia, nouvelle séri, 50. Fribourg, Switzerland: University Press, 1973.

Preller, Victor. *Divine Science and the Natural Knowledge of God: A Reformulation of Thomas Aquinas.* Princeton: Princeton University Press, 1967.

Rahner, Karl. *The Trinity*. Translated by J Donceel. New York: Herder and Herder, 1970.

Ratzinger, Joseph Cardinal. *Called to Communion: Understanding the Church Today*. Translated by Adrian Walker. San Francisco: Ignatius Press, 1996.

Rogers, Eugene F., Jr. *Thomas Aquinas and Karl Barth: Sacred Doctrine and the Natural Knowledge of God*. Notre Dame, Indiana: University of Notre Dame Press, 1995.

Ross, Susan A. *Extravagant Affections: A Feminist Sacramental Theology*. New York: Continuum, 1998.

Sauras, Emilio. "Thomistic Soteriology and the Mystical Body." *The Thomist* XV (October 1952): 543–71.

Schenk, Richard. "Omnis Christi Actio Nostra est Instructio: the Deeds and Sayings of Jesus as Revelation in the View of Thomas Aquinas." In *La Doctrine de la Révélation Divine de Saint Thomas d'Aquin*. Actes du Symposium sur la Pensee de Saint Thomas d'Aquin tenu a Rolduc, les 4 et 5 Novembre 1989, edited by Leon Elders. Studi Tomistici, vol. 37. Vatican City: Libreria Editrice Vaticana, 1990.

Schillebeeckx, Edward. *The Eucharist*. Translated by N.D. Smith. New York: Sheed and Ward, 1968.

———. "Transubstantiation, Transfinalization, Transignification." In *Living Bread, Saving Cup*, Edited by R. Kevin Seasoltz. Translated by David J. Rock. Collegeville, Minnesota: Liturgical Press, 1982.

Shanley, Brian J. "*Sacra Doctrina* and the Theology of Disclosure. *The Thomist* 61 (January 1997): 163–87.

"Substance and Attribute," In *The Encyclopedia of Philosophy*, vols. 7 and 8, edited by Paul Edwards. New York: Macmillian and Free Press, 1967.

Synave, Paul, and Pierre Benoit. *Prophecy and Inspiration: A Commentary on the Summa Theologica II-II, Questions 171–178*. Translated by Avery R. Dulles and Thomas L. Sheridan. New York: Desclée, 1961.

TeSelle, Eugene. Review of *Covenantal Theology: The Eucharistic Order of History*, by Donald J. Keefe. *America* 168 (8 May 1993): 19.

Thurian, Max. *The Mystery of the Eucharist: An Ecumenical Approach*. Translated by Emily Chisholm. Grand Rapids, Michigan: William B. Eerdmans, 1983.

———. *The One Bread*. Translated by Theodore DuBois. New York: Sheed and Ward, 1969.

———. "The Real Presence." In *Christianity Divided: Protestant and Roman Catholic Theological Issues*, Daniel Callahon et al. New York: Sheed and Ward, 1961.

———. "Toward a Renewal of the Doctrine of Transubstantiation." In *Christianity Divided: Protestant and Roman Catholic Theological Issues*. Daniel Callahon et al. New York: Sheed and Ward, 1961.

Tillich, Paul. *Systematic Theology*. Vol. 1. Chicago: University of Chicago Press, 1951.

Van Ackeren, Gerald. *Sacra doctrina*. Rome: Officium Libri Catholici, 1952.

Vaske, Martin O. *An Introduction to Metaphysics*. New York: McGraw-Hill, 1963.

Vonier, Anscar. *A Key to the Doctrine of the Eucharist*. London: Burns Oates & Washbourne, 1925.

———. *The New and Eternal Covenant*. New York: Benziger Brothers, 1930.

Vorgrimler, Herbert. *Sacramental Theology*. Translated by Linda M. Maloney. Collegeville, Minnesota: Liturgical Press, 1992.

Wallace, William A. *The Role of Demonstration in Moral Theology: A Study of Methodology in St. Thomas Aquinas*. Texts and Studies, vol. 2. Washington, D.C.: Thomist Press, 1962.

Weisheipl, James A. "The Meaning of *Sacra Doctrina* in *Summa Theologiae* I, q. 1." *Thomist* 38 (January 1974): 49–80.

White, Victor. "St.Thomas's Conception of Revelation." *Dominican Studies* 1 (January 1948): 3–35.

Williams, A.N. "Mystical Theology Redux: The Pattern of Aquinas' *Summa Theologiae*." *Modern Theology* 13 (January 1997): 53–74.

Wright, John H. *The Order of the Universe in the Theology of St. Thomas Aquinas*. Rome: Gregorian University Press, 1957.

Zuck, John E. Review of *Thomism and the Ontological Theology of Paul Tillich: A Comparison of Systems*, by Donald J. Keefe. *Journal of the American Academy of Religion* 41 (June 1973): 271–72.

INDEX